I0755019

THE STUGGLE OF '72.

THE

STRUGGLE OF '72.

THE

ISSUES AND CANDIDATES

OF THE

PRESENT POLITICAL CAMPAIGN:

CONTAINING

BIOGRAPHICAL SKETCHES OF ALL THE CANDIDATES FOR PRESIDENT AND VICE-PRESIDENT; HISTORY AND PLATFORMS OF THE GREAT POLITICAL PARTIES; FACTS ABOUT PUBLIC MEN AND MEASURES; REVIEW OF GRANT'S ADMINISTRATION; THE QUEER RECORD OF HORACE GREELEY.

BY

EVERETT CHAMBERLIN.

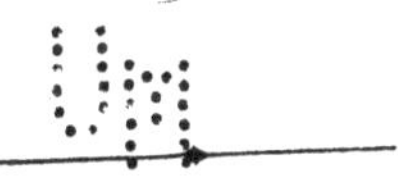

EMBELLISHED WITH MANY PORTRAITS AND HUMOROUS ILLUSTRATIONS.

UNION PUBLISHING COMPANY:
165 TWENTY-SECOND STREET, CHICAGO, ILL.
26 SOUTH SEVENTH ST., PHILADELPHIA, PA.
A. L. BANCROFT & CO., SAN FRANCISCO, CAL.
1872.

STEAM PRESS OF
OTTAWAY, BROWN & COLBERT,
7 & 9 S. Jefferson St., Chicago.

A. ZEESE & CO.,
ELECTROTYPERS,
Chicago.

INTRODUCTION.

THE Republican party of the United States has been entrusted with the management of the national affairs since 1861—a period of nearly three successive Presidential terms. During that period this party has had to meet and overcome, at almost every step of its progress, political difficulties more serious than any which the nation has ever known before since its birth; and it has met them with a success which has won the admiration of the world. And so completely has the world identified the Republican party with the stability and dignity of the nation, that the prospects of its success or defeat in pending elections have regulated the upward or downward tendencies of the national securities, and such other indices as serve to show the estimation in which a country is held abroad.

During the most of the years referred to, the Republican party has enjoyed a complete and undisputed supremacy in all the branches of the government—a condition of things very trying to the virtue of a political party. It is now threatened with a serious schism, brought about by men, some of whom have been reckoned among our best statesmen and publicists, and sympathized in by a considerable portion of the thoughtful and conservative classes of the population, the avowed object of this schism being the reformation of serious abuses alleged to exist in the administration of the government and the theories of legislation.

Is there sufficient cause to be found in the existing condition of things for the overthrow of the Republican party, and the installation of a new dynasty, to be built chiefly of the material of the long-dishonored Democratic party—founded, however, upon principles, or at least upon platforms, furnished by the disaffected Republicans? To answer this question, or rather to furnish the reader with material with which to answer it for himself, is the purpose of the present volume. In the pages which follow, the reader will find, among other things, a HISTORY OF THE REPUBLICAN PARTY with the issues it has made and the positions which it has taken, from its origin to the present time; also a HISTORY OF THE DEMOCRATIC PARTY, particularly during the years when its history has been contemporaneous with that of the Republican party; also sketches of the life and character of the several CANDIDATES FOR PRESIDENT AND VICE PRESIDENT; also, since the main question of next November is whether or not we shall have another term of President Grant's administration, a brief, though we trust an acceptably comprehensive view of the salient points of his first term, so far as it is past; also many other facts and ideas pertinent to the present exciting canvass, and such as the voter will naturally like to peruse, and lay away for reference. In short, it has been the aim of the author (or compiler, if you please) of this book, to furnish a useful compendium of facts and points for the campaign. Though the reader may discover in the manner of putting things a bias in favor of that which now is, he will not, it is hoped, encounter any misstatement of fact. The book is illustrated with portraits and cartoons, which have their own peculiar momentary interest, and for which the artist alone must have the credit, whatever it may be.

Chicago, July, 1872. E. C.

ILLUSTRATIONS.

CONTENTS.

CHAPTER V.

THE SAME, CONTINUED.

CHAPTER VI.

THE SAME, CONTINUED.

CHAPTER VII.

ULYSSES S. GRANT—HIS MILITARY CAREER.

CHAPTER VIII.

THE SAME, CONTINUED.

CHAPTER IX.

THE SAME, CONTINUED.

CHAPTER X.

THE SAME, CONTINUED.

CHAPTER XI.

THE SAME, CONTINUED.

CHAPTER XII.

THE SAME, CONTINUED.

CHAPTER XIII.

GRANT AS PRESIDENT.

CHAPTER XIV.

THE SAME, CONTINUED.

CHAPTER XV.

GRANT AS A MAN.

CHAPTER XVI.

GRANT AND THE COLORED RACE.

CHAPTER XVII.

THE SO-CALLED LIBERAL MOVEMENT.

CHAPTER XVIII.

THE SAME, CONTINUED.

CHAPTER XIX.

THE CINCINNATI CONVENTION.

CHAPTER XX.

THE SAME, CONTINUED.

CHAPTER XXI.

HORACE GREELEY.

CHAPTER XXII.

GREELEY AS A FOURIERITE.

CHAPTER XXIII.

GREELEY AS A POLITICIAN.

CHAPTER XXIV.

GREELEY AS A BOOK FARMER.

CHAPTER XXV.

IS HE FIT?

CHAPTER XXVI.

THE DEMOCRATIC PARTY.

CHAPTER XXVII.

THE BALTIMORE CONVENTION.

CHAPTER XXVIII.

HENRY WILSON.

CHAPTER XXIX.

BENJAMIN GRATZ BROWN.

APPENDIX.

HISTORY OF THE

Republican Party.

CHAPTER I.

Its Origin and Organization—The Philadelphia Convention of 1856—The First Platform—The Fremont Campaign—Lecompton—A Pro-Slavery Constitution—The Lincoln-Douglas Debates of 1858, Etc.

In its origin the Republican party was a development into organized form of the principles of freedom. In its organization it was the fusion of political elements which had always before refused to coalesce. In the year 1852 there were three parties in the Union, presenting three presidential tickets to the American people. These were the Democratic, the Whig, and the Free Soil parties. In that year the Democratic party gained an overwhelming victory, carrying a large majority of the popular suffrage, and all the votes of the electoral college except those of Massachusetts, Vermont, Kentucky, and Tennessee. Under this crushing defeat the Whig party was destroyed.

During the administration of President Pierce,

who had been elected in 1852, an event occurred which greatly aroused the country, and broke up old party ties. This was the introduction and passage by Congress of the Kansas-Nebraska Bill, repealing the famous Missouri Compromise of 1820. Large numbers of Democrats, especially throughout all the Northern States, refused to sustain this measure, and the Democratic party, so triumphant in 1852, almost everywhere met with disastrous defeat in the elections of 1854. This defeat would, doubtless, have been even more disastrous but for the fact that the disruption of parties, caused by the elections of 1852 and the Kansas-Nebraska Bill, had been too recent to allow the organization of a permanent political party. There appears to be a temporary necessity for a "make shift" organization, and this was found in the "Know Nothing" party. Of a narrow creed and with secret workings, it was necessarily of short duration.

Meantime, the anti-slavery discussion of the Abolitionists had been doing its perfect work. The Abolitionists had for many years received the hearty moral sympathies of many of the purest and ablest men in the old Whig and Democratic parties. The literature and the best journalism of the country were long thus in moral sympathy with what was generally denounced in political circles as "crazy fanaticism." A novel of great literary merit and wonderful popularity—Mrs. Stowe's "Uncle Tom's Cabin"—had taught the people to believe in the gross political immorality of slavery. And hence there was a logical fitness, and apparent national necessity for the formation of a party to be built upon the broad basis of freedom. And it was upon this broad basis, large numbers of people being now ready therefor, that the Republican party was organized early in 1856. The application of the doctrine was not in the abolition of slavery, but in its confinement to the localities in which it then existed. This involved no breach of fundamental law, and tended to accomplish two great benefits: First, the dedication of our vast Western domain to freedom; secondly, the destruction of the political despotism of the Slave Power. The first great triumph of the party was in the admission of Kansas as a free State; and this was a most refreshing demonstration—that the political despotism of the Slave Power had received a mortal wound.

FULLY ORGANIZED AT PHILADELPHIA.

But before this the party had been regularly organized in national convention. Much, also, had been done toward its organization in some of the states during the years 1854 and 1855. Its first national convention was held at the city of Pittsburgh, Penn., February 22d, 1856. An address written by Henry J. Raymond, the editor of the New York *Times*, was adopted, but no nominations were made. The regular nominating convention assembled at Philadelphia, on the following 17th of June, a fortnight after the Democratic party had nominated James Buchanan and John C. Breckinridge for the Presidency and Vice-Presidency, at a convention held in the city of Cincinnati. Over the Philadelphia convention the Hon. Henry S. Lane, of Indiana, presided. It was a large, enthusiastic and harmonious gathering. John C. Fremont, of California, was nominated candidate for President, and Wm. L. Dayton, of New Jersey, for Vice-President, each on the first ballot. The convention also adopted a platform of which the following is a copy:

PHILADELPHIA PLATFORM OF 1856.

"This Convention of Delegates, assembled in pursuance of a call addressed to the people of the United States, without regard to past political differences or divisions, who are opposed to the repeal of the Missouri Compromise, to the policy of the present Administration, to the extension of slavery into free territory; in favor of admitting Kansas as a free State, of restoring the action of the Federal Government to the principles of Washington and Jefferson, and who propose to unite in presenting candidates for the office of President and Vice-President, do resolve as follows:

"*Resolved*, that the maintenance of the principles promulgated in the Declaration of Independence and embodied in the Federal Constitution is essential to the preservation of our republican institutions, and that the Federal Constitution, the rights of the States, and the union of the States, shall be preserved.

"*Resolved*, That with our republican fathers we hold it to be a self-evident truth, that all men are endowed with the inalienable rights to life, liberty, and the pursuit of happiness, and that the primary object and ulterior designs of our Federal Government were to secure these rights to all persons within its exclusive jurisdiction; that as our republican fathers, when they had abolished Slavery in all our national territory, ordained that no person should be deprived of life, liberty, or property without due process of law, it becomes our duty to maintain this provision of the Constitution against all attempts to violate it for the purpose of establishing Slavery in any territory of the United States, by positive legislation, prohibiting its existence or extension therein. That we deny the authority of Congress, of a territorial legislature, of any individual or association of individuals, to give legal existence to Slavery in any territory of the United States, while the present Constitution shall be maintained.

"*Resolved*, That the Constitution confers upon Congress sovereign power over the territories of the United States for their government, and that in the exercise of this power it is both the right and the duty of Congress to prohibit in the territories those twin relics of barbarism—Polygamy and Slavery.

"*Resolved*, That while the Constitution of the United States was ordained and established by the people in order to form a more perfect Union, establish justice, insure domestic tranquility, provide for the common defense, and secure the blessings of liberty, and contains ample provisions for the protection of life, liberty and property of every citizen, the dearest constitutional rights of the people of Kansas have been fraudulently and violently taken from them—their territory has been invaded by an armed force—spurious and pretended legislative, judicial and executive officers have been set over them, by whose usurped authority, sustained by the military power of the Government, tyrannical and unconstitutional laws have been enacted and enforced—the rights of the people to keep and bear arms have been infringed—test oaths of an extraordinary and entangling nature have been imposed as a condition of exercising the right of suffrage and holding office—the right of an accused person to a speedy and public trial by an impartial jury has been denied—the right of the people to be secure in their persons, houses, papers, and effects against unreasonable searches and seizures has been violated—they have been deprived of life, liberty, and property without due process of law—that the freedom of speech and of the press has been abridged—the right to choose their representatives has been made of no effect—murders, robberies, and arsons have been instigated and encouraged, and the offenders have been allowed to go unpunished—that all these things have been done with the knowledge, sanction, and procurement of the present Administration, and that for this high crime against the Constitution, the Union, and Humanity, we arraign the Administration, the President, his advisers, agents, supporters, apologists and accessories, either before or after the facts, before the country and before the world, and that it is our fixed purpose to bring the actual perpetrators of these atrocious outrages, and their accomplices, to a sure and condign punishment hereafter.

"*Resolved*, That Kansas should be immediately admitted as a State of the Union, with her present free Constitution, as at once the most effectual way of securing to her citizens the enjoyment of the rights and privileges to which they are entitled, and of ending the civil strife now raging in her territory.

"*Resolved*, That the highwayman's plea, that 'might makes right,' embodied in the Ostend Circular, was in every respect unworthy of American diplomacy, and would bring shame and dishonor upon any Government or people that gave it their sanction.

"*Resolved*, That a railroad to the Pacific Ocean, by the most central and practicable route, is imperatively demanded by the interests of the whole country, and that the Federal Government ought to render immediate and efficient aid in its construction, and, as an auxiliary thereto, the immediate construction of an emigrant route on the line of the railroad.

Resolved, That appropriations by Congress for the improvement of rivers and harbors, of a national character, required for the accommodation and security of our existing commerce, are authorized by the Constitution, and justified by the obligation of Government to protect the lives and property of its citizens."

THE CAMPAIGN.

The action of the convention was heartily sustained by the Republican party, which had now become well organized in all the non-slaveholding States, and numbered many adherents in the border slave States. The campaign was characterized by great enthusiasm on the part of the Republicans. Their journals were crowded with accounts of mass meetings in various parts of the country. The current events in Kansas, in a state of civil war, were calculated to arouse the public feeling to the highest pitch; and, in fact, did so. So when the election came on, in November, it was found that Fremont and Dayton had carried all the New England States, New York, Ohio, Michigan, Wisconsin, and Iowa, and large popular votes in all the other Northern States. The popular votes of the Republican party, at its first presidential election numbered 1,341,264. James Buchanan, the Democratic candidate, was chosen President, but Millard Filmore, the "American" candidate, received the vote of Maryland and nearly nine hundred thousand popular votes in the thirty-one States which then composed the Union. Mr. Buchanan, therefore, was in a popular minority, though receiving a large majority of the votes in the electoral college.

"LECOMPTON."

The event of most political significance, perhaps, which occurred during the administration of President Buchanan, was the attempt to force slavery into Kansas, against the will of the people, under what was known at the time as "the Lecompton Constitution"—an instrument representing fraud and force only. Against this policy the illustrious Stephen A. Douglas, Senator from Illinois, revolted, and with undisguised indignation assailed the administration. In this he was most heartily in accord with the Republican party, which, with his great aid, was enabled herein to achieve a memorable victory. It was not until some years after this, however, that Kansas was admitted into the Union.

THE LINCOLN-DOUGLAS DEBATES.

The discussion of the Lecompton Constitution in Congress gave rise to two important events. First, it caused a division in the Democratic party which continued through the following presidential campaign; and, secondly, it was the indirect cause of that remarkable series of debates between Senator Douglas and Abraham Lincoln in 1858, through which the latter became first honorably known to the American public generally, thereby gaining a national renown, without which his nomination for the Presidency in 1860 would have been impossible. On account of the plucky revolt of Senator Douglas against the administration in the Kansas affair, not a few Republicans and Republican journals of note in the country thought that he ought to be returned to the Senate by the Illinois Legislature to be chosen in 1858. The Republicans of Illinois were not of this opinion, and in their State Convention of that year did the unusual thing of actually nominating Mr. Lincoln as candidate for United States Senator. It was upon this occasion that Mr. Lincoln delivered that great speech, new become historical, beginning with this remarkable exordium :

"MR. PRESIDENT AND GENTLEMEN OF THE CONVENTION:

"If we could first know where we are and whither we are tending, we could better judge what to do and how to do it. We are now far into the fifth year since a policy was initiated with the avowed object and confident promise of putting an end to slavery agitation. Under the operation of that policy, that agitation not only has not ceased, but has constantly augmented. In my opinion it will not ceasc until a crisis shall have been reached and passed. 'A house divided against itself cannot stand.' I believe this government cannot endure permanently half slave and half free. I do not expect the Union to be dissolved ; I do not expect the house to fall : but I expect it will cease to be divided. It will become all one thing or all the other. Either the opponents of slavery will arrest the further spread of it, and place it where the public mind shall rest in the belief that it is in the course of ultimate extinction ; or its advocates will push it forward till it shall become alike lawful in all the States, old as well as new—North as well as South."

Mr. Lincoln's demonstration of the tendency of the government to the latter condition through the operation of the Nebraska Doctrine and the

Dred Scot Decision, was profound, unanswerable. The speech startled the convention, and, published in all the leading journals, made a profound impression throughout the republic. It served as text for many a political harangue during subsequent campaigns, and it at once taught the country that if Senator Douglas did not have his equal in debate on the floor of the Senate, he would find him in this till then comparatively unknown lawyer of Illinois. He did, in fact, soon return home from Washington, and made a speech in the city of Chicago, in reply to Mr. Lincoln's Springfield address. To this, Mr. Lincoln speedily rejoined, and soon afterwards arrangements were made for a series of joint debates between these two celebrated men. It is certain that no State campaign was ever more animatedly conducted, or attracted more general attention. On those days when these great disputants were not engaged in joint discussion, they addressed large audiences in independent meetings, and all Illinois rang with their argumentation and eloquence. Through the elaborate reports of the newspaper press, the whole country listened, and with eager interest, to the joint debates. At their conclusion Abraham Lincoln was universally acknowledged to be among the ablest of American thinkers and speakers. His fame was exalted and national.

CHAPTER II.

HISTORY OF THE REPUBLICAN PARTY.

(CONTINUED.)

The Chicago Convention of 1860—Nomination of Lincoln and Hamlin—The Platform—The Canvass—Success of the Republicans—The South Belligerent—President Lincoln's Inaugural Address—His Cabinet, Etc.

Lincoln was, however, defeated for the Senate, Mr. Douglas being again elected by the Legislature. But when the National Convention of the Republican party assembled at Chicago in 1860, it was at once discovered that Mr. Lincoln was a formidable candidate for the Presidency. He had friends and admirers in all parts of the country. The convention itself was very large, while the attendance of visitors was so great as to crowd the city for days. The "outside pressure" for Mr. Lincoln was tremendous. He was nominated on the third ballot, amid excitement and enthusiasm the like of which has rarely been witnessed in this country. Hannibal Hamlin, of Maine, was chosen for the second place on the ticket. The platform, which, it is believed, was chiefly prepared by Horace Greeley and the Hon. John A. Kasson, of Iowa, was much more elaborate than that of 1856. As showing the growth of the party in respect of platform literature, it may be well to quote the entire document:

CHICAGO PLATFORM OF 1860.

"*Resolved*, That we, the delegated representatives of the Republican electors of the United States, in Convention assembled, in discharge of the duty we owe to our constituents and our country, unite in the following declaration :

"1. That the history of the nation, during the last four years, has fully established the propriety and necessity of the organization and perpetuation of the Republican party, and that the causes which called it into existence are permanent in their nature, and now, more than ever before, demand its peaceful and constitutional triumph.

"2. That the maintainance of the principles promulgated in the Declaration of Independence, and embodied in the Federal Constitution, "That all men are created equal ; that they are endowed by their Creator with certain inalienable rights ; that among these are life, liberty, and the pursuit of happiness; that to secure these rights governments are instituted among men, deriving their just powers from the consent of the governed," is essential to the preservation of our Republican institutions ; and that the Federal Constitution, the rights of the States, and the Union of the States, must and shall be preserved.

"3. That to the Union of the States this nation owes its unprecedented increase in population, its surprising development of material resources, its rapid augmentation of wealth, its happiness at home, and its honor abroad ; and we hold in abhorrence all schemes for Disunion, come from whatever source they may ; and we congratulate the country that no Republican member of Congress has uttered or countenanced the threats of Disunion so often made by Democratic members, without rebuke and with applause from their political associates ; and we denounce those threats of Disunion, in case of a popular overthrow of their ascendancy, as denying the vital principles of a free government, and as an avowal of contemplated treason, which it is the imperative duty of an indignant people sternly to rebuke and forever silence.

"4. That the maintainance, inviolate, of the rights of the States, and especially the right of each State to order and control its own domestic institutions according to its own judgment exclusively, is essential to that balance of powers on which the perfection and endurance of our political fabric depends ; and we denounce the lawless invasion by armed force of the soil of any State or Territory, no matter under what pretext, as among the gravest of crimes.

"5. That the present Democratic Admistration has far exceeded our worst apprehensions in its measureless subserviency to the exactions of a sectional interest, as especially evinced in its desperate exertions to force the infamous Lecompton Constitution upon the protesting people of Kansas ; in construing the personal relation between master and servant to involve an unqualified property in persons; in its attempted enforcement everywhere, on land and sea, through the intervention of Congress, and of the Federal Courts, of the extreme pretentions of a purely local interest ; and in its general and unvarying abuse of the power entrusted to it by a confiding people.

"6. That the people justly view with alarm the reckless extravagance which pervades every department of the Federal Government ; that a return to rigid economy and accountability is indispensable to arrest the systematic plunder of the public Treasury by favored partisans, while the recent startling developments of frauds and corruptions at the Federal metropolis show that an entire change of Administration is imperatively demanded.

"7. That the new dogma, that the Constitution, of its own force, carries Slavery into any or all of the Territories of the United States, is a dangerous political heresy, at variance with the explicit provisions of that instrument itself, with contemporaneous exposition, and with legislative and judicial precedent; is revolutionary in its tendency, and subversive of the peace and harmony of the country.

"8. That the normal condition of all the territory of the United States, is that of freedom ; that as our Republican fathers, when they had abolished Slavery in all our national territory, ordained that "no person should be deprived of life, liberty, and property, without due process of law," it becomes our duty, by legislation, whenever such legislation is necessary, to maintain this provision of the Constitution against all attempts to violate it ; and we deny the authority of Congress, of a territorial legislature, or of any individuals, to give legal existence to Slavery in any Territory of the United States.

"9. That we brand the recent re-opening of the African slave-trade, under the cover of our national flag, aided by perversions of judicial power, as a crime against humanity, and a burning shame to our country and age ; and we call upon Congress to take prompt and efficient measures for the total and final suppression of that execrable traffic.

"10. That in the recent vetoes, by their Federal Governors, of the acts of the Legislatures of Kansas and Nebraska, prohibiting Slavery in those Territories, we find a practical illustration of the boasted Democratic principle of Non-Intervention and Popular Sovereignty, embodied in the Kansas-Nebraska bill, and a demonstration of the deception and fraud involved therein.

"11. That Kansas should, of right, be immediately admitted as a State under the Constitution recently formed and adopted by her people, and accepted by the House of Representatives.

"12. That, while providing revenue for the support of the General Government by duties upon imports, sound policy requires such an adjustment of these imposts as to encourage the development of the industrial interest of the whole country; and we commend that policy of national exchanges which secures to the working men liberal wages, to agriculture remunerative prices, to mechanics and manufactures an adequate reward for their skill, labor, and enterprise, and to the nation commercial prosperity and independence.

"13. That we protest against any sale or alienation to others of the Public Lands held by actual settlers, and against any view of the Homestead policy that regards the settlers as paupers or suppliants for public bounty; and we demand the passage by Congress of the complete and satisfactory Homestead measure which has already passed the House.

"14. That the Republican party is opposed to any change in our Naturalization Laws or any State legislation by which the rights of citizenship, hitherto accorded to emigrants from foreign lands shall be abridged or impaired; and in favor of giving a full and efficient protection to the rights of all classes of citizens, whether native or naturalized, both at home and abroad.

"15. That appropriations by Congress for River and Harbor improvements of a national character, required for the accommodation and security of an existing commerce, are authorized by the Constitution, and justified by the obligations of Government to protect the lives and property of its citizens.

"16. That a railroad to the Pacific Ocean is imperatively demanded by the interest of the whole country; that the Federal Government ought to render immediate and efficient aid in its construction; and that, as preliminary thereto, a daily overland mail should be promptly established.

"17. Finally, having thus set forth our distinctive principles and views, we invite the co-operation of all citizens, however differing on other questions, who substantially agree with us in their affirmance and support."

THE CANVASS.

Mr. Lincoln accepted the nomination in the following letter:

SPRINGFIELD, Ill., May 23d, 1860.

HON. GEORGE ASHMUN, PRESIDENT OF THE REPUBLICAN NATIONAL CONVENTION:—

SIR:—I accept the nomination tendered me by the Convention over which you presided, and of which I am formally apprised in the letter of yourself and others acting as a Committee of the Convention for that purpose.

The declaration of principles and sentiments which accompanies your letter meets my approval; and it shall be my care not to violate or disregard it in any part.

Imploring the assistance of Divine Providence, and with due regard to the views and feelings of all who were represented in the Convention; to the rights of all the States and Territories, and people of the nation; to the inviolability of the Constitution and the perpetual union, harmony, and prosperity of all, I am most happy to co-operate for the practical success of the principles declared by the Convention.

"Your obliged friend and fellow citizen, ABRAHAM LINCOLN."

Mr. Hamlin accepted the nomination for the Vice-Presidency in a neat letter of which the following is the concluding paragraph:

"It is to be observed in connection with the doings of the Republican Convention, that a paramount object with us is to preserve the normal condition of our territorial domain as homes for free men. The able advocate and defender of Republican principles whom you have nominated for the highest place that can gratify the ambition of man, comes from a State which has been made what it is by special action in that respect of the wise and good men who founded our institutions. The rights of free labor have there been vindicated and maintained. The thrift and enterprise which so distinguish Illinois, one of the most flourishing States of the glorious West, we would see secured to all the territories of the Union; and restore peace and harmony to the whole country by bringing back the Government to what it was under the wise and patriotic men who created it. If the Republicans shall succeed in that object, as they hope to, they will be held in grateful remembrance by the busy and teeming millions of future ages.

"I am very truly yours, H. HAMLIN."

The campaign which ensued was one of the most memorable in the history of American politics. The convention of the Democratic party, which assembled at Charleston, South Carolina, failed to agree. After fifty-seven ineffectual ballotings for a candidate for President,—Senator Douglas all the time receiving a handsome majority, but not the necessary two-thirds,—the convention of storms adjourned for other storms at Baltimore. There Mr. Douglas was nominated, but the seceding delegations of several States nominated John C. Breckinridge for President, and Joseph Lane, of

Oregon, for Vice-President. Herschel V. Johnson, of Georgia, was the Douglas candidate for Vice-President, Benjamin Fitzpatrick, of Alabama, having declined the nomination of the convention.

The "Constitutional Union Party" nominated John Bell, of Tennessee, for President and Edward Everett, of Massachusetts, for Vice-President. Thus the campaign of 1860 was a quadrilateral contest. The Charleston convention and that which nominated Messrs. Bell and Everett had been held before that which placed Mr. Lincoln in nomination. Hence the campaign at once opened with "thundering all around the skies."

The members of the Chicago convention had not departed for their homes without seeing an immense procession of "Wide Awakes" parading the streets, with music, and banners and torches. In an incredibly short space of time similar organizations were formed in all parts of the North, and everywhere the Republicans went to work with earnest good will to elect their candidates. A singular interest was added to the campaign by the fact that Senator Douglas himself went upon the rostrum, and in a series of speeches to immense audiences, assailed the policy of the Republicans and the Breckinridge wing of the Democratic party. It was clear, however, to the careful observer, that Senator Douglas, despairing of his own election, desired the election of Mr. Lincoln, and at last only labored to control the organization of the party of which he had so long been a prominent member

Of the 315 votes of the electoral college, Mr. Lincoln received 180, Mr. Breckinridge 72, Mr. Bell 39, and Mr. Douglas 12. The States which sustained the Republican cause were: Maine, New Hampshire, Massachusetts, Rhode Island, Connecticut, Vermont, New York, New Jersey, (casting for electoral votes four Lincoln and Hamlin, three for Douglas and Johnson,) Pennsylvania, Ohio, Indiana, Illinois, Michigan, Iowa, Wisconsin, California, Minnesota, Oregon. Breckinridge and Lane received the votes of Delaware, Maryland, North Carolina, South Carolina, Louisiana, Mississippi, Alabama, Arkansas, Florida, Texas. Virginia, Kentucky and Tennessee voted for Bell and Everett. In addition to the three votes from New Jersey, Douglas and Johnson received the nine votes of Missouri. Of popular votes Lincoln and Hamlin received 1,857,610; Douglas and Johnson, 1,365,976; Breckinridge and Lane, 847,553; Bell and Everett, 590,631. The Republicans everywhere received the intelligence of their triumph with manifestations of enthusiastic delight.

THE SOUTH BELLIGERENT.

It was received, however, with very different feelings in the South. On the very day after the election the "Southern Confederacy" was cheered in the city of Charleston, and the "palmetto flag" was raised on shipping in the harbor. Before Mr. Lincoln had been inducted into office, several States had undertaken formally to secede from the Union; several members of President Buchanan's cabinet had resigned, some in the interest of secession, others because of their disgust at Mr. Buchanan's alleged imbecility and indecision; a number of Southern Senators and Representatives in Congress had retired from the halls, "pride in their port, defiance in their eye;" large quantities of public property had been captured by the Secessionists; a large Union army had been surrendered by a faithless general; the South below the border States was practically in armed rebellion, under the "Confederate" Government, against the Union. All this before the President-elect had uttered a word in justification of the opinion that his administration would be in any unlawful respect revolutionary or hostile to the South.

PRESIDENT LINCOLN'S INAUGURAL ADDRESS.

It was under these unhappy circumstances, that the first Republican national administration assumed control of the Government. President Lincoln's Inaugural Address was a model of moderation, forbearance, statesmanship, courage. It contains no single word of menace or of unkindness, yet declared the duty of the Chief Magistrate to transmit the government of the Union unimpaired by him to his successor. The conclusion of this notable address is of historical value:

"My countrymen, one and all, think calmly and

well upon this whole subject. Nothing valuable can be lost by taking time. If there be an object to hurry any of you, in hot haste, to a step which you would never take deliberately, that object will be frustrated by taking time; but no good object can be frustrated by it. Such of you as are now dissatisfied still have the old Constitution unimpaired, and, on the sensitive point, the laws of your own framing under it; while the new Administration will have no immediate power, if it would, to change either. If it were admitted that you who are dissatisfied, hold the right side in the dispute, there still is no single good reason for precipitate action. Intelligence, patriotism, Christianity, and a firm reliance on Him who has never yet forsaken this favored land, are still competent to adjust, in the best way, all our present difficulty.

"In your hands, my dissatisfied fellow-countrymen, and not in mine, is the momentous issue of civil war. The Government will not assail you. You can have no conflict without being yourselves the aggressors. You have no oath registered in heaven to destroy the government, while I shall have the most solemn one to 'preserve, protect, and defend it.'

"I am loth to close. We are not enemies, but friends. We must not be enemies. Though passion may have strained it must not break our bonds of affection. The mystic cords of memory, stretching from every battle-field and patriot grave to every living heart and hearthstone all over this

"CLASPING HANDS."

"We remember with gratitude the heroism of the soldiers and sailors of the Republic, (Query: The C. S. A.?) and no act of ours shall ever detract from their justly earned fame, or the full rewards of their patriotism." [*Baltimore Convention*, 1872.]

broad land, will yet swell the chorus of the Union when again touched, as surely they will be, by the better angels of our nature."

LINCOLN'S CABINET.

The Inaugural was well received by the people of the North quite generally and also by those of the Border States; but the "Southern heart" had been "fired," and the people of that section were coerced by their hot-headed leaders into most cruel and unjustifiable rebellion. Meantime, President Lincoln proceeded to administer the government with patience and wisdom. He selected a cabinet of eminent men in the party, a majority of whom had been his competitors for the nomination at Chicago, namely: William H. Seward, of New York, Secretary of State; Salmon P. Chase, of Ohio, Secretary of the Treasury; Simon Cameron, of Pennsylvania, Secretary of War; Gideon Welles, of Connecticut, Secretary of the Navy; Caleb B. Smith, of Indiana, Secretary of the Interior; Edward Bates, of Missouri, Attorney General; Montgomery Blair, of Maryland, Postmaster General.

CHAPTER III.

HISTORY OF THE REPUBLICAN PARTY.

(CONTINUED.)

General History of the Party During the War—Emancipation—The Amendments to the Constitution—The Campaign of 1846—The Baltimore Platform—The Cleveland Convention—The Democratic Convention—The Democratic Convention and Platform—The Canvass—The Death of President Lincoln—Andrew Johnson—His Treachery and Impeachment—Reconstruction Commenced.

From this time forth until the close of the war of the rebellion, the history of the Republican party is so interwoven with the history of the Union itself that it would be impossible to separate the two. Called by the people to the conduct of affairs during this momentous era in the history of the country, the policy of the party was necessarily engrafted into the conduct of the war and the material, financial, and legislative measures of the stirring and exceptional times. That the administration of affairs during this national crisis was in the main highly successful, the event of the war is ample demonstration. For not only was the Union saved, but the credit of the nation was also constantly maintained, so that notwithstanding the war, the people continued to be prosperous, and remain highly prosperous to this day. The soldiers and sailors were promptly paid. There never was any discontent either in the army or navy. The people cheerfully paid heavy taxes because they perceived that they were wisely levied, honestly collected, and faithfully disbursed to the patriotic saviours of the Republic. It were useless to relate the details of legislation and administration during these exciting years, the result so amply vindicating the statesmanship and patriotism of the party in power, but it may be well to recur to a few facts which are especially illustrative of Republican policy.

SLAVERY THE CORNER-STONE OF REBELLION.

The success of the Republican party was not the cause, but only the pretext of the war. It cannot be pretended that the election of Abraham Lincoln was not in every particular lawful. Nor can it be claimed that after election and before inauguration, he or his party had violated any law whatever, or in any way manifested any disposition to do so. Nevertheless, before his inauguration, the pretended "Confederate" Government was set up, and a provisional President and Vice-President were elected. The corner-stone of this new government, as claimed by its chief architects, was Slavery. They proposed to overthrow the Constitution and the principle of freedom at the same time; by the same blow to destroy both. Both were in the keeping of the Republican party.

The party maintained both not only, but strictly in accordance with law, gave new triumphs to freedom, and added new provisions of beneficent political effect to the Constitution.

PRELIMINARIES OF EMANCIPATION.

Among these the first in practical importance, perhaps, will be regarded President Lincoln's Proclamation of Emancipation. On the 22d of September, 1862, President Lincoln issued a proclamation in which, after reciting the provisions of certain acts of Congress, he declared that on the first of the following January he would, as Commander-in-Chief of the Army and Navy, set free all slaves in all parts of the country remaining in rebellion against the government. This proclamation created a profound impression throughout the country. Many asserted it was proof that the war was carried on, not for the restoration of the Union, but for the abolition of Slavery. This, however, the proclamation itself disproved. It is to be observed also, that on the 6th of March previous, the President had sent a message to Congress, recommending compensated emancipation, in accordance with which both Houses very soon passed the following joint resolution :

"*Resolved, etc.*, That the United States ought to co-operate with any State which may adopt gradual abolishment of slavery, giving to such State pecuniary aid, to be used by such State in its discretion, to compensate for the inconvenience, public and private, produced by such change of system."

Other legislative attempts in the same direction were also made, and there was much diplomacy on the subject between representatives of the border Slave States and President Lincoln ; but all such efforts failed to reach a practical result. A recurrence to them, however, is regarded proper, as showing that emancipation, through the war power of the government, was not adopted except as the last extremity and on account of the dire necessity of the military situation. Accordingly, after many months of wearying patience the President issued that immortal document, the "Proclamation of Emancipation," wherein, after citing the preliminary proclamation already referred to, he proclaimed:

"Now, therefore, I, ABRAHAM LINCOLN, President of the United States, by virtue of the power in me vested as Commander-in-Chief of the Army and Navy of the United States, in time of actual armed rebellion against the authority and Government of the United States, and as a fit and necessary war measure for suppressing said rebellion, do, on this first day of January, in the year of our Lord one thousand eight hundred and sixty-three, and in accordance with my purpose so to do, publicly proclaimed for the full period of one hundred days, from the day first above mentioned, order and designate as the States and parts of States wherein the people thereof respectively are this day in rebellion against the United States, the following, to wit:

[Here follows an enumeration of the Slave States, with certain reservations in favor of districts occupied by Federal troops.]

"And by virtue of the power and for the purpose aforesaid, I do order and declare that all persons held as slaves within said designated States and parts of States are and henceforward shall be free; and that the Executive Government of the United States, including the military and naval authorities thereof, will recognize and maintain the freedom of said persons.

"And I hereby enjoin upon the people so declared to be free to abstain from all violence, unless in necessary self-defense; and I recommend to them that, in all cases when allowed, they labor faithfully for reasonable wages.

"And I further declare and make known that such persons, of suitable condition, will be received into the armed service of the United States to garrison forts, positions, stations, and other places, and to man vessels of all sorts in said service.

"And upon this act, sincerely believed to be an act of justice, warranted by the Constitution upon military necessity, I invoke the considerate judgment of mankind and the gracious favor of Almighty God.

In testimony whereof, I have hereunto set my name, and caused the seal of the United States to be affixed.

Done at the city of Washington, the first day of January, in the [L. S.] year of our Lord one thousand eight hundred and sixty-three, and of the Independence of the United States the eighty-seventh.

ABRAHAM LINCOLN.

By the President:
WILLIAM H. SEWARD, Secretary of State.

LINCOLN TO THE CHICAGO CLERGYMEN.

It belongs, perhaps, rather to a biography of Abraham Lincoln than the province of history, to say that he gave to this subject his profoundest reflection, considering it not only in its legal and military bearings, but as affected by Christian civilization also. Only a few days before the warning proclamation of September 22d, the President gave audience at the Executive Mansion, to a deputation from all the religious denominations of the city of Chicago, who waited upon him to urge the propriety and necessity of emancipation. In the course of his reply to their remarks, Mr. Lincoln said:

"Do not misunderstand me because I have mentioned these objections. They indicate the difficulties that have thus far prevented my action in some such way as you desire. I have not decided against a proclamation of liberty to the slaves, but hold the matter under advisement. And I can assure you that the subject is on my mind by day and night more than any other Whatever shall appear to be God's will I will do."

It would thus appear that no great measure ever received more deliberate, earnest consideration than that sublime document by which the chains of three million slaves were at once destroyed. Congress and the people approved the measure with much unanimity. An amendment to the Constitution, forever abolishing slavery—introduced by Representative James F. Wilson, of Iowa—was speedily adopted by Congress, and soon ratified by the requisite number of State Legislatures.

Thus was freedom established throughout the land much sooner than, without the rebellion, it could possibly have been done.

THE AMENDMENTS TO THE CONSTITUTION.

It will be in logical order to speak here of two other great triumphs of the Republican party in behalf of human rights, though they were not gained for some years after the amendment by which slavery was abolished. The Fourteenth Amendment to the Constitution, the joint resolution for which passed Congress in 1866, declared that all persons born or naturalized in the United States are citizens, whose rights as such must be protected alike in all the States. By the same amendment the validity of the public debt is forever assured, and payment of the Rebel debt prohibited. By the Fifteenth Amendment, adopted in 1869, the right of franchise is secured to colored men in all parts of the Union. It is hardly too much to say that in the success of these amendments to the Constitution, following emancipation by military authority, as they did, the Republican party did more in behalf of genuine liberty and more against political and civil injustice than was ever before accomplished in a much longer period, by any party or by any nation.

THE CAMPAIGN OF 1864.

But it was not alone by great success in the management of the civil Government, and by the practical adoption in legislation of liberal and progressive ideas, that the Republican party was able to maintain its ascendancy. The conduct of the war had for some time been such as to merit the approbation of the country. The Army of the Potomac, under General Meade, had gained the great victory of Gettysburgh. With the Western armies under Grant and Sherman, victory had been the rule. With them there had been no such word as fail. By the time the presidential campaign of 1864 began, a large portion of "Confederate" territory had been regained; the Mississippi river was open to the Gulf; the backbone of the rebellion had been broken by the remarkable battle of Chattanooga; Sherman was marching on toward his rapid conquest of Georgia; Grant was thundering through the Wilderness on that notable campaign which finally resulted in the capitulation of all the rebel armies, and the glorious triumph of the Union arms.

Thus the military situation gave every promise of speedy success, when the third Republican National Convention assembled at Baltimore, June 7, 1864. Over this convention temporarily presided the Rev. Robert J. Breckinridge, the distinguished divine of Kentucky. Governor Dennison, of Ohio, was permanent President. Abraham Lincoln was re-nominated candidate for President, receiving all the votes except eleven from the State of Missouri, which were cast for General Grant. Andrew Johnson, of Tennessee, was nominated for Vice President.

The platform adopted by this convention was an admirable expression of patriotic sentiment and wisdom. It, of course, forms an important part of the political annals of the times:

THE BALTIMORE PLATFORM OF 1864.

Resolved, That it is the highest duty of every American citizen to maintain against all their enemies the integrity of the Union, and the paramount authority of the Constitution and laws of the United States; and that, laying aside all differences of political opinion, we pledge ourselves as Union men, animated by a common sentiment, and aiming at a common object, to do everything in our power to aid the Government in quelling by force of arms the Rebellion now raging against its authority, and in bringing to the punishment due to their crimes the Rebels and traitors arrayed against it.

Resolved, That we approve the determination of the Government of the United States not to compromise with Rebels, nor to offer any terms of peace except such as may be based upon an "unconditional surrender" of their hostility and a return to their just allegiance to the Constitution and laws of the United States, and that we call upon the Government to maintain this position and to prosecute the war with the utmost possible vigor to the complete suppression of the Rebellion, in full reliance upon the self-sacrifice, the patriotism, the heroic valor, and the undying devotion of the American people to their country and its free institutions.

Resolved, That, as Slavery was the cause, and now constitutes the strength, of this Rebellion, and as it must be always and everywhere hostile to the principles of Republican government, justice and the national safety demand its utter and complete extirpation from the soil of the Republic; and that we uphold and maintain the acts and proclamations by which the Government, in its own defense, has aimed a death-blow at the gigantic evil. We are in favor, furthermore, of such an amendment to the Constitution, to be made by the people in conformity with its provisions, as shall terminate and forever prohibit the existence of Slavery within the limits of the jurisdictlon of the United States.

Resolved, That the thanks of the American people are due to the soldiers and sailors of the Army and Navy, who have periled their lives in defense of their country, and in vindication of the honor of the flag; that the nation owes to them some permanent recognition of their patriotism and valor, and ample and permanent provision for those of their survivors who have received disabling and honorable wounds in the service of the country; and that the memories of those who have fallen in its defense shall be held in grateful and everlasting remembrance.

Resolved, That we approve and applaud the practical wisdom, the unselfish patriotism, and unswerving fidelity to the Constitution and the principles of American liberty, with which Abraham Lincoln has discharged, under circumstances of unparalleled difficulty, the great duties and responsibilities of the Presidential office; that we approve and indorse, as demanded by the emergency and essential to the preservation of the nation, and as within the Constitution, the measures and acts which he has adopted to defend the nation against its open and secret foes; that we approve especially of the Proclamation of Emancipation, and the employment as Union soldiers of man heretofore held in Slavery; and that we have full confidence in his determination to carry these and all other constitutional measures essential to the salvation of the country into full and complete effect.

Resolved, That we deem it essential to the general welfare that harmony should prevail in the national council, and we regard as worthy of public confidence and official trust those only who cordially indorse the principles proclaimed in these resolutions, and which should characterize the administration of the Government.

Resolved, That the Government owes to all men employed in its armies, without regard to distinction of color, the full protection of the laws of war; and that any violation of these laws or of the usages of civilized nations in the time of war by the Rebels now in arms should be made the subject of full and prompt redress.

Resolved, That the foreign immigration, which in the past has added so much to the wealth and development of resources and increase of power to this nation, the asylum of the oppressed of all nations, should be fostered and encouraged by a liberal and just policy.

Resolved, That we are in favor of the speedy construction of a railroad to the Pacific.

Resolved, That the national faith, pledged for the redemption of the Public Debt, must be kept inviolate; and that for this purpose we recommend economy and rigid responsibility in the public expenditures, and a vigorous and just system of taxation; that it is the duty of every loyal State to sustain the credit and promote the use of the national currency.

Resolved, That we approve the position taken by the Government that the people of the United States never regarded with indifference the attempt of any European power to overthrow by force, or to supplant by fraud, the institutions of any republican government on the western continent, and that they view with extreme jealousy, as menacing to the peace and independence of this our country, the efforts of any such power to obtain new footholds for monarchial governments, sustained by a foreign military force, in near proximity to the United States.

THE CLEVELAND CONVENTION.

There was some dissatisfaction with the administration of President Lincoln on the part of Republicans. These had held a convention at the City of Cleveland on the 31st of May, and had nominated General John C. Fremont for President and General John Cochrane for Vice-President. These gentlemen accepted the nominations, and for a time there was a prospect of a triangular contest. Among the most eminent men who took part in this movement were Wendell Phillips, B. Gratz Brown, (now again in the bolting business,) Frederick Douglas and James Redpath. It was winked at, but not boldly advocated, by Horace Greeley in his newspaper. The practical unanimity with which the Baltimore platform and nominations were received by the masses of the Republican party, however, demonstrated the futility of the Cleveland movement. Montgomery Blair retired from President Lincoln's cabinet, and the Cleveland ticket collapsed.

THE DEMOCRATIC CONVENTION.

The National Democratic Convention assembled at Chicago several weeks after the Republicans had entered upon the active operations of a vigorous campaign. The Union armies were at the same time carrying on vigorous and successful campaigns. Nevertheless, the Democracy adopted a peace platform. The most noteworthy resolution was the following:

"*Resolved*, That this convention does explicetly declare, as the sense of the American people, that after four years of failure to restore the Union by the experiment of war, during which, under the pretense of military necessity or war power, higher than the Constitution, the Constitution itself has been disregarded in every part, and public liberty and private right alike trodden down, and the material prosperity of the country essentially impaired, justice, humanity, liberty, and the public welfare demand that immediate efforts be made for a cessation of hostilities, with a view to an ultimate convention of the States, or other peaceful means, to the end that at the earliest practicable moment peace may be restored on the basis of the Federal Union of the States."

Gen. George B. McClellan was nominated as the candidate for President, and George H. Pendleton, of Ohio, for Vice-President.

THE CANVASS.

The canvass was one of great earnestness on the part of the Republicans. Their meetings were everywhere largely attended, but there was little manifestation of excitement. It was clear that a vast majority of the people had firmly resolved to save the republic, and by means of the re-election of President Lincoln. He carried all of the States voting except New Jersey, Delaware and Kentucky. The States of Virginia, North Carolina, South Carolina, Georgia, Alabama, Mississippi, Louisiana, Texas, Florida, Arkansas and Tennessee being in rebellion, did not participate in the election. Of the popular votes, Lincoln received 2,216,127 against 1,808,725 for McClellan, being a Republican majority of 407,402 votes.

This crushing political victory, in addition to the recent triumphs of arms, settled the question of the war. It was universally agreed that the re-election of President Lincoln meant the salvation of the republic. Thus the triumph of the Republican party was identical with the triumqh of the national cause. And as a matter of fact, it was only a little more than one month after President Lincoln's second inauguration that the Rebel armies surrendered and the pretended "Confederate" Government gave up the ghost.

THE DEATH OF PRESIDENT LINCOLN.

On the 14th of April, 1865, President Lincoln was assassinated, and expired the next morning, only five days after the surrender of the Rebel General Lee at Appomattox. By this fearful crime the nation was thrown from the highest state of enjoyment over the near prospect of peace into the deepest gloom. Had there been wanting evidence of the necessity of the abolition of slavery it would have been found in the possibility of so terrible a crime by one of its defenders. Mr. Lincoln's was "the kindest heart that ever beat," and the "deep damnation of his taking off" would forever place any cause in unmixed condemnation. Upon his death the Presidency devolved upon Vice-President Johnson. It is not to be denied that the situation at this time was one of grave responsibility and difficulty. Perhaps no man could have filled the office without making himself in some respects vulnerable to honest and well grounded criticism. But there are many reasons for believing that President Johnson's policy of reconstructing the States lately in rebellion, to which he adhered with obstinate determination, greatly added to the difficulties of the times and cast many unnecessary embarrassments in the way of a speedy, just and wise adjustment of troubles which, at best, could not have been easily arranged. As it turned out, the Republican party, instead of having one exceedingly difficult problem to solve, had two; namely, the question of reconstruction and President Johnson. In this great emergency the party performed its mission with such success as to entitle it to the favorable judgment of the country. The President was placed in a hopeless minority, and the friends of the Union in the late rebellious States were given the control of affairs. The President was afterwards impeached by the House of Representatives for high crimes and misdemeanors, but after a long and exciting trial by the Senate he was acquitted, two-thirds failing to vote for conviction. This unhappy difference between the executive and legislative branches of the government certainly, to some extent, delayed practical reconstruction, but that before the close of the first presidential term after Mr. Johnson, the seats of both Houses of Congress were all filled and the Union again fully restored and essentially harmonious, is a justification of Republican policy and statesmanship which it would be difficult to dispute. That, in addition, the result was brought about with a notable victory for the civil and political rights of millions who had been slaves, and notwithstanding the sturdy opposition of a determined executive, greatly adds to the significance of the triumph.

CHAPTER IV.

HISTORY OF THE REPUBLICAN PARTY.

(CONTINUED.)

The Campaign of 1868—Nomination of Grant and Colfax by the Republicans—An Easy Triumph Over Seymour and Blair—Grant in the Presidential Chair—Difficulties which he Encountered—The Ku Klux and the Office Seekers—Grant astonishes the Latter by His Appointments—What His Administration Accomplished.

The National Convention of 1868 was held in the city of Chicago, and was unquestionably one of the most enthusiastic occasions of the kind which has been witnessed in the country. Just before the time for the convention, there was a national gathering of the soldiers of the Union armies, which brought together vast numbers of the veteran defenders of the Republic. They remained in the city during the sittings of the Convention. The hotels and boarding houses were packed. For a week the Garden City was jammed with people. The Crosby Opera House, in which the Convention was held, one of the largest buildings of the kind in the country—since destroyed by the great fire—could not contain a tithe of the people who desired admittance.

Carl Schurz was selected as temporary chairman.

Governor Hawley, of Connecticut, was the permanent President of the Convention; an admirable presiding officer, quick and correct in decision, ever good-natured, and having a fine voice easily heard in every part of an immense auditorium. The Convention adopted a platform as follows:

THE CHICAGO PLATFORM OF 1868.

1. We congratulate the country on the assured success of the reconstruction policy of Congress, as evidenced by the adoption, in the majority of the States lately in rebellion, of constitutions securing equal civil and political rights to all; and it is the duty of the Government to sustain those institutions and to prevent the people of such States from being remitted to a state of anarchy

2. The guarantee by Congress of equal suffrage to all loyal men at the South was demanded by every consideration of public safety, of gratitude, and of justice, and must be maintained; while the question of suffrage in all the loyal States properly belongs to the people of those States.

3. We denounce all forms of repudiation as a national crime; and the national honor requires the payment of the public indebtedness in the uttermost good faith to all creditors at home and abroad, not only according to the letter, but the spirit of the laws under which it was contracted.

4. It is due to the labor of the nation that taxation should be equalized, and reduced as rapidly as the national faith will permit.

5. The national debt, contracted as it has been for the preservation of the Union for all time to come, should be extended over a fair period for redemption; and it is the duty of Congress to reduce the rate of interest thereon, whenever it can be honestly done.

6. That the best policy to diminish our burden of debt is to so improve our credit that capitalists will seek to loan us money at lower rates of interest than we now pay, and must continue to pay so long as repudiation, partial or total, open or covert, is threatened or suspected.

7. The Government of the United States should be administered with the strictest economy; and the corruptions which have been so shamefully nursed and fostered by Andrew Johnson call loudly for radical reform.

8. We profoundly deplore the untimely and tragic death of Abraham Lincoln, and regret the accession to the Presidency of Andrew Johnson, who has acted treacherously to the people who elected him and the cause he was pledged to support; who has usurped high legislative and judicial functions; who has refused to execute the laws; who has used his high office to induce

other officers to ignore and violate the laws ; who has employed his executive powers to render insecure the property, the peace, liberty, and life of the citizen ; who has abused the pardoning power ; who has denounced the National Legislature as unconstitutional; who has persistently and corruptly resisted, by every means in his power, every proper attempt at the reconstruction of the States lately in rebellion ; who has perverted the public patronage into an engine of wholesale corruption ; and who has been justly impeached for high crimes and misdemeanors, and properly pronounced guilty thereof by the vote of 35 Senators.

9. The doctrine of Great Britain and other European powers, that because a man is once a subject he is always so, must be resisted at every hazard by the United States, as a relic of feudal times not authorized by the laws of nations, and at war with our National honor and independence. Naturalized citizens are entitled to protection in all their rights of citizenship, as though they were native born ; and no citizen of the United States, native or naturalized, must be liable to arrest and imprisonment by any foreign power for acts done or words spoken in this country; and, if so arrested and imprisoned, it is the duty of the Government to interfere in his behalf.

10. Of all who were faithful in the trials of the late war, there were none entitled to more especial honor than the brave soldiers and seamen who endured the hardships of campaign and cruise, and imperiled their lives in the srrvice of the country; the bounties and pensions provided by the laws for these brave defenders of the nation are obligations never to be forgotten ; the widows and orphans of the gallant dead are the wards of the people—a sacred legacy bequeathed to the nation's protecting care.

11. Foreign immigration, which in the past has added so much to the wealth, development, and resources, and increase of power to this Republic, the asylum of the oppressed of all nations, should be fostered and encouraged by a liberal and just policy.

12. This Convention declares itself in sympathy with all oppressed peoples struggling for their rights.

13. That we highly commend the spirit of magnanimity and forbearance with which men who have served in the Rebellion, but who now frankly and honestly co-operate with us in restoring the peace of the country and reconstructing the Southern State Governments upon the basis of impartial justice and equal rights, are received back into the communion of the loyal people ; and we favor the removal of the disqualifications and restrictions imposed upon the late Rebels in the same measure as the spirit of disloyalty will die out, and as may be consistent with the safety of the loyal people.

14. That we recognize the great principles laid down in the immortal Declaration of Independence as the true foundation of democratic government ; and we hail with gladness every effort toward making these principles a living reality on every inch of American soil.

HON. HAMILTON FISH,

Secretary of State.

On motion of General John A. Logan, Chairman of the Illinois delegation, General Ulysses S. Grant, of that State, was unanimously nominated candidate for President. On the third ballot, Schuyler Colfax, of Indiana, was nominated for Vice-President, defeating Reuben E. Fenton, of New York, Andrew G. Curtin, of Pennsylvania, Henry Wilson, of Massachusetts, and others. The platform and candidates were heartily approved by the party, and the campaign at once began and was carried on to the end with great zeal. The Democratic party held its convention in the city of New York in the month of July, nominating Horatio Seymour, of New York, candidate for President and Francis P. Blair, Jr., of Missouri, for Vice-President. Grant and Colfax carried the States of Alabama, Arkansas, California, Connecticut, Illinois, Indiana, Iowa, Kansas, Maine, Massachusetts, Michigan, Minnesota, Missouri, Nebraska, Nevada, New Hampshire, North Carolina, Ohio, Pennsylvania, Rhode Island, South Carolina, Tennessee, Vermont, West Virginia, Wisconsin. Seymour and Blair carried Delaware, Georgia, Kentucky, Louisiana (by intimidation), Maryland, New Jersey, New York and Oregon. General Grant received 3,013,188 votes, Mr. Seymour receiving 2,703,600, the Republican majority being 309,588 votes.

PRESIDENT GRANT'S ADMINISTRATION.

It will not be denied by those who fairly consider the matter, that President Grant assumed control of the executive department of the Government under circumstances of peculiar difficulty. The administration of President Johnson had not been calculated to hasten a just system of reconstruction. The animosities of the war, so far from being allayed by Mr. Johnson's policy, had been aggravated, and the discontent, among the less honorable classes of society manifested itself in secret organizations which became responsible for many hideous crimes, and in some portions of the South a reign of terror. That all this has ceased, and that with the interposition of martial law, as expressly authorized by Congress, in only a single instance, is largely due to the personal influence of President Grant himself. When he entered the presidential office, many seats of Senators and Representatives were vacant—the result of the severance of relations with the Union caused by secession—and a year before the expiration of his first term, every seat was occupied, some by gentlemen who had taken active part in the rebellion, but had become qualified by the magnanimous clemency of the Government. Complete reconstruction has, therefore, for some time been a practical fact, and thorough reconciliation is rapidly being brought about. It is difficult to conceive how more could have been done in the same time.

PATRONAGE AND ITS EVILS.

But the embarrassments of the administration only began with the question of reconstruction.

The practical matter of patronage at once presented serious trouble. The President selected as his cabinet E. B. Washburne, of Illinois, Secretary of State; A. T. Stewart, of New York, Secretary of the Treasury; A. E. Borie, of Pennsylvania, Secretary of the Navy; Jacob D. Cox, of Ohio, Secretary of the Interior; John A. J. Creswell, of Maryland, Postmaster-General, and E. R. Hoar, of Massachusetts, Attorney-General. General Sherman was allowed to act as Secretary of War for a time. Mr. Stewart being found ineligible, George S. Boutwell, of Massachusetts, was appointed Secretary of the Treasury. Mr. Washburne soon resigned, and Hamilton Fish, of New York, was made Secretary of State. Soon afterwards General John A. Rawlins, of Illinois, was made Secretary of War. He was a most admirable officer, but soon succumbed to a dread disease—consumption—by which his life had long been threatened. After his death, Gen. William W. Belknap, of Iowa, was appointed. His department was assailed on a memorable occasion, and by able men, but the assault was signally and honorably repulsed, and the integrity and ability of the Secretary completely sustained. Mr. Hoar was appointed one of the Circuit Judges, under the act of Congress creating that adjunct to the Supreme Court of the United States, but the Senate, in a spasm of childish resentment, refused to confirm him, and he resigned the office of Attorney-General. Amos T. Akerman, of Georgia, was appointed to the place, but resigning in 1871,

Ex-Senator George H. Williams, of Oregon, was selected in his stead. Mr. Borie had previously resigned his position as Secretary of the Navy, to which Hon. George M. Robeson, of New Jersey, was appointed.

THE CIVIL SERVICE—DIFFICULTIES IN ITS MANAGEMENT.

The war had vastly augmented the civil service establishment. When President Grant entered the executive office, there were single bureaux of departments more extensive than had been some of the departments, or perhaps any of them, before the war. These had large numbers of officials at the national capital and throughout the country. One of the ill results of the war was this necessary increase of public offices. Many persons in every community directed their energies to office-getting as though it were a regular business. When President Grant was inaugurated, Washington swarmed with office-seekers; with many thousands of men asking the privilege of serving their country in public place. Many were necessarily disappointed, and hence arose a certain disaffection in the Republican party, which, aided by some opposed to the existing laws imposing duties on imports and the plan of internal taxation in being, culminated in the Cincinnati Convention of May, 1872, which is treated at length in subsequent chapters of this book.

Meanwhile, however, the vast patronage of the Government was distributed to the general satisfaction of the body politic, and, in the main, to the good of the service. It is believed that no more mistakes were made than were inevitable under the system in force.

Another great source of embarrassment to the Administration of President Grant—as it necessarily would have been to any administration—was the conflicting opinions among members of the Republican party upon questions which, of comparatively little moment during the war, had by this time come to be of grave importance. The patriotic public willingly endured high taxation to sustain those who were periling their lives to save the Republic and the cause of freedom. The war ended, and the armies disbanded, it was proper for the Government to cut off many of the sources of revenue. Upon the question of how this could most wisely be done, there was, and there still is, wide difference of opinion among patriotic statesmen.

If it was impossible to secure unanimity of sentiment among Republicans during the war, when it was necessary for the Executive to exercise extraordinary powers, and the people to make extraordinary sacrifices both of substance and opinion, it would require a miracle to secure such unanimity in an era necessarily requiring many changes of policy, many changes of law. The ocean is said to be more dangerous to navigators just after a storm than during its prevalence. There is an irregular wildness about the waves as they settle back to calmness, which is peculiarly perilous. Such was the political situation when President Grant assumed office. It was more difficult to administer the Government to the satisfaction of the party in power after the war than it had been during the war.

SUCCESS OF GRANT'S ADMINISTRATION.

And yet there has been constant progress and success. Taxation has been greatly reduced, and that without giving so rude a shock to systems in being, to which the trade and commerce of the country had become accustomed, as to produce a financial panic. Large numbers of officials in the internal revenue department have been dispensed with by reason of this reduction, and taxation by this mode now rests but upon a few articles. The free list in the tariff has been considerably increased, and duties upon a large number of the necessaries of life and national development have been reduced. The expenditures of the government have been considerably diminished. The national debt has been paid to the amount of three hundred millions of dollars, in round numbers, during the first three years of President Grant's administration. A large amount of the government bonds, bearing six per cent. interest per annum has been converted into a like amount of bonds bearing six per cent. interest. Thus, by the action of a Republican Congress, ably sustained by a Republican administration, have the finances of the nation been successfully conducted, and the public credit maintained against every assault, and even from time to time improved in the great commercial marts of Christendom. Nor has there been any considerable revulsion in the business of the country. The material wealth of the Republic has been constantly augmenting; its great cities have been all the time prosperous; the agricultural capacities of the nation have never ceased to grow; labor has been well paid, and the laboring man has constantly grown in the public esteem and in power; the development of all the material interests of the land has simply been stupendous. Even the South, which suffered most of the calamities resulting from the war, is in a situation of rapid recuperation, and will surely be more wealthy and progressive than ever before, ere the first centennial of American Independence.

These plain facts, which are known and read of all men, demonstrate the general success of President Grant's administration, and show that the Republican party continues to be entitled to the confidence of the American people.

CHAPTER V.

HISTORY OF THE REPUBLICAN PARTY.

(CONTINUED.)

The Campaign of 1872—Action of the Forty-Second Congress at its Second Session—$60,000,000 Taxes Taken Off—Amnesty Extended Greatly—Force Bill Discontinued—The House Votes to Abolish the Franking Privilege—Everything Investigated—Call for a National Convention—Spirit of the Party—Unanimous for Grant—The Convention is Held—Its Doings in Detail—Harmony and Enthusiasm—Platform of 1872—Grant's Letter Accepting the Nomination.

"What are you going to do in Congress next winter?" the writer asked of one of the most distinguished Senators, nearly a year ago.

"O, make Presidents," was the answer.

Such being confessedly the main purpose of both political parties during the session next preceding each Presidential election, we may properly reckon the political campaign of 1872 as having commenced with the assembling of the second session of the Forty-second Congress, on the first Monday of December, 1871.

The meaning of the Senator's expression is obvious, viz: that the Congressmen of each party would endeavor to shape legislation so as to secure the success of *their* party in the ensuing campaign; and this means, of course, where voters are as free and intelligent as in America, that the dominant party will endeavor to enact good and wholesome laws, such as the people will approve, while the minority will strive, in the debates and in multitudinous investigations and newspaper attacks, Senatorial "philippics," etc., to create the impression among the people that all the virtue resides in *their* ranks, all the vice in that of the majority and in the existing administration.

ATTACKS ON THE ADMINISTRATION.

Of this sort of tactics were the attack on the Navy Department in the House, the tirade of Charles Sumner in the Senate and other similar demonstrations against the Executive and his cabinet, and against the majority party in Congress. No less than fifteen different investigations, founded on this or that man's allegations against the conduct of the Government, in one department or another, were asked by the Democrats or the disaffected Republicans during the session. These investigations were promptly ordered by the consent of the majority—the only case where any debate occurred being on the resolution concerning the sale of arms to French agents, introduced by Mr. Sumner in the Senate, and preceded by a preamble which contained a virulent attack on the administration, and which assumed as proven all the allegations made by the enemies of the Government. This the Senate would not pass, but it did order the investigation, and gave Mr. Schurz, the instigator of the charges, the privilege of examining or cross-examining all witnesses. The investigations were, for the most part, conducted openly, and all the testimony was published; and the results (which are given at some length in a subsequent chapter) were found to strengthen, rather than weaken the position of the administration in the hearts of the people. Never was there so cogent an illustration of the proverb, "great cry and little wool," as was furnished by these investigations and the clamors which preceded them.

ACTS OF CONGRESS.

The laws enacted by the Forty-Second Congress at this session were also of a nature to strengthen the dominant party. Among the most important of these were the act reducing the taxes, internal and import, by $53,000,000 a year, estimated upon the receipts of last year; the act conferring additional civil rights upon the colored class of citizens, hitherto discriminated against by society, in despite of the manifest spirit of the recent amendments to the national Constitution; the act granting complete amnesty to 25,000 rebels of the late war, who had hitherto labored under certain political disabilities; the act extending to soldiers, widows and orphans, the benefit of the bounty laws, and the act for facilitating the entry of land by soldiers entitled to bounty; all of which became law by the President's signature. Nor is the present Republican Congress less praiseworthy for what it has left undone than for what it has done. The still rampant spirit of outlawry in many sections of the South, as proven before the Joint Committee on Southern Outrages, offered a great temptation (which was pressed by many Southern members) to continue the bill authorizing the suspension of the *habeas corpus* by the President—a privilege which terminated by limitation with the expiration of the late session. The enemies of the Republican party would have liked very much to see the majority vote to continue this law, so that an outcry against "federal usurpation" could be made. They would also have liked to see the majority committed to a bill for the federal regulation of the Southern elections, with the authorization of such measures of enforcement as should furnish grounds for some clamor about "bayonet rule." But the party refused to commit itself to such acts, and also refrained in a provoking way from doing much that was indiscreet in the way of land grants and private appropriations, out of which the Opposition orators and journals could forge any effective weapons for the campaign. In short, the freshest acts of the Republican party, even as shown in its representation in Congress—the place where, if anywhere, vulnerable points may usually be found—are probably less partisan, and no less just, moderate and virtuous than those of any political party, similarly represented, in any previous period of our history—even in the "good old days" of Andrew Jackson, or any other canonized politician whom we are accustomed to laud in our allusions. Such a record of course fortifies a party, and should always be striven after, not only before, but after national elections; and nothing will tend so strongly towards it as the principle of progressiveness and catholicity of opinion which has come to prevail among Republican statesmen, (especially in the journalistic estate and in the lower house of Congress) and which is now recognized as one of the quickening elements of the Republican creed.

THE PHILADELPHIA CONVENTION.

Still fresher than the acts of Congress, however, and perhaps more authoritative, as being the more direct expression of the popular sentiments of the party, are the acts and declarations of the National Republican Convention of 1872, held at Philadelphia, on the 5th and 6th of June. And the proceedings of this body we must now record.

The Philadelphia Convention was called by the National Republican Committee, in accordance with party usages, after a prolonged session of the Committee at Washington. The call bears date January 11th, 1872. It enumerates the achievements and the leading present tenets of the Republican party, and closes with this invitation:

"To continue and firmly establish its fundamental principles, we invite the co-operation of *all citizens* of the United States."

The National Committee, in a special resolution, sent by telegraph to all parts of the country, urged all holders of office under the national administration to abstain from participating in local conventions, or officiating as delegates; and the injunction was so generally obeyed that, notwithstanding the fact that the Opposition freely stigmatized it as the "Federal Office-holders' Convention," and Mr. Greeley's paper usually called it "Grant's Convention," there were not two dozen such office-holders in the Convention—*i. e.* a little more than one per cent. of the whole number of delegates and alternates.

THE POPULAR FEELING.

Even before this call was issued, the Senators, journalists and other public men who were displeased with General Grant's administration, or who had reasons, personal or otherwise, for desiring a change in the government, had begun to agitate the subject of such a change. This had been done chiefly by indirection, however; the only method resorted to being free criticism of Grant's administration, and a studied tone of disrespect, or a habit of sly innuendo when speaking of the President. What these Anti-Grant journalists, etc., did after discovering the drift of popular feeling within the party will be told in a subsequent chapter. That the drift was decidedly and irresistibly toward Grant as the nominee for another term of four years, was soon plainly manifest.

GRANT ENDORSED.

The Republicans of Connecticut were the first to meet after this call was issued. At their convention, at Hartford, January 24th, they avowed their "undiminished confidence in the patriotism, integrity and ability of President Grant." Those of Florida followed, on April 11th, with a resolution, unanimously adopted, instructing delegates to use "every effort to secure his [Grant's] renomination."

The Indiana Republicans, commemorating with their meeting, as usual, the sacred birthday of Washington, declared in their resolutions that the administration of General Grant had been "consistent with the principles of the Republican party, and eminently just, wise and humane"; and they accordingly instructed their delegates at Philadelphia to "vote for the renomination of Grant and Colfax."

Iowa, at her convention, at Des Moines, on the 27th of March, was no less explicit and positive in her declarations and instructions.

South Carolina had already done the same, at Columbia, on the 19th of February. And Missouri, favorite nesting-place of the so-called Liberals, declared, on the same day with Indiana, her "unswerving confidence in the integrity, patriotism, and zealous devotion of the present Chief Magistrate."

Maine, Kansas, Kentucky, Oregon, Massachusetts, Rhode Island, Wisconsin, Pennsylvania and other States joined in the chorus of approval until it echoed from ocean to ocean, and from the Gulf to the Lakes.

THE CONVENTION MEETS.

When, therefore, the Republicans of the nation

met at Philadelphia, they had a simple task before them, so far as the nomination of a Presidentali candidate was concerned. They assembled at noon, on the 5th of June, in the spacious Academy of Music, at Philadelphia, which building had been gorgeously draped and decorated for the occasion. Never did a finer and more thoroughly representative body of men assemble for a similar purpose in this country. Coming fresh from the people, they were possessed by an intense and unanimous enthusiasm for the cause which they came to organize—the reflected and concentrated glow of that great popular heart, from which all the acts of the convention seemed to spring.

It was evident that the Republican masses did not intend to be trifled with in the present crisis, and that they sent up, therefore, to Philadelphia, delegates composed of their strongest men. It was a general remark among those who came as lookers-on, and many of whom were avowedly hostile to the object of the convention, that the array of well known men—men of authority and influence, not derived from their present office—had never been excelled, if equalled, in any similar gathering. When William E. Chandler, as Secretary of the National Republican Committee, called the assemblage to order, at 12 o'clock, on Wednesday, his gavel was obeyed by nearly a score of Governors of States, by twenty-four ex-Senators of the United States, by fifteen members of Congress, two retired Cabinet officers, forty or fifty generals of the great Union army, and other dignitaries of wide public recognition too numerous to particularize. Among the Governors of States, with or without the *ex*, we can now call to mind sixteen or seventeen; viz., Claflin, of Massachusetts; Smyth, of New Hampshire; Smith, of Vermont; Hawley, of Connecticut; Burnside, of Rhode Island; Orr, of South Carolina; Parsons, of Alabama; Oglesby, of Illinois; Noyes and Hayes, of Ohio; Lane and Baker, of Indiana; Morgan, of New York; Fairchild, of Wisconsin; Howard, of Michigan; and Wells, of Virginia. Among the heroes of the War for the Union were Generals Logan, Woodford, Fairchild, Hawley, Burnside, Sol. Meredith, Thos. S. Allen, E. F. Noyes, and a host of others, many of whom have, since doffing their army blue, been honored by a grateful country with official stations, the title of which has superseded the military "handles" of their names.

But it was not of generals and politicians alone that the convention was made up. Learning had its representatives there in goodly numbers, and prominent among them were President White, of Cornell University, and Prof. Steele, of Vermont, the latter of whom had the honor of writing the most acceptable of the many platforms submitted for the use of the convention. Philanthropy and reform were there in the person of the venerable Gerrit Smith, Nestor of the Anti-Slavery army, and a man whose milk of human kindness had never been soured by personal jealousy, like that of Charles Sumner. The business community, which seems to have awakened earlier than usual to the importance of this campaign, was represented, perhaps, more ably than ever before in a similar convention. When we mention Alexander H. Rice, ex-mayor of Boston; Horace B. Claflin, the leading New York dry goods merchant; John A. Griswold, the Troy iron manufacturer; J. Y. Scammon, the Chicago banker; Horace Fairbanks, the largest manufacturer in Vermont; Wm. Orton, head of the telegraph business in the United States; Thaddeus C. Pound and J. G. Thorpe, prominent in the Wisconsin lumber business, and Eber B. Ward, the great iron manufacturer of the Northwest, we have named but a tithe of the solid business men of the country who participated in this convention as delegates. Many more were interested lookers-on, and expressed earnestly their readiness to co-operate with the convention in the work of the campaign.

Thus constituted and thus determined, the delegates came together in the historical town of Philadelphia. No better city could have been selected, on two accounts: first, there were better hotel facilities than anywhere else, except New York; and second, there was more local enthusiasm prevailing to add *eclat* to the occasion. The fall election coming on early in Pennsylvania, there were already a great many Republicans organized into clubs and prepared for public demonstrations. These, re-inforced by numerous corps from abroad—one from

Boston, one from Washington, one from Pittsburgh, and numerous others from Lancaster and elsewhere in Pennsylvania, paraded the streets with stirring music and significant banners by day, or with torches and transparencies by night, or joined in mass-meetings with unprecedented numbers and enthusiasm. Their music filled their streets with its "voluptuous swell," and their brave faces and lusty huzzas inspired enthusiasm in every breast. On Wednesday, at noon, as already mentioned, the convention assembled and organized itself for business. Hon. Morton McMichael, ex-Mayor of Philadelphia, was made temporary chairman, and, in accordance with notice previously served, the various State delegations announced to him, as called upon, their own selections for the following officers, of which each State furnished a complete set: Vice-presidents and secretaries of the convention; committees on resolutions, on credentials, on rules and on permanent organization.

The permanent officers of the convention, who assumed their functions just before the adjournment of the first session, were as follows:

President—Thomas Settle, of North Carolina.

Vice-Presidents—Alabama, Paul Strobach; Arkansas, Elijah Baxter; California, H. S. Sargent; Connecticut, Sabin L. Gage; Delaware, Isaac June; Georgia, B. F. Conley; Illinois, Emory A. Storrs; Indiana, Gen. Solomon D. Meredith; Iowa, N. H. Kevers; Kansas, John C. Carpenter; Kentucky, R. M. Keely; Lousiana, Louis F. Frazer; Maine, P. F. Rohey; Maryland, Alexander H. Rice; Michigan, Eber B. Ward; Minnesota, C. F. Benedict; Mississippi, R. W. Fleemey; Nebraska, John S. Bowen; New Hampshire, William H. Y. Hackett; New Jersey, Dudley S. Gregory; New York, H. B. Claflin; North Carolina, Edward Cantwell; Ohio, Lt. Gov. Jacob Mueller; Oregon, John P. Booth; Pennsylvania, H. W. Oliver; Rhode Island, A. E.

HON. MATT. H. CARPENTER,
U. S. Senator for Wisconsin.

Burnside; North Carolina, A. J. Rensier; Tennessee, William H. Wisner; Texas, A. B. Norton; Vermont, H. Fairbanks; Virginia, Charles T. Mallard; West Virginia, Charles Horton; Wisconsin, Hon. Lucius Fairchild; Florida, Dennis Evan; Colorado, George M. Chilcot; District of Columbia, John F. Cooke; Idaho, John R. McBride; Wyoming, J. M. Donnellon; Nevada, Gen. John Benjamin.

Secretaries—H. H. Bingham, of Pennsylvania, and forty-one others—one from each State and territory.

Committee on Platform—Alabama, R. M. Ruggles; Arkansas, W. W. Way; California, J. H. Withington; Connecticut, Gen. J. R. Hawley; Delaware, Henry F. Pickles; Florida. J. W. Johnson; Georgia, D. A. Walker; Illinois, Herman Raster; Indiana, Charles Krug; Iowa, William Vandetter; Kansas, John C. Carpenter; Kentucky, James Speed; Louisiana, John Ray; Maine, J. P. Pullen; Maryland, Thomas A. Spence; Massachusetts, J. B. D. Coggswell; Michigan, W. A. Howard; Minnesota, A. E. Hicks; Mississippi, John R. Linch; Missouri, John Stover; Nebraska, John B. Weston; Nevada, L. H. Head; New Hampshire, Osborne Ray; New Jersey, Charles Hewitt; New York, James N. Matthews; North Carolina, J. W. Hood; Ohio, B. R. Hayes; Oregon, H. R. Kincaid; Pennsylvania, G. W. Scofield; Rhode Island, William Goddard; South Carolina, R. B. Elliott; Tennessee, A. J. Ricks, Texas, J. W. Talbot; Vermont, Benjamin H. Steele; Virginia, Col. Ed. Daniels; West Virginia, Thomas B. Swan; Wisconsin, Thomas S. Allen; Colorado, Jerome B. Chaffee; District of Columbia, A. R. Sheppard; Idaho, J. Curtis; Montana, W. F. Sanders; Wyoming, J. W. Donnellton.

All that was accomplished of moment on the first day of the convention was the reporting of the permanent officers by the committee appointed for that purpose. While the Committee on Permanent Organization was out deliberating, speech-making was in order, and Senators Morton and Logan, who were occupying a proscenium box, were successively called upon and responded briefly, the former finding time, however, to enter into a careful consideration of the duties now pressing on the Republican party, and a cogent answer to those who pretend that the mission of the party is accomplished. The Senators were followed by Ex-

Governor Oglesby, of Illinois, Ex-Governor Orr, of South Carolina, and by two colored delegates, W. H. Gray, of Arkansas, and R. B. Elliott, M. C., of South Carolina. This negro oratory was a peculiar feature of the convention, and was continued to some extent on the following day—in every case with great credit to the newly enfranchised race, whose representatives had never before been heard in a national convention of one of the great political parties. The principal speakers of sable skin were the two above named and Messrs. Lynch, of Mississippi [Secretary of State], and Harris, of Georgia, all of whom were greatly to be commended for their keen insight into the main issues, and their sharp method of bringing the subject home to their auditors' comprehension. The colored race was certainly well represented in this convention, and its representatives have reason to be gratified with the impression which they made. It should be remarked here that two or three of the State delegations had colored men for Chairmen, and that the African nationality had three places upon the Platform Committee, and was also well represented upon the other committees.

NO CONTESTS.

After the speeches had been made and the Committee on Permanent Organization heard from, the "slate" made out by that body was adopted, and Judge Settle, the permanent President, made a little inaugural, which closed the first day's proceedings.

The Committee on Credentials, whose duty of settling contested seats is usually quite arduous, was not heard from until the second day. Indeed, their office proved to be a sinecure, for of all the 752 seats in the convention, not a single one was contested. Yes, there were two—from far Utah, which, of course, had to have a Mormon and a Gentile representation. The latter won, as might have been expected in view of the more than doubtful Republicanism of the Young Party. As the delegates from the land of the Saints were only two out of seven hundred and fifty-two, it can be readily seen that the contest in that quarrelsome quarter did not shake the convention very severely.

THE PLATFORM.

On Thursday morning the serious work of the convention was to commence with, it was hoped, a prompt report of the Platform Committee. This body, however, was not ready to report. Its members had met on the previous evening, and found on their table a stack of resolutions big enough to have filled the hats of all the forty-two members, and still left a surplus larger than was necessary to equip a party for the campaign. To dispose of this *embarrass de richesse*, a sub-committee of nine was appointed, and this sub-committee ground away until near morning. By that time they would have been through with their job, perhaps, had not the pressure in behalf of certain particular propositions been renewed on Thursday before the full committee. There were several complete sets of declarations and resolutions, principally those of Dr. Loring, of Boston; of George Wm. Curtis, of New York; of Prof. Steele, of Vermont, and of Prof. Edward Daniels, a member of the committee from Virginia, and editor of the Richmond *State Journal.* None of these were adopted in any considerable part. The phraseology of the platform is due more to General Joseph Hawley than to anybody else, though Judge Scofield, of Pennsylvania, was chairman of the committee. Of course the most important question was that of reconstruction, and upon this the Southern delegates were clamorous for something radical and unequivocal. Hence it was, that after declaring in the second and third paragraphs that complete civil and political liberty should be guaranted to the colored men of the South, and that the recent amendments to the National Constitution should be enforced according to their spirit, the committee afterward came to adopt, in the twelfth paragraph, a specific and positive indorsement of all the anti-Ku Klux measures of the President and Congress. There was likewise much pressure for a recognition of the cause of woman. Mrs. Lucy Stone Blackwell labored with certain members of the committee in behalf of the resolution adopted last winter by the Massachusetts Legislature. With other members, Miss Anthony became eloquent. To tell the truth, the committee were rather desirous of saying something in behalf of enlarged opportunities and education for the softer sex, with an admission coupled, if necessary, that the question of their admission to any "additional rights" was worthy of consideration. This was finally incorporated into the platform, in the fourteenth paragraph; though in such a diplomatic and general way that one is almost surprised to hear that the representatives of the oppressed sex are satisfied with it. They usually prefer stronger meat when it comes to expressions of opinion on their especial topics.

The resolution on the subject of capital and labor is essentially the same as that submitted by Wendell Phillips, and is therefore acceptable to the powerful body of voters whom he represents—the Labor Reformers.

The result of the committee's labors, as reported and adopted, *nem. con.*, is the following declaration of principles:

The Republican party of the United States assembled in National Convention in the city of Philadelphia, on the 5th and 6th days of June, 1872, again declares its faith, appeals to its history, and announces its position upon the questions before the country.

Preamble.

1. During eleven years of supremacy it has accepted with grand courage the solemn duties of the time. It suppressed a gigantic rebellion, emancipated four millions of slaves, decreed the equal citizenship of all, and established universal suffrage. Exhibiting unparalleled magnanimity, it criminally punished no man for political offences, and warmly welcomed all who proved loyalty by obeying the laws and dealing justly with their neighbors. It has steadily decreased with firm hand the resultant disorders of a great war, and initiated a wise and humane policy towards the Indians. The Pacific railroad, and similar vast enterprises, have been generally aided and successfully conducted; the public lands freely given to actual settlers; immigration protected and encouraged, and a full acknowledgment of the naturalized citizens' rights secured from European powers. A uniform national currency has been provided, repudiation frowned down, the national credit sustained under most extraordinary burdens, and new bonds negotiated

at lower rates. The revenues have been carefully collected and honestly applied; despite annual large reductions of the rates of taxation, the public debt has been reduced during General Grant's Presidency at the rate of a hundred millions a year; great financial crises have been avoided, and peace and plenty prevail throughout the land. Menacing foreign difficulties have been peacefully and honorably composed, and the honor and power of the nation kept in high respect throughout the world.

This glorious record of the past is the party's best pledge for the future. We believe the people will not entrust the government to any party or combination of men composed chiefly of those who have resisted every step of this beneficial progress.

Liberty and Equality.

2. Complete liberty and exact equality in the enjoyment of all civil, political and public rights should be established and effectually maintained throughout the Union by efficient and appropriate State and Federal legislation. Neither the law nor its administration should admit of any discrimination in respect of citizens, by reason of race, creed, color, or previous condition of servitude.

Late Constitutional Amendments.

3. The recent amendments to the National Constitution should be cordially sustained, because they are right, not merely tolerated because they are law, and should be carried out according to their spirit by appropriate legislation, the enforcement of which can safely be entrusted only to the party that secured those amendments.

Foreign Policy.

4. The National Government should seek to maintain honorable peace with all nations, protecting the citizens everywhere, and sympathizing with all peoples who strive for greater liberty.

Civil Service Reform.

5. Any system of the civil service under which the subordinate positions of the Government are considered rewards for mere party zeal is fatally demoralizing; and we therefore favor a reform of the system by laws which shall abolish the evils of patronage, and make honesty, efficiency, and fidelity the essential qualifications for public positions, without practically creating a life-tenure of office.

Land Grants, etc.

6. We are opposed to further grants of public lands to corporations and monopolies, and demand that the national domain be set apart for free homes for the people.

Revenue and Industry.

7. The annual revenue, after paying current expenditures, pensions, and the interest on the public debt, should furnisha moderate balance for the reduction of the principal, and the revenue, except so much as may be derived from a tax upon tobacco and liquors, be raised by duties upon importations, the duties of which should be so adjusted as to aid in securing remunerative wages for labor, and promote the industries, growth and prosperity of the whole country.

Soldiers' Rewards.

8. We hold in undying honor the soldiers and sailors whose valor saved the Union. Their pensions are a sacred debt of the nation; and the widows and orphans of those who died for their country are entitled to the care of a generous and grateful people. We

favor such additional legislation as will extend the bounty of the Government to all our soldiers and sailors who were honorably discharged, and who in the line of duty became disabled, without regard to the length of service or the cause of such discharge.

Protection of Naturalized Citizens.

9. The doctrine of Great Britain and other European powers, concerning allegiance—"Once a subject, always a subject,"—having at last, through the efforts of the Republican party, been abandoned, and the American idea of the individual's right to transfer allegiance having been accepted by European nations, it is the duty of our Government to guard with jealous care the rights of adopted citizens against the assumption of unauthorized claims of their former Governments; and we urge continual careful protection and encouragement, of voluntary immigration.

Franking Abuse.

10. The franking privilege ought to be abolished and the way prepared for a speedy reduction of the rates of postage.

Capital and Labor.

11. Among the questions which press for attention, is that which concerns the relations of capital and labor; and the Republican party recognize the duty of so shaping legislation as to secure full protection and the amplest field for capital; and for labor, the creator of capital, the largest opportunities, and a just share of mutual profits of these two great servants of civilization.

The Southern Policy.

12. We hold that Congress and the President have only fulfilled an imperative duty in their measures for the suppression of violent and treasonable organizations in certain lately rebellious regions, and for the protection of the ballot-box, and therefore they are entitled to the thanks of the nation.

Finance.

13. We denounce repudiation of the public debt, in any form or disguise, as a national crime. We witness with pride the reduction of the principal of the debt and the rates of interest upon the balance; and confidently expect that our excellent national currency will be perfected by a speedy resumption of specie payment.

Advancement of Woman.

14. The Republican party is mindful of its obligations to the loyal women of America for their noble devotion to the cause of freedom. Their admission to wider fields of usefulness is viewed with satisfaction, and the honest demands of any class of citizens should be treated with respectful consideration.

Amnesty.

15. We heartily approve the action of Congress in extending amnesty to those lately in rebellion, and rejoice in the growth of peace and fraternal feeling throughout the land.

Personal Liberty.

16. The Republican party propose to respect the rights reserved by the people to themselves as carefully as the powers delegated by them to the State and to the Federal Government. It disapproves of the resort to unconstitutional laws, for the purpose of removing evils, by interference with rights not surrendered by the people to either the State or National Government.

17. It is the duty of the Federal Government to adopt such measures as may best tend to encourage and restore American commerce and shipbuilding.

Commerce.

18. We believe that the modest patriotism, the earnest purpose, the sound judgment, the practical wisdom, the incorruptible integrity, and the illustrious services of Ulysses S. Grant have commended him to the heart of the American people; and with him at our head we start to-day upon a new march of victory.

President Grant.

This platform constitutes a very complete, though terse and compact presentation of all issues likely to arise during the campaign, and on which the position of the party required to be defined. It even goes beyond that, and takes ground on several new questions of which "great" political parties have usually fought shy—as for instance, the woman question, the labor question and the question of personal rights. On the last named of these, many of our German fellow citizens are decidedly sensitive, and the enunciation of principle contained in the sixteenth paragraph was accepted by Hermann Raster, of the Chicago *Staats Zeitung*, as satisfactory to the American citizens of German birth, for whom he was well qualified to speak. It is to be understood, of course, that the "rights not surrendered by the people to either the State or National Government" mean more particularly the rights of conscience, as to religion, personal regimen, etc., which some people would have the laws to interfere with.

Concerning this series of declarations a contemporary writer remarked in a letter from Philadelphia, "The platform, as a whole, gives great satisfaction, no less for its felicity of expression than for its boldness and loyalty of tone with regard to reconstructing the South, protecting the persecuted, paying off the debt, keeping up the national credit, etc., and its progressiveness in favoring amnesty to Southern political offenders, and in demanding the reform of the civil service, the abolition of the franking privilege, land-grants, etc. It leaves the Cincinnati crowd nothing to fight for—nothing but Greeley and Gratz. But they might have known as much before. They might have known, when they undertook to steal our best and newest planks for their raft of distress, that the property would be claimed by its rightful owners as soon as the proper time should come."

RE-NOMINATION OF GRANT.

In following the Platform through from its inception in the committee room to its adoption by the Convention, we have shot past the great event of the day—the renomination of General Ulysses S. Grant for President. This was accomplished by the usual routine, though the moment was so crowded with consequence as to lend a factitious interest and excitement to even the driest detail of the transaction. It was about one o'clock on Thursday afternoon, when, the Platform Committee being still dilatory with their report, the convention resolved to proceed at once to the nomination of a candidate for President. To Illinois, as the home of Grant, and to the Hon. Shelby M. Cullum, ex-member of Congress, as chairman of the delegation, was accorded the honor of making the formal presentation of General Grant's name. This was done in a speech which, for terseness and force, was worthy of the nominee himself. Mr. Cullum said:

"Gentlemen of the Convention: On behalf of the great Republican party of Illinois, and that of the Union, in the name of liberty, of loyalty, of justice and of law; in the name of economy, of good government, of peace and all of the equal rights of all; remembering, with profound gratitude, his glorious achievements on the field and his noble statesmanship as chief magistrate of the great nation, *I nominate as President of the United States, for a second term*, ULYSSES S. GRANT."

A THRILLING SCENE.

The vast assemblage could hardly wait for the few timely words which the speaker had to utter before its enthusiasm found vent in such an explosion of spontaneous applause as never was heard before in any deliberative body. The whole audience rose and waved hats, handkerchiefs, etc., and shouted promiscuously.

Then there was sufficient lull for somebody to start "Cheers for Grant and victory," and the cheers rang out with deafening volume from broad parquet, and from the four vast semi-circles of thrilled humanity, until the festoons of laurel, that stretched away to the lofty dome, shook and quivered with the sound.

The musicians caught the infection, and waved their brass horns and laced caps. There was not a square inch of space in the room but seemed to quiver with excitement and motion.

Finally from out the swelling volume of sound rose the concerted strains of music. "Hail to the Chief" was the salute of the band, as a colossal equestrian portrait of General Grant was lowered from the clouds of the scene set at the back of the stage. The picture was well executed and life-like, the main portion being bordered with medallions of Lincoln and Stanton, and full-length representations of Peace and Plenty.

Then the cheers arose again, and all was spontaneous and informal until the form of General Stewart L. Woodford, of New York, was seen upon the stage, where he appeared for the purpose of seconding the nomination of President Grant for re-election. General Woodford seemed inspired for the occasion. His words were laden with feeling, and at the same time not mere gush. They were logical and practical, and, coming from an influential and much honored citizen of the State where Horace Greeley betrayed his party, and where the faction to which he has committed himself was chiefly nourished, they were doubly welcome to the assembly.

One more speech in this behalf was made, and then the applause broke out again.

The roll of States were called and every vote of the whole 752 was solemnly recorded for U. S. Grant, the chairman of the several delegations vieing with each other in the nice bits of epigramatic eloquence, in which they laid their laurel tributes at the feet of the conqueror of the rebellion.

The result was announced, after which another surfeit of applause, out of which again rose strains of music from the band, the prelude to a stirring new campaign song, which some local genius here sprung upon the convention. It was good, and reminded certain demonstrative ones among the delegates of other songs, chiefly patriotic—melodies associated with the late war which they desired to have played and sung. "Red, White and Blue," "John Brown's Body," "Marching through Georgia," and other patriotic songs were sung and joined in with immense force by the audience—still standing.

THE VICE PRESIDENT QUESTION.

It was not until after fifteen or twenty minutes of this kind of proceedings that the Convention could bring itself down to routine business. When it did so, the work of nominating a Vice President was in hand. The chief contest for this office was between Schuyler Colfax, the incumbent, and Henry Wilson, long Senator from Massachusetts. All other candidates were merely local in their strength, and scarcely any other were voted for except as a passing compliment from the party in their own States.

There was nothing of a serious nature alleged against Mr. Colfax as a reason why he should not be renominated. Indeed, the feeling of a majority of the delegates, on assembling, was in his favor, and showed him to be still a very popular man. There was active effort made in every delegation, however, by the friends of "the Natick cobbler," who made use of the following arguments:

1. That, on general principles, a change in the

nomination for Vice-President was desirable, when the same candidate for President was presented.

2. That considerations of locality demanded the nomination of an Eastern man, after two terms with neither a President nor Vice-President from the East.

3. That Mr. Wilson possessed special elements of strength with the working men and with the negroes, which Mr. Colfax had not.

4. That Mr. Colfax had, in a letter published in the New York *Independent*, a year and a half ago, withdrawn from the field, and alleged reasons which would be used against him in the campaign.

5. That, at the same time and since, Mr. Colfax had encouraged Mr. Wilson to come out as a candidate, which he would not otherwise have done.

These considerations, especially the last two, which were vigorously advertised by an organized body of newspaper reporters from Washington, proved sufficient to defeat Mr. Colfax and secure the nomination of his principal rival. This was done on the first ballot, which, at the completion of the roll-call, stood thus:

	WILSON.	COLFAX.	MAYNARD.	SCATTERING.
Alabama	12	7	1	--
Arkansas	12	--	--	--
California	12	--	--	--
Connecticut	6	6	--	--
Delaware	--	6	--	--
Florida	5	3	--	--
Georgia	16	6	--	--
Illinois	25	17	--	--
Indiana		30	--	--
Iowa	19	3	--	--

	WILSON.	COLFAX.	MAYNARD.	SCATTERING.
Kansas	10	--	--	--
Kentucky	4	20	--	--
Louisiana	5	11	--	--
Maine	4	10	--	--
Maryland	16	--	--	--
Massachusetts	26	--	--	--
Michigan	22	--	--	--
Minnesota	10	--	--	--
Mississippi	11	4	1	--
Missouri	27	2	--	1
Nebraska	2	4	--	--
Nevada	6	--	--	--
New Hampshire	10	--	--	--
New Jersey	--	18	--	--
New York	16	53	--	1
North Carolina	20	--	--	--
Ohio	30	14	--	--
Oregon	--	6	--	--
Pennsylvania	58	--	--	--
Rhode Island	--	8	--	--
South Carolina	9	5	--	--
Tennessee	--	--	24	--
*Texas	--	--	--	16
Vermont	--	10	--	--
†Virginia	--	--	--	22
West Virginia	--	10	--	--
Wisconsin	15	5	--	--
Arizona	--	2	--	--
Colorado	1	1	--	--
Dakotah	½	1½	--	--
District of Columbia	--	2	--	--
Idaho	--	2	--	--
Montana	--	2	--	--
New Mexico	2	--	--	--
Utah	--	2	--	--
Washington	--	2	--	--
Wyoming	1	1	--	--
Total	364½	321½	26	40

* For E. J. Davis. † For John F. Lewis.

It was found, on footing this up, that the excellent incumbent of the Vice-Presidential chair was overtopped by his principal opponent by some forty-three votes. It was immediately apparent to the Colfax men that this disadvantage could not be overcome. But they had no time for effort in this direction, if they had been ever so much disposed for it; for before the result was announced, Virginia had risen and transferred her vote from her own local favorite to Henry Wilson, giving him 384½ votes in all, or seven more than were necessary to a choice. The result was sudden, but it did not demoralize or disaffect anybody. The Indiana delegation, who had worked incessantly night and day for their beloved statesman, Colfax, should have been demoralized and disaffected, if any were so; and they were heard, as soon as the lusty applause of the throng could be penetrated by any intelligible sound, recording their unanimous vote for their candidate's chief rival! This did not look like disaffection. In fact, it would seem as if the heroic determination to whip the enemy had overcome every other consideration at this convention, and that some hand higher than any that is human had overruled all turbulent passions, and envies, and bickerings, in order to facilitate this greatly desirable end.

COLFAX MAGNANIMOUS.

Before the Convention adjourned, (which occurred a very short time after the result of the balloting was declared), the chairman of the Indiana delegation, had received the following telegraphic dispatch from. Mr Colfax:

WASHINGTON, June 6.—John W. Foster, Indiana.—Accept for yourself and delegation my sincere gratitude for your gallant contest. I support your ticket cheerfully. Men are nothing—principles everything. Nothing must arrest Republican triumph until equality under the law, like the liberty from which it springs, is universally acknowledged, and the citizenship of the humblest becomes a sure protection against outrage and wrong, as was Roman citizenship of old. SCHUYLER COLFAX.

NATIONAL COMMITTEE.

Before the adjournment, which occurred at ten minutes past 4, the chair announced the following gentlemen as composing the National Committee for the ensuing five years:

Alabama	*George D. Spencer.*
Arkansas	Edwell Clayton.
California	*George C. Gorham.*
Connecticut	*Marshall Jewell.*
Delaware	James Riddle.
Florida	William H. Gleason.
Georgia	Isaac S. Fannin.
Illinois	*J. Y. Scammon.*
Indiana	*O. P. Morton.*
Iowa	*Grenville M. Dodge.*
Kansas	John A. Martin.
Kentucky	William C. Goodloe.
Louisiana	G. Cassinave.
Maine	William G. Fry.
Maryland	*C. C. Fulton.*
Massachusetts	*William Claflin.*
Michigan	*William A. Howard.*
Minnesota	*John T. Averill.*
Mississippi	O. C. French.
Missouri	R. T. Vanhorn.
Nebraska	E. T. Cunningham.
Nevada	James W. Nye.
New Hampshire	William E. Chandler.
New Jersey	*Alexander G. Cattell.*
New York	*Edwin D. Morgan.*
North Carolina	*Joseph C. Abbott.*
Ohio	*B. R. Cowen.*
Oregon	Joseph G. Wilson.

Pennsylvania	*William H. Kemble.*
Rhode Island	William D. Brayton.
South Carolina	Franklin J. Moses, Jr.
Tennessee	Horace Maynard.
Texas	
Vermont	George Nichols.
Virginia	W. H. Wells, Jr.
West Virginia	Anson Criswell.
Wisconsin	David Atwood.
Arizona	John Titus.
Colorado	Edward M. McCook.
Dakotah	William H. H. Beadle.
District of Columbia	Henry D. Cooke.
Idaho	John R. McBride.
Montana	Lucius B. Church.
New Mexico	Joseph G. Palen.
Utah	Alfred S. Gould.
Washington	L. B. Andrews,
Wyoming	William T. Jones.

Of the committee, those whose names are printed in italics belong to a sub-committee of fifteen, called an Executive Campaign Committee. The chairman of all is Ex-Governor Edwin D. Morgan, of New York; the Secretary, William E. Chandler, of New Hampshire. The committee is one of unprecedented ability and financial strength, and the organization for the campaign is already very complete—so much so that the Republican party possesses great advantages in this respect over any of its rivals in its facility for working its field of labor.

THE CANDIDATES NOTIFIED.

On the 10th of June, the President and several of the Vice-Presidents of the Philadelphia Convention, waited upon President Grant and Senator Wilson, to inform them officially of their nomination. They found the President at the White House, whither, at half-past one, he resorted for the purpose of receiving their visit, the day being the final one of the session of Congress, and the President having been on duty at the Capitol since early in the morning. Judge Settle said laconically, emulating his illustrious interlocutor:

"MR. PRESIDENT.—We are before you to perform a very agreeable duty. We are here to officially inform you of your unanimous nomination for the Presidency by the National Republican Convention assembled at Philadelphia on the 6th inst. Beyond this, I do not know that we have anything to say."

Here Judge Settle handed the President the following letter, formally notifying him of his nomination:

WASHINGTON, June 10.

"MR. PRESIDENT—SIR: In pursuance of our instructions, we, the undersigned, President and Vice-Presidents of the National Republican Convention, held in Philadelphia, on the 5th and 6th insts., have the honor to inform you of your nomination for re-election to the office of President of the United States. . As it is impossible to give an adequate idea of the enthusiasm which prevailed, or the unanimity which hailed you as the choice of the people, we can only add that you received the entire vote of every State and Territory. Regarding your re-election as necessary to the peace and continued prosperity of the country, we ask your acceptance of the nomination.

[Signed] THOMAS SETTLE, President.

PAUL STROBACH and forty-one others, Vice-Presidents.

The President said:

"GENTLEMEN: I am not now ready to respond to your letter, but will take an early opportunity to do so in writing. It is certainly gratifying for me to learn that, after holding office for three years,

HON. CHAS. F. ADAMS,

Member of the Geneva Conference from the United States.

BAKER CO. CHI.

never having before held political office, never having been a candidate for nomination, I have been endorsed by my former supporters. This is something I cannot forget. I am, of course, very grateful."

The several Vice-Presidents addressed General Grant briefly, each pledging him the hearty and energetic support of the Republicans of his State, and after some pleasant conversational sallies all around, the deputation retired. The President took his lunch and returned to duty at the Capitol, where, in the Executive room, surrounded by cabinet officers, by clerks, by Senators, importuning him anxiously about the vital question of an extra session, which the filibustering of the Democrats threatened to necessitate, he wrote out in pencil this formal letter of acceptance—a letter of which it has been said, "Every sentence is a platform":

EXECUTIVE MANSION, WASHINGTON, June 10.

Hon. Thos. Settle, President National Republican Convention; Paul Strobace, Elisha Baxter, and others, Vice-Presidents:

GENTLEMEN: Your letter of this date, advising me of the action of the convention held at Philadelphia, on the 5th and 6th of this month, and of my unanimous nomination for the Presidency by it, is received.

I accept the nomination, and through you return my heartfelt thanks to your constituents for this mark of their confidence and support. If elected in November, and protected by a kind Providence in health and strength to perform the duties of the high trust conferred, I promise the same zeal and devotion to the good of the whole people for the future of my official life as shown in the past. Experience may guide me in avoiding mistakes inevitable with novices in all professions and in all occupations. When relieved from the responsibilities of my present trust by the election of a successor, whether it be at the end of this term or next, I hope to leave to him, as Executive, a country at peace within its own border; at peace with outside nations; with a firm credit at home and abroad; without embarrasing questions to threaten its future prosperity.

With the expression of my desire to see the speedy healing of all bitterness of feeling between sections, parties, or races of citizens, and the time when the title of citizen carries with it all the protection and privileges to the humblest that it does to the most exalted, I subscribe myself,

Very respectfully,

Your obedient servant,

U. S. GRANT.

After the interview with Grant, the committee waited upon Wilson, whom they found in the room of the Senate Military Committee, of which he is Chairman. Him Judge Settle addressed in much the same manner as he had addressed the President; and Senator Wilson made the following reply, quite impromptu:

"GENTLEMEN: I will in a day or two give you an answer in writing to this communication. I take this occasion, however, to thank you and the members of the convention you represent for this manifestation of confidence, as I neither asked for or wrote to any member of the convention to give me a vote. I am all the more grateful for their generous support. I am gratified too, for the friendly tone of the Republican press of the country. For thirty-six years, in public life and in private life, I have striven to maintain the distinguishing idea of the Republican party—freedom and equality of all men. I have striven ever to be true to my country, and to the rights of our common humanity; to know no sectional interest, nor race, nor color. In the future. as in the past, I shall unfalteringly adhere to these principles, which are convictions of my judgment, heart, and conscience. I am clearly of opinion that the great soldier, who rendered such illustrious service to his country in a great civil war, will be re-elected President of the United States. His humanity to the vanquished, his firmness to vindicate the rights of the humble and defenceless, his devotion to the leading ideas of the Republican party, cannot be questioned. I esteem it high honor to be associated with him in the coming contest. While I am grateful to my friends who gave me such generons support, I honor those who adhered with such devotion to Mr. Colfax. We have been personal and political friends for nearly twenty years, and it is a source of profound satisfaction to me that our personal relations have not been disturbed by the recent contest. While I shall never cease to feel grateful to the friends who honored me by their support, I shall ever entertain sincere respect for those who deemed it to be their duty to give their support to others. I hope we shall all strive to win to our support every honest and patriotic man in the country—every man true to the rights of humanity—every man who would elevate the condition of the toiling millions, and have our republic become a great Christian nation, an example to the world. Let it be understood that our ranks are wide open to receive all devoted to the country, and who would advance its happiness and the general well-being of all sections of the land and all conditions of the people. We, Republicans, should offer the hand of reconciliation to all fair-minded and honorable men, and use all legitimate means to achieve success for the honor and salvation of the country, as well as for that of the party which saved the Union and established freedom in every part of the land."

Mr. Wilson afterwards sent the deputation a very able letter of acceptance, which is printed in an appendix near the close of this volume.

CHAPTER VI.

HISTORY OF THE REPUBLICAN PARTY.

(CONTINUED.)

The Legislation of the Republican Party, State and National—Sketch of Some of the More Prominent Acts of Congress—The Constitutional Amendments—A Brief Resume of All.

Within a short time after the organization of the Republican party it obtained political control of every free State, except Indiana. Illinois, which cast its electoral vote for Mr. Buchanan in 1856, nevertheless elected at the same time a Republican Governor, the lamented Bissell; and in 1860, Indiana passed into Republican Government by considerable majorities.

It is not within the design of this work to relate the achievements of the Republican party in the several states, wherein it gained supremacy. It may be well to remark, generally, however, that it is historically true that with the beginning of Republican ascendancy in those states there was also a beginning of a new era of progress; a more rapid development of those material interests by which national wealth is increased, the public good fostered, and the general happiness augmented; a more liberal policy inaugurated in respect to those public institutions whereby crime is repressed, suffering alleviated, and civilization advanced. All such internal improvements—railways, canals, etc.—as are of benefit to the people at large, have been liberally sustained. Generous appropriations have been made in behalf of institutions for the care of the deaf and dumb, the blind, and the insane. Many of these beneficent institutions, in fact, which so much honor our country, are due to Republican policy, against the protest of Democratic opposition. In all these Republican states, too, honesty and economy have been the rule of administration. Peculations and frauds have unquestionably occurred, but they have ever been promptly exposed and punished. The system of public schools has been extended and improved. In a word, every state which has been Republican has had its laws more or less reformed for the better; its material interest developed; its wealth increased; its political morality elevated; its substantial progress constantly assured. The legislation and administration of affairs in every Republican state demonstrate that the Republican party has everywhere been a benefactor to the body politic.

NATIONAL LEGISLATION.

Since the 4th of March, 1861, the Republican party has been responsible for all federal legislation and administration. We have already seen, by general view, how much it has accomplished; that its history has been in truth the history of the Republic. But it will not be thought out of place, or, it is hoped, tedious, here to recur to some of the more important matters of legislation which may be regarded as specially due to Republican policy.

Congress met in extra session at Washington, in accordance with a proclamation from President Lincoln, on the 4th of July, 1861. A short time afterwards the first battle of Bull Run occurred, whereby the Union General McDowell, who had, in obedience to the clamor of the New York *Tribune*, moved "on to Richmond" before he was ready for such an expedition, suffered an ignominous defeat.

Congress at once perceived that we were in a state of civil war, and proceeded to declare and legislate accordingly. On the 29th of July an act was passed which provided for men and means wherewithal to suppress the rebellion. This act gave the President ample power to call forth volunteers and to carry on the war with vigor. A week afterwards an act was passed confiscating property and setting free all slaves used in aid of the rebellion. Other acts of a practical nature were passed, so that when the campaigns of 1872 began, Edwin M. Stanton being now Secretary of War, and Grant in command in the West, results of the most gratifying nature were brought about.

In this rapid sketch of national legislation it would be well to place first an account of the amendments to the Constitution. These embody the great political and civil triumphs of the war. They will be found at length in the appendix to this work. Let it suffice here to state that the Thirteenth amendment (abolishing slavery) was passed by Congress January 27th, 1865; the Fourteenth (securing civil rights, repudiating the rebel debt, and guaranteeing the national debt), June 16th, 1866; the Fifteenth (establishing manhood suffrage), February 27th, 1869. Meantime, Congress had passed many other acts calculated to be of service to the cause of freedom and progress. Not to mention all these, reference may be made to an act which abolished the Coolie trade by American citizens in American vessels, February 19, 1862; an act forbidding the return of fugitive slaves by the army or navy, March 13, 1862; the abolition of slavery in the District of Columbia, April 16, 1862; an act authorizing the President to send diplomatic representatives of the United States to the negro republics of Hayti and Liberia; an act forever prohibiting slavery in any of the Territories of the United States, June 19, 1862; an act to carry into practical effect a treaty with Great Britain for the suppression of the African slave trade, July 11, 1862; an act incorporating a national university (Howard) at Washington city for the education of colored youth, March 3, 1863; the repeal of the Fugitive Slave Law of 1850, January 28, 1864; the act establishing the Freedmen's Bureau, March 3, 1865; the civil rights bill, April 9, 1866; an act expressly providing that there shall be no denial of the right of franchise in any of the Territories of the United States to any citizen on account of race, color, or previous condition of servitude; an act enforcing the Fourteenth amendment, and empowering the

Executive to suppress rebellious conspiracies (known as "the Ku-Klux law"), April 20, 1871; the act of general amnesty passed by the Congress which is still (1872) in existence, by which measure of magnanimity it may be said the last trace of the rebellion, so far as legislation is concerned, was obliterated.

LEGISLATION IN BEHALF OF LABOR.

Reference ought also to be made to a few acts in the direct interest of labor. The first of these in importance, perhaps, as also the earliest in date of enactment, was the Homestead law, passed May 20th, 1862, by which every actual settler was enabled to obtain 160 acres of land free of expense. The praise due to the Republican party on account of the success of this measure in behalf of the actual tiller of the soil is all the greater because President Buchanan vetoed a bill of a similar nature during the declining days of Democratic power. A similar act in behalf of labor was that donating public lands to the several States and Territories, to provide endowments for colleges for the benefit of agriculture and the mechanic arts, July 2d, 1862. The public lands of the South, amounting to about 45,000,000 acres, were also reserved to the laborer by an act of Congress. The Republican party, also set a national example for the eight hour law, by enacting that eight hours shall constitute a day's work on all the public works of the United States.

Of those acts of national legislation in behalf of the general interests of the body politic, we may mention the law of May 15th, 1862, by which a Department of Agriculture was established; the Pacific Railroad act of July 1st, 1862; the act of February 25th, 1863, providing a national currency, amply secured by stocks of the United States; the act of June 15th, 1866, whereby the commercial, postal and military communication between the different States has been greatly facilitated; the act of July 27th, 1866, in aid of a railroad from Arkansas and Missouri to the Pacific coast; the act of January 20th, 1871, authorizing the refunding of the national debt at a lower rate of interest. Of a similar nature may be regarded the law of March 2d, 1867, establishing a Bureau of Educacation, and subsequent Pacific Railroad acts.

The acts and resolutions of Congress in behalf of disabled and honorably discharged soldiers and sailors, and the widows and orphans of deceased soldiers and sailors of the Union, are very numerous. It is not insisted that these laws are due to the Republican party entirely; but it may be safely claimed that because of the supremacy of that party in the conduct of national affairs, they are more liberal than they otherwise would be.

But, without further particularization, it is believed that the legislation of the Repnblican party, in all those acts which may be called specially its own, will, when thoroughly examined, show as much in behalf of the good of the whole people, and as little against that good, as can be justly claimed for the legislation of any political organization which has had control of public affairs.

CONCLUSION.

We have thus briefly and imperfectly sketched the outlines of the history of the Republican party. We have seen that it had its origin in the principle of freedom, its organization in a practical agreement of men who had previously belonged to the various political organizations of the country. We have seen that, having once suffered defeat, it afterwards constantly received the earnest confidence of the American people. It had control of the government during the most trying period of our institutions; during those four years of terrible war, throughout which freedom and the cause of man were placed in imminent jeopardy of being lost. Never was higher trust reposed in any party; never was high trust more faithfully fulfilled. The Union was saved through a sublime victory for liberty, and by policies of practical statesmanship in finance, and the general conduct of affairs the wisdom of which must forever challenge the admiration of all candid minds. But it has not been a party of one idea. It has not only saved the Union, and made the Constitution a chart of genuine freedom, but it has accomplished many other things of great good to the country. It has supplied a uniform currency for the business of the people, with a national banking system confessedly the best we have ever had, and against which no serious criticism is uttered. It fulfilled its promises—what no other party herein had done—by building a railroad to the Pacific Ocean, and providing means for building others, by which the whole continent may be rapidly developed and made able to control the most wealthy commerce of the world. It has extended the election franchise. It has provided that every citizen who wants may have a free homestead on the public domain. It has elevated the tone of political morality. It has destroyed corrupt political "rings" with merciless severity. Ever since the close of the war of the rebellion, it has lightened the burdens of taxation, and yet is diminishing the public debt at the rate of one hundred millions annually. It has demonstrated beyond dispute its practical and valuable sympathy with the cause of labor, by adopting the eight-hour law for public workmen, and by years of devotion to the idea of the dignity of labor. There is not a citizen of the republic who is not better off because of the existence and the triumphs of the Republican party. Indeed, it is not too much to say that but for this party and its triumphs, there would be no American Union at all, but a number of discordant, belligerent States, through whose conflicts civilization would needs long meet with sad reverses, and despotism at last gain most mournful victory. The campaign of 1872 is to decide whether this party of long-tried patriotism, virtue, and great statesmanship shall give way before a party, a large majority of whose supporters have been in opposition to all the great victories of the past and blind to the great ideas of the present.

U. S. GRANT.
BAKER CO. CHI.

Ulysses S. Grant.

CHAPTER VII.

HIS MILITARY CAREER.

Early New England Ancestry—"Blood will tell"—Birth of Ulysses—Boyhood—Life at West Point—His Part in the Mexican War—A Brilliant Record—Twice Brevetted for Bravery and Efficiency in Battle—Becomes a Captain and A. Q. M.—Marries and Resigns—An Uneventful Interval—The Long Roll Sounds Again.

It is not proposed in this book to give anything beyond a brief outline of the personal history of General Grant, since an elaborate work of the sort, though, perhaps, not out of place here, has been rendered almost supererogatory by the score or more of biographies of Grant which have already been issued from the press. Aiming at nothing more than a compilation, but desiring to make that compilation as just as possible, the writer inquired of the illustrious subject of all these memoirs which was the most worthy of confidence. The President replied that he had examined but two or three, and that they were by no means trustworthy; and he specified one—the most popular of all, probably—as being particularly inaccurate. In view of this it becomes especially desirable to obtain facts for the following pages from original sources, as far as possible; and this has been done.

GRANT'S ANCESTRY.

Ulysses S. Grant, the seventeenth President of the United States of America, has at the writing of this, but lately completed his fiftieth year, having been born on the 27th of April, 1822. Perhaps it is not necessary to say anything about the family of President Grant, as the Opposition press has kept that subject well before the public since his inauguration. Nevertheless, it will be interesting to genealogists, and those who believe strongly in hereditary qualities, to learn that the ancestors of the President were sturdy, plain, New England people. His father, Jesse Root Grant, was born in Westmoreland county, Pennsylvania; but *his* father, and all his ancestors back to Samuel, son of Matthew Grant, one of the early Puritan emigrants, were born in Massachusetts or Connecticut. Matthew Grant, of the seventh generation from Ulysses, came to America from Plymouth, England, in the "Mary and John," in May, 1630, and settled in Dorchester, Mass. The heads of the third, fourth and fifth generations following Matthew were each named Noah Grant, and were born in Windsor and Tolland, Connecticut. The second Noah Grant was a famous captain in the French and Indian War, and would, doubtless, have appeared conspicuously among the heroes of the Revolution, had he not fallen by an Indian's bullet, while out scouting, in 1756. His son Noah served through the War for Independence, having enlisted at the first call. Of this Noah, the President's father, Jesse Root Grant, is the oldest son. He was born, as above remarked, in Westmoreland county, Penn. (twenty miles above Pittsburgh, on the Monongahela), on the 23d of January, 1794. The old man is still hale at 78 years, and able to discharge the duties of the post-office at Covington, Kentucky, a city of 30,000 inhabitants, on the Ohio, opposite Cincinnati. Apprenticed when sixteen years old, to an Ohio tanner, whose trade he learned, Jesse Grant took up his residence, shortly after coming of age, at Point Pleasant, Clermont county, Ohio. Here, in 1821, he married Hannah Simpson, a woman who contributed to the conjugal capital stock of qualities a large degree of piety, firmness, and strength of character; her husband contributing plentiful vitality, quickness of discernment, and that general cleverness which takes a man along well through the world and keeps him on good terms with his fellow men; these, combined with an unswerving integrity and independence of habits which never left him, no matter in what emergency.

THE BOY GRANT.

Of this marriage, contracted in June, 1821, was born, on the 27th of April, 1822, Ulysses Grant, whose name, reckoning according to the wideness of its celebrity, stands third in the long list of statesmen, generals, and philosophers which our country is able to boast. It is not proper to attempt in this sketch a detailed account of the boyhood life of Grant, which has already become familiar to millions of readers through the efforts of his many biographers. Suffice it to say that he soon developed several noticeable qualities—physical courage, self-possession, honesty, and modesty; one particular talent—that of horsemanship, which he possessed to a remarkable degree; and one special passion—a dislike to tannery work. He was not lazy, however, nor yet untractable; nor had he any vices which his father ever discovered. One fact which the old man recalls with satisfaction, was the boy's freedom from the taint of profane or intemperate language.

A CADET AT WEST POINT.

By the time he had arrived at the age of sixteen, Ulysses had acquired at the common school of Pleasant Point the rudiments of a common school education, and had read the Life of Washington, but not many other books. Fortunately for the American Union (as it has turned out since,) Jesse Grant knew a member of Congress well enough to secure the appointment of his boy to the West Point Military Academy—subject, of course, to the prescribed examination. It was while passing through the hands of this Congressman, and through the forms incident to its owner's muster as a cadet, that the name of young Grant underwent that singular change, from Hiram Ulysses, the boy's baptismal title to Ulysses Simpson. The obliging Member was precisely like other obliging Members in his inability to remember the full names of all the promising sons of his respectable constituents. He did know, however, that the principal Christian name of his hopeful young *protege* at Point Pleasant was ULYSSES; and remembering also that the surname of the mother was SIMPSON, he jumped at a conclusion, as many another Congressman has done, and decided that the full name was ULYSSES SIMPSON. Thus it was written down in the application; thus it went down on the muster rolls and records pertaining to the matriculation of the newly-fledged cadet; and thus it had to be borne during the period at the Academy, since the officers declined to comply with Ulysses's request and restore the name to its original form.

Grant's military life commenced at 17, the time of his admission, in July, 1839, to West Point—the class of 1843. His career at the Military Academy was characterized by these features: he was quiet, self-poised, plodding, and not brilliant, except in horsemanship. He was a green youth from the backwoods, and, of course, there was a disposition among his more free and easy classmates to snub him, and "put him through," as young gentlemen from sixteen to eighteen are fond of doing. He also came in for his share of the "hazing," in which the class above was bound to indulge toward the fresh class; but his self-respect and self-possession helped him easily through all these, and he was in good standing with his classmates before the term had progressed far. He had few intimates, however, and among these were Ingalls, now high in the Quartermaster's department of the army, Franklin and Steele, both distinguished as corps commanders during the late war, and Augur, one of the finest soldiers in any army, and a cavalry officer of considerable distinction.

Of the intellectual qualities exhibited at West Point by young Grant, the most noticeable was his cool, unerring, judicial faculty, (such that his classmates, in case of a dispute, were accustomed to say, 'We'll leave it to Uncle Sam"—Grant's *soubriquet* among the boys.) Another, he was much above the average of his class in mathematics; but then it must be admitted that the average was uncommonly low for West Point. Of the hundred who entered along with him, Grant was one of the thirty-nine who got through, and of these thirty-nine he stood the twenty-first on the list at graduation. When his class rank and the rank of his class amongst other leading Academy classes are taken into consideration together, there is nothing remarkably favorable to be inferred concerning his intellectual standing at that time. But it has generally proved the case that the most brilliant cadets have not turned out the ablest generals, or the ablest men, when set to work in the world of affairs.

GRADUATES.

Among the military men who were contemporaries of Grant at West Point were Geo. B. McClellan, Kirby Smith and Thos. Jeff. ("Stonewall") Jackson, of the class of 1844; Rosecrans, Longstreet, Doubleday and Van Dorn, of the class of 1842; Buell, Rodman (inventor of the gun,) Reynolds and Lyon, of the class of 1841; and Sherman, Thomas and Earle, of the class of 1840. Grant graduated on the 30th of June, 1843, capping the climax of the feats of horsemanship performed by the cadets before the board of visitors by leaping the famous horse "York" over a hurdle six feet and three inches in height. Receiving his commission of Brevet Second Lieutenant—the same which is, by regulation, awarded to all graduating cadets—young Grant betook himself to his home in Ohio, and afterwards to St. Louis, the home of his classmate and (now) brother-in-law, Frederic T. Dent; his principle industry for a time being "waiting orders" and paying court to the young sister of his friend, Miss Julia Dent, fifth child of his host, Col. Frederic Dent. Between this young pair—the girl being then seventeen—an ardent attachment sprang up, which ultimately resulted in their union, notwithstanding the very moderate prospects of the swain and the high social standing of his sweetheart had seemed to Miss Julia's parents a serious obstacle to such a union.

SUMMONED TO ACTION.

On leaving West Point, the young subaltern was assigned to the Fourth Infantry—a fine old regiment, with a record stretching back into a former century; and when in the early summer of 1845, the difficulties with Mexico began to culminate in war, the regiment was rapidly moved to a point near the frontier of the hostile country, and Grant was summoned from his wooing to a much sterner scene.

In August of that year the Fourth took up a station near Corpus Christi, waiting for the shock to come. On the 1st of October, Grant received a commission as full Second Lieutenant in the Seventh Infantry; but with the *esprit du corps* which characterizes good soldiers, he asked to be retained, if possible, in the Fourth, and his request was granted. On the 1st of December, Brevet Second Lieutenant Grant received his commission as full Second Lieutenant in his favorite corps. It could not have been admiration for his colonel, which made Grant so devoted to the Fourth; for Colonel Whistler, who commanded, was a miserable toper, and was constantly failing and disappointing Gen. Taylor, who commanded the army.

THE CAMPAIGN IN MEXICO.

Grant's first engagement was at Palo Alto, on the 2nd of May, 1846. The skirmish of Resaca de la Palma followed the next day, and the army of Invasion—squad of invasion, it would have been called in the late civil war—went on its triumphant way toward Monterey, which Taylor stormed and captured on the 21st of September, 1846. By this time, Lieutenant Grant had been detailed as quartermaster, and soon after as adjutant of the regiment, both of which duties he discharged simultaneously and satisfactorily. At Monterey, after the storming party to which Grant belonged had entered the city, it was discovered that there was no ammunition with which to keep up the fight—the Mexicans contesting the ground inch by inch, and keeping up a rattling hail of bullets from house tops and windows. To supply this pressing want, Grant put his fancy horsemanship to good use, and made a ride which has become historical, through showers of bullets and over walls and ditches, to Twiggs' headquarters for ammunition. He is said to have escaped only by hanging, Indian fashion, along one side of his steed.

WITH SCOTT.

In the following spring, Grant's regiment was assigned to the force of General Winfield Scott, who had landed at Vera Cruz and assumed command of the movement against the Mexican capital, leaving Taylor with barely five thousand men to hold Monterey and the mountain country around, while he (the commander-in-chief) undertook his famous and brilliant campaign from Vera Cruz to Mexico. The way was won by dint of sharp tactics on Scott's part, and extraordinary endurance and bravery on the part of his men, who in the hard-fought engagements at Cerro Cordo, Contreras, Churubusco, Chapultapec and Molino del Rey, achieved no little glory for American arms. They achieved it not without severe sacrifices, however. Of Grant's regiment, which was attached to Worth's splendid division, and which went to Mexico five hundred and eleven strong, one hundred and ninety perished in the campaign. In such a campaign it is obvious that a young officer need not lack opportunities to distinguish himself.

TWICE BREVETTED FOR GALLANT DEEDS.

Grant, though a quartermaster, detached from the line, insisted upon joining in all the actions, and threw himself into the thickest of every fight. As a consequence, he won at Molino del Rey a brevet as First Lieutenant, and at Chapultapec, a still further brevet as captain. He was mentioned in the reports of his brigade commander as acquitting himself most nobly on several occasions under my observation." On the 18th of September, 1847, the city of Mexico was captured, and General Scott made a triumphal entry with his troops. In this triumph joined many officers, then serving as mere subalterns for the most part, who were destined afterwards to figure most conspicuously in the great civil war of 1861–5,—some on the side of the Union, and some (alas! for them) on the side of disunion and rebellion. Among these were Generals

Grant, McClellan, Hancock, Buell, Steele and Lyon, of the Federal, and Generals Lee and Beauregard, of the Rebel army. In Taylor's force were many more young men of destiny, including Braxton, Bragg, Pillow, and Hardee, of the regular, and Jeff. Davis, of the volunteer army. A roll-call of all the officers mustered in the streets of Mexico on the morning of that triumphal entry would, if repeated a few years afterwards, have been answered from the heads of a hundred corps and divisions of the two great hostile hosts either of which swallowed up scores of armies, like that which we sent to Mexico. The campaigns of Scott and Taylor were thought to be very important in their immediate political consequences. They were far more important in developing generals for the great struggle to which this Mexican affair was a mere preliminary skirmish—or rather, a simple drill exercise.

MARRIED AND SETTLED.

With the capitulation of Mexico the war with the Mexican Republic ended; but it was not until the middle of the following summer that the treaty of peace was ratified by both countries, and the Army of Occupation withdrawn. Grant arrived home on furlough in August of that year, and on the (to him) very importamt errand of marrying Miss Dent—an arrangement to which the parents of that young lady had, perhaps, become more reconciled by the brilliant military record of the proposed son-in-law. At all events, the pair were married, and "settled down"—so much as an army quartermaster may be said to settle down—in quarters of their own, at Detroit—the first station to which Captain Grant was assigned. The Bedouin-like wanderings to which the exigencies of the service condemned him, were too much for even the strong devotion to a military life with which Grant had become imbued; and in 1854, after having been successively assigned to Sacketts Harbor, N. Y.; Detroit; Fort Columbus, N. Y.; Benicia, Cal.; Fort Vancouver, Oregon; and Fort Humboldt, Colorado; and having then obtained the full rank of Captain of the Fourth Infantry,* he resigned his commission, and betook himself to a citizen's life. When, in the fall of 1854, he retired from the army, to manage the little unimproved farm at "Hardscrabble," near St. Louis,—a name which seems to have fitly characterized the place and its proprietor's farming course,—Grant was the father of two boys, and a devoted domestic *pater familias* Indeed, it was only his devotion to wife and children that induced him to relinquish that military life for which he was so well qualified, and to which his tastes had been so thoroughly trained.

THE FIRST GUN—GRANT RESPONDS.

Grant now spent nearly seven years—dull and unprofitable years apparently—in the pursuits of

* His commission, as such, bears date August, 1853.

civil life; first, on the farm near St. Louis, afterwards in that city as partner of a Mr. Boggs, in the real estate business, and finally as a partner with his father in the leather business, at Galena. It was his vocation as a tanner which led his admirers in after days to form Tanner's clubs in furtherance of his election as President. He was called from his hides and "findings" by the guns which battered down Sumpter; and a few days after the memorable commencement of hostilities Grant had raised a company at Galena, drilled them, and tendered his services, both at Washington and to the Governor of his State, at Springfield. Governor Yates took him into his service, on the recommendation of Elihu Washburne, as Adjutant General. He soon after tendered him the command of the Twenty-first Illinois Volunteer Infantry, and Grant, after waiting a few days for the War Department to make use of him in the regular army, if it chose, accepted the commission. Being sent to Quincy, Ill., and afterwards into Northeastern Missouri, to defend various railroad points, Col. Grant's regiment was assimilated with other troops into a brigade, and he was selected by General Pope, commanding the district, as acting Brigadier.

CHAPTER VIII.

GRANT'S MILITARY CAREER.

(CONTINUED.)

Colonel of the Twenty-first Illinois Volunteers—Brigadier General—His Fellows of that Rank—Captures Forts Henry and Donelson—Is Promoted to Major General—Battle of Shiloh.

THIS was early in July, 1861, and in August Grant received a commission as full brigadier general. His commission dates from the May preceding. He was one of the first "batch" of brigadier generals of volunteers, and amongst the rest were Heintzelman, Franklin, Couch, Kearney, Sherman, Pope, Buel, Sigel and twenty-five others, the most of whom became more famous as politicians than as soldiers. Grant's district embraced the Mississippi and its valley from Cape Girardeau to New Madrid, and the lower part of the Ohio Valley, including all of Western Kentucky. Establishing his headquarters at Cairo, the most important strategic point in all that valley, Grant threw a force over into Paducah just in time to save that point from being occupied by Bishop Polk's rebels, who would doubtless otherwise have soon shelled him out of Cairo, and made havoc generally.

THE BATTLE OF BELMONT.

Grant's first engagement was on the 7th of November, at Belmont, a small town on the west, or right, bank of the Mississippi, opposite Columbus, Ky. This engagement wore the appearance of a defeat, since it ended by the Union force retreating to their starting point, leaving their dead and wounded in the enemy's hands. Subsequent reports, however, put a different phase upon it, as it was made to appear what was the object of the expedition. This, according to the official report of General Grant, was mainly to demonstrate upon Polk's works, and prevent him from reinforcing some troops against whom Pope was operating in Missouri. If so, its object was accomplished, though not without severe loss to the attacking party; viz., 84 killed and 300 wounded and missing out of a command of 2,850 men. Of the five regiments of infantry, one battery and two squadrons of cavalry engaged, the 7th Iowa Infantry suffered most seriously. The rebel loss is stated by some authorities as high as one thousand men; and the rebel force was certainly larger than ours. The affair was of the nature of a forest skirmish, and was waged with great courage and desperation on both sides. It was, however, magnified into a grave defeat, the public mind being morbidly excited after the disasters of Big Bethel and Bull Run, with which the war opened. It proved to be almost the only engagement of this great commander's many trying campaigns which could be construed into a defeat, even by the most captious of his detractors

CAPTURE OF FORT HENRY.

The brilliant engagements ending with the capture of Forts Henry and Donelson, of which Grant was the directing genius, occurred in the February following, having been set on foot some weeks earlier. By the middle of January the Rebels had established a pretty continuous and well defended line (so far as numerical forces were concerned), stretching from Manassas to Columbus. Lying in this line were several important strategic points—none more so than Forts Henry and Donelson—two strong earthworks which had been thrown up and were rapidly being finished off as first-class forts, situated respectively on the Tennessee and Cumberland rivers, where those great navigable streams approach within twelve miles of each other, and not far south of the boundary between Tennessee and Kentucky. Against these Grant moved early in February, with twenty regiments of infantry, one regiment and four independent companies of cavalry and four batteries of artillery, as land forces, aided by six river gun boats, of the pattern then just originated, under Commodore Foote. Fort Henry was easily taken, the gallant Commodore having indeed secured its capitulation before the land forces arrived in front.

FORT DONELSON.

The easily won victory of Fort Henry was followed by the capture of Fort Donelson, won at the end of two day's hard fighting. Fort Donelson was defended by Generals Floyd and Pillow, with a force of sixteen to eighteen thousand men and a very heavy armament of columbiads and field pieces. The work was a very strong one, every way worthy in the engineering skill which had placed and planned it to defend the most important stragetic point west of the Blue Ridge. The movement upon Donelson from the fort on the Tennessee was made on the 11th of February; but the engagement on land was not commenced until the 15th. (The gunboats had been pounding away during the two previous days, and had damaged seriously the water batteries of the fort, and at the same time experienced severe punishment themselves.)

Grant's forces consisted of the divisions of Generals McClernand, C. F. Smith, and Lew. Wallace. The first of these was furiously attacked by a force of 10,000 rebels, hurled suddenly against them at day break. The engagement thus inaugurated was continued all day with varying fortune, Grant sending McClernand heavy reinforcements from Smith and Wallace, and at the same time pushing the attack on the right of the enemies lines, which had been left weakened by the massing in front of McClernand. A dashing charge was made, led by Smith in person, and all the positions carried. This was the turning point in the engagement. Night closed in and the attack was to have been renewed and the advantage followed up in the morning; but with the morning came a flag of truce with a note, proposing a capitulation. It was from Simon B. Buckner—not from Floyd, nor yet from Pillow, both of whom had ignominiously fled during the night.

GRANT'S CORRESPONDENCE IN THE FIELD.

The correspondence which ensued between the victorious and the defeated commanders has become famous, and, being remarkably laconic, may be properly given here. Buckner who was much more of a soldier by nature than his superiors, and who was evidently disgusted at their course, lost no time in sending Grant the following note:

"HEAD-QUARTERS, FORT DONELSON, February 16th, 1862.

"SIR:—In consideration of all the circumstances governing the present situation of affairs at this station, I propose to the commanding officer of the Federal forces the appointment of commissioners to agree upon terms of capitulation of the forces and fort under my command, and in that view suggest an armistice until twelve o'clock to-day.

"I am sir very respectfully, your obedient servant,

"S. B. BUCKNER,

"Brigadier-General, C. S. A.

"TO BRIGADIER-GENERAL GRANT, commanding United States forces near Fort Donelson."

To which Grant made this memorable reply:

HEAD-QUARTERS, ARMY IN THE FIELD,

"CAMP NEAR DONELSON, February 16th, 1862.

"TO GENERAL S. B. BUCKNER, Confederate Army:

"Yours of this date, proposing an armistice and appointment of commissioners to settle terms of capitulation, is just received. *No terms other than an unconditional and immediate surrender can be accepted. I propose to move immediately upon your works.*

"I am, sir, very respectfully, your obedient servant,

"U. S. GRANT,

"Brigadier-General, U. S. A., Commanding."

And soon the final answer came from Buckner:

"HEAD-QUARTERS, DOVER, TENN., February 16th, 1862.

"TO BRIGADIER-GENERAL U. S. GRANT, U. S. A.:

"SIR:—The distribution of the forces under my command, incident to an unexpected change of commanders and the overwhelming force under your command, compel me, notwithstanding the brilliant success of the Confederate arms yesterday, to accept the ungenerous and unchivalrous terms which you propose.

"I am, sir, your very obedient servant,
"S. B. BUCKNER,
"Brigadier-General, C. S. A."

It may be added, in passing, that the style exhibited in the communication to Gen. Buckner fairly exemplifies Grant's style of correspondence in similar exigencies throughout the war. He was always laconic, but not affectedly so. He always embraced all the essential points at issue, but never expanded upon them, nor indulged in mere bragadocia or stilted grandiloquence, such as characterizes the orders and proclamations of many commanders, both great and small. Grant's brevity of epistle is a result of his simplicity of diction rather than of any scarcity of ideas, and of his apparently intuitive perception, rather than labored analysis of the elements of each critical situation.

The victory at Fort Donelson was dearly bought, though no less so than could have been expected from the exceeding strength of the work to be taken and the courage with which the Confederate troops fought. Of the Union forces, 446 were killed, 1,735 wounded and 150 made prisoners; while the rebels lost in killed 231, in wounded 1,007 and in prisoners nearly 14,000—a few having escaped along with the cowards, Floyd and Pillow.

PUBLIC REJOICINGS.

This victory occasioned more rejoicing throughout the North, especially the Northwest, than any other victory of the war, except the great final triumphs which it was given to the hero of the Donelson fight to win also. Spontaneous meetings were held everywhere and all manner of jubilant public demonstrations were indulged in. The anniversary of Washington's birthday came within a day or two after the public obtained the particulars of the fight; and there has never been so fervently patriotic a celebration of the birthday of the Father of his Country as took place on the 22nd of February, 1862. The writer had the privilege of listening, at Milwaukee, to a very eloquent oration from Hon. Matthias H. Carpenter, in which the elogium in memory of the great dead was gracefully interwoven with a tribute to our northern soldiery and to their intrepid leader in Tennessee. Little did his hearers then think, when mingling their tears of gratitude to the living and of bereavement for the dead, that the same gifted orator would, ten years after, be called upon to defend the fame of the same gallant General from attacks of slander and innuendo made in the United States Senate, and inspired by motives far less worthy of charity than those which made necessary the attack upon Donelson!

PROMOTED TO MAJOR GENERAL.

The victory achieved at Forts Henry and Donelson was most prolific of good results. The navigation of the Tennessee and Cumberland rivers was assured by it, and the Rebel line of occupation was so effectually penetrated that it had to be withdrawn fully two hundred miles on the average, necessitating the abandonment, within a few days, of the strongholds of Columbus, Bowling Green, and Nashville, all of which were speedily occupied by the Union armies. For this achievement Grant was promoted to be a Major General of volunteers. His name was also greatly promoted in the affections of all loyal people, who, whether or not they appreciated the strategic advantages of his position, or the military difficulties which he had overcome, did appreciate the value of a trustworthy leader for the troops whose fighting qualities had been so bravely demonstrated. And it was very refreshing to the souls of the patriotic to learn of a signal victory to the national arms after hearing scarcely aught for months but disaster to a cause and an army that deserved only good fortune.

SHILOH.

Six months afterwards—as soon as the new levies of troops, now rapidly pouring in from the North, under Lincoln's call for half a million of men, could be organized and drilled a little—came the battle of Pittsburgh Landing; or, as the Rebels called it, Shiloh. This was a step in the aggressive campaign which had been inaugurated (though unfortunately with Halleck, the least aggressive of generals, to direct it) against the strong and threatening forces of the Rebels. These forces had been strengthened by the arrival of Beauregard from Manassas, with 15,000 troops; and an army of at least 60,000 was raised at Corinth, under command of General Albert Sidney Johnston, probably the ablest of all the Rebel generals. To dislodge this army, and to prevent it from assuming the offensive, was the task of Grant. To this end he crossed the Tennessee at Savannah and took up a position on the left bank of the river at Pittsburgh Landing. The ground, a series of wooded ridges and ravines, flanked by creeks, was selected by General C. F. Smith, with reference to its defensibility against the attack which the enemy was deemed sure to make. The attack came rather sooner than was expected, on the morning of the 6th of April, and before Buell's army, which formed a part of Grant's force, could come up from Savannah. The organization and officering of the contending armies were as follows:

REBELS.

Force, 45,000.
Commander-in-chief, Gen. A. S. Johnston.
Second in Command, Gen. P. T. Beauregard.
First Corps, Lieut.-Gen. Leonidas Polk.
Second Corps, Lieut.-Gen. Braxton Bragg.
Third Corps, Lieut.-Gen. W. T. Hardee.
Reserves, Maj.-Gen. G. B. Crittenden.

UNION FORCES.

Force, 38,000.
Commander-in-chief, Maj.-Gen. U. S. Grant.
First Division, Maj.-Gen. John A. McClernand.

Second Division, Brig.-Gen. W. H. L. Wallace.
Third Division, Maj.-Gen. Lewis Wallace.
Fourth Division, Brig.-Gen. S. A. Hurlbut.
Fifth Division, Brig.-Gen. W. T. Sherman.

(The Division of Gen. Lew. Wallace, 5,000 strong, was not engaged during the first days.)

In the disposition of Grant's forces for the battle, Gen Prentiss occupied the left, resting on the left bank of the river, near the mouth of Lick Creek. At his right, his line stretching in a curvilinear direction to Owl Creek, was Gen. Sherman, supported in the rear by McClernand, while W. H. L. Wallace was posted with his command a mile in the rear, so as to command the bridge across Owl Creek. (or Snake Creek, into which it has emptied) and at the same time act as a reserve for use in case the attack should be pressed too hotly upon the left and center. To guard the flank and rear, Lew. Wallace was stationed with his division in column by brigades across the Burdy road, near Crump's Landing, six miles below.

The story of the battle was briefly this (for we must not go into detail in regard to each of Grant's battles—there were too many of them): The fight was precipitated by a collision between a small reconnoitering party sent out from Prentiss's headquarters, and the advance guard of the enemy, who had already assembled for the attack. The two or three companies of scouts were driven in pell-mell. and Prentiss's force a good deal disordered by the suddenness of the onset. They rallied, however, and, with help from McClernand, were soon able to make a stand. The battle was waged fiercely all the forenoon, all along Sherman's and Prentiss's lines (the latter officer was taken prisoner early in the day, together with a considerable portion of his command), and again about four o'clock in the afternoon, when the Rebels made a furious charge on our left. This last was directed by Beauregard, General Johnston having fallen mortally wounded at half past two o'clock. The plan of the Rebel commander was to turn Grant's left flank and crowd him away from the river altogether; and to this end the whole force of the enemy was hurled impetuously against the raw levies who made up the larger part of Grant's army. But they fought with all the firmness and more than the desperation of the coolest veterans. The discharge of musketry and artillery was deafening and continuous, from daylight till dark, and the wooded ridges and ravines which formed the battle ground were covered with the dead and wounded, men and horses. Night closed in upon two defeated and shattered armies. That is, the Union forces were driven back a mile all along, and were in a bad plight for fighting on the morrow; and as for the Rebels, when Grant, reinforced by a few regiments brought by Buell, and by the division of Wallace, now tardily arrived from Crump's Landing, ordered an advance and an attack at daybreak, it was found that the "Johnnies," too, had fallen back, and were so weak as to afford next to no resistance to the onset. A pursuit was ordered under Sherman; but the storm of Sunday night had rendered the roads impracticable for cavalry, and the pursuit was not pressed. Beauregard, who, according to contemporary accounts, had made his boast that he "would water his horses that night in the Tennessee or in h—l," was in full retreat *away* from the Tennessee, and presumably in the direction of the other place named.

During the terrible engagement of Sunday—one of the most severe of modern times—General Grant had been always noticeable for his activity and energy, though always cool and seemingly oblivious to danger. He seemed ubiquitous, and more than once averted disaster by his presence and timely directions. Prodigies of valor were displayed by officers and prodigies of endurance by the men. General Sherman had three horses shot under him and received two wounds, but kept his saddle in spite of them. At night, after giving directions for the morrow, Grant (who, by the way, had been suffering for two days with a sprained ankle, which disabled him either from walking or mounting without help), lay down on the field and slept, with a log for his pillow, and the sleety rain falling upon him. But this was no worse for the General commanding than for his noble troops —not so bad as for the thousands of them who lay wounded upon the field, the most of them in hostile hands, as they believed. The losses of the Union army in this bloody engagement amounted to 1,700 killed, 7,495 wounded and 3,022 missing; while those of the Rebels were still greater in killed and wounded, but aggregating about 1,500 less than ours.

GRANT'S GENERALSHIP CRITICISED.

General Grant's management of this affair has been a subject of much acrimonious discussion. The friends of Halleck and Buell, jealous of the fame which Grant was already winning, made a persistent exhibition of all the unfavorable features of the engagement—such as the severe mortality among our troops (the rebels lost still more), the surprise of Prentiss and Stuart, and especially the absence of General Grant during the first three hours of the engagement. The only criticism which seems to stand the test of subsequent investigation and very free discussion by men of military science is that, in view of the proximity and supposed force of the enemy, Grant should not have entrenched himself in front. This mistake, however, was shared by Sherman and by other officers of now acknowledged genius; and it was counterbalanced by such qualities and feats on the part of the Commander-in-chief, during the progress of the fight, as were unquestionably the means of winning it in more than one crisis when another commander would have lost. The charge was made that the army was not efficiently directed during the first day of the battle; and Don Carlos Buell, who arrived quite at his leisure, at four o'clock that afternoon,

caused it to be understood that he then found the army practically without a head. Nothing could be farther from the truth. Grant's orders, from the time of leaving Savanna at five o'clock in the morning and ordering up Nelson's division (the advance of Buell's army) to the time of directing the triumphant advance on Monday morning, were those of a clear-headed and far-seeing general, as well as an active and courageous soldier. At ten o'clock on Sunday forenoon, when Sherman was so hotly pressed, Grant was with him, sustaining him with his counsel, at other critical junctures and places during the day, he was always to be found, reforming the line and giving directions; at four o'clock in the afternoon he met Buell at the Landing; at five o'clock he placed in position a brigade just arrived from Nelson's Division across the river; in the evening he met Buell and Sherman for consultation, and gave orders for the attack on the following morning. When Buell arrived, his question to Grant was. "Well, General, what preparations have you made for retreating?" And Grant's answer, "I haven't despaired of whipping them yet," and his order to hurry up the troops from Savanna showed, when coupled with the result of the next day's advance, that Grant understood the situation much better than his critic.

It should be borne in mind that this battle of Shiloh was the first general engagement since the disastrous battle of Bull Run, in which a large, well organized and well commanded force of the rebels had been met by our boys, and that the result was, at all events, such as to completely erase the painful impression produced by the panic into which the Northern army had been thrown. General Wm. Tecumseh Sherman, now General-in-Chief of the army, (and who warmly defends the course of Grant at Shiloh), is of opinion that just such a deadly engagement as this was necessary, to demonstrate the perfect *morale* of our men when on the field and without entrenchments—a very important element in the conduct, plan and management of all military operations.

CHAPTER IX.

GRANT'S MILITARY CAREER.

(CONTINUED.)

Halleck in Command—Corinth Captured—Battle of Iuka—Desperate Fighting at Corinth—The Rebels Out-Generaled—Grant as an Administrator—Vicksburg Striven After—Two Unsuccessful Attempts to Reach it—Grant "Takes the Responsibility," and Wins the Most Decisive Victory of the War.

On the 8th of April, 1862, General Halleck, in charge of the department, took the chief command of the combined armies of Grant and Buell. Sherman, with a large cavalry and infantry force, made a reconnoisance on the line toward Corinth, and, after a brief, but brilliant skirmish, compelled an outlying force of the enemy to retire, and destroyed their camp. Several movements of a similar character were made by our forces during the month of April. On the 30th, the town of Purdy was occupied, two important bridges were blown up, and the siege of Corinth began to assume definite shape. Beauregard made good use of his time in concentrating his forces and strengthening his fortifications.

The Grand Army of the Tennessee was organized early in May, under the supreme command of General Halleck, as follows: The Army of the Tennessee, under Grant, was on the right; Buell, with the Army of the Ohio, occupied the center, and Pope's Army of the Mississippi was on the left. There were in all sixteen divisions, eight of which were in the army of General Grant, whose right wing was commanded by General George H. Thomas. Grant was made second in command, under Halleck, a promotion which was warmly approved by the soldiers of the Grand Army.

CAPTURE OF CORINTH.

The investment of Corinth proceeded with creditable rapidity. From the 8th of May to the 16th, there was almost continual skirmishing between the advance guards on both sides. On the 17th, Sherman captured Thorsell's House, a strong point which was held by a large Rebel force. The place was immediately occupied by our victorious troops. On the 21st Thomas A. Davis's division, after a very sharp engagement, captured an important bridge, within shelling distance of the Southern lines, north of Philips's Creek. Sherman's division drove a strong body of the enemy on the 27th, and on the 28th the columns commanded by Thomas, Pope and Buell, under the chief direction of General Grant, advanced within easy gunshot range of the Rebel stronghold. The loss on our side was severe, but the fight sickened the enemy, who, on the succeeding day, evacuated Corinth, conceiving that it would be impossible to defend it successfully against the skillful disposition and impatient valor of our investing force. The fifth division of Grant's

Army of the Tennessee was the first to plant its colors on the captured ramparts. The enemy were vigorously pursued, but their flight was so rapid that nothing could be done with them, beyond destroying railroad communications and capturing supplies. General Sherman again signalized himself in this pursuit, and at Holly Springs damaged the enemy's communications with such effect that their future movements were much embarrassed. The pursuers were then recalled and the Grand Army rested on its arms.

When Memphis capitulated, in the month of June. 1862, Grant visited that city, and placed a Provost-Marshal in charge of it. He immediately issued such orders as effectually checked the rebellious practices of a majority of the citizens. The guerilla outrages were greatly mitigated and illicit trade with Rebels in arms was peremptorily prohibited The families of such persons as held official position, civil or military, under the Rebel Government, were ordered to move south beyond our lines, unless they signed a prescribed parole and guaranteed good behavior in the future. Other important orders were also issued, all of which had a happy effect on our cause, and showed favorably for the executive ability of General Grant.

GRANT SUPREME IN THE SOUTHWEST.

General Halleck bade farewell to the Grand Army of the Tennessee on the 17th of July, and proceeded to the National Capitol, where he assumed a still higher office, that of Commander-in-Chief of the Union Armies. The Department of the Mississippi was then subdivided, and Grant was placed in command of the Department of West Tennessee, his headquarters being at Corinth. This was the idlest military period of Grant's active career in the War of the Rebellion. From July until the middle of September nothing of importance, from a fighting standpoint, occurred. Some skirmishes took place, in which our troops where uniformly the victors. The army was perfected in discipline, and the rebel positions were fully reconnoitred, preparatory to another campaign.

On the 11th day of August 1862, the following significant order was issued:

GRANT'S ADMINISTRATIVE ORDERS.

On the 11th of August, 1862, General Grant issued an important order (published in full in a subsequent chapter) relating to the employment of negroes who came into camp as fugitives from slavery. He soon afterwards caused the adoption in his army of a system of educating and caring for the negroes, which was substantially that adopted afterwards by Congress in the formation of the Freedmen's Bureau. On the 16th of the same month another order was issued providing for the enlistment of all skulkers, from States within the Union, who would be subject to the draft if at home. Their enrollment was to be allowed for in the quotas of their proper districts. Traffic with the enemy, or with sympathizers with the rebellion, was forbidden, under heavy penalties.

BATTLE OF IUKA.

On the day of the famous battle of Antietam, September 17, 1862, General Grant ordered an advance against the rebel commander, Sterling Price, who had concentrated his forces near Iuka, on the Memphis and Charleston Railroad. Price had with him about 15,000 men, and was endeavoring to deceive Grant into the belief that he intended to follow Buell's army, which was then retiring upon Nashville. He wanted to draw Grant away from Corinth, upon which place Van Dorn's rebel column was marching with rapid strides. Price's plan, which Grant instantly penetrated, was to join his forces to Van Dorn's and so recapture the fortified camp which the rebel army had evacuated in the early part of the campaign. Grant was aware, from information he received through his scouts, that it would require at least four days' rapid marching to bring Van Dorn before Corinth. In that time he hoped to surround and capture Price,—so he laid his plans accordingly.

General Ord, with about 3,500 men, having left garrisons at Corinth and other points of importance, was ordered to move on the left of the railroad to Iuka. General Ross, posted at Bolivar, was ordered, by telegram, to follow that route also, raising the Union force, which was destined to attack Price from the North, to something over 6,500 men.

Stanley's division, of Rosecrans's command, with Mizner's troopers, was ordered to move by way of Jacinto, and so take the enemy in flank, while Hamilton's brigade was ordered to move around by the Fulton road, so as to encompass the enemy on the south and cut off his retreat, or, at least, throw him into hopeless confusion.

The forces were pretty nearly equalized, but the enemy had the advantage of position. At 4 o'clock on the morning of September 18, the grand movement of our troops commenced. Rosecrans, that same night, having marched all day over bad roads and through a heavy rain-storm, rested his tired soldiers at Jacinto. He continued his advance early next morning, and, after sharp fighting at Barnett's Corners, marched direct on Iuka and encountered Price in force on the center ridge which helped to defend that position. The fighting lasted until darkness set in, and, during the long struggle, three guns, belonging to an Ohio regiment, were frequently taken and retaken, but finally, at night, the enemy held them.

Grant rode with Ord's column, expecting, when he reached the objective point, to be in full communication with Rosecrans. That general had, however, encountered greater difficulties than he calculated upon. The roads on the line of his advance were miserable. The rebels were well posted and in formidable force and the messengers sent by either general, being unused to that tangled country, lost their way in the woods so that the communications sent after operations began, were late in arriving. Thus Ord's force could not be brought into action in time to capture Price and his army, but the approach of our soldiers from the North made the rebel commander retreat in hot haste in the direction of Bay Springs, twenty-seven miles south from the battle field. He had lost one of his best officers, Gen. Little; his diversion in favor of Van Dorn was defeated; he had lost over 2,000 of his men, in killed, wounded and prisoners.

Grant, although the effort to surround Price had failed, had effectually punished his audacity, demoralized his forces and prevented his proposed attack on Corinth, at least for that time.

Meanwhile Van Dorn was marching from the West, hoping to eat up Grant's forces without even a note of warning. Price's fugitive army, having made a tremendous circuit, joined Van Dorn at Dumas and the combined forces moved northward on Pocahontas, where they were still further strengthened by the rebel division of Mansfield Lovell. The enemy then marched by the railroad, through Chewalla, upon Corinth.

THE BATTLE, ABOUT CORINTH.

Grant, being in a state of uncertainty as to which route the rebels would decide to advance upon, had provided for the safety of all the posts within his command. Rosecrans had been marched back from Jacinto and reached Corinth on September 26. Ord was stationed at Bolivar, which was a threatened point, and from which he could readily support Rosecrans in the event of a strong attack upon his position. Hurlbut's division sentinelled the country toward Pocahontas, while General Grant's headquarters were at Jackson.

The works at Corinth had been improved, under Grant's orders, in a manner that rendered them defensible by a small, as well as by a large army, for which they were originally intended. Every precaution was taken, and Corinth was a very hard rock against which Van Dorn was determined to dash his unfortunate soldiers.

The 3d of October brought the enemy in force on the Chewalla road. The reconnoitering troops, after a heavy fight, were driven in on the outer intrenchments, which they stubbornly defended. Davis's brigade lost two heavy guns in the retreat, and the yelling foe halted within range of our ramparts. Van Dorn immediately telegraphed Jeff. Davis that he had gained a surprising victory. The rebels made merry in their camps that night, and devoured their hoe cake with gusto.

Next morning, the memorable 4th of October, dawned on one of the most fiercely contested battles of that murderous war. The enemy, during the night, had erected several batteries in our front, and had closed up their lines to within 1,000 yards of our works. Their generals addressed them in stirring words, and they were wild for the onset.

Our men stood cool and firm, making no demonstrations, but evincing a calm courage that was well borne out on that sanguinary day.

The enemy opened the ball with a fierce cannonade from the batteries erected on our right, which was held by the division of General Hamilton, supported by Dillon's battery. Davies's division, supported by the Powell battery, occupied the centre, while Stanley's division, protected by the batteries of Williams and Robinett, defended the extreme left of our line. The attack on Davies was the first grand movement of the day, and it was one of the most determined on record. The rebel columns, headed by Price, rushed upon our left centre, despite our tremendous fire, like furious bisons. They fell in whole sections, but nothing in the way of cannon balls and cannister could drive them back. Davies's division was too hard pressed, and began to waver, but Rosencrans rushed to its aid, and, fighting magnificently, drove back the savage hordes. The latter, however, rallied again, advanced with fresh fury and actually entered the outskirts of the town, where they were finally mowed down and bloodily repulsed by a section of artillery, which was gallantly supported by the Tenth Ohio and Fifth Minnesota infantry.

Price had thus disastrously failed, but Van Dorn, not to be outdone in foolhardy valor, led a terrific attack on our left, which, after a terrible struggle, was driven back in confusion. Again the glorious maniacs, led by brainless officers, are hurled into the very flaming mouth of destruction. Nothing daunted, on they came, strewing the intervening ground with their dead and wounded, mown down like summer grass. Their charging shout was heard even above that infernal din. But all was in vain. Torn with round shot, shattered with grape, mown down by shell, and literally overwhelmed by a concentrated fire of musketry, those dauntless troops, worthy of wiser leaders and a better cause, were at length compelled to retreat, from sheer exhaustion. Our brave fellows, having received the stirring order to charge upon the foe, advanced at a double-quick, and quickened the enemy's flight. They retreated on Pocahontas, where, early on the morning of October 5th, they were attacked by the division of General Hurlbut, which Grant had dispatched on that route to intercept them. The enemy were driven back over the Hatchie river, toward Corinth. Ord now arrived and took command. The pursuit was very vigorous. The Rebels retreated to Crum's Mill, six miles above, where they recrossed the Hatchie in a fearfully disorganized condition. Their ruin being complete, Grant recalled the pursuers and issued a congratulatory order to the troops who had participated in the dreadful conflict. This order is worthy of being preserved:

GENERAL ORDERS, NO. 88.

HEADQUARTERS DEPARTMENT OF WEST TENNESSEE.
JACKSON, TENN., October 7, 1862.

It is with heartfelt gratitude the general commanding congratulates the armies of the West for another great victory, won by them on the 3d, 4th, and 5th instant, over the combined armies of Van Dorn, Price and Lovell.

The enemy chose his own time and place of attack, and, knowing the troops of the West as he does, and with great facilities for knowing their numbers, never would have made the attempt, except with a superior force numerically. *But for the undaunted bravery of officers and soldiers, who have yet to learn defeat,* the efforts of the enemy must have proven successful.

Whilst one division of the army, under Major-General Rosecrans, was resisting and repelling the onslaught of the Rebel hosts at Corinth, another, from Bolivar, under Major-General Hurlbut, was marching upon the enemy's rear, driving in their pickets and cavalry, and attracting the attention of a large force of infantry and artillery. On the following day under Major-General Ord these forces advanced with unsurpassed gallantry, driving the enemy back across the Hatchie, over ground where it is almost incredible that a superior force should be driven by an inferior, capturing two of the batteries (eight guns), many hundred small-arms, and several hundred prisoners.

To those two divisions of the army all praise is due, and will be rewarded by a grateful country.

Between them there should be, and I trust are, the warmest bonds of brotherhood. Each was risking life in the same cause, and, on this occasion, risking it also to save and assist the other. No troops could do more than these separate armies. Each did all possible for it to do in the places assigned it.

As in all great battles, so in this, it becomes our fate to mourn the loss of many brave and faithful officers and soldiers who have given up their lives as a sacrifice for a great principle. The nation mourns for them.

By command of

MAJOR-GENERAL U. S. GRANT.

JOHN A. RAWLINS, A. A. G.

The plans of General Grant had succeeded beyond his most sanguine hopes. He had confided to Rosecrans, for the defence of Corinth, the following troops: Hamilton's division, containing the brigades of Buford and Sullivan; Davies's division, brigades of Oglesby and Hackelman; Stanley's division, nine regiments; McArthur's and Oliver's brigades, commanded by McArthur. Batteries: First Missouri; Third Michigan; Company F, United States artillery; Tenth and Eleventh Ohio; Eighth and Twelfth Wisconsin; Three Missouri companies, together with the strong batteries already mentioned.

With the commands of Hurlbut and Ord he had operated in rear of the discomfited foe and completed his demoralization. The enemy had lost in killed 1,423 officers and enlisted men; nearly 6,000 in wounded and 2,300 prisoners, while fourteen regimental colors and two pieces of field ordnance were among the trophies of this brilliant victory. Our loss was relatively slight, amounting to only 2,000 in killed, wounded and missing. General Hackelman was killed and Generals Ord and Oglesby were both severely wounded.

President Lincoln telegraphed his congratulations, and asked how it all summed up. It cleared Grant's road to Vicksburg. The country again did honor to the Western heroes, and Corinth became a synonym of hope to all loyal citizens of the United States.

AGAIN PROMOTED.

The War Department recognized the services of General Grant by making him, on October 16, 1862, Commander of the Department of the Tennessee, embracing the State of Mississippi to Vicksburg, together with Cairo, Fort Henry, Fort Donelson, and those portions of Kentucky and Tennessee west of the river of the latter name.

Grant established his headquarters at Jackson, Tenn., and, on the 26th of October, issued a general order placing the District of Memphis under control of General W. T. Sherman; the District of Jackson under charge of General W. S. Hurlbut; the District of Corinth under command of General C. S. Hamilton, and the District of Columbus under the orders of General T. A. Davies. These Districts comprised four geographical divisions, each commander being held responsible to the head of the Department. The Army of the Mississippi was continued as a separate organization, and matters of detail were clearly disposed of.

In addition to the foregoing, on November 1, General Grant issued a general order which regulated the movements of trains and limited the equipments of the soldiery to the smallest possible weight and bulk. He set his face against the encumbrance of numerous baggage wagons; discountenanced dandyism in the office, and set an example to all his forces by going through the approaching campaign destitute of everything superfluous in the way of personal baggage.

VICKSBURG NEXT!

The fall of Memphis had left the Mississippi open, from Minneapolis on the North, and from New Orleans on the South, to Vicksburg and the country surrounding it, which was held by the rebel forces under John C. Pemberton.

Vicksburg, key of the Mississippi, was now the splendid prize toward which the undaunted mind of Grant was directing all its attention.

The attempt to cut a new channel for the Mississippi, and leave Vicksburg high and dry inland, had failed. Farragut had been operating around Vicksburg with his fleet, about the middle of the summer; he had even silenced some of the enemy's batteries; but low water had eventually compelled him to take his flotilla down the river to New Orleans.

Pemberton's main army covered Vicksburg on the line of the Mississippi Central Railroad, the strong points of his position being Abbeville, behind the Tallahatchie river, and Holly Springs, Miss. His advance guard was posted between Grand Junction and La Grange.

THE FIRST ASSAULT.

Several reconnoisances had been made by our troops, under Grant's directions, and, on November 4th, that general's plans having been completed and his forces concentrated, he pushed briskly forward and, encountering Pemberton's advance at La Grange, drove it back, with great loss, on Holly Springs. This movement flanked the enemy at Grand Junction, on the Memphis and Charleston Railroad, and they rapidly fell back from that position. Grant urged forward his elated troops, and succeeded in capturing Ripley, Orizaba and Hudsonville, thereby uncovering the enemy's strong positions of Holly Springs and Coldwater.

Sherman was advancing from Memphis with a splendid army, and an expeditionary force from Arkansas, under Generals A. T. Hovey and Washburne, was taking the Rebel army in flank. Thus, surrounded on almost every side, Lovell, who commanded that portion of the Rebel army, abandoned the line of the Tallahatchie and fell back in confusion, without making even a respectable effort to defend his position.

It would be impossible, in a book of this extent, to give details of the brilliant manœuvring on the part of General Grant's forces, which led to this result. The Rebels had fallen back to Grenada, and Northern Mississippi appeared to be almost entirely under control of our forces. Grant moved forward on the Rebel lines at Grenada, and was preparing for a final assault upon Pemberton, when an unexpected disaster, due to the treason or cowardice of a subordinate, destroyed all his plans, uncovered his rear to the enemy and threatened to destroy his communications. It came about in the following manner:

Hovey, after the retreat of the rebels, had been ordered to return to Helena, and, when Van Dorn, who commanded a division of Pemberton's army, was aware of this fact, he resolved upon a bold expedition in rear of Grant's forces, with the intention of capturing the posts of Columbus, Trenton, Jackson, Bolivar, Corinth, Holly Springs and other places of lesser importance, and, by this means, compelling Grant, in order to save his line of communication with the North, to fall back and so relieve Pemberton, whose front and flanks were being roughly assailed by the indefatigable captor of Fort Donelson.

Van Dorn lost no time in putting his plan into execution. He fell like a thunderbolt on Cold Water, Davis's Mills and Middlesburg, but was bloodily repulsed in each endeavor. Unfortunately the strong and important post of Holly Springs, which contained many valuable stores, and which was garrisoned by the Eighth Wisconsin infantry, was under the command of a man who was utterly inadequate to the task before him Van Dorn surrounded the place on the 20th of December, and at once moved to an assault upon it. Murphy, the commander, deeming his regiment too weak to resist the shock, despite the protestations of his officers and men, disgracefully surrendered the place, almost without firing a shot.

Grant was then at Oxford, Miss., thirty miles away, and, when this disastrous news reached him, fearing a movement of the enemy in his rear, he fell back to Holly Springs, which Van Dorn had evacuated, after burning or carrying off everything of value.

Grant immediately issued a ringing order, in which he denounced the surrender of the place, and refused to accede to terms of parole agreed upon between the inefficient commander and the rebel general, unless some modifications were made by the latter. He also congratulated the garrisons that held out, most warmly. The wretched Colonel was dismissed in disgrace from the service of the United States.

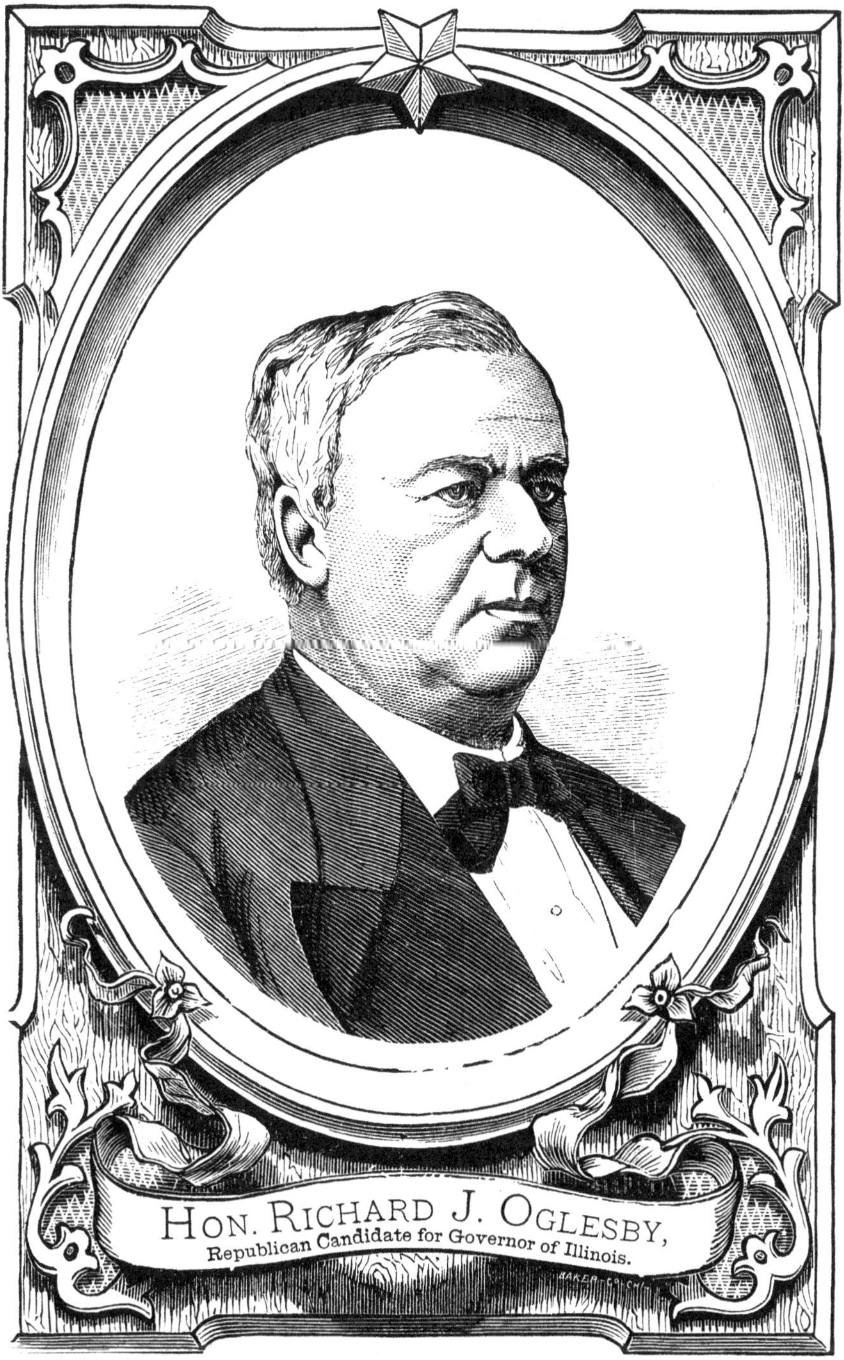

HON. RICHARD J. OGLESBY,

Republican Candidate for Governor of Illinois.

BAKER-CO.CH

SHERMAN'S UNSUCCESSFUL ENDEAVOR.

Prior to the mishap at Holly Springs, the first act in the drama having been successfully performed, Grant proposed to the Commander-in-Chief to hold Pemberton beyond the Yalebooka river, while forces from Helena and Memphis were moved on Vicksburg. Halleck acceeded to this proposal, and, on the 8th of December, General Sherman, who commanded the right wing of the army, and who had formed a junction with Grant, near Waterford, Miss., on December 1, received the following order:

HEADQUARTERS DEPARTMENT OF THE TENNESSEE,
OXFORD, MISS., Dec. 8, 1862.

MAJOR-GENERAL W. T. SHERMAN, Commanding Right Wing:

GENERAL—You will proceed with as little delay as possible to Memphis, Tenn., taking with you one division of your present command. On your arrival at Memphis, you will assume command of all the troops there, and that portion of General Curtis's force at present east of the Mississippi River, and organize them into brigades and divisions in your own way. As soon as possible, move with them down the river, to the vicinity of Vicksburg; and, with the co-operation of the gunboat fleet under command of Flag-Officer Porter, proceed to the reduction of that place, in such manner as circumstances and your own judgment may dictate.

The amount of rations, forage, land transportation, etc., necessary to take will be left entirely with yourself. The quartermaster at St. Louis will be instructed to send you transportation for thirty thousand men. Should you still find yourself deficient, your quartermaster will be authorized to make up the deficiency from such transports as may come into the port of Memphis.

On arriving in Memphis, put yourself in communication with Admiral Porter, and arrange with him for his co-operation.

Inform me at the earliest practicable day of the time when you will embark, and such plans as may then be matured. I will hold the forces here in readiness to co-operate with you in such manner as the movements of the enemy may make necessary.

Leave the district of Memphis in the command of an efficient officer, and with a garrison of four regiments of infantry, the siege-guns, and whatever cavalry may be there.

(Signed) U. S. GRANT, Major-General.

In pursuance of this order, General Sherman prepared, in concert with Admiral Porter, the first expedition against Vicksburg. On the day after the surrender of Holly Springs, (December 21st, of which unfortunate event he was in total ignorance), this gallant officer embarked his expeditionary force at Memphis and Helena. He had with him four splendid divisions of infantry, with artillery and a small force of cavalry. On the 27th the main body of his forces debarked at Johnston's Landing, on the Yazoo river, about eight miles north of Vicksburg. The result of the assault on the Rebel positions along Haines's Bluff, is well known. Unsupported from the interior by Grant, who had been compelled by the Holly Springs disaster to fall back, as before stated, Sherman did all that man could do, and failed, but not ingloriously. He buried his dead, picked up his wounded and re-embarked his troops, to rejoin Grant, whose vexation was great, but whose gallant spirit was in no wise damped by disappointment.

CHAPTER X.

GRANT'S MILITARY CAREER.

(CONTINUED.)

Re-organization of the Army—The Slaves Emancipated—The Second Campaign against Vicksburg—Difficulties by Water—Porter Runs the Gauntlet with his Gunboats—Attack on Grand Gulf—Battle of Port Gibson—Vicksburg Described—Feints—The Battles of Champion Hills—The Town Invested—The Grand Assault—The Outer Works Carried—The Rebel Commander Capitulates—"Unconditional Surrender" Again—Vicksburg and its Spoils—Port Hudson Too—The Victor's Crown.

FORMATION OF CORPS D'ARMEE.

Notwithstanding the results of these attempts to reduce the Rebel stronghold of the Southwest, the Government at Washington had learned to confide in General Grant, and, as a consequence, re-inforced him heavily. The army was immediately divided into distinct corps, on the Napoleonic plan, which is so admirably adapted to prevent confusion and develop the military talent of subordinate commanders. Numerous divisions were not suited to the measures which the war, then assuming gigantic proportions, called for.

Accordingly, on December 22d, 1863, orders were issued from headquarters, dividing the troops in the Department of the Mississippi into four *corps d' armee.* The divisions of G. W. Morgan and A. J. Smith, with all troops operating on the river, below Memphis, except those included in the Fifteenth Corps, comprised the Thirteenth Army Corps, under the command of General McClernand, Generals M. L. Smith and F. Steele's divisions, with the forces in the "District of Memphis," were formed into the Fifteenth Army Corps, Major-General W. T. Sherman commanding. The divisions of McArthur, Quimby and Ross, with the cavalry of Colonel A. L. Lee, and the commands of Davies and Sullivan, comprised the Sixteenth Army Corps, commanded by Major-General Hurlbut. The Seventeenth Army Corps was made up from the divisions of J. W. Denver, John A. Logan, and J. G. Lauman, with Grierson's cavalry and General Dodge's command in the Corinth district. Major-General J. B. McPherson commanded this organization.

Subsequently, McArthur's and Quinby's divisions were transferred from the Sixteenth to the Seventeenth, and those of Denver and Lauman from the Seventeenth to the Sixteenth Corps.

NEGRO EMANCIPATION.

When, on the 22d of September, 1862, Abraham Lincoln issued that proclamation which has immortalized his name, declaring that on the first day of the new year, 1863, all persons held as slaves within the States which were in arms against the Federal Government should be free, General Grant, like a good soldier and faithful citizen, heartily seconded the Administration, and allowed, wherever his department extended, no obstacle to be thrown in the way of the Administration policy. He encouraged the organization of colored troops, and used all his influence to subdue the senseless prejudice which then exsited against that unhappy race.

SECOND MOVEMENT ON VICKSBURG.

General Grant felt much chagrined over the failure of the first movement on Vicksburg, but, dauntless as ever, immediately set on foot plans by which the next attempt might be rendered brilliantly successful. He had a choice of five routes by which to move on the Rebel citadel from the interior and secure a base of operations. The first of these routes was the Williams Canal, which the gallant general of that name cut across the peninsula, on the Louisiana side of the Mississippi, in the preceding year. This canal was situated six miles below Vicksburg, and, could it be made available, would infinitely lighten the labor of capturing the coveted stronghold. Work was recommenced on this channel on the 2d of February, 1863, and was continued with energy until the 8th of March, when the Mississippi arose in its wrath and, breaking through the mouth of the "cut off," overwhelmed everything and compelled our engineers to desist from that project.

Of course the Rebels were elated at our misfortune; but Grant, although annoyed, was not disheartened, and immediately gave orders to try Milliken's Bend, where large bayous run from that point on the north to New Carthage on the south. From the latter point Roundabout Bayou ran into the Tensas River. This place was worked upon for a week, but, finding it impossible to effect a passage, Grant ordered the digging and dredging discontinued.

Lake Providence, situated 75 miles from Vicksburg, immediately south of the Arkansas State line, was the next point on which engineering skill was tried. This sheet of water is six miles long, two miles wide, and is only one mile west of the great river. A water channel, called Bayou Baxter, connected it with Bayou Macon, which latter is connected with the Tensas river, which communicates with the Washita and Red rivers, and so into the Mississippi. A canal was cut through the short strips of land, already referred to, but without effect. The project was soon given up.

The Yazoo Pass, eight miles below Helena, a very winding channel, running eastward from the Mississippi into Moon Lake, whence by a tortuous course, it again runs eastward until it empties into the Coldwater, which in turn empties into the Tallahatchie river, was next attempted. After incredible exertions and an attempt by a portion of the Thirteenth and Fifteenth corps, under Generals McPherson, Quinby and Ross, to storm Fort Pemberton, which obstructed navigation at the head of the Pass, this project had to be abandoned on the 23d of March.

A WAY AT LAST.

After vainly attempting to utilize States Bayou, the success of which adventure would give to his army all the base of operations he required, Grant finally determined to occupy New Carthage, which was accessible by land, and the possession of which point would insure the safety of his water communication. McClernand's corps—the Thirteenth—was moved forward on March 29, but at Smith's plantation, two miles from the desired position, McClernand, to his intense disgust, found that the levee at Bayou Vidal had burst, and that New Carthage was, as a consequence, surrounded by a deep channel of water. Grant, however, by marvelous exertions, provided a way out of the difficulty. He led his troops around the bayou and gained what he had toiled for so long—a base of operations. His supplies had to be hauled over execrable roads, thirty-five miles, all the way from Milliken's Bend. No such feat had been accomplished in warfare since the days of Bonaparte.

"THE ARMY AND NAVY FOREVER."

The 16th of April, 1863, was destined to be splendidly signalized by one of the most superb naval manœuvers that had ever, up to that time, been chronicled. Grant, by his untiring zeal, had provided for the march of the army down the western bank of the Mississippi, so that he could get south of Vicksburg, the only point, as he correctly estimated, from which that fortress could be successfully attacked. The great problem was, after marching the army down the river to a sufficient distance, how to procure transportation to the eastern bank, and, at the same time, protect the landings.

Acting under Grant's instructions, Admiral Porter, on April 16, declared himself ready to run south on the river, past the batteries of Vicksburg! He had seven iron clad gunboats and one of the old pattern. He also had three transports, laden with supplies. He protected the bulwarks of his boats by piling on hay and cotton, in bales. The Admiral arranged the gun boats to run past in single file, prepared to broadside the enemy's batteries if discovered. The transports were arranged on the starboard side, so as to sneak past under cover.

PORTER RUNS THE GAUNTLET.

It was within an hour of midnight when the vanguard of the brave flotilla appeared around the bend. Vicksburg, to all appearance, slept upon her arms, and the entire fleet came even with her guns before she made a sign.

Then, when, as the rebels thought, they had Porter fairly within their power, as if hell itself had opened, the batteries of the fortress belched their fire upon the daring flotilla, the guns from which pealed back a dauntless answer. The spectacle was sublime. The hills along the left bank of the river gave back the thunderous echoes, while the dark waters reflected the cannons' flash and the angry glare of exploding shells. The enemy kept up a continuous cannonade, which seemed to grow louder every second, while the gunboats of Porter returned, with interest, the iron hail from fort and battery. This running battle lasted two hours and a half, by which time Porter, with most of his fleet, was safe below. The transports were more or less damaged; one of them, the Henry Clay, was burned to the water's edge. This was the only serious loss sustained in prosecuting this glorious adventure, upon the success of which so many vital issues depended.

On the 22d of the same month, Gen. Grant, inspired by the brilliant success of the first expedition, ordered six other transports, having in tow twelve barges laden with forages, to be run past. The experiment was tried and resulted very encouragingly. One transport only, the Tigress, was sunk by the fire from Vicksburg, while five boats were damaged. The greater portion of the stores and forage were safely carried through. Volunteers bravely manned the transports in each expedition. Grant, in his official report, refers in complimentary terms to these men, and calls attention to the gratifying fact that skilled mechanics, of all branches, could be procured from the armies, whenever their services were needed.

THE ATTACK ON GRAND GULF.

The General, having seen the passage of the

fleet safely accomplished, moved his army, by a circuitous road, down the Louisiana shore, to Hard Times. This place is just above Grand Gulf, and its distance from Milliken's Bend, is at least seventy miles. Grant had with him here, on April 29, the 13th corps, under McClernand, and the 17th corps, under McPherson. The enemy's fortifications were very strong at Grand Gulf, and Porter, with his gunboats, was called upon to assist in reducing the place. When the fleet had silenced the enemy's batteries, it was calculated that McClernand's corps, which had been crossed to the other side of the river, could carry the forts by assault.

Porter proceeded to attack the forts in a most gallant manner. He advanced his boats to within hailing distance of the batteries, and gradually narrowed the space. Then opened an infernal fire from both sides. Our sailors exhibited superb courage, and the Rebels kept up a tremendous cannonade. After this practice had lasted some hours, it was found impossible to reduce the place by bombardment or storm just then, and the affair ended in a drawn battle. Grant, from a tug-boat in the river, witnessed the engagement.

THE CROSSING AT BRUINSBURG.

Next morning found Grant marching down the river to a point opposite Bruinsburg, on the Mississippi side of the river. The corps of McClernand had been already recrossed to the western bank. The gunboats and transports ran the Rebel gauntlet at Grand Gulf, and were ready to co-operate. With extraordinary celerity, McClernand's corps was again flung across the river and, not waiting for a moment's refreshment, these gallant troops immediately commenced their march and occupied the highlands above Bruinsburg, without any show of resistance. McPherson's corps followed, Grant crossing with them. The troops were in high spirits, and glad to be once more about to face the enemy, whom fortune had so long protected. That same night the Rebels were encountered in force about seven miles northeast of Bruinsburg, and, after some hot fighting, were compelled to retire.

Next morning, May 1st, General Bowen's Rebel division was encountered by our advance, strongly posted at a place called Port Gibson. This led to a serious battle.

GRAND GULF OCCUPIED.

The enemy were posted on two roads, which branched on ridges right and left in such a manner as to protect Grand Gulf. The Rebels made a determined opposition, fighting vehemently for several hours, until, at length, General Grant had to send portions of McPherson's corps to reinforce McClernand, who had stood the brunt of the engagement. The fighting continued until night, when the enemy retreated, thoroughly whipped, beyond Bayou Pierre, having first taken care to blow up all the bridges, and doing much damage in the line of our advance. McPherson, by morning, had constructed a floating bridge across the bayou, and his corps followed the Rebels on the road to Harkinson's Ferry. Grand Gulf was immediately evacuated, being badly fortified on the land side. The enemy left fifteen heavy guns behind them. The capture of this place, so strong from the river side, gave great joy to our soldiers, and was a brilliant earnest of what was to follow.

THE KEY OF THE MISSISSIPPI.

The great Rebel stronghold of Vicksburg has been so frequently described that its extent and importance must be fully known to every American citizen who has "kept track" of our tremendous civil war. Still, to keep the thread of this story, a slight description of the Southern Sebastapol may not be out of order.

The city stands on an extensive bluff, situated above one of the sharpest curves on the Mississippi River, which, at that time, its guns completely commanded, barring that great water thoroughfare to our arms. The line of bluffs extend from Yazoo River on the north to Warrenton on the south, a distance of some fifteen miles. These bluffs, with the Yazoo and Mississippi river-fronts, formed an almost impregnable line of defense on its northern approaches. Bayous, swamps, ravines, and other natural obstacles, added to the immense strength of the position. It was the Southern Sebastapol, and required an

American Pelissier to conquer its stubborn resistance.

In 1863, the land side of the great fortress was equally formidable, and General Grant at once recognized the necessity of fighting several battles with the outlying forces of Pemberton before the thorough investment of the place could be accomplished.

CO-OPERATING MOVEMENTS.

Simultaneously with Grant's movement by way of Bruinsburg, Sherman made his celebrated feint movement by way of Haines's Bluff, thus dividing the rebel corps so much that they were unable to support each other with alacrity in the movements which followed. This demonstration of Sherman's was only the precursor of several others of a similar nature, all along the rebel line, so that poor Pemberton was utterly confounded and unable to pierce the real design of his opponent.

The Federal corps were moved on the Napoleonic principle, that is, never so separated that combination at a critical time would be rendered difficult. Grant, with his searching gaze, followed every move, and knew precisely where each division was before the grand movement began.

THE BATTLES AROUND VICKSBURG.

On May 13, McPherson attacked the rebel General Gregg at Raymond, and gained a complete victory. Sherman immediately joined the victorious general, and both pushed on to Jackson, upon which point the enemy had retreated and were concentrating reinforcements. McClernand was held in reserve at Raymond. On the 14th, Sherman and McPherson came up with the rebel out-posts near Jackson, where they learned that Joseph E. Johnston was in command.

The action was short, sharp and bloody. Johnston was utterly defeated, narrowly escaped capture, and retreated in great disaster. Grant, accompanied by his eldest son, then a mere boy, joined the combined corps after the battle, and immediately put the army in motion toward Champion Hills, where Pemberton held a strong position, having most of his forces well in hand. Sherman's corps was in the rear, having orders to destroy all rebel property, of a public character, lying in the line of march. McClernand had received orders to co-operate in the movement on Champion Hills, but did not arrive until the conflict was decided. One of his divisions, however, under General Hovey, got on the field in time, and materially assisted Logan's and Quinby's divisions of McPherson's corps in winning the battle. Pemberton fought obstinately, and his men showed their customary valor, but nothing could withstand the impetuous courage of our troops, and once more Pemberton showed a light pair of heels. He determined, however, on making one more grand effort before retiring within the main fortifications of Vicksburg. Grant directed the pursuit, which continued until night-fall. This battle was fought on May 16.

Next evening was fought the battle of the Big Black, where the enemy occupied formidable positions on both sides of the river, but, after a long resistance, an undirected charge of Carr's division of McClernand's corps struck them with panic, and they fled in tumultuous disorder toward their stronghold. Pemberton and his officers did all that men could to stay the tide of flight, but in vain.

INVESTMENT OF THE REBEL STRONGHOLD.

Sherman, having learned the result of the battles last fought, crossed his corps, on pontoons, at Bridgeport on the 18th, took possession of Walnut Hills and the Yazoo river, driving the enemy before him within sight of the walls of Vicksburg.

McPherson crossed on floating bridges above the Jackson road, and McClernand, by the same means, below. The former followed Sherman, and the latter, marching through Mount Albans, occupied the left of the line, on the south, while McPherson and Sherman, the latter occupying the right of the line, completed the investment on the north.

This series of manœuvres, directed by General Grant, placed the Key of the Mississippi within his grasp; and never, in the history of warfare, had a campaign been more skillfully planned or more brilliantly executed.

Admiral Porter, with his fleet, having learned the position of affairs, immediately co-operated, so that Pemberton was effectually cooped up by land and water.

THE ASSAULTS OF THE 19TH AND 21ST OF MAY.

Grant, conceiving that the enemy were in a very demoralized condition after their recent defeats, determined on giving them no rest, especially as his army was eager for an assault on Vicksburg, and hated the prospect of a long siege, with all its attendant discomfort and drudgery. The brave fellows preferred to risk their lives in a bold attempt rather than dig trenches, advance parallels, and act rather as prisoners than warriors.

On the afternoon of the 19th, Sherman's corps attacked the fortifications, in front of our right, with great vigor. The rebels made a gallant stand, and, at nightfall, our soldiers were withdrawn from the attempt. The assault was renewed along the whole line on the 21st, Porter's fleet pounding the rebel batteries and firing shot and shell into their citadel from the side of the river. Each army exhibited unsurpassed valor. McClernand imagined that he had captured two forts, and badgered Grant upon the field about reinforcements and divisions in his favor. The General, who saw the position better than McClernand, doubted the accuracy of his statement, but reinforced him with Quinby's division and against his inclination, ordered Sherman to make another assault. The result was a repulse, andour army, when night came, had gained nothing, but mourned the loss of many gallant soldiers. McClernand, imitating the egotism of Bernadotte on an occasion almost similar, issued a complimentary order to his corps, in which he was disrespectful to his superior officer. Grant, very properly, removed the gasconading general from command, and transferred the command of his corps to General Ord, a brave and modest soldier.

THE REGULAR SIEGE COMMENCED.

Our losses in both assaults numbered over 3,000 in killed and wounded. Grant immediately made his dispositions for a regular siege, and the army, cured of its ardor for assaulting Vicksburg, settled down patiently to its task of digging trenches and pelting Pemberton with iron hail from behind them. Meanwhile, re-inforcements from the Ninth and Sixteenth corps, under Generals Washburn and Parke, arrived from Memphis and St. Louis.

The investment now commenced in earnest, and Pemberton found himself in anything but an enviable position. Sherman, with a portion of his corps, went to observe General Joseph Johnston, who was reported marching to raise the siege; but Joseph, whatever might have been his original intention, did not give his alert enemy a chance to overhaul him. He let Vicksburg "severely alone," until it was too late to save it.

FORT HILL CAPTURED BY STORMERS.

By June 25th, a mine, which had been pushed forward, in spite of amazing obstacles, was exploded in front of Fort Hill, and our forlorn hope, consisting of detachments from the Forty-fifth Illinois and Twenty-third Indiana, supported by Leggett's brigade, rushed in with a terrific shout and possessed themselves of that important outwork. Grant, in support of the stormers, ordered a cannonade along the whole line and from the fleet. It seemed as though the earth was being rent. The astonished Rebels paused for a moment and then commenced a deadly struggle with the gallant men who had planted the "Stars and Stripes" above the ramparts of Vicksburg. The effort proved vain, for McPherson supported Leggett, and Fort Hill remained in the possession of Grant's forces.

Another mine, of even greater proportions, had been constructed in the meantime, and on July 1st it was exploded, causing the demolition of a redan, and killing a number of Rebels who were manning the ramparts or engaged in countermining.

PEMBERTON PARLEYS.

This last success, in addition to the terrific bombardment constantly kept up from all sides by our army, caused consternation in Vicksburg. Provisions were giving out, and, in a word, Pemberton's position was desperate. In his despair, he blamed Johnston for not supporting him, and vowed never to surrender Vicksburg while a pound of beef, or other food, remained, or while a man was left to defend the walls. This was on the 2d of July. Grant, having occupied the portion of the enemy's works uncovered by the mine, prepared for the

HON. GEO. S. BOUTWELL,
Secretary of Treasury.

BAKER-CO. CHI.

grand assault. On the morning of the 3d, at 8 o'clock, a flag of truce was displayed by the enemy, in front of A. J. Smith's position. Half an hour later, General Bowen and another officer of the Rebel army placed in Grant's hands a proposition from Pemberton to surrender Vicksburg! The Rebel general wished for the appointment of commissioners for the purpose of treating, but Grant utterly refused to comply with his request. He agreed, however, to meet Pemberton on neutral ground, that afternoon, and arrange terms.

At this famous interview Grant was attended by Gens. McPherson and A. J. Smith. Pemberton was accompanied by Gen. Bowen and Col. Montgomery. The rebel asked what terms Grant could give. The Union General at once replied—"UNCONDITIONAL SURRENDER!"

Pemberton expostulated and even threatened to renew his defence. Grant was quite collected, and told him to follow his own counsel, but warned him that the siege would be pressed with merciless vigor. Finally the two Generals walked apart, and, after a short consultation, Pemberton agreed to lay the matter before a counsel of war and send his answer next noon.

VICKSBURG CAPITULATES.

After consultation with his corps commanders, Grant submitted to Pemberton, in writing, the terms of surrender, which were, as is well known, courteous and liberal in the extreme. The General, however, utterly refused to make any stipulation in regard to the treatment of citizens or their private property. Pemberton endeavored to procure some modifications, but Grant was obstinate, and on the following morning, July 4, 1863, Pemberton surrendered Vicksburg and the army which had defended it, with all the arms, stores, etc., which it contained.

The rebels, who stacked their arms under the eye of McPherson's corps, numbered 31,600 men. No less than 172 guns fell into the hands of the victor. McPherson's men immediately occupied the evacuated works, and in the afternoon Grant made his triumphal entry. The rebels received him sullenly, and well they might. Since the investment had commenced, 37,000 prisoners, including 19 generals and about 4,000 officers of lower grades had been taken. In killed, wounded and missing, the enemy, since the campaign opened, had lost 12,000 men, with 300 pieces of cannon and an immense amount of public property, including railroads, steamboats, locomotives, and other matters of great value.

At last—(since Fort Sumpter was fired upon it could not be said)—the Mississippi, to use the expression of Lincoln, flowed "unvexed to the sea," and the rebel territory was rent in twain. The news of Vicksburg, with that of Gettysburg, crowded the wires, and, on that auspicious Fourth of July, "Grant and Meade" were the names that swelled upon the breeze far and wide throughout the loyal States.

THE VICTOR'S CROWN.

The meed of victory soon reached the victor. The cool and veteran Halleck compared Grant's exploit with Napoleon's at Ulm and Ratisbon. The generous and genial Lincoln wrote him the following letter, so worthy of his great mind and noble heart:

EXECUTIVE MANSION, WASHINGTON, July 13, 1863.

TO MAJOR-GENERAL GRANT:

MY DEAR GENERAL—I do not remember that you and I ever met personally. I write this now as a grateful acknowledgment for *the almost inestimable service you have done the country.* I wish to say a word further. When you first reached the vicinity of Vicksburg, I thought you should do what you finally did—march the troops across the neck, run the batteries with the transports, and thus go below; and I never had any faith, except a general hope that you knew better than I, that the Yazoo Pass expedition and the like could succeed. When you got below and took Port Gibson, Grand Gulf, and vicinity, I thought you should go down the river and join General Banks; and when you turned northward east of the Big Black, I feared it was a mistake. I now wish to make a personal acknowledgment *that you were right and I was wrong.*

Yours, very truly, A. LINCOLN.

The Southern press, when commenting on the surrender, spoke respectfully of Gen. Grant and even allowed that his terms to Pemberton were generous, considering how completely that unfortunate general was in his power.

THE CAMPAIGN ENDED.

On the 9th of July, the rebel General Gardner surrendered the important fortress of Port Hudson to Gen. Banks, having first learned that Vicksburg had fallen.

Sherman followed Johnston, who, when too late,

had approached toward Vicksburg and was manœuvering in the vicinity of Jackson. The rebel issued a boastful order to his troops on July 9 and awaited Sherman's attack. On the 13th the rebels made a desperate sortie from Jackson and were repulsed. Sherman then prepared for a general assault—but his opponent did not await the result. Johnston evacuated his works on the night of the 17th, and next day Sherman entered them in triumph.

This virtually ended the campaign, and Grant was promptly rewarded by being appointed a Major-General in the regular army of the United States, his commission dating from July 4th, 1863. The officers of his command presented the successful commander with a magnificent sword. Afterward an obelisk was erected on the spot, outside of Vicksburg, where the interview between Grant and Pemberton took place.

CHAPTER XI.

GRANT'S MILITARY CAREER.

(CONTINUED.)

Grant Busies Himself with Administration—Is Promoted to the Command of Four Armies—Prepares to Attack Bragg at Lookout Mountain—Plan of the Battle—A Dashing Assault—Grant "Refuses to be Embarrassed"—The Battle Above the Clouds—A Mighty Charge—Phil. Sheridan Distinguishes Himself—Victory—Its Trophies—Gratitude of the Nation.

GRANT AS AN ADMINISTRATOR.

The few succeeding summer months were occupied by General Grant in managing the general executive business of his department, checking smugglers, baffling traitors and punishing extortionists. He gave no countenance to stragglers, and put the contraband Negroes to good use in the colored regiments, or else in constructing camps, driving train wagons, repairing railroads, etc. His administration of public affairs was highly successful throughout the region over which he had authority. He compelled unprincipled captains of Mississippi steamboats to disgorge money fraudulently obtained from officers and enlisted men, who were compelled to voyage by the river. Never was such strict discipline and thorough honesty enforced in that State or in Tennessee. He made a tour of observation in August, and received an enthusiastic ovation from the loyal portion of the citizens of Memphis. He thanked them in a modest, manly, patriotic letter, in which he bore noble testimony to the courage and endurance of the brave troops who had followed his fortunes.

He returned to Vicksburg and went to Natchez and from thence to New Orleans. He arrived in the Crescent City on September 2d, and on the 3d, the trade of the Southwestern metropolis was declared free; that is, with the ports of the Northwest. Military restriction on commerce was removed, and everything wore an aspect of returning peace and prosperity.

AN UNLUCKY ACCIDENT.

On September 4th, General Grant reviewed the Thirteenth Army Corps, in company with General Banks, who commanded the department. During the review the strange horse which General Grant rode stumbled and threw him heavily, injuring him so severely that it was feared his future active service in the field was somewhat doubtful. The Government had intended to place him in command of the troops marching on Georgia, and his accident caused Lincoln and the country at large great anxiety. His case, fortunately, did not prove so serious as was first anticipated, and in a few weeks he was again fit for duty.

GRANT PLACED IN COMMAND OF FOUR ARMIES.

Then he went up the Mississippi to Cairo, having stopped at Vicksburg and other points, to arrange the route of the troops who were to form part of the corps then concentrating in and around Chattanooga, Tenn. He made provisions for a medal commemorative of the fall of Vicksburg, and then proceeded to Indianapolis, where the following communication from the War Office was handed him:

WAR DEPARTMENT, ADJUTANT-GENERAL'S OFFICE,
WASHINGTON, October 16th, 1863.

By direction of the President of the United States, the Departments of the Ohio, of the Cumberland, and of the Tennessee, will constitute the Military Division of the Mississippi. Major-General U. S. Grant, United States Army, is placed in command of the Military Division of the Mississippi, with his headquarters in the field.

Major-General W. S. Rosecrans, United States volunteers, is relieved from the commaud of the Department of the Army of the Cumberland. Major-General G. H. Thomas is hereby assigned to that command.

By order of the Secretary of War,
E. D. TOWNSEND, A. A. G.

On the 18th, Grant issued his general order, at Louisville, Ky., assuming the above command, and announcing that the headquarters of the Military Division of the Mississippi would be in the field.

HE ORGANIZES THE GRAND ARMY.

The States of Michigan, Illinois, Indiana, Ohio, Kentucky, Tennessee, Mississippi, Northern Alabama, and Northwestern Georgia were included within the limits of the new department. He had under his command four fine armies—"The Army of the Tennessee, (conquerors of Vicksburg) "The Army of the Cumberland," "The Army of the Ohio," and the Eleventh and Twelfth corps detached, under Hooker, from the Army of the Potomac. These last named troops were afterward consolidated into the splendid Twentieth corps.

The corps of this magnificent command were officered by the following able generals: Fourth Army Corps, General Gordon Granger; Ninth, General Porter; Eleventh, General O. O. Howard; Twelfth, General Slocum; Fourteenth, General J. M. Palmer; Fifteenth, General John A. Logan; Sixteenth, General Hurlbut; Seventeenth, General McPherson, and Twenty-third, General Munson.

This was the largest army that had ever been controlled by one general on the American continent. Those who were jealous of Grant predicted his ruin. Those who knew him best, and who had fought under him, were enthusiastic in their congratulations and strong in hope. With his usual sagacity, Grant had placed in command of his four armies Sherman, Thomas, Hooker, Burnside, and, in after days, Foster.

BRAGG BRACES HIMSELF FOR BATTLE.

General Braxton Bragg, the rebel commander, had gathered a force equally large and prepared to defend the road to Georgia, with all the resources at his command. The unfortunate issue of the battle of Chickamauga, fought and lost by Rosecrans, had enabled the rebels to occupy Lookout Mountain and Missionary Ridge, which eminences commanded the route to Atlanta, and from thence to the sea.

THE SITUATION AT CHATTANOOGA.

Thomas, commanding the Army of the Cumberland, occupied Chattanooga, and, as the rebels threatened to make an attack in force on that point before Grant could arrive, the latter telegraphed Thomas to hold it at any cost. The sturdy old hero promptly replied over the wires—"I will hold the town till we starve!"

This expression alluded to the fact that his men were on half rations, it being a matter of much risk and difficulty to convey supplies over a wretched road from Stevenson, in Northern Alabama, to the village of Chattanooga.

GRANT'S PLAN OF OPERATIONS.

Grant arrived at the destined point on October 23, and found that Thomas had taken very skillful measures to defend the place. Hooker had been concentrated at Bridgeport, on the Tennessee river, and was prepared to secure the river and main wagon road between Brown's Ferry, just below Lookout Mountain, and the headquarters of Hooker's army. Other dispositions for defence had been made, but the moment Grant arrived everything was put in working order, and, after a careful survey of the enemy's position, he resolved to assume the offensive, so soon as all his force arrived on the ground. The General thus briefly explains a portion of his tactics:

"The next morning after my arrival at Chattanooga, in company with Thomas and Brigadier-General W. F. Smith, Chief Engineer, I made a reconnoissance of Brown's Ferry, and the hills on the south side of the river and at the mouth of Lookout Valley. After the reconnoissance, the plan agreed upon was for Hooker to cross at Bridgeport to the south side of the river with all the force that could be spared from the railroad, and move on the main wagon-road, by way of Whitesides to Wauhatchie, in Lookout Valley. Major-General J. M. Palmer was to proceed by the only practicable route north of the river from his position opposite Chattanooga to a point on the north bank of the Tennessee river and opposite Whitesides, then to cross to the south side, to hold the road passed over by Hooker. In the meantime, and before the enemy could be apprised of our intention, a force under the direction of Brigadier-General W. F. Smith. Chief Engineer, was to be thrown across the river at or near Brown's Ferry, to seize the range of hills at the mouth of Lookout Valley, covering the Brown's Ferry road, and orders were given accordingly."

HAZEN'S HAPPY HAZARD

Brigadier-General Hazen, a dashing young officer, took charge of Smith's expedition, and, after a series of brilliant stratagems, landed the 1,800 picked men composing the expeditionary force at two points on the enemy's side of the river, captured the pickets and seized the spurs of the ridge near the river. Four thousand men who had marched along the north bank of the Tennessee, while their comrades, floated down the river on pontoon boats, were ferried across from Brown's Ferry, to support the forlorn hope, and, at 10 o'clock on the morning of October 28th, General Smith had laid down his pontoon bridge, which was nine hundred feet long. The captured points were strongly intrenched, giving full play to our artillery, and compelling the enemy between Lookout and Shell Mound to evacuate their positions.

OTHER MOVEMENTS.

Hooker advanced that same day and occupied a

portion of Lookout Valley. Palmer, according to the programme, followed in his rear, protecting the route on which the army had advanced.

These advantages alarmed Bragg. They also alarmed Jeff Davis, and that worthy, in person, came down to inspect the situation. Our army was now abundantly supplied with provisions, and felt in fighting humor.

Longstreet made a night attack on Geary's division of Hooker's Corps, but Hazard hurried up to his comrade's aid, the Rebel attack was dashingly repulsed, and Hooker followed up his success by seizing all the hills lying west of Lookout Creek.

BRAGG MAKES A BLUNDER.

Prompted by his bad angel, Bragg imagined that he was doing a brilliant thing when he detached Longstreet's corps to attack Burnside at Knoxville. He hoped by this movement to embarrass Grant. That general, however, refused to be embarrassed. He knew that Burnside was enough for Longstreet, and he also knew that Sherman's corps (the Fifteenth) was near at hand to re-inforce his own army. Halleck besought Grant to re-inforce Burnside; but our stubborn hero would not play into the enemy's hand, and resolved to thrash Braxton Bragg and his army without loss of time. He knew that to defeat Bragg's army would be to compel Longstreet's retreat from Knoxville. So he held to his own plans and refused to be ordered around by telegraph. Burnside lured

Longstreet on, doing just what Grant required of him.

Sherman's army had arrived on November 23d, and having marched from Bridgeport, crossed the river at Brown's Ferry, then moved cautiously up the north bank and established itself at an important point near the South Chickamauga.

THOMAS ADVANCES.

Bragg having given indications of falling back, Grant determined to test the matter, and for this purpose ordered Thomas to demonstrate on the enemy's lines in front of his position. Thomas, beside his own corps, had with him the major portion of Howard's command, and demonstrated to such effect that he carried Orchard Knob by a brilliant charge of General Wood's division of Howard's corps. The Rebels did not expect a serious attack, and were actually taken by surprise. The division of Buckner's corps, sent to re-inforce Longstreet's attack on Burnside, was recalled, and General Braxton Bragg prepared to meet the grand shock which he now saw was rapidly approaching.

SHERMAN AND HOOKER MOVE.

Taking advantage of the darkness, in the early morning of November 24th, Sherman's army, after a series of movements, crossed the Tennessee and South Chickamauga rivers, and, early in the forenoon, had taken position below the north end of Mission Ridge. The position was well fortified, and formed a good base for the operations which were to follow.

Hooker moved on the same day, his part being to capture Lookout Mountain, cross the valley of Chattanooga to Rossville, and then co-operate with Sherman's attack on Mission Ridge, by way of Rossville Gap. The enemy's pickets on the Northern slope of Lookout were driven higher up the mountain, and the Tennessee river was rendered safe to all our boats, thus effectually destroying the Rebel blockade.

"ABOVE THE CLOUDS."

Hooker, like Thomas, had surprised the enemy, and followed up his success, fighting that action which is known in American history as "The battle above the clouds." The spectacle of the fight, as seen from Chattanooga, was superb, but the results were more superb still, for the enemy's left was turned, and Hooker, leaving a force to hold the mountain, advanced on the extreme right of our line, to take part in the main attack. Thomas occupied the centre, at Orchard Knob, and Sherman held our left, in front of Tunnel Hill.

Grant, during the prosecution of these unrivaled plans, was, or seemed to be, everywhere present. His energy was untiring, and he left nothing to subordinates that could in any way jeopardize the safety of the army.

Wednesday, November 25th, ushered in the final struggle, on which the fortunes of both generals, and, in great measure, of both causes, were staked. Grant had fairly outwitted his opponent, and the latter felt it. To add to his misfortunes, Bragg permitted himself to be again out-generaled, in this way: Sherman made the attack on the Rebel position, in front of Tunnel Hill, and Bragg, conceiving that that was to be the main point of attack, commenced moving brigades and regiments from his centre, to aid, as he thought, in annihilating Sherman's army. Grant allowed the Rebels to proceed with their tactical mistake until it was too late to rectify it.

THE GRAND ATTACK.

Grant watched for the advance of Hooker on the Rossville road, and at 20 minutes past three o'clock the signal informed him that "Fighting Joe" had fulfilled his part of the contract, and was in line on the right ready to fall upon the foe. He had been unavoidably detained by a broken bridge across Chattanooga Creek, but he made up for this late in the day.

Scarcely had the head of Hooker's advance appeared, when the signal for the storming of Mission Ridge, being six guns fired at intervals, was given. On the weakened centre and disheartened left of Bragg's army the soldiers of Thomas and Hooker were hurled, charging right up the slopes of the Ridge in defiance of the deluge of fire which the enemy rolled down upon them. Sherman, on the left, renewed his attack with ten-fold energy.

Consternation seized on the rebel army. Their general proved himself a brave soldier, if not a skillful one, and his exertions to restore the battle were tremendous. But it was all of no use. With enthusiastic shouts our soldiers stormed the crest of the Ridge, and the rebel left fled in panic before Hooker's assault. Their entire line soon gave way, and, after one of the grandest struggles on record, the battle of Chattanooga was won. Grant, elated as he must have been by his splendid success, remained calm as ever, directing the pursuit and taking measures to clear off the wreck of the battlefields.

In this battle, among the many brave and noble men who distinguished themselves as generals was Phil. H. Sheridan, who commanded a division of Granger's corps. He had a horse killed under him, but, undaunted, he stepped upon a gun and retained his position, so that he could view the fight, until the battle was over. He made a brief but stirring address to his division, which cheered every heart, and, from that day, Grant knew that he had found his thunderbolt—his cavalry leader.

The retreat of the enemy was followed by Sheridan's division. Bragg left 6,000 prisoners in our hands, not counting stragglers; 40 guns; 7,500 small arms, and a large amount of ammunition. The retreat would have been followed up more closely had it not been that Grant feared to leave Burnside isolated in Knoxville.

Burnside had fought gallantly, in retreat, and confronted his enemy with confidence. Sherman and Granger were sent to reinforce him. Longstreet, learning of Bragg's defeat, assaulted Knoxville desperately on November 28, and was bloodily repulsed. The advance of the supporting Federal generals compelled the rebels to raise the siege and retreat in great haste to a safer locality.

END OF THE CHATTANOOGA CAMPAIGN.

On December 10, 1863, General Grant issued a congratulatory order to his army, and predicted the speedy downfall of the so-called Confederacy.

With this campaign the active military campaign of Braxton Bragg terminated. His after efforts in the Rebel cause were obscure and unchronicled.

Meanwhile the thanks of the Executive and of Congress were awarded to the victor of Chattanooga. These thanks were supplemented by a magnificent gold medal, voted by Congress, commemorative of General Grant's great victories, and symbolical of the respect and gratitude of the American people.

CHAPTER XII.

GRANT'S MILITARY CAREER.

(CONTINUED.)

Created Lieutenant General—Goes to Washington to Receive his Commission—Two Memorable Speeches—Grant Takes Command—With the Army of the Potomac—In the Wilderness—How he Kept Flanking Lee—An Alert Enemy—The Assault Upon Petersburg—A Failure—The Winter, and How it Was Passed—The End Near—Grant Discovers his Antagonist's Purpose, and Thwarts Him—Sheridan "Pushes Things"—Lee Surrounded—He Surrenders—Collapse of the Confederacy.

CREATED LIEUTENANT-GENERAL.

Such had been the signal abilities displayed by General Grant. The success which had uniformly attended his campaigns, and the confidence and enthusiasm which his name everywhere evoked, that it was deemed best for the public service to place him in the general command of all our armies. Accordingly the committee on Military Affairs of the House of Representatives reported a bill to revive the rank of Lieutenant General.

The fact that during our whole previous history only two soldiers had been thus honored, will give some idea of the confidence which this new rank implied. Washington and Scott were his glorious predecessors, and Gen. Grant was fully entitled to wear the honors a grateful country had tendered her greatest captains.

The bill establishing the new rank was as follows:

Be it enacted by the Senate and House of Representatives of the United States of America, in Congress assembled, That the grade of lieutenant-general be, and the same is hereby, revived in the Army of the United States of America; and the President is hereby authorized, whenever he shall deem it expedient, to appoint, by and with the advice and consent of the Senate, a commander of the army, to be selected during war, from among those officers in the military service of the United States, not below the grade of major-general, most distinguished for courage, skill, and ability; and who, being commissioned as lieutenant-general, *shall be authorized, under the direction of the President, to command the armies of the United States.*

While the bill was under discussion, Mr. Ross offered an amendment recommending General Grant for the new rank. The amendment was adopted by a large majority, and on the 2d of March, 1864, General Grant was confirmed by the Senate as Lieutenant-General, giving him rank over all our other generals.

GENERAL GRANT GOES TO WASHINGTON.

He was immediately notified, and late in the afternoon of Tuesday, March 8th, he arrived in Washington, for the purpose of receiving his commission and instructions. His arrival was unheralded, and he took his seat at the dinner-table of Willard's Hotel unnoticed.

Though four years in the service, and the most successful and popular of all our generals, he had been so little in Washington that he was known to but few. It happened, however, that there was seated near him at the table a gentleman who had made his acquaintance at New Orleans. He soon spread the information, and in a few minutes the

HON. ELIHU B. WASHBURN,
U. S. Minister to France.

dining-room was ringing with cheers for the hero of Vicksburg. General Grant modestly acknowledged the honor, and soon withdrew.

RECEIVES HIS COMMISSION.

The next day he was received by President Lincoln in the cabinet chamber and presented with his commission. In doing this, President Lincoln said: "*General Grant*—The Nation's appreciation of what you have done, and its reliance upon you for what remains to be done in the existing great struggle, are now presented with this commission, constituting you Lieutenant-General in the army of the United States. With this high honor devolves upon you also a corresponding responsibility. As the country herein trusts you, so, under God, it will sustain you. I scarcely need to add, that, with what I here speak for the nation, goes my own hearty personal concurrence."

To this, General Grant responded as follows: "*Mr. President*—I accept the commission, with gratitude for the high honor conferred. With the aid of the noble armies that have fought on so many fields for our common country, it will be my earnest endeavor not to disappoint your expectations. I feel the full weight of the responsibilities now devolving on me; and I know that if they are met, it will be due to those armies, and, above all, to the favor of that Providence which leads both nations and men."

THE DIFFICULTIES OF HIS POSITION.

The position to which General Grant was thus called was one of grave responsibility, attended by numerous and serious embarrassments. A confiding nation had, as it were, placed its destinies in his hands, and the public expectation was such that only great achievements would satisfy it. The enemy was brave, active, vigilant, full of confidence in its own power, and actuated by a blind faith in its commander. Having the advantage of position, acting on the offensive or defensive with equal facility, possessing the means of communication which enabled it to rapidly shift its armies from one exposed point to another, it was, though inferior in numbers in the aggregate, able to meet its opponents with equal forces on the most important field of operations.

HIS PLAN FOR THE CAMPAIGN.

Fully conscious of these points of advantage possessed by his enemy, General Grant immediately formed his plans for meeting them.

First—To counterpoise the Rebels' interior advantages and prevent them from shifting their forces to relieve the most hard-pressed points in their line of defense, he resolved to attack their whole line simultaneously at all points.

Second—To make constant and unrelenting war upon his main enemy's armies, particularly the forces General Lee in Virginia and of General Johnson of in Georgia, believing, and that correctly, that these once destroyed or captured it would be impossible for the Confederacy to continue further armed resistance to the Federal forces.

GENERAL GRANT GOES TO THE FRONT.

Having matured the details of these plans, General Grant hastened to join the Army of the Potomac which it was decided should contest with General Lee the issue of the war.

On the 18th of March he issued the following order:

HEADQUARTERS OF THE ARMIES OF THE UNITED STATES,
NASHVILLE, Tenn., March 17, 1864.

In pursuance of the following order of the President,

"EXECUTIVE MANSION, WASHINGTON, March 10, 1864.

"Under the anthority of the act of Congress to appoint to the grade of lieutenant-general in the army, of March 1, 1864, Lieutenant-General Ulysses S. Grant, United States Army, is appointed to the command of the armies of the United States.

ABRAHAM LINCOLN."

I assume command of the armies of the United States. Headquarters will be in the field, and, until further orders, will be with the Army of the Potomac. There will be an office headquarters in Washington, to which all official communications will be sent, except those from the army where the headquarters are at the date of their address.

U. S. GRANT, Lieutenant-General.

To crush the Rebel army of Northern Virginia, the flower of the Confederate forces, commanded by General Lee in person, was the task General Grant had chosen for the army directly under his command. The first step in this endeavor was to issue orders the all-pervading tenor of which was to attack Lee whenever opportunity offered, and follow him wherever he went, fighting or harrassing him without cessation, allowing him no time for rest or opportunity for recuperation.

HOW TO ATTACK LEE.

Two plans of attack were considered:

First: To cross the Rapidan below Lee's army, move rapidly upon his right flank, and turn or crush it.

Second: To cross above Lee's army, threaten his left flank, and force him to accept a general engagement or retreat.

While either plan possessed many strong points in its favor, there were considerations which rendered each somewhat hazardous. After due deliberation, the first was adopted.

General Sherman was to keep General Johnston's army well employed. General Banks was to operate in the Department of the Gulf, while General McPherson assumed command of the Army of the Department of the Tennessee. The general orders to these commanders were to constantly face the enemy, keep him so well engaged that not a man or a gun could be sent to re-enforce any of the yielding points of their line elsewhere.

THE WORK OF PREPARATION.

For a few weeks the camps of the Army of the Potomac resounded with the notes of preparation. Re-enforcements were gathered in, supplies were accumulated, and the organization perfected. Grant made constant tours of inspection, cultivated the confidence of the army, and kindled anew its faith and enthusiasm. He was in almost daily conference with the authorities at Washington, receiving their suggestions and explaining his own plan of operation. When everything had been arranged, he took the field, and just eight weeks from the time of receiving his commission he issued the order of advance, to turn if possible the right flank of the enemy.

THE POSITION OF THE ARMY.

The position of the Army of the Potomac at the commencement of this movement was along the north bank of the Rapidan, confronting and watching the army of General Lee. The forces of the latter were strongly entrenched on the opposite bank, his corps admirably disposed, and all his exposed points adequately guarded. Thus secured, he defiantly awaited the development of the plans of his new adversary.

This, as we have said before, was to cross the river below, and, by a sudden movement, turn his right flank and cut him off from Richmond; then by fiercer battles beat him, and destroy his army. Failing in this, his plan was to force his left, and by this flank movement follow him to Richmond.

THE WILDERNESS.

In making the movement desired, it was necessary that our troops should pass over a broken table-land called the Wilderness, covered with patches of timber—a dense undergrowth; ravines and fallen trees affording a natural covert for the enemy, and rendering our own movement slow, tedious, and full of danger. It was almost impossible for cavalry to operate there, and our artillery was rendered mostly useless. It was hoped that by a sudden movement our army would be able to cross this dangerous field without encountering Lee's legions.

A FIERCE STRUGGLE.

On the 3d of May a stirring address was issued to the army, and at midnight the movement commenced. Our forces were successfully crossed at Germanna and Ely's Ford. The crossing was a surprise, but Lee soon recovered and pushed forward two columns to contest our advance; it thus became evident that the ugly Wilderness could not be passed without a fierce battle, and General Grant prepared for the struggle. As soon as the enemy's advance was known, General Warren, who led the Union advance, was ordered to halt, concentrate his forces, and attack vigorously whatever he should find in his front, while several other divisions were put in motion for his support. Warren drove the enemy, but the almost impenetrable nature of the wood prevented the arrival of the supports, and the advantage was lost. Thus encouraged, the enemy made frantic efforts to crush General Warren before aid could arrive; but they were handsomely foiled. Soon re-enforcements for both armies began to come up, and the battle raged more fiercely than ever. While our gallant troops were heroically resisting the headlong outset of the enemy, General Hancock reached the field with the Second Corps, and the battle was resumed with increased fury, and continued with varying success until nightfall.

As soon as he had received reports from his corps commanders, General Grant issued orders to have everything in readiness for a general attack at precisely 5 o'clock the next morning, each commander being directed to vigorously assault whatever it found in its front.

It is not our purpose to describe in detail the battle of the Wilderness. It is sufficient to say that another day of heroic fighting followed without decisive results for either party. Lee, it is true, had been forced from the Wilderness, but he had withdrawn to a new line of defence, little inferior in strength to the one he had been forced to abandon.

THE FLANK MOVEMENT.

General Grant instantly determined upon a flank movement by the way of Spottsylvania Court House. Scarcely had our columns begun to move before traitors in camp found means to communicate the fact to General Lee, or else that able general penetrated the design; for he hurried all his available force in the same direction, and prepared to oppose us. Desultory fighting followed, and on the 10th a terrible general engagement ensued, of which, though the advantage was on the side of the Union arms, the result was not decisive.

The next day General Grant sent the following dispatch to the Secretary of War:

HEADQUARTERS IN THE FIELD, May 11, 1864, 8 A. M.

We have now ended the sixth day of very heavy fighting. The result, to this time, is much in our favor.

Our losses have been heavy, as well as those of the enemy. I think the loss of the enemy must be greater.

We have taken over five thousand prisoners by battle, while he has taken from us but few, except stragglers.

I PROPOSE TO FIGHT IT OUT ON THIS LINE, IF IT TAKES ALL SUMMER.

U. S. GRANT, Lieutenant-General,
Commanding the Armies of the United States.

The next day, being the 12th, General Hancock was ordered to make another assault upon the enemy's works, which proved one of the most brilliant of the campaign. General Edward Johnson's entire division, with its general, two other brigades, Brigadier-General Geo. H. Stewart and thirty guns were captured. The Rebels, largely re-enforced, made frantic efforts to retrieve the fortunes of the day, but with poor success; and at nightfall the fighting ceased.

CONGRATULATIONS TO THE TROOPS.

The result of the last day's work had been so decidedly in our favor that General Meade deemed it proper to issue the following order:

HEADQUARTERS ARMY OF THE POTOMAC,
May 13, 1864.

SOLDIERS—The moment has arrived when your commanding general feels authorized to address you in terms of congratulation.

For eight days and nights, almost without intermission, in rain and sunshine, you have been gallantly fighting a desperate foe, in positions naturally strong, and rendered doubly so by intrenchments.

You have compelled him to abandon his fortifications on the Rapidan, to retire and attempt to stop your onward progress; and now he has abandoned the last intrenched position so tenaciously held, suffering a loss in all of eighteen guns, twenty-two colors, and eight thousand prisoners, including two general officers.

Your heroic deeds and noble endurance of fatigue and privations, will ever be memorable. Let us return thanks to God for the mercy thus shown us, and ask earnestly for its continuation.

Soldiers! Your work is not yet over. The enemy must be pursued, and, if possible, overcome. The courage and fortitude you have displayed renders your commanding general confident your future efforts will result in success.

While we mourn the loss of many gallant comrades, let us remember the enemy must have suffered equal, if not greater, losses.

We shall soon receive re-inforcements, which he cannot expect. Let us determine to continue vigorously the work so well begnn, and, under God's blessing, in a short time the object of our labors will be accomplished.

GEORGE G. MEADE,
Major-General commanding.

Official, S. WILLIAMS, A. A. G.

Approved, U. S. GRANT, Lieutenant General.
Commanding the Armies of the United States.

THE PROGRESS OF THE CAMPAIGN.

The campaign had now lasted nearly two weeks, with almost constant fighting; and although the enemy had been steadily forced back, he had retired sullenly, fought gallantly and still presented a defiant front. To avoid the hazard and loss of another direct assault, General Grant resolved upon another flank movement, the purpose of which was to turn the enemy's left, and force him to confront him upon the former battle-fields of Cold Harbor and Gaines's Mills. Incessant fighting marked the progress of this movement, and Grant's abilities as a commander were never more severely taxed. He was called upon to manœuvre a large army in an extremely difficult and thoroughly hostile country, in the face of a brave, sagacious and desperate enemy fighting for the salvation of his capital and the very life of his cause. The flanking movements we had inaugurated, and in which we must persist until we should reach more permanent ground south of Richmond, constantly exposed our flank, and our troops must be kept well together, always ready to form in line of battle to repel the enemy's attack.

FLANKING AGAIN.

Carefully watching every exposed point, General Grant moved his army to the North Anna river and crossed it, when he again found Lee in a strong position. Finding, after a severe engagement, that his works could only be carried with heavy loss, General Grant again flanked him, and swinging around toward Cold Harbor and Gaines's Mill, gradually approached Richmond, and at the same time again forced Lee to leave his strongly entrenched position.

BATTLE OF COLD HARBOR.

At Cold Harbor the two armies met, and fought one of the most fierce and deadly battles of the war. The enemy again successfully resisted our assault, and then Grant decided to cross his army to the south side of the James river by the enemy's right flank, and cut his communications and lines of supply. As the first important step in the programme, Generals Butler and Gilmore were directed to seize Petersburg, an important railway point, and destroy the bridges. A succession of untoward circumstances followed, and before General Grant could reach the field in person to repair the mistakes of his subordinates, the enemy had rendered the position too strong for assault. Into that stronghold the enemy gathered his strength, and around it the great captain drew his lines, thus laying upon the devoted city of Richmond the first coil of that anaconda grasp, ever tightening and never to be released until the object of assault should be strangled and lie lifeless in his embrace.

AROUND PETERSBURG.

From the 28th of June, 1864, to the 29th of March, 1865, the grand armies confronted each other at Petersburg. In the meantime numerous raiding parties had gone out in every direction, harassing the enemy, breaking his line of communication, capturing his trains and wearing him out by unremitting assaults or threats of assault, at all points of his line.

General Grant became convinced early in March, that General Lee was only waiting the opportunity to evacuate Petersburg, and if he could elude our army, join General Johnston in North Carolina, and with the united forces, inaugurate a new, long and bloody campaign.

To prevent a consummation so full of peril, now became Grant's sole purpose. General Sherman, who was operating against Johnston, was summoned to Petersburg for consultation, and instructed to press the latter without cessation, and allow no opportunity for any concerted action with General Lee.

THE FINAL STRUGGLE.

For himself, he put everything in readiness for any emergency. His camp was cleared of the sick, and all superfluous baggage. The several divisions were reviewed, the organization perfected, and, thus prepared, he waited the first signal of the Rebel retreat. His plan was to attack him the moment the movement began, and rout him if possible; failing in this, he was to mass his cavalry, destroy the communications between Lee and Johnston, and not only prevent their junction, but beat them in detail.

On the 28th of March, orders were issued for General Sheridan to move. The following is an extract from Sheridan's instructions:

"You may go out by the nearest roads in rear of the Fifth Corps, pass by its left, and passing near to or through Dinwiddie, reach the right and rear of the enemy as soon as you can. It is not the intention to attack the enemy in his intrenched position, but to force him out if possible. Should he come out and attack us, or get himself where he can be attacked, move in with your entire force in your own way, and with the full reliance that the army will engage or follow as circumstances will dictate. I shall be on the field, and will probably be able to communicate with you. Should I not do so, and you find that the enemy keeps within his main intrenched line, you may cut loose and push for the Danville road. If you find it practicable, I would like you to cross the Southside road, between Petersburg and Burkesville, and destroy it to some extent. I would not advise much detention, however, until you reach the Danville road, which I would like you to strike as near to the Appomattox as possible. Make your destruction of that road as complete as possible. You can then pass on to the Southside road, west of Burkesville, and destroy that in like manner."

NO ESCAPE FOR LEE.

In the meantime our lines continued to contract around the Rebel stronghold, and had been so strengthened that General Grant felt almost certain that the time had at last come for capturing Richmond, and, what was more important, defeating Lee and forcing him to a surrender.

He accordingly sent to General Sheridan the following significant dispatch:

GRAVELLY RUN, March 29, 1865.

GENERAL—Our line is now unbroken from the Appomattox to Dinwiddie I now feel like ending the matter, if it is possible to do so, before going back. I do not want you, therefore, to cut loose and go after the enemy's roads at present. In the morning, push round the enemy if you can, and get on to his right rear. The movements of the enemy's cavalry may, of course, modify your action. We will all act together as one army here, until it is seen what can be done with the enemy.

U. S. GRANT, Lieutenant-General.

MAJOR-GENERAL P. H. SHERIDAN.

THE BATTLE OF FIVE FORKS

On the 30th, Sheridan pushed forward and fought the Battle of Five Forks, striking the rear of the enemy and inflicting much loss upon him. Other successes followed. Lee's lines were forced at several points, and at last the grand Army of Northern Virginia was pushed from its entrenchments, and went streaming westward in great confusion along the main road by the Appomattox. The Federal troops pursued sharply, dealing heavy blows at every opportunity.

TERROR IN RICHMOND.

The night of the 2d of April was one of great terror and consternation in Richmond. The disaster to General Lee could no longer be concealed, and the proud Rebel capital was known to be defenceless. On Sunday, the 2d, it was evacuated, and on the following morning our victorious troops entered.

Lee, with the remnant of his army hastened along the Danville road, hoping to reach Johnston in North Carolina. Sheridan made a forced march and planted himself directly across the line Lee was following, while the main army was pressing him closely on the other side. Unable to cope with either antagonist, nothing was left the Rebel army but to drift hopelessly westward and put off for a few hours the evil day.

THE SURRENDER.

From the 4th to the 7th of April, the dissolving Rebel army struggled against its inevitable fate. Believing that the end had at last come, General Grant sent the following letter to General Lee:

April 7, 1865.

General:—The result of the last week must convince you of the hopelessness of further resistance, on the part of the army of Northern Virginia, in this struggle. I feel that it is so, and regard it as my duty to shift from myself the responsibility of any further effusion of blood, by asking of you the surrender of that portion of the Confederate States army known as the Army of Northern Virginia.

U. S. GRANT Lieutenant-General.

GENERAL R. E. LEE.

Early on the morning of the 8th, before leaving, Grant received at Farmville the following:

April 7, 1865.

GENERAL:—I have received your note of this date. Though not entertaining the opinion you express on the hopelessness of further resistance on the part of the Army of Northern Virginia, I reciprocate your desire to avoid useless effusion of blood, and, therefore, before considering your proposition, ask the terms you will offer on condition of its surrender.

R. E. LEE, General.

LIEUTENANT-GENERAL U. S. GRANT.

To this Grant immediately replied:

April 8, 1865.

GENERAL:—Your note of last evening, in reply to mine of same date, asking the condition on which I will accept the surrender of the Army of Northern Virginia, is just received. In reply, I would say, that *peace* being my great desire, there is but one condition I would insist upon—namely, that the men and officers surrendered shall be disqualified for taking up arms again against the Government of the United States until properly exchanged. I will meet you, or will designate officers to meet any officers you may name for the same purpose, at any point agreeable to you, for the purpose of arranging definitely the terms upon which the surrender of the Army of Northern Virginia will be received.

U. S. GRANT, Lieutenant-General.

GENERAL R. E. LEE.

General Lee promptly replied as follows:

April 8, 1865.

GENERAL:—I received at a late hour your note of to-day in answer to mine of yesterday.

I did not intend to propose the surrender of the Army of Northern Virgiania, but to ask the terms of your proposition. To be frank, I do not think the emergency has arisen to call for the surrender. But as the restoration of peace should be the sole object of all, I desire to know whether your proposals would tend to that end.

I cannot, therefore, meet you with a view to surrender the Army of Northern Virginia, but so far as your proposition may affect the Confederate States forces under my command, and lead to the restoration of peace, I should be pleased to meet you at 10 A. M., to-morrow, on the old stage-road to Richmond, between the picket lines of the two armies.

R. E. LEE, General.

TO LIEUTENANT-GENERAL GRANT.

The following is Grant's rejoinder:

April 9, 1865.

GENERAL R. E. LEE, Commanding C. S. A.:

GENERAL: Your note of yesterday is received. As I have no authority to treat on the subject of peace, the meeting proposed for 10 A. M., to-day, could lead to no good. I will state, however, General, that I am equally anxious for peace with yourself; and the whole North entertain the same feeling. The terms upon which peace can be had are well understood. By the South laying down their arms they will hasten that most desirable event, save thousands of human lives, and hundreds of millions of property not yet destroyed.

Sincerely hoping that all our difficulties may be settled without the loss of another life, I subscribe myself, U. S. GRANT, Lieutenant-General.

General Lee's response was as follows:

April 9, 1865.

GENERAL: I received your note of this morning on the picket line, whither I had come to meet you and ascertain definitely what terms were embraced in your proposition of yesterday with reference to the surrender of this army.

I now request an interview in accordance with the offer contained in your letter of yesterday for that purpose. R. E. LEE, General.

To LIEUTENANT-GENERAL GRANT.

The following letter closed the correspondence on the part of General Grant:

APPOMATTOX COURT-HOUSE, Va., April 9, 1865.

GENERAL: In accordance with the substance of my letter to you of the 8th instant, I propose to receive the surrender of the Army of Northern Virginia on the following terms—to wit: Rolls of all the officers and men to be made in duplicate, one copy to be given to an officer to be designated by me, the other to be retained by such officer or officers as you may designate. The officers to give their individual paroles not to take up arms against the Government of the United States until properly exchanged; and each company or regimental commander to sign a like parole for the men of their commands. The arms, artillery, and public property to be packed and stacked, and turned over to the officers appointed by me to receive them. This will not embrace the side-arms of the officers, nor their private horses or baggage. This done, each officer and man will be allowed to return to his home, not to be disturbed by United States authority so long as they observe their paroles, and the laws in force where they may reside.

U. S. GRANT, Lieutenant-General.

GENERAL R. E. LEE.

The rebel General's reply was as follows:

HEADQUARTERS ARMY NORTHERN VIRGINIA,
April 9, 1865.

GENERAL:—I have received your letter of this date, containing the terms of surrender of the Army of Northern Virginia as proposed by you. As they are substantially the same as those expressed in your letter of the 8th instant, they are accepted. I will proceed to designate the proper officers to carry the stipulations into effect. R. E. LEE, General.

LIEUTENANT-GENERAL U. S. GRANT.

The terms of this correspondence were carried out without delay. How desperately the war had been carried on by the rebel leaders is shown by the fact that, though the names of 150,000 men were borne on Lee's muster-rolls a few weeks before, there were but 27,000 found to surrender to Grant. Desertion had told the story; and this was brought about only by failing supplies and a hopeless cause. Of arms and ammunition, however, there was a rich supply, and these were turned over to Grant, as trophies of his victory over the ablest and best beloved general of the Confederacy, and one but for whose staunchness and sagacity, the victory would have been much more easily won.

GRANT'S MILITARY GENIUS.

We do not propose to enter here upon a minute analysis of General Grant's military methods, or discuss the question of his genius as a general. This has been done in more technical works, as Coppee's Life of Grant, Swinton's able work on the battles of the late civil war, and various treatises by both American and European writers. In Mr. Greeley's "American Conflict," second volume, the reader will find a brief but vigorous defence of Grant's plan of the Virginia Campaign, so hastily sketched above; and in his journal—the New York *Tribune*—of July 2d, 1864, he paid the following glowing tribute to the man who "bróke the back of the Slaveholder's Rebellion:"

"We loathe man-worship, yet every day's experience strengthens our faith in Lieutenant-General Grant. The task devolved on him is arduous; he is confronted by an able general and a gallant veteran army who enjoy enormous advantages in their defensive attitudes, the nature of the country and their intimate knowledge of its topography; yet from the hour of his crossing the Rapidan, General Grant has gone steadily, sturdily forward, repelling impetuous attacks, assaulting (when necessary) strongly fortified positions; withdrawing unobserved from the immediate front of his wary antagonist and effecting the most daring and difficult flank movements, thereby achieving the fruits of victory without encountering the carnage which is the usual cost of success—and all this with a stern quietude that indicates reserved force and a consciousness of power adapted to any emergency. We are not apt to be over sanguine; we realize that victory is often a happy accident and that occurrences purely fortuitous often derange and defeat the ablest combinations; but, having noted his bearing under every phase of fortune, his quick improvement of advantages and his skillful reparation of mischances, we cannot doubt that he has true military genius, and that he will do whatever one man can do to break the back of the Slaveholder's Rebellion."

HON. OLIVER P. MORTON,
U S. Senator for Indiana.

CHAPTER XIII.

GRANT AS PRESIDENT.

Difficulties Encountered on his Induction to the Chair of State—General Policy of the Administration—The Will of the People Supreme—Economy the Rule—Some Figures—Grant and the Civil Service—Important Reforms—Grant and Amnesty—Policy toward the Colored Race—The Treaty with England—History of the Negotiations—Grant's Indian Policy—The Olive Branch Armed with a Switch.

Some of the peculiar difficulties with which President Grant had to contend at the outset of his administration were alluded to in a previous chapter; the two chief being reconstruction and the unhappy state of the civil service. Each of these was partly the natural growth of the war and partly the legacy of Andrew Johnson's cross-grained administration; and the treatment of either of them would have furnished a very good eight years' job to a moderately active President. But General Grant, though commencing his administration very modestly, so far as all his public utterances went, has undertaken not only these Herculean labors which thrust themselves forward the most prominently, but numerous other beneficent works within the sphere of his duties as Executive. Many of these he has happily accomplished; others he has advanced creditably, and seems sure to secure both Congressional and popular co-operation in their behalf within a year or two; while a single one, having met serious opposition in the legislative branch,—which General Grant, unlike his predecessor, consents cheerfully to recognize as a co-ordinate branch of the Government,—has been quietly dropped, in lieu of the persistent scolding to which Congress became so accustomed during the incumbency of Johnson.

GRANT'S VIEW OF HIS DUTIES.

Grant's general policy, as mapped out by himself, for himself, at his inauguration, has been made familiar to all. "The office," he said, "has come to me unsought. I commence its duties untrammeled. I bring to it a conscientious desire and determination to fill it to the best of my ability to the satisfaction of the people. On all leading questions agitating the public mind I will always express my views to Congress, and urge them according to my judgment; and when I think it advisable will exercise the constitutional privilege of interposing a veto to defeat measures which I oppose. But all laws will be faithfully executed, whether they meet my approval or not. I shall on all subjects have a policy to *recommend*, but none to *enforce* against the will of the people. Laws are to govern all alike, those opposed to as well as those who favor them. I know no method to secure the repeal of bad or obnoxious laws so effective as their stringent execution."

In other words, he proposed to discharge the

duties of an Executive without attempting to trench upon those of the Legislature. He rightly judged that as an Executive merely (with his slight semi-legislative function added, of signing or vetoing acts of Congress) he could find ample scope for all his ability and energy, even though he were the ablest and most energetic of statesmen.

ECONOMY IN ADMINISTRATION.

As is well known, one of the main tenets of the Republican faith is Economy in administration. As is also well known, the annual expenses of the Government, at the installation of President Grant, had become very large—partly through the inevitable increase of business, especially of the Revenue Department incident to the long war, and partly through the demoralization brought about by Johnson. To reform this as far as possible, and to reduce the annual outgo to the minimum, was the early effort of President Grant.

During the year ending July 1, 1866, the annual revenues of the Government, raised from duties and from excise taxes, reached the enormous sum of $558,000,000. This sum has been so reduced that, although we are still paying off $100,000,000 annually of the national debt and defraying all the interest as it comes due, the Government only asks about $240,000,000 per year from the people for all purposes. Part of the reductions have been made by Congress, to be sure; but they could not have been made if the collection of duties and of internal revenue had been carried on in the lax and dishonest fashion of Johnson's time. To collect an annual revenue of $46,000,000 from spirits and tobacco in 1867–8, for instance, cost $1,200,000 more under Johnson's administration than it did to collect $87,000,000—nearly twice as much—in 1870–1 under Grant's administration. (And it is the former office-holders of Andy Johnson who are now most active in forwarding Greeley's cause; and who are promised by the Chicago *Tribune*—the great civil service reformer!—that they shall not be prevented from enjoying their "spoils" when Greeley comes into the White House.)

The aggregate reduction of internal revenue since 1866 has been as follows:

Act of July 13, 1866	$65,000,000
Act of March 2, 1867	40,000,000
Act of February 3, 1868	23,000,000
Act of March 31, 1668, Act of July 20, 1868,	45,000,000
Act of July 14, 1870	55,000,000
Total	$228,000,000

Adding to this the tariff reduction of July, 1870, amounting to $30,000,000, and that of the measure just passed, amounting to about $53,000,000, and we have a grand total of $310,000,000, annual taxes taken off, since July 1, 1869. This reduction has been voted by a Republican Congress. What has been voted since March 4, 1860, has been done with the consent of President Grant's Secretary of the Treasury, and has been done because the efficient collection of the taxes, without unnecessary expense, has caused the same tax to yield much better than it did in Democratic days.

Then, as to the cost of collection: Mr. Eugene Hale, of Maine, in a recent speech in Congress, introduced the following statement made to him by Revenue Commissioner Douglas:

"In reply to your verbal request, I have the honor to hand you the following as the number of each grade of officers of this bureau whose services have been dispensed with from March 4, 1869, to January 1, 1872:

Collectors (consolidation of districts)	9
Assessors (consolidation of districts)	9
Assistant Assessors	1,355
Distillery Storekeepers	129
Distillery Surveyors	209
Tobacco Inspectors	625
Total	2,334

"From the best information in my possession I am of the opinion that the saving to the Government by this reduction will equal, if it does not exceed, $1,200,000 per annum."

Another exhibit:

Expenses of Government, year ending July 1, 1866	$520,809,416.99
" " " " " " " 1867	357,542,675.16
" " " " " " " 1868	377,340,284.86
" " " " " " " 1869	322,865,277.80
" " " " " " " 1870	309,653,560.75
" " " " " " " 1871	295,177,188.25

(This includes interest on the public debt.)

It will be seen from this exhibit that in 1868, when Andy Johnson fell fully into the arms of the Democracy, the expenditures of his administration were $20,000,000 larger than in 1867; while the first year of President Grant's administration—1869—shows a decrease of $54,000,000. This was followed, in 1870, by a decrease of $13,000,000, and of $14,000,000 in 1871.

Another: The subjoined figures show the expenditures of the Government for carrying on the civil administration during each tenth year:

YEAR.	POPULATION.	EXPENDITURES.	PER CAPITA.
1800	5,305,925	$10,813,971 01	$2 03
1810	7,239,814	8,474,753 37	1 17
1820	9,638,131	18,285,534 89	1 89
1830	12,866,020	15,142,108 26	1 17
1840	17,069,453	24,314,518 19	1 42
1850	23,191,876	40,948,383 12	1 76
1860	31,443,321	58,489,037 16	1 86
1871	38,555,983	57,117,332 43	1 48

(The figures for 1860 and 1871 are exclusive of permanent public improvements.)

Thus it is seen that it cost the people about 26 per cent. more *per capita* to carry on the various Departments of the Government when the Democrats were in power, and had been so eight years, than it did when the Republicans had the job. This will do for illustrations of President Grant's efforts in behalf of *Economy*. We have shown that Grant's administration, while paying off $100,000,000 per year of the national debt and defraying promptly the annual interest on the remainder, has reduced the total annual expenses some $310,000,000, and the expenses of special departments in a way to show that the present Executive has made it a constant and successful study to develop the greatest possible amount of revenue at the least possible cost.

MAINTAINING THE PUBLIC CREDIT.

Unquestionably it is to this economy of administration, and to the steady policy of the Government in nursing tenderly the Public Credit, that the great material prosperity of the country during the years of Grant's administration is due. His selection of a Secretary of the Treasury proved to be a most happy one, and Mr. Boutwell has by his honesty, his firmness and his inventive genius done much to straighten out our finances and relieve the burdens of the people. One of the best achievements of his administration has been the funding scheme, whereby more than a thousand millions of our debt will soon have been converted from 6 per cents into 5 and 4½ per cents, thereby saving in interest, say $12,000,000 per annum. This reduction could never have been accomplished except through a great strengthening of our national credit in Europe, consequent upon the continued ascendency of the Republican party, and the wise, conservative administration of General Grant. Indeed, the very popularity of Grant has contributed to this strengthening of the public credit, since the capitalists abroad perceived in that popularity a guaranty that his administration was not likely to be upset at next November's election, and the candidate of the reckless, repudiating, Tammany-fostering Democrats installed in the White House. The clamor of the anti-Grant press and the recent temporary delay in the Alabama negotiations may serve to keep this foreign confidence disturbed somewhat during the summer and early fall; but after Grant's re-election, the funding of the remainder of the debt will go on as before.

CIVIL SERVICE REFORM.

In his second annual message to Congress, President Grant wrote thus:

"Always favoring practical reforms, I respectfully call your attention to one abuse of long standing, which I would like to see remedied by this Congress. It is a reform in the civil service of the country. I would have it go beyond the mere fixing of the tenure of office of clerks and employees, who do not require "the advice and consent of the Senate" to make their appointments complete. I would have it govern, not the tenure, but the manner of making all appointments. There is no duty which so much embarrasses the Executive and Heads of Departments as that of appointments; nor is there any such arduous and thankless labor imposed on Senators and Representatives as that of finding places for constituents. The present system does not secure the best men, and often not fit men, for public place. The elevation and purification of the civil service of the Government will be hailed with approval by the whole people of the United States."

With particular reference to the heads of Bureaus and other officers of like grade, he called the attention of Congress to the vastness of the interests committed to them, and to the inadequacy of their salaries to the responsibility imposed on them. He asked for a change in this respect, and said to Congress, "There has been no hesitation in changing officials in order to secure an efficient execution of the laws, sometimes, too, when in a mere party view, undesirable political results were likely to follow; nor any hesitation in sustaining efficient officials against remonstrances wholly political."

Is not this the Civil Service Reform which the anti-Grant men are now claiming as the corner stone of their platform?

In a later message, President Grant wrote:

"It has been the aim of the Administration to enforce honesty and efficiency in all public offices. Every public servant who has violated the trust placed in him has been proceeded against with all the rigor of the law. If bad men have secured places it has been the fault of the system established by law and custom for making appointments, or the fault of those who recommend for Government positions persons not sufficiently well known to them personally, or who give letters indorsing the characters of office-seekers without a proper sense of the grave responsibility which such a course devolves upon them. A civil service reform which can correct this abuse is much desired. In mercantile pursuit, the business-man who gives a letter of recommendation to a friend, to enable him to obtain credit from a stranger, is regarded as morally responsible for the integrity of his friend, and his ability to meet his obligations. A reformatory law which would enforce this principle against all indorsers of persons for public place would insure great caution in making recommendations. A salutary lesson has been taught the careless and the dishonest public servant in the great number of prosecutions and convictions of the last two years."

When finally Congress, in the spring of 1871, passed an act, or a fragment of an act, looking toward a definite reform of the methods of appointing to civil office—which act authorized the President to constitute a board or commission for the careful investigation of the whole subject and the drafting of a system of operations—General Grant proceeded with alacrity to carry out the act according to its spirit. He selected for members of the commission, Messrs. George William Curtis, Joseph Medill, A. G. Cattell, E. B. Elliott and J. H. Blackfan—the first two distinguished journalists of the very highest character, whose journals had expressed a decided interest in the proposed reform; the third an Ex-United States Senator, and a public man of much experience; and the last two old bureau officers, familiar with the workings of administrative machinery. The commission sat and sifted the subject very carefully and, at length, was able to report a partial system, which, so far as it went, was a great advance upon the old methods.

THE CIVIL SERVICE AS IT WAS.

As generally understood, the recognized rule of past administrations, regulating appointments to clerkships at Washington, or to more important offices at local points throughout the country, has been *political pressure* simply. If the political pressure in behalf of A. was only strong enough, B. had to be turned out of his clerkship to make room for him, no matter if B. were much the better clerk. This pressure usually came from Senators and Representatives in Congress, who *demanded* such and such appointments from the Government as their rightful property, wherewith to pay off the debts incurred in getting themselves elected to office. This practice was very demoralizing, not only to the civil service, but to politics generally—since it debased the considerations upon which men were nominated to office, and often resulted in the election of tricky, log-rolling, bargaining politicians, when the people would rather vote for men of parts and character. It also embarrassed the President with a great deal of patching and peddling which belonged properly to the members themselves—or, rather, to nobody at all.

THE NEW REGIME.

The President therefore entered with zeal, though not with undue haste, or with overmuch flourish, into the work of reforming the civil service by giving employees of the Government a better tenure of their offices, and by fixing according to fitter and more calculable rules, the method of their appointment. The rules framed last winter by the Advisary Board of the Civil Service for the classification, qualifications, etc., of clerks and other employees and officers of the Federal departments at Washington, have been in operation there some months; and a set of rules, founded on them, had a short time before putting this book to press, been adopted for the New York Custom House service. Hereafter all applicants for office in the Government service in New York must make application in writing, giving name, age, occupation past and present, accompanied by certificate of character from two responsible persons, and a physician's certificate of health and fitness for clerical labor. The manner in which these applications are drawn up will go far to decide the fitness of the applicant for appointment. Every application which does not conform with the requirements of the rules, or which shows manifest lack of qualification, will be summarily rejected by the examining boards. The names of those whose applications are satisfactory will be placed on what is termed the "eligible list." The persons whose names are on this list will be notified to appear for examination whenever a vacancy is to be filled, unless it should be impracticable to examine all of them, in which case a practicable number of those apparently best qualified will be selected and summoned for examination. In making up the eligible list and in selecting the practicable number, the board will be guided entirely by the merits of the applications, without regard to political considerations. The names of the three persons standing highest on the list will be certified to by the board for the vacancy, and from the names thus certified the appointment must be made.

The regulations of the advisory board, applying to all departments of government service, further required that such appointments, excepting persons appointed by the President, with the advice and consent of the Senate, postmasters and persons appointed to any position in a foreign country, shall be made for a probationary term of six months, during which the conduct and capacity of such persons shall be tested; and if, at the end of such probationary term, satisfactory proof of their fitness shall have been furnished, they shall be re-appointed. The regulations are stringent, as it was the purpose of the advisory board and of the President, who was from the beginning in entire accord with them, to make the experiment with perfect sincerity and good faith. The object is to get the best service possible; and this method is the result of the best reflection and experience which could be brought to bear upon it. In the service of the Treasury department alone the number of appointments to which the rules will be applicable when vacancies arise, is stated at fourteen thousand. The morale of this branch of the service was never so high as it is now. The excellence of its organization and the business-like character and efficiency which pervaded it was recognized even by the opposition until its organs had political reasons for blackening it.

The object of these rules is not merely to furnish a series of tests by which the maximum amount of ability and other qualifications can be secured in the employee appointed to a place under the Government. If this were so, it would be exceedingly problematical whether the competitive examination system were worth, in benefits derived from it, the pains and expense bestowed upon it. But the system has another and far higher use, in that it furnishes (together with the system of promotions in line) a fixed and definite process by which places under the Government are filled *without the interference of political favoritism;* and it must always be recollected that the gravest of the evils to be got rid of is not inefficiency of the service as it exists, but the demoralization of general politics by the introduction of the spoils doctrine. There are other methods of curing this evil—such as a law of Congress protecting all office-holders in their places during a certain fixed term of (say) four years, subject to removal for bad behavior only; the election of postmasters by the people, and the abolition of internal revenue collectors and assessors altogether, and the selling of all the necessary stamps by postmasters (something which the President has favored); and it is likely that some or all of these additional measures will have to be resorted to before the serpent is scotched altogether. There is no doubt that the President is in earnest in his devotion to this reform; and doubtless the reason why he has moved with moderate pace in it is because he has seen that the people, and especially Congress, had not yet fairly waked up to it until quite recently.

SKEPTICS AND REACTIONISTS.

There are still some public men of both parties, who affect to distrust the possibility of any valuable reform of the service through the means indicated in the foregoing paragraphs. The Advisory Board they characterize as "schoolmasters" and the regulations for examination and probation are, they charge, but so many devices for preferring a few dry-veined bookworms before men of practical acumen, in the assignment of candidates to places. They have also some cant to utter about these regulations being an insult to the intelligence of the American people; but just where the "insult" comes in, when, in truth, the whole system is intended to protect the interests of the people against the rapacity of the politicians, would, perhaps, puzzle the reactionists to point out. The Republican party has now, through its legally constituted delegates in national convention, approved of the reform, and no good Republican Congressman can rightfully refuse to give his co-operation. The people should see to it in the pending campaign, that the genius of real civil service reform prevails, both at the primaries and at the polls; that the management of the former is not relegated to men who work for pay promised them by candidates, in the shape of postoffices and assessorships; and that all candidates who attempt to forward their own chances in such a way are left at home, and not sent to Washington to corrupt our legislation.

THE PRESIDENT'S POLICY TOWARD THE SOUTH.

General Grant's policy toward the reconstructed States has been a liberal and a careful one. Realizing that pacification and reconciliation were the great requisites of those communities, he has endeavored to stimulate loyalty among the lately disloyal, and industry and development among the great mass of blacks lately endowed with the powers of citizenship. And it has also been the aim of the administration to protect both of these classes, so far as they would allow it, from the effects of their own extremism, as shown in the surrender of most of the State governments to adroit, but unprincipled "carpet-baggers." President Grant has watched with favorable interest all measures for the education of the negro race, and was, in fact, the original proposer of the plan embodied in the bill of Congressman Hoar, passed by the House of Representatives last session, and intended especially for the benefit of the South. This bill proposed to divide in proportion to the illiteracy of the respective States the proceeds of all public lands sold hereafter.

AMNESTY.

The magnanimity which Grant as a conquering general showed to Lee and his troops at Appomattox, has distinguished his demeanor toward them and their sympathizers since. He has, from time to time, proposed measures of amnesty to the Rebels still left more or less under the political ban (none are absolutely disfranchised); and last December he sent this recommendation to Congress:

"More than six years having elapsed since the last hostile gun was fired between the armies then arrayed against each other,—one for the perpetuation, the other for the destruction, of the Union,—it may well be considered whether it is not now time that the disabilities imposed by the fourteenth amendment should be removed. That amendment does not exclude the ballot, but only imposes the disability to hold office upon certain classes. When the purity of the ballot is secure, majorities are sure to elect officers reflecting the views of the majority. I do not see the advantage or propriety of excluding men from office merely because they were, before the rebellion, of standing and character sufficient to be elected to positions requiring them to take oaths to support the Constitution, and admitting to eligibility those entertaining precisely the same views, but of less standing in their communities. It may be said that the former violated an oath, while the latter did not. The latter did not have it in their power to do so. If they had taken this oath, it cannot be doubted they would have broken it, as did the former class. If there are any great criminals, distinguished above all others for the part they took in opposition to the Government, they might, in the judgment of Congress, be excluded from such an amnesty. This subject is submitted for your careful consideration.

"The condition of the Southern States is, unhappily, not such as all true, patriotic citizens would like to see. Social ostracism for opinion's sake, personal violence or threats towards persons entertaining political views opposed to those entertained by the majority of the old citizens, prevent immigration and the flow of much needed capital into the States lately in rebellion. It will be a happy condition of the country when the old citizens of these States will take an interest in public affairs, promulgate ideas honestly entertained, vote for men representing their views, and tolerate the same freedom of expression and ballot in those entertaining different political convictions."

This is plain language, and as liberal in sentiment

as the most advanced of the so-called liberals can boast, and yet the loyal men of the country will feel far safer in seeing such precepts carried out under the administration of one who has displayed always a nice appreciation of the rights of both races of the South, than under one who proposes to sail into the White House upon a breeze which blows only in behalf of the old Rebel element at the South, and a popularity which results from his favoring Secession and bailing Jeff. Davis.

Congress heeded the recommendation of President Grant, and passed several amnesty bills, in a single one of which about 25,000 Rebels were re-admitted to all the privileges of citizenship, including office-holding.

Grant's record on Amnesty is such, in short, as to make him much stronger in the South than his principal adversary in this contest; though not, perhaps with the old political class of Rebels, who seem fully as blind now as they did in 1860 and 1861. With the Confederate soldiers, who fought nobly for what they were taught to believe was their country, it will doubtless be otherwise; and as for the Blacks, who constitute a majority in the South, not one in ten of them is going to be beguiled into voting for the candidate of the Democracy, especially if it be Greeley. They regard Grant as next to Lincoln, their deliver; and of Greeley they say, "If he had had his say in '60 and '61, and you'd let de Southern States, depart in peace,' den we'd done been slaves to-day, shuh,

No, we can't go for Mr. Greeley." And their logic has common sense in it, as negro logic usually has.

THE TREATY WITH ENGLAND.

The foreign policy of President Grant has been one of peace. In one of his messages, he says, "As the United States is the freest of all nations, so, too, the people sympathize with all peoples struggling for liberty and self-government. But while so sympathizing," he adds, "it is due to our honor that we should abstain from enforcing our views upon unwilling nations and taking an interested part without invitation in the quarrels between different nations, or between governments and their subjects." This principle—an old maxim with the American government—is the President's answer to those feverish, fretful newspaper organs in New York, which have always (apparently in the interest of some speculators in Cuban Republic bonds) been teasing the Government to interfere with Cuban affairs, and bring on a war with Spain. It is also a sufficient reason for the President's prompt interference to check the irruption of Fenians from our borders upon British soil in 1869. The President himself came near forgetting it in the case of Baez, Cabral and the Haytien government, where the cause of the first-named chieftain promised soon to become our own cause, through annexation; but he recollected himself in time to save his record in this respect.

The principal matter of foreign policy with which

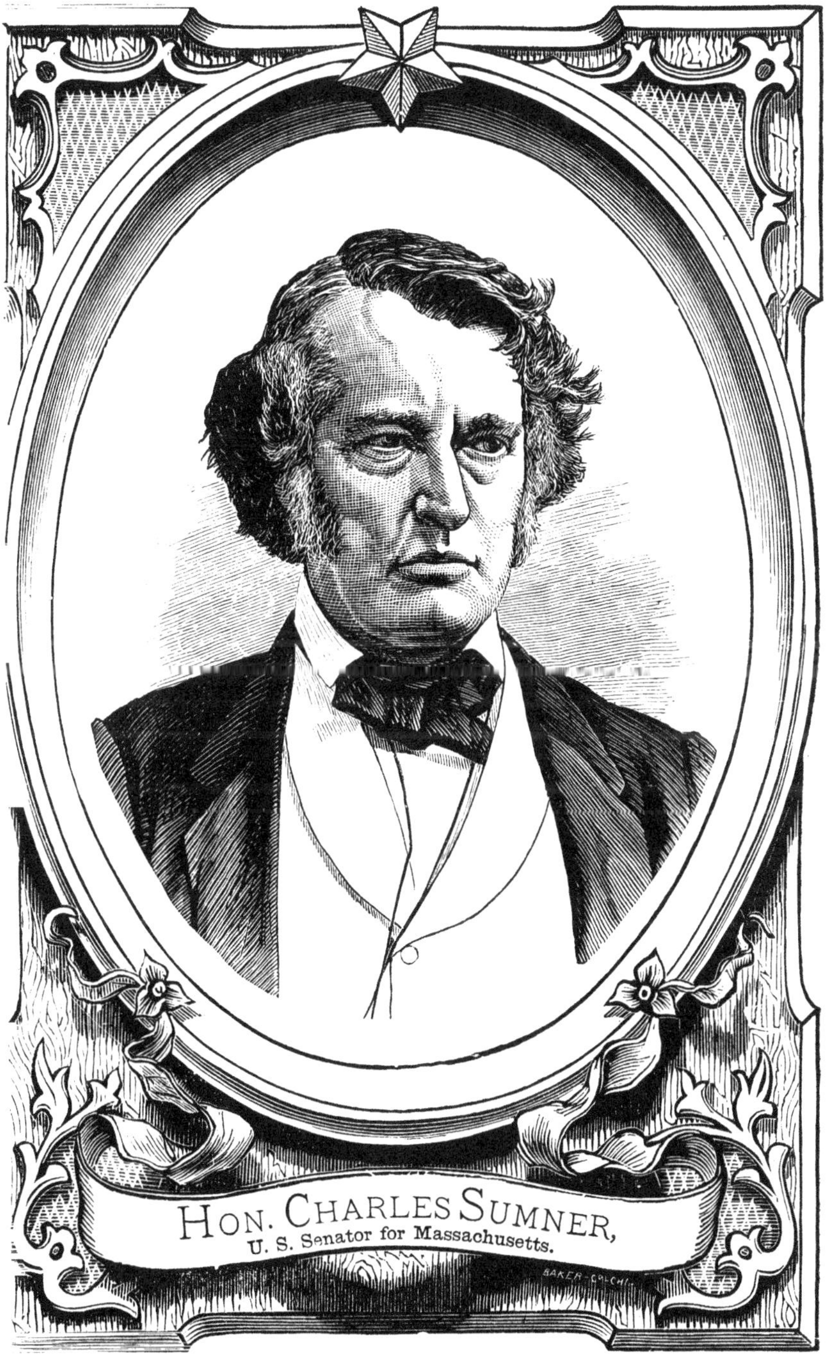

HON. CHARLES SUMNER,
U. S. Senator for Massachusetts.

General Grant's administration has had to do, however, is the negotiation of the much-talked-about treaty with England, intended to bring about a settlement, without bloodshed, of four questions which had long vexed the diplomacy of the two nations. These were:

1. The claims alleged against Great Britain, by reason of the Rebel privateers fitted out in British ports, and known as the "Alabama Claims."

2. The question of Fishermen's rights along the Banks of New Foundland, there being an old dispute as to how near to the Canadian shore American fishermen were, by former treaties, entitled to approach

3. The navigation of the Great Lakes and other navigable waters lying within either government's territory, by the navy and merchant marine of the other.

4. The location of the San Juan boundary (between Washington Territory and British Columbia.)

To arrange for the settlement of these questions a Joint High Commission was appointed by the two governments and assembled at Washington in February, 1871, completing its labors on the 8th of May when the treaty of Washington was signed by the members of the Commission. The treaty was ratified June 17th, 1871. (An abstract of all its important provisions, together with some interesting papers bearing upon the question before the

Geneva Tribunal of Arbitration, is given in the appendix to this volume.)

The third of the questions referred to above was settled by the treaty itself and confirmed by the action of the Canadian Parliament. The first was made the subject of a special commission, which has not yet concluded its labors. The fourth was referred to the Emperor of Germany as arbitrator, and his decision was, at the writing of this, about to be promulgated. The first question is the only one about which there has been any national soreness, and this chiefly on the part of Great Britain, the people of which country seem less able than their liberal statesmen to "put themselves in our place," in considering such a question. On the first session of the Tribunal of Geneva, in December, 1871, it was found that the counsel on our part, J. C. Bancroft Davis, Esq., had filed claims for *indirect damages* growing out of the maintenance of the Confederate cruisers on the high seas after the last aggressive movements of the Rebel land forces at Gettysburg; "indirect damages" meaning the general expense of prolonging the war, the loss to individuals by enhanced insurance, the loss to the nation by the transfer of her shipping to foreign flags, etc. This order of claims was so stoutly resisted by Great Britain (she claiming that they were ruled out by the treaty and protocol), that the proceedings of the Tribunal were interrupted, and a long correspondence commenced between Earl Granville, the British Secretary for Foreign Affairs, and

Secretary of State, Fish, on behalf of our Government, relative to the adoption of an understanding on which we could proceed with the arbitration. This correspondence, commencing February 3d, 1872, with a letter of remonstrance from Earl Granville to Mr. Fish, is very voluminous, and in it every position is contested, as it were, inch by inch, by the two diplomats; but the tone is remarkably deferential throughout, indicating a determination on the part of both governments not to sacrifice the opportunity of settling the misunderstanding by peaceful arbitration.

On the 25th of April, it was apparent from General Schenck's telegram to Secretary Fish that the British Government had determined to repudiate the Treaty. On the 27th, however, Secretary Fish had received from Sir Edward Thornton, British Minister at Washington, a hint that the British Government would be glad to consent to a supplemental article disposing of the claims upon neutrals for Consequential Damages by excluding them forever from consideration between the two nations, and of course directing their withdrawal in this present case. This was agreeable to our Government, since the United States is usually a neutral power, and hence the one most likely to suffer from a liability to such enormous claims.

In accordance with the proposition which was further elaborated and discussed in a score of communications by cable which passed between the 25th of April and the 10th of May, 1871, such a supplemental article was presented to the American Senate, and approved by that body.

Concerning the wording of the supplemental article proposed by Great Britain and assented to by the United States, with certain slight verbal alterations, there was again a vast amount of correspondence and discussion. The British Parliament, especially, became greatly agitated over the subject, and the British Government began to display much more deference to the clamor of the Tories than it had done heretofore. As a consequence, the Treaty would soon have failed, through the withdrawal of Great Britain from the negotiations (our Government having refused to higgle any longer over mere sentimentalities) had not the Tribunal, at its session in the latter part of June, announced its decision adversely to any claims for indirect damages, and thereby at once relieved the fearful forebodings of John Bull and done away with the supplemental article which had been the bone of contention for the past two months. It is now believed that the upshot of the proceedings will be to award the United States justice in the matter of the Alabama Claims; and at the same time very beneficial results will be obtained from the enforcement of other provisions of the Treaty, and a lamentable war with Great Britain, which seemed to have been long culminating and threatening, be avoided. If so, this negotiation of the Treaty of Washington, with its advantages, if any, on our side, as everybody says, especially in Europe, will be among the greenest laurels of President Grant's administration.

GRANT'S INDIAN POLICY.

President Grant is generally credited, and justly, with having inaugurated a very successful and beneficent policy toward our Indian wards, in the plains and mountains of the West. When Grant came into office, the Indian Bureau was still, what it had long been, a slough of political mire, breeding, pecuniary corruption. It was the home of jobbery and peculation, and lo! the poor Indian had to stand the victim of it all. Cheated by one agent and pampered by another, his natural vindictiveness, quarrelsomeness and recklessness were inflamed still more by his treatment, and hence we heard of massacres upon the border, and of frequent ruptures of our relations with these savage tribes, which it was the custom of the Government to treat as distinct nations. At the same time we were failing utterly to reclaim the unfortunate savages from the low condition of their birth.

General Grant undertook to reform some of these things. His idea was that some of the Red Men, nearly civilized, and others favorably disposed that way, could, by careful teaching and exclusion from bad influences, be hastened on the road to enlightenment and Christianization; that others, like the Apaches and Piegans, too debased in the scale of being to be wrought upon in this way, could best be held in their places by a firm hand, wielded by the War Department; while others, like the Sioux, intelligent, but warlike and intractable must be handled with gentle firmness—treated with through a peace commission backed up by a division of cavalry; and all were alike susceptible to the influence of honest dealing and uniform treatment. General Grant, having had considerable experience with the Indians himself, and having noticed the success of the missionaries of the Society of Friends, in dealing with the Red Men, appointed several members of that society to be superintendents and agents at the Indian posts. At the same time he invited the other religious denominations to name candidates for whose character as humane and honest men they could vouch; and these recommendations were also heeded in the appointment of Indian officers. A general Peace Commission was also appointed shortly after the accession of Grant to the Presidency, consisting of George H. Stuart, Felix R. Brunot, Wm. Welsh, Wm. E. Dodge, E. S. Tobey, John V. Farwell, Robert Campbell, Henry S. Lane, and Nathan Bishop. (John DeLang and Vincent Collyer have since been substituted for Messrs. Welsh and Lane.) It has been the duty of this commission to visit turbulent tribes, ascertain what is their grievance, and, if possible, remedy it. The members, who are all eminent Christians and philanthropists, labor gratuitously for the sake of humanity; and their efforts have been crowned with so great success that the Government has had, comparatively, no trouble with the intelligent tribes, while the Indians themselves have suffered far less from bad management than heretofore. Their latest report (for the year 1871) bears this testimony to the success of the peace policy:

THE PEACE POLICY—ITS ADVANTAGES.

"Increased experience in dealing with the Indians only tends to confirm the board more and more in the wisdom of the policy of peace so uniformly advocated by the President, and supported by the liberality of Congress and the humane sympathies of the people; and the board confidently look forward to the day when the bitterness which now assails this policy in some parts of the United States, where it is least understood, will fill a page in history as unnatural and curious as that which records the old hatred against freedom and the friends of the slave."

The policy of confining the tribes strictly to their own reservations, and protecting them in the undisturbed possession of those reservations, is also a characteristic of the present Administration; and it is unquestionably an indispensable prerequisite of peace. Another innovation upon past practices, and one calculated to render the Indians more domestic and industrious, is the plan of subdividing their reservations into individual "eighties"—some heads of families thus getting several quarter-sections of land. This is done in the case of those (like the Creeks, Choctaws, etc.) manifesting any disposition favorable to husbandry.

But while holding out the olive-branch of peace to the red men, as our humane instincts tell us should be done, we all know that olive-branches will not do the business with *all* Indians and on *all* occasions. When the sword has been found to be necessary, General Grant has applied it vigorously. The very silly efforts made in behalf of certain treacherous and bloody Apaches by Vincent Colyer, an over-sentimental member of the Peace Commission, have apparently ceased to have any weight at Washington, and orders have now been issued to General Crook, who commands our troops in Arizona, and who understands the weaknesses of the Apache creatures, to proceed with them thoroughly and teach them a good lesson. The Sioux tribes, to the north of the Union Pacific Railway, inhabiting the valley of the Yellowstone, have also threatened to become belligerent, on account of the projection of the Northern Pacific road across the Northern limits of their allotted domain. To these went recently General B. R. Cowen, Assistant Secretary of the Interior, and other able men, composing a Commission; and it is certain that if the Sioux malcontents refuse to listen to the arguments and remonstrances of these men, they will smell powder promptly. The administration evidently realizes that; while you may well give the Indian to understand that you love him and care for him, it will not on any account do to have him understand that you fear him, or will yield to him when he makes a threat of force.

CHAPTER XIV.

GRANT AS PRESIDENT.

(CONTINUED.)

Grant and the Workingmen—Grant and Education—The Postal Telegraph System—Grant and the Colored Race—Down with Polygamy—Grant the Immigrant's Friend—Messages in their Behalf—Rights of Naturalized Citizens—The Houard Hubbub—Grant and San Domingo—How would Greeley have Worked it?—Grant and the Veto Power—Legislative Jobbery—Sumner's Vile Insinuations—Is the White House a Military Headquarters?—Sumner Put Down with a Plain Tale—Greeley's Tributes to Grant.

GRANT AND THE WORKINGMEN.

President Grant has not the special reputation as the workingman's friend which is enjoyed by his companion upon the National Republican ticket. He is evidently a friend of the laborer, but does not "howl about it," like some public men solicitous of votes. It is very cheap to declaim a little in behalf of the workingman, and then to go off and let him get his rights the best way he can. Grant talks but little in any behalf, yet he never has written a message without finding space for a word in behalf of labor. Here are extracts which show either that Grant is a statesman of comprehensive glance, or else that he has not forgotten the days when he was a working, studying tanner:

"By the late war, the industry of one-half of the country had been taken from the control of the capitalists and placed where all labor rightfully belongs—in the keeping of the laborer."

"The opinion that the public lands should be regarded chiefly as a source of revenue is no longer maintained. The rapid settlement and successful cultivation of them are now justly considered of more importance to our well-being than is the fund which the sale of them would produce. The remarkable growth and prosperity of our new States and Territories attest the wisdom of the legislation which invites the tiller of the soil to secure a permanent home on terms within the reach of all. The pioneer who incurs the dangers and privations of a frontier life, and thus aids in laying the foundation of new commonwealths, renders a signal service to his country, and is entitled to its special favor and protection. These laws secure that object, and largely promote the general welfare. They should, therefore, be cherished as a permanent feature of our land system."

"I renew my recommendation that the public lands be regarded as a heritage to our children, to be disposed of only as required for occupation and to actual settlers."

"The true prosperity and greatness of a nation is to be found in the elevation and education of its laborers."

Nor does Grant stop with saying to the workingmen, "Be ye warmed and filled." A few weeks ago a deputation of carpenters from New York—employed there upon the Government buildings—waited upon him at the White House. He listened to their requests, which were for a shortening of the hours of their labor. An act of Congress provided for this, and the President lost no time in seeing that the workingmen were endowed with all the rights to which they were entitled under it. It is, doubtless, his fidelity to their interests in several instances like this, as also his steady hand at the helm, which keeps the ship of State well righted and all her crew safe and comfortable, which makes the workingmen of the country so zealous and unanimous for Grant and Wilson—a ticket put in nomination by their organization at New York.

EDUCATION.

Popular education and the elevation of labor go hand in hand—a truism which the President has referred to in some of the extracts already quoted. But he has not stopped with "offering a few remarks" concerning the importance of education. He has proposed a definite measure of practical utility, in extending the blessings of learning—the plan of dividing the proceeds of the sales of public lands, already referred to in the paragraph referring to the policy toward the South.

POSTAL TELEGRAPH.

Allied to this subject in interest is the postal telegraph scheme, which is rather likely to come into operation on some scale or other, and under government patronage, before another year elapses. The privilege of rapid communication without the burden of an enormous tax for the nourishment of giant monopolies, is one of the essential concomitants of our civilization. It is enjoyed by nearly every prosperous European people, and must not be much longer withheld from the people of the United States. The adoption of postal telegraphy by our Government has for some time enlisted the sympathy and the effort of President Grant; and it should now, if he be at all interested in self, engage him all the more, since one of the earliest effects of a nearly free government telegraph would be to break down a monopoly in telegraph news which has enabled four or five bloated newspaper corporations to control certain strata of public opinion as despotically as the Khan of Tartary controls his subjects, and to use such control for the one grand purpose of disparaging Grant and the Republican party. Fortified in the strength which their monopoly of news gives them, these four or five corporations *command* the public ear—not win it by fair competition—and being responsible to nobody, use their power solely for their own private ends. They are the least democratic institution in the country; and a popularization of the telegraph, through the Government's efforts, is therefore needed in the interest of pure Republicanism.

GRANT AND THE NEGROES.

There has been a feeble effort on the part of the dectractors of President Grant, especially since they set up a candidate of their own for whom they hoped to attract some of the colored vote, to belittle Grant's work for the colored race. This effort has already failed, and the shafts of detraction have fallen harmless; for it has been shown by the record that Grant has been a true friend of the colored race; that he was active in their behalf long before the Emancipation Proclamation of Lincoln was issued; and that his course toward that people has been one of uniform and intelligent friendship. It will be referred to more in detail in a subsequent chapter.

PURSUING POLYGAMY.

The remaining one of those "twin relics of barbarism," slavery and polygamy, still curses a single territory of the Union. But its days are numbered; and General Grant, who evidently feels deeply the scandal and reproach upon our institutions, can comfort himself with a record on his own part, which has exhausted all the legitimate powers of the Executive office in the effort to root out the evil. His appointees to federal office in Utah have, unlike the most of their predecessors, been staunch opponents of polygamy, refusing to yield to the blandishments which have been thrown around them by the wily monarch of Mormondom. His judicial officers—one of them at least—may be charged with going a step beyond the bounds of judicial propriety in his attempt to throttle the monster of Polygamy. The attempt was worthy, so far as the motive was concerned; but the method formed a dangerous precedent, and when the President was asked to back it up by the interference of the strong Executive arm, he declined. It is a curious fact, however, that the Chicago *Tribune*—one of the journals which howls loudest about federal usurpation and arbitrary government—was continually urging on the Administration at Washington, and Judge McKeon at Salt Lake, to acts unquestionably despotic, arbitrary and unconstitutional. It is tolerably certain, however, that without such acts, and the demoralizing effects sure to follow them, the extermination of the vice of Polygamy will be accomplished within General Grant's second term. If so, it will be due to the Pacific Railroad—a Republican measure; the general statute against Polygamy—another Republican measure; and the staunch anti-barbarism and incorruptibility of President Grant's appointees to the Territorial offices.

GRANT AND THE IMMIGRANTS.

President Grant has interested himself, ever since entering upon the duties of the Presidency, in the amelioration of the condition of immigrants to our shores. The abuses which have been practiced upon these people have been manifold, whether on shipboard or at Castle Garden, where they are landed and forwarded to their destinations. The President has been prevented from doing much in their behalf, however, for these reasons; that for the abuses on ship-board, co-operation with foreign nations is necessary; while the Castle Garden distributing establishment is within the jurisdiction of the sovereign State of New York. The President has been active in his endeavors to make practical some reform. He gave Congress, in his first annual message, the following account of what had been done by himself in co-operation with the heads of other governments, from whose points the imigrant vessels principally sail:

" On the accession of the present Administration, it was found that the minister for North Germany had made propositions for the negotiation of a convention for the protection of emigrant passengers, to which no response had been given. It was concluded that, to be effectual, all the maritime Powers engaged in the trade should join in such a measure. Invitations have been extended to the cabinets of London, Paris, Florence, Berlin, Brussels, The Hague, Copenhagen, and Stockholm, to empower their representatives at Washington to simultaneously enter into negotiations, and to conclude with the United States, conventions identical in form, making uniform regu-ations as to the construction of the parts of vessels to be devoted to the use of emigrant passengers, as to the quality and quantity of food, as to the medical treatment of the sick, and as to the rules to be observed during the voyage, in order to secure ventilation, to promote health, to prevent intrusion, and to protect the females, and providing for the establishment of tribunals in the several countries, for enforcing such regulations by summary proccss."

In his message to the Forty-Second Congress at its last session, he continued to agitate this subject, the following paragraph:

"The number of immigrants ignorant of our laws, habits, etc., coming into our country annually has become so great, and the impositions practiced upon them so numerous and flagrant, that I suggest Congressional action for their protection. It seems to me a fair subject of legislation by Congress. I cannot now state as fully as I desire the nature of the complaints made by immigrants of the treatment they receive, but will endeavor to do so during the session of Congress, particularly if the subject should receive your attention."

And this was followed up on May 14 by a special message, in which the President wrote these earnest, philanthropic words:

"In my message to Congress, at the beginning of the present session, allusion was made to the hardships and privations inflicted on poor emigrants on board ship and upon their arrival on our shores, and a suggestion was made favoring national legislation for the purpose of effecting a radical cure of the evil. Promise was made that a special message on this subject would be presented during the present session, should information be received which would warrant it. I now transmit to the two Houses of Congress all that has been officially received since that time bearing on the subject, and recommend that such legislation be had as will secure—

"*First*, Such room and accommodation on shipboard as as is necessary for health and comfort, and such privacy as will not compel immigrants to be unwilling witnesses to so much vice and misery; and, *Second*, Legislation to protect them on their arrival at our seaports from knaves who are ever ready to dispoil them of the little they are able to bring with them.

"Such legislation will be in the interest of humanity, and seems to be fully justifiable. An immigrant is not a citizen of any State or Territory on his arrival, but comes here to become a citizen of our great republic, free to change his residence at will, to enjoy the blessings of a protecting government, where all are equal before the law, and to add to the national wealth by his industry. On his arrival he does not know States or corporations, but confides implicitly in the protecting arm of the great free country of which he has heard so much before leaving his native land.

"It is a source of serious disappointment and discouragement to those who start with means insufficient to support them comfortably until they can choose a residence and begin employment for a comfortable support, to find themselves subject to ill treatment and every discomfort on their passage here, and at the end of their journey seized on by professed friends, claiming the legal right to take charge of them for their protection, who do not leave them until all their resources are exhausted, when they are abandoned in a strange land, surrounded by strangers, without employment, and ignorant of the means of securing it. Under the present system this is the fate of thousands annually. The exposures on shipboard and the treatment on landing is driving thousands to lives of vice and shame who, with proper humane treatment, might become useful and respectable members of society.

"I do not advise national legislation in affairs that should be regulated by the States, but I see no subject more national in its character than provision for the safety and welfare of thousands who leave foreign lands to become citizens of this republic. When their residence is chosen they may then look to the laws of their locality for protection and guidance. The mass of immigrants arriving on our shores, coming as they do on vessels under foreign flags, make treaties with the nations furnishing these immigrants, necessary for their complete protection. For more than two years efforts have been made on our part to secure such treaties, and there is now reasonable ground to hope for success.

[Signed] U. S. GRANT."

POLICY TOWARD NATURALIZED CITIZENS.

Coupled with this interest in behalf of immigrants is a wise policy toward naturalized citizens, whose rights, as American citizens, the President stands ready at all times to vindicate. But he goes further than some of his predecessors have done, and declares that he will not hazard the rights of genuine American citizens, by interfering in behalf of those bogus American citizens who come to America and take out naturalization papers merely for the purpose of availing themselves of our government's jealous protection, while they return to their native country, "make believe" as loyal subjects of their renounced sovereign, and, all at once, when called upon for some service, or taken to task for violation of the laws of those lands, produce an American passport as their charter of freebootery. Of this class is (probably) the Doctor Houard, who has recently attracted some attention as an alleged American citizen deprived of his liberty by the Spanish Government. He has been operating almost exclusively, of late years, as a Cuban citizen (which means a Spanish subject), conspiring against the government under which he lived; and it is in his behalf that President Grant has been asked to call out the American Navy (which happens to be considerably weaker than the Spanish), and with it batter down the walls of Castle Moro, of Cadiz, and all other Spanish strongholds. It is more than probable that Houard is one of that class of whom Grant says, "While I have a voice in the direction of affairs, I shall not consent to imperil this sacred right [of citizenship] by conferring it upon fictitious or fraudulent claimants."

SAN DOMINGO.

The President's early enunciation of his purpose

as Chief Magistrate—"I shall on all subjects have a policy to *recommend*, but none to *enforce* against the will of the people"—received a marked illustration in his course concerning San Domingo. He saw, as he believed, a favorable opportunity for acquiring dominion over the western portion of that island. The necessity of a foothold in the West Indies, especially as a rendezvous and coaling station for our vessels of war, in case of hostilities along the Southern coast, or against any nation having such advantages, had been painfully manifest to all the officers concerned in the conduct of the government during the late war against the Rebels. The richness of the soil of San Domingo and the eagerness of the people to join our Republic, were also known to Grant; and upon the strength of these facts, he took the preliminary step toward the framing of a treaty with the President of the West Indian Republic—subject, of course, to ratification by the Senate of the United States and by a *plebiscite* of the Dominican people. Very warm opposition to the treaty was developed, however, in this country, especially in the Senate, where Charles Sumner made several of his famous philippics, accusing the President of all manner of high crimes and misdemeanors; and although a commission of honorable citizens, whom Congress sent thither to investigate the subject, pronounced unqualifiedly in favor of annexation, the President declined to push his project. Of course, he did not hesitate on account of Sumner's clamor; but

he had apparently become satisfied that the *people* were not yet ready for the annexation of any West Indian territory, and hence, he could not consistently insist upon his policy of annexation. Mr. Greeley would have done otherwise, if any of his agricultural or social crotchets had impelled him to undertake a similar enterprise; for he has often boasted his courage in "flying in the teeth of prejudice."

INTERFERENCE WITH LEGISLATION.

The veto power which the Constitution, for wise reasons vested in the President, has been used by Grant in only a few instances, and then never in the way of "enforcing a policy of his own" against the manifest sentiment of the country, or of its legislative representatives. Only a few weeks before the adjournment of the recent session of Congress, President Grant returned several bills without his approval. They were of the sort known as *jobs*—chiefly in behalf of certain claimants of damages growing out of the late war. There were a large number of these before Congress at its late session, and it looks as if in future sessions their number will be legion, unless the flood is checked by firm and hon est action on the part of Congress, the Executive, or both. Everybody at the South whose property was injured by the war, is now proposing to file claims for damages. The aggregate would be many hundred millions—a doubling up of the national debt, may be. The Court of Claims will not allow them, and the claimants besiege Congress, relying on the practice of "log-rolling" to push through their bills and get them allowed. That is, every Southern member is obliged to vote for all the bills presented by every other Southern member, because each has a set of bills of a similar nature, of his own, none of which could go through on their merits, and hence all must join interests, or "log-roll" together, in order to secure the necessary vote. Nor will this be sufficient unless the Southerners combine with such Northern and Western members as have local jobs to push through—harbor improvements, post-office buildings, railroad land grants, etc., and who, by "hitching horses" with the Southern members, fasten still another lot of disreputable jobs upon the national treasury. The better sense of every honest Congressman is against this, yet it takes a very large measure of personal and official honor to resist the temptation to log-roll, when the local interests which the Congressman is supposed mainly to represent depend so directly upon such combinations. It is thus that jobs get through Congress in spite of the honest judgment of that body; and until some effective legal prohibition for log-rolling is devised (and this is one of the duties with which the Republican party must charge itself) the country must depend upon the Executive for occasional timely interferences, through the exercise of the veto power. We have already pretty nearly scotched out the Land Grant iniquity (to which Horace Greeley, and against which the Republican Party, is committed) and the most threatening development of the log-rolling evil now manifesting itself is the Southern War Claims. But for the timely intervention of the veto by President Grant during the latest days of the last session of Congress, several grossly improper claims would have been legalized by Congress, and dangerous precedents established, which might have swept millions out of the Treasury.

GRANT'S "MILITARY RING."

Probably the loudest of all the clamor made by the jealous Senators and their newspaper *claqueurs* against President Grant is that which refers to his employment of three detailed military officers to help do the office work of the White House. It must be understood, in the first place, that Grant has made the effort, as a rule, to fill his cabinet places, and also such minor offices as came directly within his purview, with men whom he *knew* to be personally trustworthy, instead of men who were recommended by the politicians as "persons to be provided for." This is the very essence of the much-sighed-for civil service reform; and yet it is the very thing in President Grant's management about which the *soi disant* reformers have howled the most savagely. In the next place, it should be remembered that the clerical work of the Executive office has increased enormously since the war brought into existence an army of 60,000 officials throughout the country; and that the growth of the country itself, and the increase of traveling facilities, rendering it convenient for a hundred men to visit the national capitol where one visited it twenty years ago, have also contributed to multiply the duties of those who keep the office of the country's Chief Magistrate. At the same time, the law has made no provision for a corresponding increase of the *personnel* of the White House. This difficulty has had to be got over by General Grant and his immediate predecessors as best it could.

So much being premised, we will quote a paragraph from the famous philippic of Charles Sumner, in the United States Senate, on the 30th of May, 1872—a speech which may be fitly pronounced the most scurrilous and venomous—the greatest elaboration of eloquence upon the smallest basis of facts—ever perpetrated in that chamber. Said Sumner, attempting to epitomize in a paragraph for campaign use, the principal allegation against President Grant:

"The military spirit which failed in the effort to set aside a fundamental law as if it were a transient order, was more successful at the Executive Mansion, which at once assumed the character of military headquarters. To the dishonor of the civil service, and in total disregard of precedent, the President surrounded himself with officers of the army, and substituted military forms for those of civil life, detailing for this service members of his late staff."

To which Senator Carpenter replied, as soon as he could obtain a copy of Mr. Sumner's tirade—held back from the Senate, though printed and circulated amongst the anti-Republican press many days before:

"I propose to consider several of the articles of impeachment which are set in array by the Senator's speech against the President. And first let me consider the charge that the President has turned the Executive Mansion into a military headquarders. What are the facts? Three officers of the army may be found in the White House. Babcock, a major of engineers, detailed in pursuance of an act of Congress to act as commissioner of public buildings and grounds; and Dent and Porter, officers belonging to the staff of General Sherman. Three more modest and courteous gentlemen cannot be found in the United States. They were members of General Grant's military family during the war, and they love him, as do all those who have ever served with him. In so far as they can assist the President, it is with them a labor of love to do so, and only a labor of love, for neither one of them receives one cent of compensation for such service. If they were all dismissed from the White House to-day, Babcock would have an office in some other public building, and receive the same salary as at present. Dent and Porter would be occupying rooms in the War Department, dividing with other assistants of General Sherman labor not very severe in these piping times of peace, and which would be lighter still when still further divided. It has been attempted by the Senator to exalt these gentlemen into some official importance; but they are merely clerks at the White House, assisting the President, with the permission of General Sherman, their official chief; and here let me repeat that neither of them receives a cent for such assistance beyond his pay as an officer of the army.

"Now for the precedents. General Washington appointed General Knox, his old comrade in arms, Secretary of War; General Jackson was assisted by Major Donalson; General Taylor by his son-in-law, Colonel Bliss, and President Johnson by four officers of the army, detailed for service at the White House."

THE FACT ABOUT GRANT.

The fact is, President Grant is much simpler and less military in his habits as President than Andrew Johnson was, notwithstanding the demagoguery of the latter led him to affect a great many extreme democratic notions. Senator Carpenter is authority for the following statement illustrative of this fact:

"When General Grant took possession of the White House it was patrolled by sentinels day and night; so was the War Department; so was the residence of Mr. Seward. The first night General Grant slept at the President's

House, after retiring, he heard the tramp of soldiers in the hall below, and presently the command, 'Halt; order arms,' and the crash of muskets on the floor. The General, not knowing what it meant, ran down stairs to ascertain. There he found an officer in command of a squad of soldiers; and on asking an explanation, the General was informed that it was the night guard of the Executive Mansion, which for a long time had been stationed there every night. But General Grant informed the officer that he could take care of himself, and ordered him to take his soldiers to their quarters. He waited till his armed friends had left, then locked the door and went to bed. The next day the whole business of sentinal service was discontinued, and not a soldier has been on duty at the White House since. General Grant also ordered away from Washington all the companies of soldiers which were on duty here when he was inaugurated; and not a company of troops can now be found in or around Washington city."

In the light of these facts, the eloquent Senator, quoting the language of Sumner, which we have transcribed above, continues:

"Allow me to call attention again to the precise language; and here let me repeat that this speech of the Senator from Massachusetts is not to be estimated as you would estimate a speech thrown off in the heat of an extempore debate. This wrath was carefully distilled; this speech was prepared with great and protracted labor.

"Here is a deliberate arraignment, and what is here is either deliberate truth or deliberate falsehood; one or the other. When he alleges, as he does here, that "to the dishonor of the civil service and in total disregard of precedent, the President surrounded himself with officers of the Army, and substituted military forms for those of civil life, detailing for this service members of his late staff," the Senator from Massachusetts penned, revised, corrected, printed, published, sent to the world a deliberate truth or a deliberate falsehood. Which was it? Was there no precedent for his being served by a few clerks who were willing to aid him without pay, from mere personal affection? Did not Andrew Johnson have four Army officers detailed for service in the White House? Had not Andrew Johnson been surrounded with sentinels and the White House guarded like a military fortress; and in all the complaints that were made against Andrew Johnson, did any man charge him with violating the law in having his house protected at night by sentinels? Was any complaint made upon the ground that three or four Army officers were serving him in the capacity of clerks in the White House? If there was, I never heard of it, and yet we know that in that heated and angry time those who opposed Andrew Johnson were not over-scrupulous about the charges they brought against him, and still such a thing was never laid to his charge, although, as I have shown, instead of what has been done, and is being done now, being without a precedent, it is less in every respect than was done during the entire administration of Mr. Johnson without criticism from anybody whatever.

"But again, this is a charge not only that the Executive Mansion has assumed the character of military headquarters, but that he has substituted military forms for those of civil life. I take it to be the duty of this Senate, I take it to be the duty of the members of the other House, I take it to be the duty of all lovers of truth and justice, who reside for a portion of the year in Washington, and know the facts, to bear testimony to the American people whether this arraignment of President Grant is a truth or a falsehood. Senators, how has the White House been made to assume the character of military headquarters? Do you encounter any sentinel at the door? Do you see any orderly on the stairs? Do you see a gun or a musket or a shoulder-strap in the White House from top to bottom? Not one. The whole charge is baseless as a dream."

GRANT AT THE HEAD OF HIS CABINET.

None have the temerity to accuse Grant of being a demagogue; yet it is quite common to hear him blamed with being in the hands of political tricksters, who shape his administration for party ends. Hear the testimony, upon this point of the Hon. E. Rockwood Hoar, who was Attorney General under Grant, and whose word is authority absolute. Said Judge Hoar, in a recent speech in Faneuil Hall:

"I presume I am in part indebted for the honor of the invitation to come here to the fact, that for one year and part of another, I had the honor of being a participator in the councils of his Administration, and I desire to testify, and I believe that what I say in Massachusetts will be accepted as fact, that during the whole period in which I was in the Cabinet councils I never heard any measure of the Administration discussed or considered except with a single reference to the public interest. I never heard a personal suggestion in regard to his influence upon one man or another man, but the consideration simply was what would be best for the country. And when I remember the simple, clear-headed, practical, modest man, who sat at the head of the table there, and then hear him talked of by Mr. Sumner, I think Mr. Sumner must be referring to somebody else."

Perhaps we cannot better close this chapter than by incorporating in it some of the many tributes paid to Grant's success as Chief Magistrate, by his present opponent in the presidential contest—the first of them from a speech delivered after General Grant had made up his record as President; the second printed in the New York *Tribune* in February, 1871; and the last contained in Mr. Greeley's speech in New York, January 5th, 1871, and before he took that famous Southern trip which stirred up the Presidential bee in his own bonnet.

Said Horace Greeley:

"Upon General Grant's accession to the presidency, a great number of those who had supported his election, with some who had not, sought office at his hands, or expected him to bestow it unasked. He was unable to gratify their aspirations. Their lamentations, mingled with the howls of the disappointed, made up a very doleful dissonance, whereof the only meaning deducible runs thus: 'General Grant is found wanting—his administration is a failure.' 'Failure?' how? in what? Have we not peace and plenty in the land? Is not our flag displayed and respected on every sea? What foreign foe molests or threatens us? Who fears insurrection at home or invasion from abroad? Yes; General Grant has failed to gratify some eager aspirations, and has thereby incurred some intense hatreds. These do not and will not fail; and his administration will prove at least equally vital. We shall hear lamentation after lamentation over his failures from those whose wish is father to the thought; but the American people let them pass unheeded. Their strong arm bore him triumphantly through the war and into the White House, and they still uphold and sustain him."

Said Horace Greeley again:

"We like General Grant; but we care far more for Republican ascendency than for any man's personal fortunes. It is, in our view, of great importance that the opposition shall be kept out of power, while it is of comparatively small moment that A or B should tenant the White House: for a Democratic national triumph means a restoration to power of those who deserted their seats in Congress and their places under the last Democratic President to plunge the country into the Red Sea of secession and rebellion. Though you paint an inch thick, to this complexion you must come at last. The brain, the heart, the soul, of the present Democratic party is the Rebel element of the South, with its Northern allies and sympathizers."

Said Horace Greeley, further:

"As to the administration of General Grant, I recognize no one as a Republican who is not grateful for its judicious, energetic and successful efforts to procure the ratification of the Fifteenth Amendment, that keystone of our political arch, whereby the fruits of our great triumph over rebellion and slavery are assured and perpetuated.

"That the President has made some mistakes in appointments is obvious—it would be strange, indeed, if one so inexperienced in the conduct of political affairs had wholly escaped them. Whatever blame may justly attach to this, falls rightfully on us, who took him from the head of the army and made him our civil chief magistrate, fully aware that he had never voted a Republican ticket, if, indeed, he had voted at all. While asserting the right of every Republican to his untrammeled choice of a candidate for next President until a nomination is made, I venture to suggest that General Grant *will be far better qualified for that momentous trust in* 1872 *than he was in* 1868. Such, gentlemen, are the ideas and convictions which have compelled me to take my place among you, and accept the responsibility you have imposed upon me [Chairman of a Republican Central Committee.]. Let us take care to act with substantial unanimity, and with such evident moderation and fairness that our friends throughout the State and the Union shall see and feel that we are doing our utmost to *unite and strengthen the Republican party*, and animate it with well-grounded and sanguine hopes of future triumphs."

CHAPTER XV.

GRANT AS A MAN.

Some Personal Traits—A Glance at the White House—The President's Daily Programme—Grant's Personal Appearance—His Habits—His Conversation—A Little Story—His Mental and Moral Qualities—A Friendly Portrait—How the Painter Came Afterward to be Unfriendly—Grant and Sumner Contrasted.

This chapter will be devoted mainly to the personal traits of President Grant, though some portions of it will necessarily have a close connection with the matter of the two previous chapters, inasmuch as it will be a running sketch, from observation, of how he carries himself in the White House, which is at once his office and his home.

THE WHITE HOUSE.

The reader will suppose himself to be on a visit to that great cynosure of American eyes, and goal of American ambitions, the White House, and to be armed with such letters, or escort, or personal fame, as shall secure his introduction to the Chief Magistrate. Not much is required in this way—merely enough to keep downright idlers and adventurers from occupying the President's time to the exclusion of those who have some business with him. You seek out the Executive Mansion, located on Pennsylvania Avenue, just west of the magnificent Treasury Building, and opposite the luxuriantly growing Lafayette Park. A broad, semi-circular walk admits you through the grounds of the Mansion, which is found to be a fine, spacious edifice, with over a hundred feet of front, built of freestone painted white, and adorned with plain, heavy, round columns, enclosing a roomy portico, with driveway and landing for carriages. Inside, the impression is not remarkably pleasant. The halls are vast and reachy, and the main reception room, directly at the left of the front entrance, is usually quite deserted, except by occasional stragglers. Here, however, on certain days of the week, the promiscuous public is received by the President and his lady. This room is richly furnished, and its eight immense pier glass mirrors are interspersed with as many portraits of former hosts of the White House, all of them smartly framed, but not all well painted. At the foot of the broad staircase, you encounter one or more ushers, apparently of the Celtic race, and quite affable, though not otherwise prepossessing. They are utterly devoid of everything which could be construed into "style" or "pomp"—no livery, no ceremony, no look, even, of the trained house servant. Indeed, these fellows appear as if they were but recently broken into this duty, and that their latest calling had been farming, or teaming, perhaps.

Up stairs—whither any one goes who assumes the right to go—another reception room is reached, wherein are usually found throughout the forenoon and until two or three o'clock, an average of half a dozen gentlemen, awaiting their turn for an audience with the President. You seat yourself among them and hand your card, or your letters, to General Frederic Dent, one of those shameful brothers-in-law of whom we hear so much, who acts as chamberlain, or usher-in-chief. Dent is genial and withal a trifle loquacious, so that few visitors fail to be entertained in some way. Your card is taken in to the President, who sits in the Cabinet chamber, and you await the result, as the rest are doing.

"IMPERIALISM" ILLUSTRATED.

The waiting room you discover to be also an office for two or three clerks. To the rear of it is a hall or ante-room, in which are two more servants. These are colored, fat, ungainly and illy-dressed; and the visitor begins to inquire in his own mind where is that imperial pomp—that military parade—which Mr. Sumner's speeches had led him to expect. Not here, certainly. We will wait and get a glimpse of it as we approach the Executive presence itself. If we are a Cabinet Minister, a Senator, a Congressman or a high bureau officer, we go into the Cabinet Chamber without much ceremony—perhaps through the office of Gens. Porter and Babcock, which flanks the Cabinet Chamber and communicates with it. The forenoon hours are ostensibly devoted to the privileged characters named, all of whom have legitimately much business with the Executive; but Grant manages to sandwich in a considerable number of lay visitors between the official callers.

IN THE CABINET CHAMBER.

Supposing such to be your opportunity. You pass into the chamber, hallowed by hundreds of state meetings of gravest moment, like that when Lincoln presented a draft of his immortal Proclamation for the consideration of his Cabinet; and you feel, most likely, an awe begotten of such associations. Nor is this lessened by the thought that you was now in the presence of the Chief Magistrate of a great nation, and the most succesful of modern generals. That is he, at the further end of the long table. Perhaps his face disappoints you; for it is thicker and a shade older than the prints show him, or than you recollect him, in the hand-shaking days, just after the war, or perhaps it is his stature, which is a trifle below the medium height. His face is ruddy, his beard close-cropped, as usual, and his straight brown hair is combed back with scrupulous care, but no grace. He throws a glance at you with his quick, clear, deep eyes—they are blue and liquid, but capable of piercing like a poniard—and seems to be satisfied with your measure at once.

GRANT IN CONVERSATION.

You are asked to sit, and conversation commences at once. Here you make another discovery, viz: that Grant is not the sphinx which Mr. Sumner and other detractors have painted him. He manifests an intelligent interest in his visitor's affairs, or, if the talk take a public turn, expresses himself freely on the questions of public moment. The writer cannot forbear an illustration of this from his own experience, which also shows that Grant is not destitute of the story-telling faculty which distinguished Abraham Lincoln, even while occupying the same chair.

The conversation had drifted into politics and the question was propounded of Greeley's ability to win over the Democratic party to his support. The President did not answer this categorically; but he was reminded of "a little story," which served the same purpose.

"Shortly after the close of the war," he said (and we quote Grant's language, as nearly as possible, from memory) "and before much had been learned about the way Southern society was going to settle down, I sent these two young men, Generals Porter and Babcock, down through the Gulf States on a tour of observation. In some places, the planters, anxious to produce a good impression, got up meetings of the colored folks and had speeches made, by way of inaugurating an 'era of good feeling,' or showing that one had already commenced. At one of these meetings, the principal planter in the place harangued the boys (with one word for them and two for Porter and Babcock), telling how the war had changed the relations between the masters and the slaves: but that they (the masters) were still the natural guardians of the negro people, etc. 'We accept the situation,' he said; 'the South is whipped and the slaves are free. But they are going to stick to their old friends. Ain't they, Tom?' said he, speaking to an old colored man who, he thought, was on his side.

"But Tom didn't see it in the same light as the master, exactly. And so Tom addressed the meeting. He said 'he'd been to a great many meetin's afore, and seed a great many folks get converted; but he noticed that when they did that, they always jined de church, and didn't ask de church to jine them.'"

The inference was that if Greeley had been converted to Democracy, the natural course, as it would appear to the members of that flock, would be for him to join the Democratic church, and not ask the church to join him.

GRANT NO IMITATOR.

Grant will not probably, however, establish a reputation as a story-teller, if for no other reason than because he would dislike to seem to be an imitator, even of Lincoln. A high officer of the national government, whose station brought him near to the Presidents (and from whom we have the incident directly), took occasion, during the early months of his administration, to drop hints of how Lincoln used to do this and how he did not do that. Grant bore this a little while, but finally stopped it with "Well, now, you know, Mr. ———, that I can't be Lincoln if I try ever so hard. I think I had better be myself, and do the best I can." This shows—not that Grant did not hold Lincoln high in esteem as a model—for he is a great admirer of that statesman—but that he recognized the truth of the maxim that "no man is ever great by imitation."

PHYSICAL CHARACTERISTICS AND HABITS.

General Grant again disappoints his visitor (at first) in his voice, which is low and almost croaking—not the bluff, hearty voice which one expects to find in a soldier. Nevertheless it is the voice for a President to have—that is, which goes with the qualities necessary in a good Executive. It indicates—and correctly—a man not obtrusive with his thoughts or opinions until he has got all he needs of the thoughts and opinions of others. It indicates the man who husbands his energies, as he must do who plods through the enormous amount of work now incumbent on a faithful American President, and yet seem to have plenty of leisure. It indicates the studious man, who goes to the bottom of every question presented to him, nor shrinks from puzzling long, if necessary, over any knotty question of fact or law. The peculiar quality of Grant's voice soon ceases to attract his visitor's notice, which is absorbed in the matter of his speech.

Before leaving President Grant's physical and

superficial characteristics, we may mention a fact or two concerning his daily habits. These are not noticeable, except for their simplicity and their very lack of noticeable features. Rising at about the average hour of his fellow citizens of the sedentary or professional class, President Grant breakfasts simply and is ready for business as soon as the public or the officials having transactions with him, can arrive for the purpose. He sits in the Cabinet Chamber until well into the afternoon, after which, having lunched lightly, he usually drives—oftener single than otherwise—in a modest little buggy and behind a young bay mare, which General Dent extols, but which an Iowa horse fancier, who has lately inspected the President's stud, pronounces not much above the ordinary. We will, however, pay enough deference to Grant's judgment of horseflesh to place the colt on record as one of the best of her race.

After this drive, which occupies, perhaps, two hours, the President occupies himself miscellaneously until dinner time. This meal is often shared with guests, usually at the White House informally. The President's dinners are good, but not elaborately bountiful. For company there are usually two courses of wine, in which the President indulges, if at all, very abstemiously—merely tasting his glass for sociality's sake. After dinner, in summer, comes a walk, oftener solitary than otherwise; though, of course, so conspicuous a man is constantly receiving greetings from those whom he does or does not know. His evenings, in time of

SHAKESPEARE ON THE DEMOCRATIC SITUATION.

ANTONIO. G——Y.—Well, Shylock, shall I be beholden to you?
SHYLOCK. B——T.—Signor Horatio, many a time, and oft

You call us liars, villains, cut-throat dogs,—
Well, then, it now appears you need our help.
What should I say to you? Should I not say

Congress, are devoted to hard work upon bills, letters, and other dry and laborious details, which often keep the President employed far into the night. He is represented as a most assiduous worker, never affixing his name to a paper whose contents he has not carefully investigated. With such habits, it is not to be wondered at that the man suffers occasionally from neuralgia; but this ailment has not increased since his undertaking the duties of Executive. His much smoking, which is often alluded to, seems to be, as in many cases it undoubtedly is, a necessity, or, at least, no bane, of his physical system; just as, in other cases, it is a rank poison.

GRANT AT CHURCH.

Grant is a regular attendant at church, to which he walks, when accompanied by his family, through the church—the Metropolitan Methodist—is about a mile distant from the White House. His dress has nothing noticeable about it; his aim being evidently to follow the style of his fellow citizens, just as that of his rival in the present political campaign has been to be unlike the rest of mankind in affecting a long white coat and a general studied negligence of attire. Grant is by no means a showy person in a crowd—his short, stooping form and downcast look and the general commonness of his mien failing to seize the eye of the passer-by.

GRANT'S INTELLECT AND TEMPERAMENT.

When we consider U. S. Grant's mental and

moral characteristics, we discover more which pertains to the great general and succesful President. And even of these it is probably the perfect balance of all, rather than the special development of any one, which has brought their possessor such uniform success. Grant's temperament is a combination of the various orders, though perhaps the phlegmatic predominates; and his intellectual qualities seem constructed, like his physical, for enduring great and long-continued pressure. Those who have been much with him have almost incredible accounts to give of his capacity for carrying on several mental operations at the same time; as of hearing a report from an officer, and writing simultaneously an important order on a totally different subject; and of retaining in his mind all the details pertaining to a great battle, without a past event misplaced, or a singular particular of his plans crowded out or jostled in the least. His mathematical mind seems never to become confused, and his impulses are so balanced by judgment as never to step in and upset the plans which his calculation had arranged.

A TRIBUTE FROM AN ENEMY.

Some of the points of General Grant's character are thus sketched, apparently from life, after careful study, and we reproduce them here with especial relish, since they were endorsed, (if not written), by Mr. Charles A. Dana, of the New York *Sun*, who has since, for reasons which the public understand pretty well, become one of the most unscrupulous of Grant's traducers:

"There is no noise or clash or clamor in the man; his voice is as quiet and orderly as a woman's, and his language judiciously chosen. He was never heard to give utterance to a rude word or vulgar jest; no oath or fierce, fiery imprecation has ever escaped his lips. No thundering order, no unfeeling or undignified speech; and no thoughtless or ill-natured criticism ever fell from him. When angry, which is rarely the case, or, at least, he rarely shows his anger, he speaks with well-ordered but sbudued vehemence, displaying his passion by compressed lips and an earnest flash of the eye. But it must be said of him that of all men he is the slowest to anger. He has been heard to say that under the severest insult he never became indignant till a week after the offence had been given, and then only at himself for not having sooner discovered that he had been insulted or misused. This arises rather from an unconscious self-abnegation than from any incapacity for choler.

"It is precisely this quality which has made him so successful in the personal questions which have arisen between him and his subordinates. They have usually mistaken his slowness for dullness or a lack of spirit, and have discovered their mistake only after having become rash and committing a fatal error. Grant is unsuspicious and pure-hearted as a child, and as free from harmful intention; but he is stirred to the very depths of his nature by an act of inhumanity or brutality of any sort; while meanness, or ingratitude, or uncharitableness, excites him to the display of the liveliest indignation. He is not slow in his exhibition of disgust for whatever is unmanly or unbecoming."—*Dana's Life of Grant.*

The same writer goes on to dilate upon Grant's habits, tastes, and mental characteristics; and though the picture is apparently tinted with warm personal admiration, it cannot be said, by those who know the subject, that it is over-drawn.

"Grant's personal habits and tastes are exceedingly simple; he despises the pomp and show of empty parade, and in his severe simplicity and manly pride he scorns all adventitious aids to popularity. He lives plainly himself, and cannot tolerate ostentation or extravagance in those about him. His mess was never luxuriously, though always bountifully furnished with army rations, and such supplies as could be transported readily and easily in the limited number of wagons that he permitted to follow his headquarters. His appetites are all under perfect control. He is very abstemious, and during his entire Western campaign the officers of his staff were forbidden to bring wines or liquors into camp. He has been represented as one of the most taciturn of men, and in one respect he is such. He never divulges his thoughts till they are matured, and never aspires to speech-making; and even in private conversation he falls into silence if he suspects that he is likely to be reported. He is the most modest of men, and nothing more annoys him than a loud parade of personal opinion or personal vanity; but with his intimate friends, either at home or around the camp fire, he talks upon all subjects, not only fluently but copiously, but in the most charming and good natured manner. His life has been too busy to read history or technical works, but he has always been a close and careful reader of the newspapers. He has a retentive memory, and is deeply interested in all matters which concern the interests of humanity, and particularly his own country. Upon all such subjects, in fact, upon all the vital questions of the day, he thinks carefully and profoundly, and expresses himself with great ease and good sense. His understanding is that of incisive character that soon probes a question to the bottom, no matter how much the politicians or newspapers may labor to confuse it, while his judgment is so deliberate, honest, and truthful in its operations, that it may be implicitly relied upon to arrive at a fair and unbiased conclusion."

THE MILK IN SOME COCOA NUTS ACCOUNTED FOR.

It may be timely to remark that this panegyric was not succeeded by denunciation from the same source until its author had personal reasons, not entirely unconnected with a rejected application for a federal appointment, for maligning the man whom he had so unqualifiedly praised. And here another quotation from Grant's colloquial talk is in order. During the same interview at which the story about the Southern planter and his negroes was told, a Virginia gentleman came in for the purpose of reporting to the President the state of politics in the Old Dominion. The defection of Ex-Governor Pierrepont, in West Virginia, was referred. To the President interrupted with a remark which seemed more tempered with the pleasure of having discovered a rule or a fact in human nature than with any feeling of personal resentment. "It is a curious fact," he observed, "that in nearly every one of these cases of disaffection among Republicans, the man's action can be traced directly to some motive entirely personal to himself—usually the refusal of office to himself or some of his particular friends"; and he proceeded to mention other cases besides that of the West Virginia Ex-Governor. It is a fact that the names of seven out of every nine of the members of the Cincinnati Convention appear upon the books at the White House as applicants for office.

GRANT'S LEARNING.

It cannot be claimed in behalf of General Grant that he is deeply read in abstruse sciences, even in those which Mr. Sumner would consider indispensable to statesmanship; but it is true that he is no ignoramus in such matters, and that what technical knowledge he does possess is not so much a damage to him, as that possessed by some of his enemies and rivals is to them. A President should not be a theorist or a book-worm. His lore should not be gulped down from musty books, where it was distilled full-flavored—and, perhaps, poisoned in the flavoring—years, perhaps ages, before. It should be gathered, as the bee gathers its honey, in actual contact with men. Thus acquired, it is assimilated with the judgment and becomes a faculty of instantaneous perception—an instinct, almost. The difference between Grant's life and that of such a man as Charles Sumner, is expressed in these opposite sets of circumstances. While Sumner, born to plenty and reared in an atmosphere of scholarship and semi-aristocratic ease, became at once a book-worm, and learned nothing of men, because he never came in contact with but a single point of their natures, Grant was thrown from the first among practical affairs, and passed through an almost unintermitting school of human life and experience, calculated to develop those *practical* qualities essential to a good Executive. While Sumner was immersed in books, books, books, Grant was everywhere encountering men, men, men; studying their strong and their weak points, and learning lessons from both. That he improved his opportunities is shown from the quickly, keenly penetrating "common sense" which he, as President, has brought to bear, almost unerringly, upon the questions of state which have presented themselves for his solution. A man of practical common sense, and of well-balanced impulses is better in the President's chair than a man who has Vattel at his tongue's end and Grotius dog's-eared in his library.

CHAPTER XVI.

GRANT AND THE COLORED RACE.

The Real Question for the Colored Man's Consideration—Grant's Record as to Treatment of Negroes—Early Orders, Letters, Etc.—He Shuts Down at Donelson upon Fugitive Slave Hunters—Issues Practical Military Orders in Behalf of Freedmen in Advance of the Government—Organizes the First Freedmen's Bureau—Encourages the Formation of Negro Regiments—Favors a Negroes' Paradise at Milliken's Bend—His Expressions as President—Appointments of Colored Men to Office, Etc.

Considerable effort has been made by the partisans of Mr. Greeley to excite among the colored voters some jealousy of Grant, and thereby make votes for Greeley, whom they propose to foist upon the negroes by means of his old anti-slavery record. The argument which these sophists use against General Grant is, that he was not known as an Abolitionist before the war. They also make an assertion, founded upon no trustworthy authority which can be discovered, that Grant expressed himself, early in the war, in decided opposition to emancipation as an object of the war. But even if this apocryphal assertion should be proven, it will not go very far, since Abraham Lincoln, whom the negroes justly regard as the particular benefactor of their race, expressed himself, less than a month before issuing his preliminary Emancipation

Proclamation, as in great doubt of the correctness of that policy.

THE REAL QUESTION.

But be these things as they may, it will be generally admitted that the main question for colored voters now is, who has actually shown in his *acts* the most friendship for our race? Who is *now* with our friends, and who with our enemies? If Grant is the representative of the party which emancipated the colored race from slavery, and which now favors their elevation to the highest functions of citizenship, he is the colored man's candidate *par excellence*. If Horace Greeley, no matter what his past record may be, is *now* acting with the party of the slave-holder, the party of the Ku-Klux, and the party of Rebel rights as against national power and loyalty, then Mr. Greeley is the man for the colored voter to help defeat as effectually as Mc Clellan was defeated in 1864, or Seymour in 1868.

Nevertheless, it is worth while to look over General Grant's record as to the colored race, since it is found not merely to corroborate his present favorable attitude toward the race, but also shows that Grant was one of the negro's earliest, staunchest, most practicably valuable friends. And in doing so, we shall use, in the main, the language of a colored citizen of Washington, who has made the matter the subject of careful investigation. Writing in reply to an article in the personal organ of Governor Warmoth, of Louisiana, obviously written for the purpose of misleading the minds of the black population on this subject, he brings up the following facts:

THE PROCLAMATION OF LINCOLN—GRANT'S EARLY ACTION.

Mr. Lincoln, in his proclamation, warned the Rebels that he would, on the first day of January following, proclaim emancipation in those States where the people shall be in rebellion against the United States. That glorious proclamation he accordingly issued; but Kentucky, Tennessee and portions of Louisiana and Virginia were not included in it.

General Grant commanded the armies which were moving southward from Cairo and operating in Territory affected and unaffected by the proclamation. I find by consultation with an ex-officer in that army, who knew all the orders issued, that General Grant was always up with or in advance of authority furnished from Washington, in regard to the treatment of persons of color, then slaves.* Thus a large number of the Blacks, through

*The following order, issued at Fort Donelson as early as February, 1862, is an evample:

"HEADQUARTERS DISTRICT OF WEST TENNESSEE,
"FORT DONELSON, Feb. 26, 1862.

"General Orders, No. 14.

"I. General Order No. 3, series 1861, from headquarters department of the Missouri, is still in force and must be observed. The necessity of its strict enforcement is made apparent by the numerous applications from citi-

his orders, were furnished employment within his lines, or transportation to homes and places of comfort for themselves and families, and education for their children, in the North. And when he reached northern Mississippi, or the region where the people of color were more numerous, I find that he issued, November 11, 1862,—before the emancipation proclamation, and before authority was furnished from Washington, and solely on his own conviction of the military necessity and right,—an order caring for the "contrabands."

THE FIRST FREEDMEN'S BUREAU.

Those of the negroes fleeing from slavery had been not inaptly designated contrabands of war by General Butler. Those of us who participated in or witnessed these scenes can recall with sufficient vividness the exodus from slavery to liberty through the Federal lines wherever the soldiers in blue appeared. General Grant saw the demoralizing effect upon the army of thousands of men, women and

zens for permission to pass through the camps to look for fugitive slaves. In no case whatever will permission be granted to citizens for this purpose.

"II. All slaves at Fort Donelson at the time of its capture, and all slaves within the line of military occupation that have been used by the enemy in building fortifications, or in any manner hostile to the Government, will be employed by the quartermaster's department for the benefit of the Government, and will under no circumstances be permitted to return to their masters.

"III. It is made the duty of all officers of this command to see that all slaves above indicated are promptly delivered to the chief quartermaster of the district.

"BY ORDER OF BRIG. GENERAL U. S. GRANT.

"JOHN A. RAWLINS, A. A. G."

children pouring through the camps. He recognized, too, the humane considerations which would not allow even in those disturbed and fearful scenes, the starvation of those negroes, in regard to whom, as slaves, the Government had not yet fixed its policy Selecting an officer for the purpose, in special orders No. 15, dated Headquarters 13th Army Corps, Department of the Tennessee, Lagrange, Tenn., Nov. 11th, 1862, he directed this officer to "take charge of the contrabands who came into the camp, organize them into suitable companies for work, see that they were properly cared for, and set them to work." He ordered suitable guards detailed for their protection, and the officer to report to him in person. He followed this with ample orders to the Commissary General and Quartermaster General for the issue of rations, clothing for men, women and children, and implements necessary for use in their labor.

In General Orders No. 13, dated Headquarters 13th Army Corps, Department of the Tennessee, Oxford, Miss., 17th Dec., 1862—still a month before the Emancipation Proclamation—he made the same officer, Colonel John Eaton, Jr., General Superintendent of these affairs for the Department, with authority to designate assistants—and, in a word, increasing his authority, specifying more fully the details of his duties, the kind of labor in which the contrabands were to be employed, and enforcing their compensation. They were to fill every position occupied by the soldier, save what depended upon his enlistment. Their wives and children were to be cared for and given employment also as far as possible.

Indeed, looking over a report of the General Superintendent, which was printed in the winter of 1865, and favorably received by the *North American. Review*, I find that each military post came to have an office, and that office had one officer to care for supplies furnished them, another for the enforcement of justice in their behalf, another for their medical attendance, another for their education. All abandoned property was ordered to be used for them. In all these benefits, it is to be noticed, white refugees shared also.

Here was the full germ of the Freedmen's Bureau apparent in the orders of General Grant before the Emancipation Proclamation, not as a theory, but as a practical solution of the relation of slaves in the South to the suppression of the rebellion, and in the interest of the welfare of all concerned. Here, in the midst of the terrible scenes of war, still slaves so far as law and the action of Government are concerned, the poor fugitives were, as far as possible, protected in their families and lives, sheltered and clothed, their sick furnished medicines, and the well furnished with employment, that they might learn self-support.

ORGANIZING NEGRO REGIMENTS.

After slavery was declared abolished, as spring approached, the Government determined to employ the contrabands as soldiers, and Adjutant General Thomas was sent out with proper authority to organize regiments in the Mississippi Valley. Already one company of colored troops had been organized, furnished with arms and put on duty.

General Grant was at Milliken's Bend, La. His General Order, No. 25, in relation to these black soldiers, says:

"Commissaries will issue supplies, and quartermasters will furnish stores on the same requisitions and returns as are required from the troops. It is expected that all commanders will especially exert themselves in carrying out the policy of the administration, not only in organizing colored regiments and rendering them efficient, but also in removing prejudice against them." Was this opposing the organization of troops?

General Grant, in his letter to General Lee, Oct. 19, 1864, although declining to discuss the slavery question, declares, "I shall always regret the necessity of retaliating for wrongs done our soldiers, but regard it my duty *to protect all persons received into the army of the United States, regardless of color or nationality!*"

I learn from an ex-officer, who was thoroughly cognizant of the facts, that in the midst of the fearful labors around Vicksburg, General Grant always found time to attend to the calls necessary to make upon him in regard to the colored people or colored troops; that he gave every aid to the development of their industry and the means of their improvement.* He favored no Utopian schemes, and sought apractical solution of every difficulty. in the way of the welfare of the colored people. It will not be forgotten by them that, when before Vicksburg he and his associates in the chief command of the troops who night and day were pressing the siege, found time to listen to an extended report of the officer he had placed in charge of our people in the November previous.

GRANT TO LINCOLN.

This report he afterwards forwarded to President Lincoln with a private letter, dated June 11, 1863, in which he says: "Finding that negroes were coming into our lines in great numbers, and receiving kind or abusive treatment, according to the peculiar views of the troops they first came in contact with, and not being able to give that personal attention to their care, and use the matter demanded, I determined to appoint a General Superintendent over

* "A NEGRO PARADISE."

"One evening in the midst of the siege of Vicksburg, General Grant was sitting by the trunk of a great tree near his tent, talking to his Superintendent of Freedmen of their affairs, telling him in detail of a Great Bend in the Mississippi, 25 miles below the town, indicating how easily it could be protected, saying considerable portions of the land then deserted was owned by Jeff. Davis and his brother, Joe, whose plantation was often visited as a model by foreigners, suggested that his Bend should be occupied by the freedmen, and be made a "negro paradise." So it was. Soon it was divided into small farms for their cultivation, houses built, schools opened, the administration of order left chiefly to the colored people, and the whole protected against guerrillas by colored troops. Now, Joe Davis's former slave and foreman, one of these free cultivators of the Bend, owns and successfully carries on the Davis plantation, having purchased it from his former master."

the whole subject, and give him such assistants as the duties assigned him might require. I have given him such aid as was in my power, by the publication from time to time of such orders as seemed to be required, and generally at the suggestion of the Superintendent."

He speaks of the results up to that date as of great service to the blacks in having them provided for, when otherwise they would have been neglected, and to the Government in finding employment for the negro whereby he might earn what he was receiving, and, in closing, directs special attention to the portion of the report which would suggest orders regulating the subject which a Department Commander is not competent to issue.

The officer who delivered this letter and report to Mr. Lincoln, states that Mr. Lincoln received them with the greatest satisfaction, asking many questions about General Grant's views upon the whole subject of the treatment of the colored people, and on thus learning something in detail of the success of General Grant's plans and the usefulness, in his judgment, of colored soldiers, he repeated the expressions of his gratification that a General who was winning such military successes over the Rebels was able, from a military standpoint, to give him so many practical illustrations of the benefits of the emancipation policy.

WHAT WAS DONE WITH THE CONTRABANDS.

I find it stated in a printed copy of a letter to

Mr. Levi Coffin, then in England, written by the General Superintendent, and dated at Vicksburg, only a year after its fall, that this supervision, embracing the territory within the lines of our army, from Cairo, down the Mississippi to Red River, together with the State of Arkansas,—numbered in its care, during the past year, 113,650 freedmen.

"These are now disposed as follows: In military service, as soldiers, laundresses, cooks, officers, servants and laborers in the various staff departments, 41,150; in cities, on plantations, and in freedmen's villages and cared for, 72,500. Of these, 62,300 are entirely self-supporting—the same as any industrial class anywhere—as planters, mechanics, barbers, hackmen, draymen, etc., conducting enterprises on their own responsibility, or as hired laborers. The remaining 10,200 receive subsistence from the Government. 3,000 of them are members of families whose heads are carrying on plantations, and have under cultivation 4,000 acres of cotton, and are to pay the Government for their subsistence from the first income of the crop. The other 7,200 includes the paupers (those over and under the self-supporting age, the crippled and sick in hospital) of the 113,650, and those engaged in their care; and, instead of being unproductive, have now under cultivation 500 acres of corn, 750 acres of vegetables, and 1,500 acres of cotton—besides the work done at wood-chopping, etc."

"There are reported in the aggregate some over 100,000 acres of cotton under cultivation. Of this, about 7,000 acres are leased and cultivated by blacks. Some of these are managing as high as 300 or 400 acres. It is impossible to give, at the present date, any definite statement of many of the forms of industry; 59,000 cords of wood are reported to me by Colonel Thomas, Superintendent and Provost Marshal of Freedmen, as cut within the lines of 110 miles on the river banks above and below this place. It would be only a guess to state the entire amount cut by the people under this supervision; it must be enormous. The people have been paid from 50 cents to $2.50 per cord for cutting. This wood has been essential to the commercial and military operations on the river.

"Of the 113,650 blacks, here mentioned, 13,320 have been under instruction in letters; about 4,000 have learned to read quite fairly, and about 2,000 to write. So our people were helped by General Grant's policy through this terrible transition."

August 16, 1864, General Grant wrote Mr. Washburne the celebrated letter so widely quoted, in which he affirms that the Confederate leaders had robbed the cradle and the grave to carry on the war, urging that our friends in the North could have no hope for peace from separation; and among the special reasons in reply to "*peace on any terms*," he affirms that the South would demand the restoration of their slaves already free; they would demand indemnity for losses sustained; they would demand a treaty which would make the North slave hunters for the South; they would demand pay for every slave that escaped to the North.

In his last and noted order to the great army, dated June 2, 1865, General Grant distinctly recognizes the good results they had accomplished; affirms that they had "overthrown all armed opposition to the enforcement of the laws, and the proclamation forever abolishing slavery—the cause and pretext of the rebellion."

May we not justly say, will it not be the unquestioned sentiment of history that the liberty which Mr. Lincoln declared with his pen General Grant made effectual with his sword—by his skill in leading the Union Armies to final victory?

GRANT'S EARLY EXPRESSIONS CONCERNING SLAVERY.

But I prefer that General Grant shall speak for himself, by here quoting from his private letter to Mr. Washburne, and published without the General's knowledge or permission, dated August 30, 1863, in which he said: "The people of the North need not quarrel over the institution of slavery.

What Vice President Stephens acknowledges as the corner-stone of the Confederacy, is already knocked out. Slavery is already dead, and cannot be resurrected. It would take a standing army to maintain slavery in the South, if we were to make peace to-day guaranteeing to the South all their former constitutional privileges.

"I never was an abolitionist—not even what could be called anti-slavery—but I try to judge fairly and honestly, and because patent to my mind, early in the rebellion, that the North and South could never live in peace with each other except as one nation. *As anxious as I am to see peace and that without slavery, re-established, I would not therefore be willing to see any settlement until this question is forever settled.*"

In a letter written by Mr. Lincoln to General Grant, April 30, 1864, is this emphatic sentence: "I wish to express in this way my entire satisfaction with what you have done up to this time."

GRANT'S POLICY AS PRESIDENT TOWARD THE NEGROES.

But since he became President how faithfully has he carried out his pledges in which the colored race are most directly interested?

In his Inaugural, March 4, 1867, we find these wise words, in regard to suffrage and the 15th Amendment:

"The question of suffrage is one which is likely to agitate the public so long as a portion of the citizens of the nation are excluded from its privi-

leges in any State. It seems to me very desirable that this question should be settled now, and I entertain the hope and express the desire, that it may be by the ratification of the 15th article* of amendment to the Constitution."

Indeed, his language often points to his clear apprehension of the fact, that peace could only be fully restored by removing the cause of disturbance. In his message in regard to Mississippi and Virginia, April 7th, 1869, while he urges the restoration of the States to their proper relations to the Government as speedily as possible, he clearly states that it must be conditioned that the people of those States shall "be willing to become peaceful and orderly communities, and to adopt and maintain such constitutions and laws as will effectually secure the civil and political rights of all persons within their borders."

True to all his instincts, all his declarations and acts, in his first annual message, he has for the Blacks, as freedmen, a kind word, and declares, "the freedmen, under the protection they have received, are making rapid progress in learning, and no complaints are heard of lack of industry on their part where they receive fair remuneration for their labor;" and among the reasons which he finds for gratitude to the Giver of all good, is a country "with a population of forty millions of free people, all speaking one language; with facilities for every mortal to acquire an education; with institutions closing

* For which, it will be remembered, Mr. Sumner did not vote.

to none the avenues to fame or any blessing of fortune that may be coveted; with freedom of the pulpit, the press and the school." Again, he declares that the "second great object of the Government is to secure protection to the person and property of the citizen of the United States in each and every portion of our common country, wherever he may choose to move, without reference to original nationality, religion, color, or politics, demanding of him only obedience to the laws, and proper respect for the rights of others."

Though, as he said, it is unusual to notify the two houses by message of the promulgation of the ratification of an amendment to the Constitution, yet he sent one in regard to the ratification of the 15th Amendment, in which he said, "Institutions like ours, in which all power is derived directly from the people, must depend mainly upon sheir intelligence, patriotism and industry. I call the attention, therefore, of the newly-enfranchised race to the importance of their striving in every honorable manner to make themselves worthy of their new privilege. To the race more favored heretofore by our laws, I would say, withhold no legal privilege of advancement to the new citizen. The framers of our Constitution firmly believed that a Republican Government could not endure without intelligence and education generally diffused among the people. 'The Father of his Country,' in his farewell address, uses this language: 'Promote, then, as a matter of primary importance, institutions for the general diffusion of knowledge. In proportion as the structure of the Government gives force to public opinion, it is essential that public opinion should be enlightened.' In his first annual message to Congress, the same views are forcibly presented, and are again urged in his eighth message.

"I repeat that the adoption of the 15th Amendment to the Constitution completes the greatest civil change and constitutes the most important event that has occurred since the nation came into life. The change will be beneficial in proportion to the heed that is given to the urgent recommendations of Washington. If these recommendations were important then, with a population of but a few millions, how much more important now, with a population of forty millions, and increasing in a rapid ratio.

"I would, therefore, call upon Congress to take all means within their constitutional powers to promote and encourage popular education throughout the country; and upon the people everywhere to see to it that all who possess and exercise political rights shall have the opportunity to acquire the knowledge which will make their share in the government a blessing and not a danger."

GRANT'S APPOINTMENTS OF COLORED MEN TO OFFICE.

An inquiry into the appointments of colored men to office under General Grant, gives results more satisfactory than I anticipated. No records, so far as I learn, appear to be kept of the color of the appointees.

I can only ascertain facts by my own personal knowledge, and from the personal knowledge of others acquainted with the appointees. It is impossible for me to fix the exact number, but I find them in all Departments of the Civil Service. Two have been appointed foreign ministers; several collectors of customs; some assessors of Internal Revenue; and so on down through all the various grades of the service—as route agents, post-masters, clerks, messengers, etc., according to the intelligence of the applicants.

I should have been glad to have obtained the exact number of colored appointees. In one Department at Washington, I found 249, and many more holding important positions in its service in different parts of the country. In other Departments, the facts ascertained were correspondingly gratifying, as I pursued the inquiry (continues the writer), meeting some new man at every step, and left it satisfied, as I think any colored man would be, that there has been a hearty disposition to disregard all past prejudices, and treat us in the matter of appointments according to our merits. The appointments to West Point, as overcoming the army prejudices, are well known, and too significant to be overlooked. Indeed, I closed the inquiry thoroughly satisfied, and believe that any man of my race could be with the same facts before him, that, with General Grant at the head of the Administration of the country, we are assured in due time, not only of all our rights, but of all our privileges.

GRANT TO THE CIVIL RIGHTS CONVENTION.

In view of the foregoing facts, the following excellent letter should be added:

EXECUTIVE MANSION,
WASHINGTON, D. C., May 9, 1872.

Gentlemen: I am in receipt of your invitation extended to me to attend a mass meeting to be held for the purpose of aiding in securing civil rights for the colored citizens of our country. I regret that a previous engagement will detain me at the Executive Mansion, and that I shall not be able to participate with you in person in your efforts to further the cause in which you are laboring. I beg to assure you, however, that I sympathize most cordially in any effort to secure for all our people of whatever race, nativity, or color, the exercise of those rights to which every citizen should be entitled.

I am, very respectfully,

U. S. GRANT.

Here the communication of the colored citizen ends. It is by no means exhaustive of the facts showing the absence from General Grant's mind of any sentiment except a kindly one for the negro race. His interference in behalf of the colored troops during the campaign before Richmond, for instance, had the effect to save thousands of them from being put to work by the Rebels like galley slaves upon the fortifications. Learning that colored soldiers were being used in this manner whenever captured by the Rebels, General Grant immediately issued orders for the employment of an equal number of Confederate prisoners upon the Dutch Gap canal. He of course notified General Lee of this retaliatory measure, and the notification had the desired effect. It brought an order for the relief of the colored Union prisoners, and an explanatory letter from Lee to Grant, to which the following is Grant's reply:

"HEADQUARTERS ARMIES OF THE UNITED STATES,
"October 29, 1864.

"General R. E. LEE, C. S. A.,
"Commanding Army Northern Virginia.

"*General:* Understanding from your letter of the 19th, that the colored prisoners, who are employed at work in the trenches near Fort Gilmer, have been withdrawn, I have directed the withdrawal of the Confederate prisoners employed in the Dutch Gap canal.

"I shall always regret the necessity of retaliating for wrongs done our soldiers; but regard it my duty to protect all persons received into the army of the United States, regardless of color or nationality. When acknowledged soldiers of the Government are captured they must be treated as prisoners of war, or such treatment as they receive will be inflicted upon an equal number of prisoners held by us.

"I have nothing to do with the discussion of the slavery question; therefore decline answering the arguments adduced to show the right to return to former owners such negroes as are captured from our army.

"In answer to the question at the conclusion of your letter, I have to state that all prisoners of war falling into my hands shall receive the kindest treatment possible, consistent with securing them, unless I have good authority for believing any number of our men are being treated otherwise. Then, painful as it may be to me, I shall inflict like treatment on an equal number of Confederate prisoners.

"Hoping that it may never become my duty to order retaliation upon any man held as a prisoner of war, I have the honer to be, very respectfully, your obedient servant,

"U. S. GRANT, Lieutenant General."

CHAPTER XVII.

THE SO-CALLED LIBERAL MOVEMENT.

How and When it Originated—The Grand Hobby—Attempt to Split the Republican Party in 1868—Trumbull's Backbone Stiffened—A Regular Siege—Approaching the Citadel by Parallels—Sumner's Grievance—His Ejection from the Senate Foreign Affairs Committee—A General Misunderstanding—How it Happened—The Civil Service Purists—The Bee in Trumbull's Bonnet—The Newspaper Ring—"We Four and No More."

It is a great mistake to suppose that the schism created and engineered by a dozen individuals, and dignified by the name of the "Great Liberal Movement," originated in any disaffection growing out of the administration of the government by President Grant. The movement had its origin before ever Grant was nominated for President by the Chicago Convention of 1868. Its germ was the theory of Free Trade, which so disturbed some of its more ardent advocates in the early Spring of 1868, that they would then have been very glad to disrupt the Republican party and scatter to the four winds the glorious record of that patriotic organization, with all the beneficent measures then in the womb of that party's future, for the sake of an opportunity to air themselves upon their favorite hobby of Free Trade, or, as they had then just begun to call it, Revenue Reform. This was the way it was done:

THE GAME IN 1868.

Early in 1868, the impeachment of Andrew Johnson came on. The American Free Trade League, comprising among its members the editors of the Chicago *Tribune*, New York *Evening Post* and Chicago *Evening Post*, as well as all the prominent Democratic journals, and numbering the papers specified among the most valued and industrious of its organs, was then just fairly launched in its active campaign work, and, under the leadership of Mahlon Sands and the editors above named, was beginning a vigorous warfare in behalf of its vital theory.

It was soon perceived that the conviction and removal of Andrew Johnson would leave in the Presidential Chair, for the remaining ten months of Johnson's term, the Hon. Benjamin F. Wade, then President *pro tem* of the Senate. Now, Wade was a staunch Protectionist, as indicated by his votes in the Senate, and the Free Traders immediately saw that it would never do to have him occupying the Presidential Chair, with an almost certainty of being made the Republican candidate for Vice-President at Chicago, in May. Accordingly, we saw the Chicago *Tribune* and *Evening Post* suddenly veer about, a few days after the Senate took the trial of Johnson in hand, and enjoin moderation upon the Senate as earnestly as they had demanded a red-hot prosecution from the House a fortnight or so before. Fortunately for their cause, there were really some very weak points in the impeachment of Johnson, which presented a good excuse for such Senators as chose, from one motive or another, to vote for acquittal. One of these was Lyman Trumbull, of Illinois, who had, we have no doubt, honest scruples about the propriety of removing Johnson by force. Nevertheless, Trumbull lacked backbone, and there is no telling what he would have done, but for the stiffening up which he received from home. Letters from Horace White, and from one other newspaper knight (since deceased) whose support was important, assured Trumbull that he would be sustained by the (then) most influential of the home newspapers of Republican name. Sustained by such assurances, Trumbull, to the surprise of the country, voted "nay" on the question of Johnson's conviction. Of the Republican Senators, Grimes, Fessenden, Ross, Henderson, Van Winkle and Fowler voted with him—part of them certainly from conscientious motives. By their votes Johnson was acquitted, and Ben Wade was kept out of the Presidential Chair.

AT THE CHICAGO CONVENTION.

Now for the next act in the drama. The revenue "Reformers," though they had exorcised their *bete noir* from the place of authority, still were not happy. There was still a high tariff majority in Congress, and was likely to be, at least in the Senate, for many years—perhaps until the anxious "Reformers" had, to quote the thought of Sidney Smith, wrapped their taxed shrouds about them, and lain down in taxed coffins to their final rest. There seemed little prospect of bringing about the Free Trade millenium so long as the Republican party continue to sit, like Mordecai, at the king's gate. The Democratic party was better material, as Free Trade had been one of the vital dogmas of the Democrats, in their virtuous days. But the Democrats had a war record which would damn them to all eternity, if they should have the temerity to keep fighting under their old colors. To cleave a slice off from the Republican party and work it over into a grand hash along with the cold meats of the Democracy, was the problem of Messrs. Sands, White, *et al.*

The National Republican Convention of 1868 assembled. It was the hope of the agitators that a split might be brought about through a bolt, organized on one of three pretexts, viz:

1. The nomination of Wade for Vice President.

2. The adoption by the Convention of a resolution sharply censuring the seven Republican Senators who voted against convicting Johnson.

3. The refusal of the Convention to adopt a resolution, presented by Carl Schurz, in favor of the speedy enfranchisement of the Rebels.

None of these delicately edged wedges, however, could be made to enter the glorious old trunk. It resisted them all. Wade was not nominated, the resolution of censure was not passed, and Schurz's resolution, far from being rejected, or quarreled over, was readily adopted, notwithstanding it was irregularly presented.

In short, the gentlemen who were waiting for a rupture found the party disgustingly unanimous and enthusiastic; so much so as to render hopeless the prospects of a successful schism *that* year. The idea was accordingly abandoned, or rather, held in abeyance, while the schemers sought new instrumentalities and new opportunities. They made a sort of mock fight during the campaign of 1868, and, after Grant was swept into the White House on a flood of popular enthusiasm, the like of which had rarely been seen, they immediately proceeded to right their foundered craft, and take advantage of the reflex wave to get back off the shoals on which the election had landed them.

THE NEWSPAPER SYNDICATE.

It was not long before that newspaper "quadrilateral," which has since become famous—chiefly through blowing its own trumpet—began to take form. This powerful concern has varied in form and magnitude somewhat since commencing its operations for the destruction of the Republican party. As first organized, it consisted of, first, the Springfield (Mass.) *Republican;* second, the New

York *Evening Post;* third, the Cincinnati *Commercial*, and, fourth, the Chicago *Tribune*,—the editors of which, and of the few other journals which have co-operated with them from time to time, were actuated by various motives. With White and Nordhoff (representing the second and fourth of the dailies named) the grand object was Free Trade and the disruption of the Republican party. With Bowles and Halstead, representing the two others, it was less a theory of politics than a theory of journalism which constituted the motive power. They believed in being independent—in driving a free lance—and they enjoyed the prospect which the proposed free criticism of the administration afforded them for making their journals spicy and readable. Halstead is much more wanton than Bowles, and of the last it is but justice to say that his standard of journalism is exceptionally high, though his views of what is practicable, as well as of what is patriotic, may be erroneous. He aims to be frank and fair in all things, and, accordingly, he has not attempted in his paper, since the machinations of the ring resulted in the nomination of Greeley, to conceal his disgust with that nomination.

LOVE FEASTS.

This newspaper ring, or syndicate, soon began to hold occasional meetings and compact themselves into a tolerably well organized mutual admiration society. Their proceedings were nominally in behalf of Revenue Reform, though afterwards some other elements, deemed available for a Presidential canvass, were worked into the cake, as a leavening or flavoring ingredient. Speaking of cakes reminds us of the banquets which these phenomenally elevated statesmen-journalists used to hold at Delmonico's or Wormley's, and at which they practiced bravely at the (to them) untried art of oratory. To these conferences Democratic editors and politicians, like Manton Marble, were admitted; and it was in cultivating the good graces of this "syndicate" that Charles Sumner—always lusting after newspaper puffs—first nerved himself to attack Grant in those bitter speeches and "interviews" with newspaper folk, which began to appear in the fall of 1870.

BATTERIES OF SLANDER.

Thus the "syndicate" went on pecking away at the foundations of the Republican organization, and doing their best endeavors, by blows repeated seven days in the week and fifty-two weeks in the year, to so weaken the grand old columns that new ones would have to be put in their place, and an opportunity be thus afforded for the introduction of something from the "syndicate's" famous quarries for new foundation stones. They never went to press without a cutting criticism or a sly inuendo in the editorial columns, or a whole volley of loosely constructed slanders from their special correspondents, aimed at the Administration of President Grant.

In the fall of 1870, a very loud hue-and-cry was raised about Grant's San Domingo scheme, and it was freely charged in the papers of the syndicate that General Babcock, one of Grant's *quasi* secretaries, who had the most active part in managing the details of the preliminaries to annexation, was corruptly interested in certain (or rather some very uncertain, vaguely imagined and never specified) financial speculations, dependent on the annexation of the Island. Charles Sumner, who traversed his record as a negrophilist in order to make a point against the Administration which had failed to accept his dictation concerning a certain federal appointment, made a lecturing tour Westward in October and November, 1870, during which he disseminated among his admirers, in private conversations, the insinuation that Grant himself had been speculating in lots in the Bay of Samara. This was a lie; and to take the curse off it, when it was brought home to him in the Senate, he perpetrated another, wherein he denied the paternity of the first.

The San Domingo matter was the most meaty bone of contention that the "syndicate" got hold of in the whole weary three years of waiting for such; but they did not scorn to accept less promising trifles. They criticised the financial policy of Boutwell; they criticised the President's appointment of relations to office; they criticised the New York Custom House through and through—criticised Grant because he did not change collectors, and criticised him all the worse when he did change them; they criticised indiscriminately the legislation of Congress, laid it all to Grant and named it "Grantism," knowing that Grant was the hardest Republican candidate for them to beat, and feeling that if they could force him out of the field their chance was good, with Democratic co-operation, to win. In short, it is not too much to say that the "syndicate" allowed no act, either of Congress or of the administration, to pass by without picking some flaw in it and presenting its worst aspect to the public.

CONFUSING LOCAL ELECTIONS.

Another method was resorted to in addition to this wholesale and indiscriminate misrepresentation. This was to confuse the issue in as many State and local elections as possible, by organizing a bolt from the regular Republican nominations, and a coalition with the Democrats on what the bolters humorously termed a "Reform" ticket. With the help of the sore-heads, added to that of the syndicate and the Democrats (never greatly in the minority in large towns), the conspirators were able sometimes to carry their ticket (though no reforms were ever heard of); but they oftener failed, except as the mere effort was a success in itself, since it confused the questions before the public and helped a little toward obliterating the party lines which the people had learned during the war to recognize so well as identical with the lines between loyalty and disloyalty. These efforts were, in fact, the series of parallels by which the besiegers of the Republican fortress proposed to approach, slowly and gradually, until they could mine our works and blow our fortifications and their defenders, into a thousand fragments. And so, perhaps, they might have done, but for the premature explosion of their magazine at Cincinnati.

ALLIES IN THE SENATE.

The syndicate captured, during the fall and winter of 1870, four Senators, of whom, as might be expected, from what has preceded, Sumner and Trumbull were two. The others were Carl Schurz, whose first disaffection came about more honestly and legitimately than that of any of the rest, and who is still by far the least selfish and most ingenuous of the quartette; and one Tipton, a Nebraska nobody, who abandoned a backwoods pulpit to make a clown of himself in the more conspicuous arena of the United States Senate.

Bombardment commenced in earnest in the Senate during the last session of the Forty-first Congress, in the winter of 1870–71. Sumner got out his heavy siege gun and, loading it with San Domingo ammunition, fired some shots at the White House which were certainly intended to demolish that edifice with all its occupants. Schurz threw a few shell, also, and Tipton brought his penny popgun to bear, with such effect as might have been expected. Sumner displayed great vindictiveness in his speeches, and great arrogance and contempt for his fellow Senators in his method of proceeding—dodging the rules of the body, dictating and overbearing his colleagues, and displaying all the airs of a demi-god, along with the tricks and habits of a narrow, tricky partisan.

SUMNER'S "MARTYRDOM."

It was this arrogant and unpleasant manner of the Massachusetts Senator—something which the Senate had long felt, but which was, of course, but little alluded to in that body—which, as much as aught else, earned for Sumner his omission from the Committee on Foreign Relations, of which he had been chairman for several terms. Nevertheless, the cause assigned by the caucus committee charged with the making up of the standing committees was, not Mr. Sumner's general factiousness, arrogance, impetuousness and personal vindictiveness, but this: that he was in notorious opposition to a prominent measure of the Administration, and that to make him chairman of the committee which was to have this measure under consideration, and be, in fact the Senate's agent therein, would be a severe and unnecessary censure of the Administration. Another reason was also alleged, which was taken up with considerable effect by the Sumnerites, viz., that Sumner was not on speaking terms with the Secretary of State, who, necessarily, has much to do with the Chairman of the Senate Committee on Foreign Relations, and should, to make the Government efficient and harmonious in its action on foreign questions, be able to work side by side with that official.

In spite of all these reasons, any of which ought to be sufficient for the Senate's electing another man than Sumner to the place if it chose, the personal and faction friends of that Senator succeeded in creating an impression in the minds of many, even of those who did not sympathize with Sumner's factious opposition to the Administration, that that Senator had been "struck down" by a caucus committee in very much such an outrageous manner as he had been struck down by the ruffian Brooks in old chivalry days. Among those who spoke in his behalf was Senator Wilson, his colleague, a staunch Administration man, whose generous heart prompted him to resent what was really a severe blow to his colleague's personal ambition, without, apparently, considering that it was a rebuke which Sumner's unreasonable conduct had brought upon himself, and which his unwholesome purposes had made absolutely necessary to the proper conduct of the Senate's business. If Sumner had been a sympathetic, a magnanimous, or a chivalrous man, the answering qualities in his fellow Senators would have gained him respite from this deserved rebuke. He was not such a man, and he therefore failed.

THE PRESS ON THE AFFAIR.

The act which deposed him from his pet Committee (though it was not a deposing, but simply

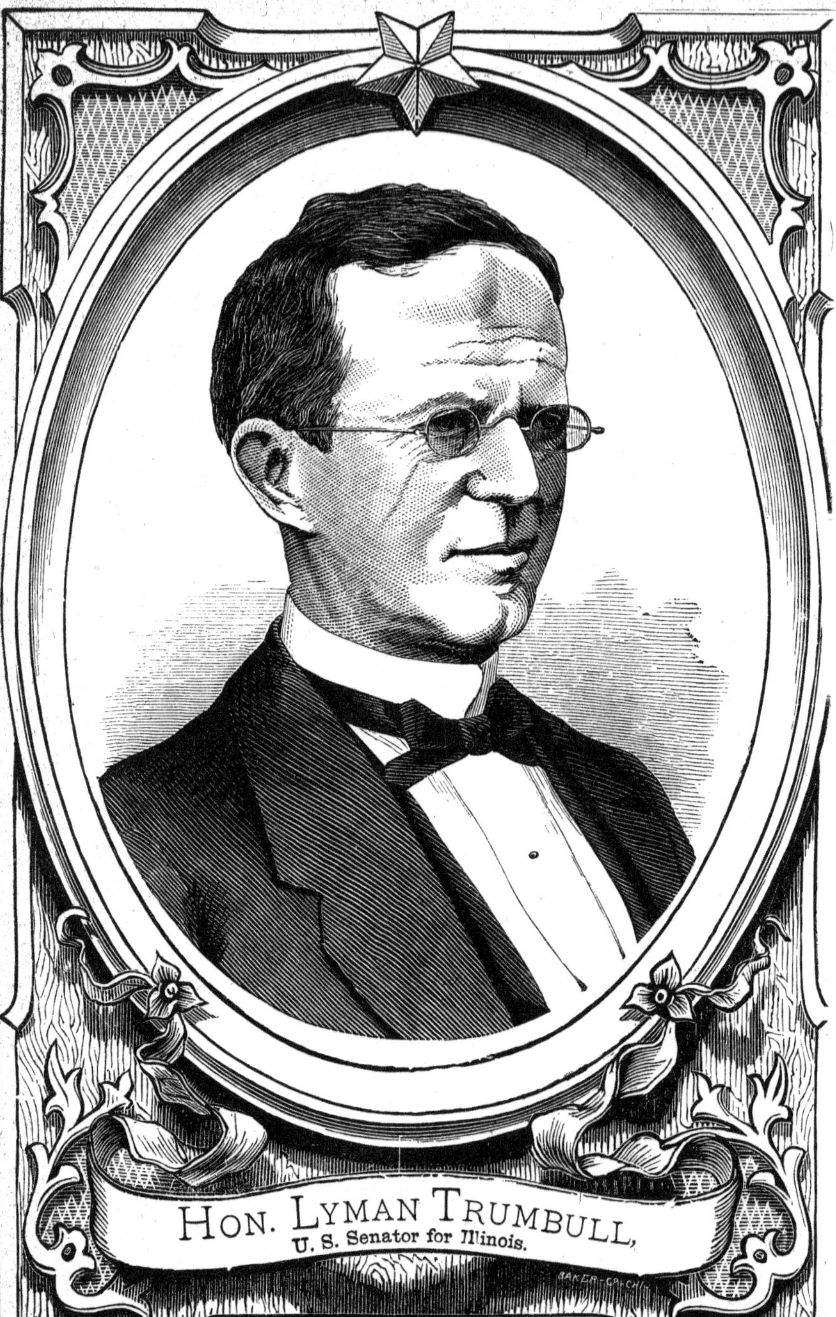

HON. LYMAN TRUMBULL,
U. S. Senator for Illinois.

a failure to re-elect to an additional term) was trumpeted to the country by the newspaper syndicate as an act of outrageous tyranny and of Presidential vindictiveness. It so happened that through the peculiar predilections of the press, the country obtained, generally, an erroneous impression of the motives involved in this act. The Democratic press and the syndicate had an obvious interest in representing the act as a heinous one, in order that it might tell against Grant and the Republican leaders in the Senate; and at the same time a majority of the Republican press were misled by their old-time admiration of Sumner as an anti-slavery orator, into sympathizing with him as they would not have done if they had known the many facts which Senatorial courtesy prevented from appearing in the debates. The consequence was that Sumner won out of the affair no little reputation as a martyr — a character in which he successfully figured until his morbid, malignant, mis-aimed speech in the Senate, on the 30th of May, 1872, exposed the true character and motives of the man.

THE SIEGE CONTINUES.

The disorganizers continued to construct their parallels of approach to the Republican citadel. Having seized a commanding position in the Senate, they operated there the most energetically. During the last session of Congress, no less than fifteen investigations into the conduct of the government, were under way at Washington or elsewhere, by direction of Congress. These have been already alluded to in Chapter V. It is also explained there how they resulted in the vindication of the Administration from any serious blame. The most malignant of these investigations were ordered on the motion of the renegade Republicans of the Senate. During the Spring session of 1871, Mr. Sumner had made, in the Senate, no less than eleven speeches on the subject of San Domingo—not counting those which he was continually seeking to smuggle into the proceedings in the shape of preambles to resolutions—a trick in which he was usually successful, through the forbearance of the Senate, he being a "martyr." These were reinforced by others from Schurz, all of which were faithfully echoed by the syndicate.

What San Domingo was to the disorganizers during the session of '71, the French arms sale was during that of '72; the hope, on the part of the "Liberals," being that they might find material, in the sale of damaged or superannuated ordnance to the French, to excite the enmity of the German voters of this country against the Administration.

TRUMBULL.

Senator Trumbull did not fail to put in an appearance, when occasion offered, as a light skirmisher upon the flanks of the Republican army. The hobby upon which Trumbull rode oftenest was State Rights. Mounted upon this, or upon the chair of the Judiciary Committee, he was able to discern quibbles of "unconstitutionality" and masked batteries of Federal usurpation where two or three years before, he would have sworn the field was as clear as a June morning. Trumbull's status in July, 1871, is to be learned from an "interview" published in the Chicago *Tribune*, his special organ, and hence assumed to be authentic. In that interview, he seems to forget the State Rights trouble, which had attracted so much of his solicitude in the Senate, and which has since come to form the only distinctive plank in the platform of the new party. He is reported thus:

Trumbull—"I think the great question of the Presidential campaign will be the finances, taxation, and civil service reform. These subjects are uppermost in the minds of the people."

"Is Secretary Boutwell's policy popular here in the West?"

Trumbull—"Yes, to some extent it is. I don't altogether believe in it myself, but still there are a great many people who feel proud of the manner in which Boutwell is paying off the debt. I think it a mistake to keep so much gold in the Treasury and to use it in buying our indebtedness. It is a wonder somebody has not assailed the policy of the Secretary going into the market and buying the government indebtedness at a discount."

"The last government loan seems to be a failure."

Trumbull—"Yes, I expected as much. You see the trouble is men won't give up a 6 per cent. bond for a 5 or a 4, not if they can help it. Besides, our government should first improve its credit at home before it goes abroad to borrow money. We have a currency consisting of promises to pay, and no provision made to pay them. We should first of all bring these up to the gold standard. That would improve our credit. On the whole, however, Boutwell's management of the Treasury gives very general satisfaction. It will be the trump card of the administration when it comes before the people for a verdict. There is a general conviction that the revenue is more faithfully collected than ever before, and, as I said, the people feel a good deal of pride in this matter of paying off the debt."

He then points out to his amanuensis, the faithful reporter, the evils of the civil service. He is then questioned about the Presidency, and replies that it looks as if the Republicans had settled down upon Grant for renomination; "but," he adds—and here the Trumbullian eye must have twinkled with anticipation of what came so near happening at Cincinnati—"you can't tell what may happen in a year." And he presently adds, after an intervening interrogatory or two, "It is too early in my judgment, to predict who will be the nominee of the Republican party." From this, it is obvious that Trumbull then felt confident that some conservative statesman, whose initials were L. T., could be forced upon the Republican Convention of 1872 by bringing the parallels nearer and nearer, and making the fire of bombardment hotter and hotter through the next session of Congress.

CHAPTER XVIII.

THE SO-CALLED LIBERAL MOVEMENT.

(CONTINUED.)

The Ring Reinforced—Greeley gets a Bee in his Bonnet, too—The Possum Policy of the Democrats—The Blair Family Smell the Battle Afar Off—The Movement Begins in Missouri—Some of the Pioneers—Sore-heads—The Cincinnati Convention Called—The Response—The Spring Elections—The Democracy Weakens Perceptibly—Greeley Smiles upon the Movement.

By this time the newspaper syndicate had been reinforced by several valuable allies. Horace Greeley himself had joined them for one. The way in which he became converted to their cause, through his own ambition to be President, will be told in that portion of this book which we have devoted to the personal history of Mr. Greeley. The fact must be mentioned here, however, that since the summer of 1871, when Greeley returned from the South, imbued with the idea that he was personally stronger there than any other public man, his *Tribune* had nothing favorable to say of Grant's Administration; and the vials of wrath which it had so carefully husbanded when Tammany needed denunciation, were emptied out upon the New York Custom House and upon the National Administration, as the responsible guardian thereof. One or two journals, hitherto Democratic, also whispered that they could be counted upon, in whatever hazard, as partners in the formation of a new party under a name other than that which the ancient Democracy has so long abused. These journals were the Missouri *Republican* and the Louisville *Courier-Journal*, the former of which, at any rate, had a record unquestionably and unvaryingly Democratic.

THE DEMOCRATS PASSIVE.

This promise of passivism on the part of the Democrats was soon acquiesced in by nearly all the influential papers of that party, including the *World*, of New York, and the *Times*, of Chicago; by several prominent politicians, also, though the Simon-pure old hunkers—wheelhorses of the party coach—were slow to give in their adherence. John Quincy Adams, Jr., who had served the Democrats once or twice by lending them the name of the Adams family (very much as the profligate Charles Surface proposed to serve a boon companion by selling his ancestors' pictures), wrote an able letter, which was published in the Missouri *Republican* of the 29th of November, 1871, favoring what had then come to be known as the "Missouri Policy." It was otherwise designated as the Passive Policy, or "Possum Policy"—the latter phrase referring aptly to the habit of the opossum to play dead, as a strategem to escape punishment for his depredations. Montgomery Blair, who, ever since being turned out of Lincoln's cabinet, had yearned for an opportunity to crush the Republican party between his thumb and finger and the thumbs and fingers of the rest of the Blair family, also wrote a letter which was published in the *World* of December 8th, advocating a passive policy on the part of the Democrats.

THE TOCSIN SOUNDS.

The first note of the "Liberal" campaign of 1872 was sounded in December, 1871. This was the call of William M. Grosvenor and other members of the Missouri Liberal Republican party, so-called, for a convention of that party, to be held at Jefferson City on the 24th day of January for purposes of organization, etc. The idea of a Liberal party had its origin in the disappointment of Gratz Brown and others who were defeated as candidates before the regular State Republican convention of 1870, and who therefore formed a coalition with the Democrats and lately enfranchised Rebels, with Brown as their candidate for Governor. This coalition was merely temporary in its nature and purpose; but it worked so well, and its Republican members were so likely to be ostracised by their party henceforth, that a portion of the members of the central committee, and nearly all the State officers whom the coalition had elected, determined to perpetuate the arrangement, if possible. Grosvenor, who headed the call above referred to, was an earnest Revenue Reformer and a politician of the *dilletante* order, who had been discharged from the editorship of the St. Louis *Democrat*, and who had become very bitter against the Republican organization. He afterwards, from lack of other occupation, became the principal working manager of the "Liberal" schism, with his headquarters at Washington.

The call for the Missouri convention of January 24th was signed by fifteen members of the State Liberal Committee (the other members claiming that their authority as a committee had terminated with the campaign of 1870) and by B. Gratz Brown and twenty-five other members of the State Government or the Legislature. It was an eloquent document; its signers lashed themselves into patriotic fury with such invocations as these:

"It is our proud duty not to retreat from the field of our triumph, but to beckon forward the hosts of liberalism in other States to the overthrow of that Radical domination which, in the nation even more than in the State, wars against vital principals of true republicanism.

"The honest men of all parties may unite in a victorious assault upon the greatest combination of all, that which sits enthroned at Washington with a sceptre ready for its grasp, enriching favorites by monopolies and grants, wielding government patronage, and dictating to States in elections and conventions.

"The time seems to us ripe for an uprising of the people, in kind not unlike that which swept this State in 1870. Look where you will, from county to county, and from State to State, the men who have been prominent in shaping policies and moulding public opinion are waiting for some movement that shall give promise of a brighter future, etc., etc., etc."

The Convention was held; was a respectable gathering; and resulted in the call for the Cincinnati Convention, to meet on the 1st of May, a little over a month before the time fixed for the assembling of the Republican Convention at Philadelphia.

THE MALCONTENTS OF 1872 AND 1864.

This Cincinnati Convention has been compared with that of Cleveland, in 1864, at which John C. Fremont was nominated for the Presidency. The circumstances of the two have, indeed, many points of similarity. The ostensible design of this one was to prevent the renomination of Grant by the Republicans. The design of that was to head off the renomination of Lincoln by the same party. Each was called, therefore, a short time in advance of the convention whose action it was sought to influence. The callers of the Cleveland gathering were loud in their denunciation of the "imbecile and vacillating policy" of Lincoln's Administration and demanded prompt measures to "rescue the imperiled nationality, and the cause of impartial, universal freedom, threatened with betrayal and overthrow." Similarly, the Cincinnati callers lashed themselves into fury over the usurpation, the corruption, and manifold other alleged sins of the existing Administration. And the *personnel* of the two enterprises was largely the same. Gratz Brown was a prominent figure in each; so was John Cochrane, of New York, the crazy secessionist Democrat of 1861, the equally crazy Radical of 1864, and the still more crazy Conservative of 1872; and, it may be added, the favorite fugleman of Greeley on nearly all occasions, and the trustworthy patriot on none. Another name on the Cleveland call was that of Cluseret, the French Communist, whose cowardice alone saved his neck from the halter. Again, Horace Greeley took an exceedingly favorable interest in each of these malcontent gatherings; but it is hardly necessary to mention this, as Mr. Greeley is understood to favor all bolts by "natural selection," as Darwin would say.

The Cleveland Convention proved a most lamentable farce. Fremont was nominated for President, and resigned his commission as Major-General in the army; and the rattlehead, Cochrane, was set up for Vice-President, as the rattlehead, Brown, has since been set up. The result upon the Baltimore Convention of 1864 was indicated by the unanimous renomination of Abraham Lincoln, save for the dissenting vote of Missouri. It became evident that Fremont could not muster a single electoral vote. Then Greeley, with infinite effrontery, wrote to the Republican Governors of States, proposing the withdrawal of Fremont if the Republicans would consent to the withdrawal of Lincoln, who (Greeley was sure) could never be re-elected! Fremont himself soon saw the ridiculousness of his situation and took himself out of the way.

The parallel referred to between the Cleveland and Cincinnati Convention, does not continue throughout, since the latter had a much better recourse to a combination with the enemy, which course, indeed, the leaders of the movement greatly preferred for reasons already hinted at.

THE DEMOCRACY AGAIN.

Nor was the Democracy at all loath to avail itself of the advantage of a coalition. The Spring elections in New Hampshire and Connecticut did not serve to strengthen their faith in their ability to combat the Republicans successfully. Up to April the most of the party organs had apparently maintained the idea that, with the help of the persistent criticism and slanders which the Disorganizers had been heaping upon the Administration of President Grant, the Democrats might still hope to beat the old enemy against whom they had contended so long and so pluckily in vain; but with the decision of the New Hampshire election, this hope utterly vanished. Of the four principal organs of the Democracy in the country—The New York *World*, the Chicago *Times*, the Cincinnati *Enquirer*, and the Missouri *Republican*—the last named had for months been favoring the Passive policy; the others responded to New Hampshire in these words: The *World:*

"The Democratic party is satisfied with this result. It confirms the certainty of Grant's renomination, precludes the taking up of any other candidate who might reunite the Republican party, and though last not least, it removes the last vestige of danger that any portion of the Democratic party will protest against the complete abandonment of dead issues."

The *Times:*

"It is a circumstance tending to convince even the most irrational and pig-headed of Democrats that the political organization called the Democratic party is utterly and irredeemably powerless to achieve a change in the Federal Administration. It is a fact proving, to the full extent that it proves anything, that however much a considerable body of liberal-minded Republicans may dislike the military President and his military regime, they dislike the Democratic party more. It is needless for any Democratic abstractionist to say that they are influenced by unreasonable prejudices. What is to be considered is the fact; not whether the causes of the fact are rational or irrational."

The *Enquirer* was at first disposed still to hold out, and urged:

"It is not in this little and remote New England State that the great battle of 1872 is to be fought, but is in New York, Pennsylvania, Ohio, Illinois, Indiana, and Missouri that the contest will be decided. It is in those States, with a different population from New England, that we shall win."

But this journal soon after wheeled into the Passive line, and put on so docile a demeanor, that it was e'en willing, or at least ready, to take up Greeley himself, as the bearer of the coalition standard.

Mr. Greeley received the call of the Missouri malcontents with a mixture of real smiles and simulated frowns. In his paper of the 29th of January, he said:

"The *Tribune* is likely to be *against* the Bolters, since they are almost certain to make hostility to Protection one of the planks of their platform, and *that* the *Tribune* can never abide, no matter who may be the rival candidates for President. Now that Emancipation is a fixed fact, Impartial Suffrage nearly so, and Universal Amnesty inevitable, there is no remaining National issue which is half so important in the view of the *Tribune* as that of Protection *vs.* Free Trade. We have no shadow of doubt that the overthrow of Protection would be speedily followed (as in 1816–20, and again in 1833–'7) by a sweeping industrial collapse and commercial bankruptcy, which would carry hunger and distress into the homes of millions of our countrymen. To such a calamity the *Tribune* cannot contribute, even passively, for anyconceivable consideration."

This does not seem very favorable to the Disorganizers, of whose platform Free Trade was certainly the corner-stone; but the sting was taken out of his rebuke of this feature by the paragraphs which followed, and in which Mr. Greeley handled very roughly the conduct of the Administration and the policy of Congress, adding, in his exclamatory style, "Men and brethren! a new leaf must be turned over, or there are breakers ahead. The proposed Cincinnati Convention may prove a fiasco, or it may name the next President"; and hinting that if "Roscoe Conkling & Co." are allowed to run the "Grant machine" a few months longer, it will be all up with the Republican party, and that Cincinnati will surely win. Altogether, this editorial of Greeley's forms a congeries of inconsistencies, like his political record in the large.

Under such auspices the Cincinnati Convention assembled. Its proceedings will form the subject of the next two chapters.

CHAPTER XIX.

THE CINCINNATI CONVENTION.

The Place—Gathering of the Clans—No Concert of Action—The Tariff Question—The Rival Candidates—Greeley's Name Received with Laughter—The Davis Hordes—Caucuses of the Syndicate—Opening of the Convention—A Side Show—Row in the New York Delegation—How Greeley's Strikers Captured that Body—Flank Movements—A Woman in the Case—Trouble, of Course—A Turbulent Session—Permanent Organization—Carl Schurz's Speech—Good Advice which was Not Followed.

The selection of Cincinnati as the place of holding the *soi disant* liberal convention was most agreeable to the people of that city. For this, there were various reasons, some of propriety, others of interest. The "new departure" had taken place from this point not so many months before that it had slipped the memories of observant politicians. This city and vicinity was a hot-bed of discontent with the present Administration. The region abounded with the flash element in politics.

There were lawyers of repute, ambitious of national distinction, like ex-Judges Hoadley, Stello, and Matthews, in neither of whom inhered persistency of purpose, or qualities that command permanent success. Their sworn allegiance to any cause was the sure precurser of its speedy downfall and decay. Judge Stallo, representing the extreme phases of German freedom of thought, has never been trammeled by church or party. To these effervescent orators was added Judge Cox, an excellent gentleman and average lawyer, but not above revenge for offended vanity, and willing to accept any honorable means to compass the defeat of Grant.

THE LOCAL PRESS.

The newspapers of the Queen City were leavened with discontent. The *Enquirer* being a Democratic journal, was the hereditary enemy of the incumbent of the Presidential office. The *Commercial*, a fierce iconoclast, was eager for anything that seemed to promise the loss of others and its own gain. Even the *Gazette* was known to desire a change of national standard-bearers, although hoping it would be effected within the old organization. The Germans of Northern Ohio, like all their countrymen in the United States, for obvious reasons, are directly influenced and controlled by the journals published in their language. Whatever sparks of discontent were latent among them had been assiduously fanned into flame by the *Volksblatt*, *Courier*, and *Volksfreund*, the three daily German newspapers of the city. Fred Hassaurek, editor of the first, is an ex-office-holder of long standing, and has had ever an eye for spoils. The *Courier*, an infant newspaper, just beginning to walk the devious paths of journalism, had its own reasons for desiring a change in the national management. The *Volksfreund* was Democratic, and an old and bitter enemy of the party in power.

LOCAL FUSION OF PARTIES.

Nowhere else in the country were the two great national parties so ready for fusion. One State Democratic Convention had adopted a platform expressing desire for conciliation and compromise, and the party had once suffered defeat on the issues of the new departure in a gubernatorial canvass. To offset this reverse, there had been a local victory upon a united ticket of rather pronounced character. The convention was therefore sure of a certain amount of local support and sympathy in case its action was sound and sensible. If a body of men which was to give voice to the opposition to Grant, and place a candidate in the field to defeat him, could not find moral encouragement and assistance, and accomplish its results with eclat in Cincinnati, the weakness of the cause which it espoused would be at once apparent, and its fall assured.

WANT OF CONCERTED ACTION.

The circumstances under which the convention assembled were anomalous. When such bodies gather in the ordinary course of events, their policy is generally foreshadowed. If the delegations from the various States are not definitely and openly instructed, their predelictions become known through some of the many channels by which private political sentiment reaches the public and becomes its property. In the present instance all was different. The feeling of opposition to the Administration was merely inchoate and unformed. The antipathy of the press was sporadic, although personally virulent wherever developed. A political change was hoped for, and in that change many hoped to come to the surface. How strong the opposition to Grant might be in special localities,—what private ambitions would be developed—toward what candidates for office the majority would incline,—who would be strongest with the masses,—were questions that must be asked and answered, without any existing *data* for sound reasoning. The opponents of the Administration had not even settled upon their grievances.

What was to be done was to find a common basis of action, and feasible means of carrying out their designs. Those who had special measures to the support of which they desired to win the new party, as personal interests to aggrandize, came upon the ground early. Rooms were engaged at the hotels two or three weeks in advance by representatives of various States, and they were soon filled. With praiseworthy hospitality the citizens of Cincinnati opened the doors of private houses to receive strangers. Quarters for the ample accommodation of several thousand guests were soon placed at the disposal of the committee having the matter in charge.

MISSOURI DELEGATION.

The Missouri delegation, headed by Grosvenor, were the first active partisans in the city. They came in the interest of Gratz Brown, whom they hoped to put upon the ticket as a candidate for president. They took rooms at the St. James, where they kept their camp fires burning from dawn until after midnight. Among the early arrivals with Colonel Grosvenor were Mr. Enos Clark, one of the earliest movers in the emancipation cause in Missouri, Joe Pulitzer, editor of the *Westliehe Post*, of St. Louis, and General John McNeil, whose connection with the shooting of certain guerrillas at Palmyra, Missouri, early in the rebellion, has made his name historical. Considering themselves the parents of the Liberal movement, the delegation for awhile labored under the delusion that their points could be easily carried. Logic that militated against their favorite candidate was most distasteful.

They arrived about the 26th of April, and as delegates, were thus limited in number, received for several days the almost exclusive attentions of the reporters of the city press. What Grosvenor thought, and said, and prognosticated, was supposed to have more than the reliability of ancient prophecy, and to be pregnant with the fate of the nation. It formed for many days, while opinions, and projects were crystallizing, the stock-in-trade of the local papers, and of the correspondents of the press of other cities, whom a keen desire for news had brought thus early to the front of battle. Brown never had any chances for the nomination, but his friends did not perceive it until his name was fairly fetid in the nostrils of the convention.

FREE TRADE ARRIVALS.

The parlors of the Missouri delegation at the St. James were made glad by the cheerful presence of several free-traders from the East, who came thither because of the declared proclivities of the former in the same direction. The first arrivals of this kind were Mahlon Sands, Secretary of the National Free Trade League, and Henry D. Lloyd, a fair-faced, juvenile *attache* of the same organization. Prime, of the Illinois branch of the same association, came soon afterwards. Atkinson, Bird and Davis, of Massachusetts, of similar sympathies, and with faces of characteristic Boston thinness, came on Saturday evening, the same train bringing David A. Wells, an almost maternal fondness for foreign pig-iron being the ruling passion in his breast. Other prominent free-traders came from Missouri, New York, Massachusetts and Chicago on the last day of the week, making it apparent that whatever occurred, those who favored revenue reform did not intend that their case should go by default. They seemed determined that this their great and perhaps only opportunity should not be missed.

ILLINOIS DELEGATION.

The Illinois delegation, bearing the banner of Judge David Davis with much clamor, was the second to appear upon the scene. Their forces were the best organized upon the ground, their leaders being politicians, tried in the furnace of the Chicago fire, and some of them annealed in the operations of the Relief Society. They established their bureau in an upper parlor of the Burnet House, looking out upon the bowlders of Third street. From this center the busy workers in the Davis interest laid their pipes and extended their wires to other delegations supposed to be at all infected with the Davis interest. Here the solemn old pump, Long John Wentworth, went and came, and swayed to and fro, like a double-jointed lighthouse.

Here the vapid Fairbanks displayed his elegant shape and aired his attenuated rhetoric. Here a representative of the Chicago *Times*, labored in the cause of the Associate Justice with earnestness and not a little asperity. The bald poll of Wirt Dexter, like an iceberg just floated from northern seas, flashed in the southern sunlight. Leonard Swett, the organizer of defeat, was seen flitting uneasily about, as he injected a subtle word here, a pertinent suggestion there, into the daily informal deliberations of the junto. The adherents of Davis continued strong in their confidence of his nomination until the very eve of the convention.

TO THE WHITE HOUSE
N.Y. TRIBUNE
FREE TRADE
CHICAGO TRIBUNE
H.G. PROTECTIO
CINCINNATI
TO PROTECT ION 10 MILES

JOURNALISTS AND POLITICIANS.

On the Saturday preceding the first of May everything was in a state of bewildering uncertainty. The Davis delegates were sincerely confident of success, and the Brown delegates professed equal serenity of faith. But the ordinary observer was simply bewildered by the scarcity of facts, and the abundance of possibilities. Only fragments of delegations about whom hung shreds of politicians were in the city. There were rumors of the expected presence of many persons of distinction.

It was expected that the inherent modesty of Democratic politicians would keep them at a distance from a meeting in which they had not been invited to participate. Force of habit was too strong with a few. Belmont, eager in the support of Adams, like a tethered horse, moved about Cincinnati as a pivot. One day report had him snip-shooting in southern Indiana, and the next transferred him to the Blue Grass region of Kentucky, where he gave himself up to the purchase of blooded horses with such a degree of absorption, that it seemed impossible he would ever condescend to politics again. About the time of the assembling of the convention, he went back to New York, and ceased temporarily to be a theme of newspaper comment.

Anna Dickinson was said to have engaged rooms at the Carlyle House, but she failed to make an appearance. Horace White, of the Chicago

Tribune, reached Cincinnati on Saturday morning, making a strong accession to the Free Trade element already present. The Saturday night trains added large numbers to the floating population, and on Sunday things began to gather shape; the chaos commenced slowly rounding into form.

THE TARIFF QUESTION.

The leaders in the liberal movement had from the first recognized that the real rock in their path, on which their bark was in danger of shipwreck, was the tariff question. They therefore approached it warily, and with an attempt at skillful pilotage. The free-trade men, being first upon the ground in force, had the preliminary shaping of the business. The first meeting to consider the question was held in the ladies' parlor of the St. James Hotel, at eleven o'clock on Sunday morning, April 28th. Not an avowed Protectionist was in the room. There were present Mahlon Sands, Henry D. Lloyd and Illinois Prime, all paid employees of the National Free Trade League, and all pledged, of course, to every possible effort to get the free trade question in some desirable shape into the platform. Atkinson and Bird, of Boston, were there, quiet, well-bred, earnest. Judge Hoadley formed a segment of the circle into which the party was formed—restless in manner, and looked at askance by the others, as a sort of political bull in the liberal china shop.

The bland face of David A. Wells, almost as placid and moonlike as the visage of his great opponent in the matter of revenue from customs, Horace Greeley, illumined the ring, and near it the pale, distressed features of Horace White attracted general attention. Carl Schurz, who had arrived during the previous night, was in the little assembly, quietly observant, and plainly studying how not to say it. General J. D. Cox occupied the chair. There were present, besides, at the services of this holy Sabbath occasion, Mr. Dorsheimer, of Buffalo, General Brinkerhoff, General Burnett and Colonel George Ward Nichols, of Cincinnati, and one or two others even less noteworthy than these last.

The discussion was informal, and only indicated the preferences and predilections of each in regard to the points in debate. Judge Hoadley was pronounced in favor of a vigorous free trade plank in the platform, and had drafted a resolution looking to that end, which he presented to the meeting. He was supported by General Burnett. Horace White preferred that free trade should not be made needlessly prominent in the platform; free trade was only a matter of degree; as for absolute free trade, it was not a question of the present, but an issue of the future.

Schurz favored some negative declaration in regard to it. The sentiments of the meeting were divided, and those in attendance separated with expressed wishes for conciliation and harmony, to meet again the next day at the same hour and in the same apartment. But the apple of discord had been thrown among them. High Protectionists appeared at subsequent meetings, and the question came near proving what the best advised feared, the cause of actual disruption and fatal disaster.

MATTERS CRYSTALLIZING.

On Monday the town was filled with delegates, their satellites and manipulators. Diligent reporters and correspondents began with some success the process of winnowing the grains of fact from the chaff of imagination and falsehood. Missouri was still true to Brown, and Grosvenor claimed that he had the promise of votes in other delegations. The Davis men had not yet begun to have the premonitions of defeat. The friends of Trumbull had secured rooms at the Burnett House, opening from one of the main corridors convenient for the button-holing and entanglement of unwary and plastic delegates. They had assurances of help from various quarters, and were not without reasonable hope of advantage. The son of the Senator from Illinois was ubiquitous, and sanguine, claiming that he had had repeated assurances of cordial support from Schurz.

The friends of Greeley, warmly sympathetic, but scarcely hoping to win, had begun to enumerate their adherents upon their fingers. Cox was talked of as a compromise candidate in case of failure to agree upon those whose chances seemed best at the outset. A few persons, the chief fuglemen being Alexander Long, a Democratic lawyer of Cincinnati, with a record of treachery in war times, attempted to evoke the ghost of Chase from the political grave to which that gentleman had been long consigned.

Wm. S. Groesbeck, of Cincinnati, a polished orator and finished gentleman of the antique school, was faintly hinted as one who would becomingly fill the office of president. Mr. Groesbeck put the crown from him with quite as much grace, and with almost as much sincerity as did Cæsar in the Capitol, but he was seen talking often to delegates in his stately fashion, and was presumed to have at least a fleeting interest in what was transpiring. Of all the candidates named, it was understood that none of them was willing to take the second place on the ticket except Brown, and perhaps Greeley. Any two of the names would have made it strong, but their unyielding ambition had made such a collocation impossible.

LOCAL STRENGTH OF ADAMS.

The local influence was all thrown in favor of Adams. Scarcely any other name was mentioned by the Cincinnati press in connection with the Presidential nominatlon. The *Commercial* supported him with energy, returning to the charge with renewed vigor each morning, and writing up his life laboriously. The *Enquirer* pursued a similar course, but its style and manner were less pronounced. Adams was a favorite of the German newspapers, which declared their preferences mildly.

The publication of his letter to D. A. Wells, produced a momentary shock, but did not seem, after the first day of its appearance, to affect its chances. The name of Greeley was received with mildly-suppressed laughter whenever mentioned. Outside of his own friendly circle Brown was not thought to have a shadow of a chance. The Davis and Adams men sneered at the chances of Trumbull.

On Monday, nearly all the delegates were in the city, comfortably disposed of and conferring with one another in regard to the course that should be pursued. Fenton was on hand, secretly working for Greeley. His headquarters were in a room at the Burnet House, but he boarded with his private secretary at a house in Broadway. He spent his time in quietly but vigorously counteracting the effects of the aggressive Western delegates in the direction of tariff reform. George W. Julian was prominent among the Indiana delegates, but was not understood to be working in the interest of any particular candidate. The difference in the Illinois men became an absolute rupture. The money spent in the interest of Davis, and the shameless effort to pack the convention in his favor rent the delegation with dissention and caused great scandal outside of it. It was the only case in which money was known to have been openly used to further the cause of a candidate. The region of Bloomington was said to be almost depopulated of its inhabitants, who had come to Cincinnati to shout for Davis. At a meeting of the delegation from this State, on Tuesday, a compromise was effected by which Davis should have in the convention twenty-one of the delegates, Trumbull, ten and a half, and Palmer ten and a half. As Palmer's chances for the nomination had entirely evanesced, this gave half of the voting delegates to Trumbull, and was considered a great concession on the part of the friends of Davis, who were sufficiently numerous to have everything in accord with their own wishes.

THE SITUATION ON TUESDAY.

The Illinois delegation was not peculiar as regarded internal discord. The quiet manipulation of Greeley by his New York friends was distasteful to the Free Trade portion of the delegates from the State. The animus of the former was very decided, and finally ended in excluding these opponents entirely from the convention. This was the situation on the eve of Wednesday, the day of the convention:

Adams strong in Ohio, Massachusetts, Connecticut, Kentucky, Michigan, Tennessee, Wisconsin, Maine, and having portions of their delegations, Davis having half of Illinois, a part of Indiana, North and South Carolina, and a few other votes, Trumbull having half of Illinois, nearly all of Indiana, Kansas, and some scattering ballots, Greeley, New York, New Hampshire, Vermont, and undefined strength among his southern delegates, Brown had his own State, with Georgia and Arkansas, and

Curtin, Pennsylvania, with rumors of supporting Greeley and Davis as its second choice. The tariff question was undecided, but was understood to be still in abeyance, with a growing preponderance of Eastern influence against the out-and-out revenue reformers. The power of New York and Pennsylvania had already made itself profoundly felt. None of the prospective candidates were present, delicacy forbidding.

PERSONAL REBUFFS.

A little incident which occurred to Richard Smith, editor of the Cincinnati *Gazette*, caused considerable gossip. That gentleman applied for admission to one of the meetings which daily assembled at the St. James to crystallize opinion on the tariff, and other important questions, but was refused. He sent back word by the messenger that in the course of a long political experience he had never been excluded from a reputed Republican meeting before, and he advised the gentlemen in council to question their own hearts and see if there was not something wrong.

FIRST DAY OF THE CONVENTION.

The spacious Industrial Hall—the place appointed as the session of the Convention—was moderately filled on the first day of the convention. The scene was one of considerable animation. The delegates occupied about half the floor, and were separated from vulgar outsiders by a rude railing.

A large concourse of spectators, among whom there were a few ladies, was in the galleries.

The hall was tastefully docorated, and to add to the general enjoyment of the occasion, a brass band was stationed behind the platform, screened from public view by the wealth of flowers and greenery, and the voluptuous swell of the melodies of many lands floated from their retreat during the progress of liberal business. A thick coating of sawdust and tan-bark upon the floor, laid to deaden the oratorical reverberations, gave to the place the air of a decorous beer-garden.

On all sides were to be noted the most studied affectation of courtesy. All ill-feeling, seemed for the time allayed, and all heart-burning temporarily smothered.

TEMPORARY ORGANIZATION.

It was a few minutes past twelve o'clock when W. M. Grosvenor, Chairman of the Liberal Republican Executive Committee of Missouri, arose and called the convention to order. The order demanded did not become intensified into silence, and it was difficult to hear his shrill tones in remote parts of the hall. The applause which his appearance elicited was not enthusiastic. The speaker made a brief, vigorous appeal for harmony, of which, acquainted with the hidden mainsprings of the movement, and the hidden elements of discord, he knew well the need.

Having nominated Hon. Stanley Matthews as

temporary chairman of the convention, the owner of the primal voice in its deliberations withdrew his tangled black locks and his oriental visage from the view of the audience.

OPENING SPEECH OF STANLEY MATTHEWS.

The Hon. Stanley Matthews, a wayward son of Southern Ohio, and constitutionally unfitted for party leadership, was well received and heartily elected to fill the position for which he was named. He made a fifteen minute speech, in which he proceeded, first, to deprecate the possibility of his being looked on as a prophet, and secondly, to apologise for ever having affiliated with the Republican party, in which connection he said " it was Sir Walter Raleigh, I believe, who, in reference to the pride of ancestry, said that those who boast the most of their progenitors were like a plant which he had discovered in America—the best part was under ground." [Applause.]

The remainder of the speech was without pith or point, dealing only in shabby generalities, and resembling the aimless political experience of its author.

The speech finished and decorously applauded, Mr. Matthews addressed himself industriously to the duties of the gavel. Colonel Grosvenor announced the following temporary Secretaries: Geo. Ward Nichols, of Ohio; George W. Palmer, of New York; and Joseph Pulitzer, of Missouri.

The audience seemed restless, much frayed at

the edges, and plainly anxious to emerge once more into the open air.

THE CONVENTION AFRAID OF ITSELF.

The proceedings thus far were too tame to win prolonged attention. The kernel of the nut was not yet reached. The convention was evidently afraid of itself, and desirous of keeping all inflammable matter from the explosives which every one knew to be lying just beneath the surface. Time, time was what was wanted to work up the latent strength of candidates, to fix upon a suitable person for permanent president, and most important of all, to mature a platform. The irrepressible Grosvenor offered a resolution that when the convention adjourn it adjourn to meet at 10 o'clock the next morning, and that in the meantime the several State delegations elect from among their number delegates double the number of votes to be cast by their respective States in the Electoral College; and that when this convention meet again the names of the delegates so selected be reported to the temporary Chairman. The resolution was adopted. Carl Schurz was loudly called for, but speech-making at this stage of the proceedings was not in his thoughts. He came to the front, said a few words, and vanished from the gaze of his auditory.

Without taking a vote upon the question, the chairman declared the convention adjourned until ten o'clock on Thursday morning.

RENEWAL OF CAUCASSING.

The Burnett House was the scene of the greatest animation. Its extensive corridors and handsome parlors were filled with excited crowds of individuals, surging out and in, and flowing hither and thither in torrents all the long spring afternoon, and far on into the noisy night, A few of the States had held final caucuses and had nothing more to say. But most of the delegations re-assembled to settle some vexed point hitherto left undecided.

In the Ohio delegation an informal ballot was taken, which resulted: Adams, 43; Greeley, 1. Indiana instructed her delegation to cast their first Vice-Presidential ballot for Julian. The Missouri delegates still adhered to the fortunes of Gratz Brown against hope. Kentucky, whose preference was for Adams, decided to urge Cassius M. Clay for permanent President of the convention. Michigan declared her preference for Adams. Hon. J. B. Grinnell, Chairman of the Iowa Delegation, had long been anxious for the nomination of Greeley, and very conspicuous during the Chappaqua philosopher's progress through the rural districts of the West, in the summer of 1871.

A majority of the delegates, however, at their last caucus, decided to vote first for Trumbull, reverting to Greeley as their second choice. Minnesota decided to vote for Trumbull. Warmoth told the reporters that Louisiana was for Greeley.

The smaller delegations reaffirmed their decisions already given as the result of Wednesday's caucusing.

TROUBLE IN THE NEW YORK DELEGATION.

The meeting of the New York delegation was especially interesting. Pursuant to a call of the Chairman, it met at headquarters at two o'clock in the afternoon. The free-traders had some time ere this been silenced. General Cochrane offered the following:

"*Resolved,* That we, delegates of New York, cast the entire vote for Hon. Horace Greeley for President, and until such times as we, members of the delegation, prefer to the Chairman a request that we delegates retire for consultation, after which the other votes of the delegates shall be cast for Horace Greeley, according to the direction of the majority."

In the discussion that followed, the great strength of Greeley in the delegation was apparent. Mr. Dorsheimer advised that the delegation vote as a unit for him. Mahlon Sands declined to go into convention with a padlock, that inconvenient symbol of tyranny, upon his lips. Mr. Goodrich, of King's county, expressed the opinion that the will of the majority should decide the vote of the entire delegation. General Cochrane, with sonorous voice, and in a decided manner, declared that Greeley and the delegation were identical.

Judge Henry R. Selden, of Rochester, unused to the turmoil of politics, and the devious ways of the caucus, dissented from the views of the majority. He thought that the minority should not be tabooed, although he was himself willing to abide the wish of the majority. Mr. Henry D. Lloyd, the young man who, with Mahlon Sands, represented the Free Trade League, spoke violently against Greeley, whom he deemed unfit to occupy the Presidential chair. He objected further to the majority rule, but was cut off in the midst of his eloquence by the strategic move of some rigid parliamentarian.

Another caucus was held at early candle-light, and another later in the night. At the first, General Cochrane presided; Judge Selden at the second. At the first the names of the voting delegates were presented by a committee and endorsed duly. It was ascertained through a member of the delegation that the Greeley men numbered about one hundred and forty, and the Adams men about forty.

The delegates were nominated by a committee (composed of Greeley men) appointed by the Chair (a Greeley man), under instructions that in those Congressional Districts from which there were representatives present the committee should appoint the delegates according to the instructions of such representatives. When the committee reported, the name of Mr. Lloyd, who had been chosen by a two-thirds majority of the members from his district, appeared among the number of delegates. Mr. Sinclair Toucey, of New York, then arose and inquired of Mr. Lloyd whether he would vote for Mr. Greeley. Mr. Theodore Tilton then arose and said if he were asked such a question he would remain silent till doomsday. Some further discussion then took place, and Mr. Lloyd not answering, Mr. Toucey moved that Mr. Lloyd's name be stricken from the list of delegates. The question was put, and, on a division of the house, was lost.

A flank movement on John N. Pomeroy, another delegate who refused to bow the knee to the white-coated Baal, was more successful. His name was expunged from the record.

VARIOUS PERSONAL MATTERS.

On Thursday it transpired that Fenton had left silently but suddenly for New York on the previous day. Exactly what he had been doing, except that he had been working for Greeley under cover, like a mole, precisely why he had left the city, was not plain to the common understanding. On Thursday Matteson, of the Chicago *Times*, received a letter from Wilbur F. Storey, in which it was declared that the Democracy of Illinois would support no other candidate but Davis. The German Democrats seemed more pronounced for Adams as the time of the nomination approached.

In attendance upon the convention, and hoping to be recognized in its deliberations, were Miss Susan B. Anthony, conspicuous for her gold spectacles and her faded loveliness, and Mrs. Laura De Force Gordon, of San Joaquin, California. A hum, a bustle, and a rush, occurred wherever they went. Mrs. Gordon was a champion of her own sex on general principles, a declared Internationalist, and had been a candidate for the State Senate in California, for which office she had received two hundred votes. The two ladies, being in the parlors of the Burnett House on the evening of May 2d, were invited to address the eager crowd that pressed around them. Before, however, they had had time to clinch a single point with their feminine logic, their auditory was ruthlessly swept from the elegant drawing-room by a squad of police, whose aid for the purpose had been invoked by the proprietors.

The close of the first day of the convention's sessions showed no particular change in respect of candidates to the casual observer. The lines of the various factions were, however, more tightly drawn, and personal bitternesses were greatly intensified. Partisans were preparing, in case of disaster, to throw the responsibility upon those who refused to support their candidate. During all the day, and a large part of the night, discussion, not entirely free from bitterness, was going on over certain portions of the platform.

SECOND DAY OF THE CONVENTION.

The weather was pleasant on the second day of the convention. The committee of arrangements having decided to admit to the floor, outside the hall, persons of all classes without tickets, the standing room in the lower part of the building was all occupied. The galleries were well filled, ladies handsomely dressed, and armed with lorgnettes, forming a prominent feature. Not less than eight thousand people were present. Before the assembly was called to order, Theodore Tilton, bowing gracefully, his head covered with ambrosial curls, escorted Miss Anthony and Mrs. Gordon to the platform. The appearance of the trio in conjunction called forth applause mingled with hisses.

Persons who had leisure looked around for people of note. There were many such to be seen here and there among the delegates. Warmoth, of Louisiana, the Apollo of carpet-baggers, moved easily about among the host, tall, handsome, nonchalant, dignified. General Cochrane, of New York, was conspicuous in his place in the New York delegation, of powerful physique, animated look, bronzed complexion, and voice that enforced attention whenever heard in the deliberations. All were anxious to see Alexander McClure, of Pennsylvania. His massive head and expansive brow indicate and his *blase* air showed that he could give the vote that might decide the welfare of the nation with as much coolness as he ever cast a die. Mrs. Gordon, dressed in gray, with a straw hat, gay with superflous ribbons, that fluttered like defiant pennons when she walked, took occasion to be much seen on the platform and in the aisles. If a bold usher ventured an inquiring look she congealed him with a stern stare, and an imperious nod.

Judge Matthews called the convention to order at ten o'clock. The immense mass of surging humanity settled itself into comparative quiet.

General McNeil, of Missouri, moved that a committee on permanent organization consisting of one from each State, be appointed, each delegation to designate its member.

A motion to amend, so as to allow delegates from the Territories to be represented on the committee, caused an excited discussion, in which General Cochrane joined ponderously, and the crepitant tone sand incisive manner of Judge Hoadley, grated harshly on the fine sensibilities of the convention.

Mr. Samuel E. Brown, of Colorado, ended the brief debates with some pertinent words, affirming the rights of Territories, and the amendment was adopted.

The appointment of the other essential committees was moved and carried.

MRS. GORDON.

The Chair produced by some unaccountable process of legerdemain, from some unperceived portion of his anatomy, a sheet of commercial note paper, delicately inscribed, and read as follows:

To the Chairman of the National Liberal Republican Convention:

DEAR SIR—The undersigned has the honor to submit for your consideration the following claims that entitle her to a seat in your convention. She is a citizen of the United States, and a resident of San Joaquin County, California, and fully sympathizes with the objects and aims of this convention. Heretofore she has acted with the Republican party, but believing, in common with the members of this convention, that there are grave errors to correct, and many reforms needed in said party, she is desirous of uniting her action with them for the purpose of accomplishing so desirable an object.

She represents further, that, according to opportionment, California is entitled to ten delegates and ten votes in the convention ; but, besides herself

NEGRO CITIZENSHIP
CIVIL SERVICE REFORM
ONE
GRANT & WILSON
PROTECTION OF THE BALLOT
ABOLITION OF FRANKING
GRANT

there are only four citizens of that State present to represent the people thereof; and, being desirous that California shall be as fully represented as practicable, she applied to one or two of the members present at this convention from that State for recognition as a delegate with themselves; and, finding them indifferent to her claim, or doubtful of the convention accepting the female citizens as members, she therefore appeals directly to the honorable officers and members of the National Republican Convention, and respectfully asks to be admitted as a member and delegate to the convention from the State of California, and entitled, under the rules thereof, to all rights and privileges as such.

With assurances of the most earnest sympathy in the purposes of the convention,

I am most respectfully yours,

LAURA DE FORCE GORDON, of California.

Amid applause and acclamation, the delicate document was referred, to the Committee on Credentials.

THE COMMITTEES.

The Committees on Credentials and Permanent Organization, which were then announced, contained no men known outside of their states, unless it were R. P. Spaulding, of Ohio.

The gentlemen whose names follow constituted the Committee on Platform:

Alabama, Samuel F. Rice; Arkansas, Edwin Bancroft; California, Wm. H. Russell; Connecticut, D. A. Wells; Florida, James B. C. Drew; Georgia, James Johnson; Illinois, Horace White; Indiana, Thomas C. Whitesides; Iowa, J. B. Grinnell; Kansas, E. G. Ross; Kentucky, John Mason Brown; Louisiana, J. M. Dirheimer; Maine, J. S. Lyford; Maryland, A. W. Bradford; Massachusetts, F. W. Bird; Michigan, J. P. Thompson; Minnesota, Theodore Halscher; Mississippi, W. I. Yesbitt; Missouri, Wm. J. Grosvenor; Nebraska, W. P. Roberts; Nevada, George D. Lyon; New Hampshire, Ed. D. Baker; New Jersey, James M. Scoville; New York, Theodore Tilton; North Carolina, Louis Haines; Ohio, George Hoadley; Oregon, J. W. Johnson; Pennsylvania, Hon. Wm. M. Ball; Rhode Island, Ed. Harris; South Carolina, S. A. Pearce, Jr.; Tennessee, G. P. Thruston; Texas, A. J. Hamilton; Vermont, Chas. Clemens; Virginia, W. W. Wood; West Virginia, W. P. Hubbard; Wisconsin, G. M. Woodward; District of Columbia,

John D. Defrees; Colorado, S. E. Brown; Dakota, George A. Pryor; Montana, F. C. Evarts; Utah, A. W. Galvia.

THE NEW YORK ROW.

Judge Selden, of New York, obtained the floor, and presented a paper which he said was a protest of his friends of the minority of the delegation from his State against the action of the majority, and which he desired to be presented to the Committee on Credentials. The paper recited the facts already herein given, and stated besides, that—

"In the First Congressional District, Edward H. Seaman was nominated by the delegation present from that district as one of the representative delegates, and after it was ascertained that Mr. Seaman was opposed to the nomination of Horace Greeley, another person, known as "Rocky" Moore, was substituted for him by the committee." Also "that the delegates present from the Eighth Congressional District met, as directed by the Chair, and nominated, by a vote of eight out of thirteen delegates, then and there present, James L. Bishop and Thomas Duffy as their representative delegates, and that this choice was duly reported to and disregarded by said committee, and by the whole number of members in its election, and that the representative delegates reported by the committee and elected by the whole body from this district were never nominated at any meeting of the resident delegates thereof, as required by the instructions of the convention and by a resolution of our members."

It was further stated "that in the Twenty-seventh Congressional District, the one delegate present recommended himself and Theodore Bacon as representative delegates; that upon ascertaining that Mr. Bacon was opposed to the nomination of Mr. Greeley, the committee substituted, without consultation with any resident of the Twenty-seventh Congressional District, the name of a person known to concur in the views of the majority; and still further, *that no persons were present as members of the convention from several congressional districts, and that, in the election of representative delegates to fill these vacancies, all persons understood to be opposed to the nomination of Mr. Greeley were studiously ignored.*"

The inconvenient document was duly referred as requested by the inexperienced politician who presented it. It was found to have been signed by twenty-six gentlemen, including nearly all the respectable New Yorkers present.*

THE CONVENTION TURBULENT.

A scene of disorder ensued, which exceeded the limited abilities of the chairman.

The committees, having been appointed, needed time to prepare their reports, and there was really no business before the convention. Various trivial motions were made, but few of which were entertained; and finally, on motion of McClure, of Pennsylvania, a recess was finally taken until three o'clock, there being no other way of disposing of the tumultuous assemblage.

AFTERNOON SESSION—SECOND DAY.

The convention reassembled at three P. M., and was called to order by Judge Matthews.

The report of the Committee of Permanent Organization was read by Judge Spaulding, of Cleveland. It announced that the committee, with entire unanimity, had fixed upon Carl Schurz as permanent chairman.

The announcement was received with loud and continuous cheering. Mr. Schurz was escorted to

*There is no doubt whatever that the New York delegation was secured for Greeley, and his nomination thus brought about, by simply packing the delegation, or rather, making up the mob which came to Cincinnati from New York, of the disreputable Fenton Republicans, chiefly from New York city, who had fought with Greeley (and with Tammany) in previous campaigns. These swamped with their numbers the Revenue Reformers and other progressive men who were drawn to Cincinnati by principle, rather than spoils.

the stand by a gentleman, whose only badge of distinction was the reeking stump of a cigar, tightly pinched between his lips. Judge Matthews shook hands with his successor, and presented him to the convention with the briefest possible formula of introduction.

PRESIDENT SCHURZ AND HIS SPEECH.

Mr. Schurz then delivered his speech. Its opening sentences were pregnant with astonishment at the size of the convention, and the thought that such an assemblage was possible. The American people had just emerged from a mighty struggle in the full pride of their national strength, surrounded by hidden dangers and insidious evils, of which the masses were not aware. Corruption, fostered by the war, had invaded the goverment, and public opinion was woefully lenient in regard to it. The government was disregarding the laws, and those in authority were, through the public services, tyrannically interfering with private affairs; men in high places were seeking selfish advantages, thus corrupting our politics, and the cries of partisanship were drowning the voice of criticism. Amnesty was refused to the South, so much in need of restoration, and party spirit justified the ungenerous use of power. Would the American people longer suffer themselves to be driven like a flock of sheep? The answer was, No! Love of liberty was not dead, nor did it intend to die. These questions, he said, were answered in thundering tones by the convention there assembled. The volume of the response had exceeded all expectations. The conscience of the people that seemed dead had arisen to new life. Nothing could withstand so genuine an uprising. The breath of victory was in the very air. The opportunity presented to crush corruption, and give the country a pure government was grand. But all selfishness must be cast backward. The occasion was momentous, and the responsibility fearful.

"If [said the speaker] you disappoint the high expectations brought forth by that spontaneous impulse, you have not only lost a great opportunity, but you have struck a blow at the confidence the people have in themselves, and for a long time popular reform movements will not rise again under the weight of the discredit which you will have brought upon them. Is it possible that such should be the result of our doings? It is possible if we do not rise to the full height of our duty. It is possible if, instead of following the grand impulse of the popular heart, we attempt to control and use this movement by the old tricks of the political trade, or fritter away our zeal in small bickerings and mean, selfish aspirations.

* * * * * * * * *

"Reform must become a farce in the hands of those who either do not understand it or do not care for it. If you mean reform, intrust the work to none but those who understand and honestly do care, and care more for it than their own personal ends. Pardon me if I express myself on this point with freedom and frankness. I have not, I assure you, come here for the purpose of urging the claims or advancing the interest of any one man against all others. I have come here with sincere and ardent devotion to a cause, and to use my best endeavors to have that cause put under the care of men who are devoted to it with equal sincerity, and possess those qualities of mind and heart which will make it safe in their keeping. I earnestly deprecate the cry we have heard so frequently, 'Anybody to beat Grant.' There is something more wanted than to beat Grant—not anybody who might, by cheap popularity, or by astute bargains and combinations, or by all the tricks of political wire-pulling, manage to scrape together votes enough to be elected President. We do not merely want another, but we want a better, President than we now have. We do not want a mere change of persons in the administration of the Government: we want the overthrow of a pernicious system; we want the eradication of flagrant abuses; we want the infusion of a loftier moral spirit into our political organism; we want a Government which the best people of this country will be proud of. Not anybody can accomplish that, and therefore away with the cry, 'Anybody to beat Grant!'—a cry too paltry, too unworthy of the great enterprise in which we are engaged."

We give in this sketch the words of this really statesmanlike and patriotic speech, chiefly for the sake of showing how completely the convention, by its subsequent course, disobeyed its worthy precepts.

The following gentlemen officiated as the chief secretaries: General W. E. McClane, of Indiana; John X. Davidson, of Minnesota; D. T. Wright, of Maine; J. D. Rhodes, of Ohio; and each State was represented by a Vice-President.

The Committee on Credentials reported the names of those entitled to seats, and adversely to the contestants in the New York delegation Mrs. Laura De Force Gordon was not recognized as a delegate, but the committee recommended that she be tendered the freedom of the hall. The contestants in the California delegation were declared not entitled to seats as delegates, on the ground that they simply hovered on the verge of California civilization. Shortly after, Mrs. Gordon, from a place on the floor, attempted to protest against her exclusion. After many times repeating the formula "Mr. President," with the assistance of a kind German friend, she gained the attention of the Chair, but only to be courteously told that, the committee having ignored her plea, the Chair could not listen to her address. She still persisted, but was ungallantly hissed into silence.

After this amusing episode the report of the committee was adopted without change.

The Committee on Rules reported that they had organized by electing Theodore Tilton as their chairman; that the chairman of each delegation should declare the vote of the delegation according to the manner in which each member voted; that a majority of votes should be necessary to a choice, and that the yeas and nays should not be called, but if necessary there should be a division of the convention by a call of the States.

OPPOSITION TO FORMAL NOMINATION.

At this point a vigorous effort was made to force the nomination. Mr. H. J. Stansbery suggested that the convention proceed to ballot for nominees; and that, as it was impossible to expect the concurrence of all the delegates on the questions which were now before the country, the nominees themselves be considered the platform. The suggestion was interpreted as a plea for Democratic assistance. It was violently opposed by John Cochrane, and favored by Mr. McClure, of Pennsylvania.

The chair stated that the committee had taken a recess until five o'clock without perfecting a platform. Mr. Dembite, of Kentucky, thought that they understood the matter as well now as they would at five o'clock; he preferred that a nomination should be made here, and not in the hotel down town.

These efforts, being a sort of skirmish drill preliminary to the general battle, were finally ended by a motion of General Cochrane to lay the whole matter on the table, which prevailed upon a call of the states.

The gentlemen who desired to nominate prematurely, having failed in their attempt, endeavored to effect their purpose by a shower of resolutions, all of which were referred, without reading, to the Committee on Platform, with the exception of one presented by Colonel McClure, which was adopted. This declared that the convention would not proceed to ballot for candidates before a platform had been adopted.

Besides the meaningless generalities embodied in these various expressions of private opinion, there were declarations for the one term principle, enactment of penal laws, punishing by fine and imprisonment all persons found guilty of bribery and corruption, abrogation of the government patronage system, and improvement of morality among the officers and servants of the people, etc. A portion of these specific principles were embodied in a series of resolutions, prepared and presented by Mr. Braughn, who innocently moved that they be adopted as the platform of this convention.

The vast assemblage laughed heartily, and the tropical delegate took his seat discomfited.

CHAPTER XX.

THE CINCINNATI CONVENTION.

(CONTINUED.)

"The Apple of Discord"—Struggle Over the Tariff—The Temporary President Demands a Free Fight—Reformers Beaten on Both Candidate and Platform—The Balloting for President—Blair's Game—Arrival of Gratz Brown—Greeley Forging Ahead—Schurz Denounces Him Before the Missouri Delegation—White Might Have Saved His Own Humiliation, but Did Not—Greeley Nominated and Blair Triumphant—Brown Also—Chagrin of the Reformers—Their Utterances—Carl Schurz Plays a Plaintive Air, and the Curtain Falls.

EVENING SESSION—SECOND DAY.

A recess was taken until half-past seven o'clock in the evening. At that hour the convention reassembled. A prolonged stay in Cincinnati was beginning to tell on the purses of delegates, and protracted sessions on their patience. A large portion were in no humor for longer delay.

The chairman stated that the Committee on Platform would not be ready to report until morning, and suggested that the time be pieced out with speeches such as are usually made when candidates are named.

General Cochrane, taking advantage of the situation, moved that members proceed to name their candidates, and be allowed ten minutes in which to proclaim their virtues and demonstrate their availability. The motion prevailed by a scarcely perceptible majority. No one taking immediate advantage of the permission to nominate, Mr. Parks, of New York, presented a resolution recommending extension of civil rights to all, and universal amnesty. The resolution was referred. Mr. Allen followed with a resolution advising the appointment of executive committees in all the States.

TARIFF AND OTHER TROUBLES.

Gilbert H. Peck, of New Jersey, presented a resolution in favor of a reform in the manner of levying import duties, steadfast resistance to centralization, and many other generalities. An Indiana delegate, devoted to serious business, presented a resolution, which was adopted, declaring that the convention would not defeat the objects for which it was assembled by adjourning without a nomination of candidates for the position of President and Vice-President.

Mr. Groesbeck, of Virginia, offered a resolution against a restriction of the presidential office, and affirming that every American, with a true heart in his bosom, was eligible to the office.

A resolution presented by Mr. L. N. Peterson, of Richmond, Pa., favored an amendment to the constitution, providing for the election of a President, Vice-President and U. S. Senators, directly by the people.

Others were presented, all of which, with the exceptions named, were referred to the Committee on Platform. Among the rest was one referring the question of tariff to the Congressional districts.

It is uncertain how long this thing might have continued, every member seeming to have a resolution in his pocket, had not Mr. Hickman, of Pennsylvania, called for the regular order of business, which was understood to be the presentation of candidates. But the undercurrent of feeling against a nomination at that time was very vigorous. A motion to adjourn was for the moment defeated.

A delegate from North Carolina suggested a call of States alphabetically, and an adjournment if no delegates were named. A slight gloom had overspread the convention, but this sally provoked laughter.

Colonel Hudson, of Terre Haute, Ind., gaining the attention of the Chair in spite of the confusion, said he had been informed by a member of the Committee on Platform that they were unable to agree. As it was apparent that the convention hesitated to nominate candidates, and the Committee on Platform seemed to be "stalled" on the tariff question, that question already having been decided, it would be quite proper for the committee to report at once, that being the only impediment. A delegate suggested that the tariff resolution presented was not adopted, only referred. "Then, sir," said Colonel Hudson, "upon that question of the tariff and its presentation in the resolutions just referred to the committee, I move you, sir, a suspension of the rules [laughter] that this convention, at this very moment, may take up that stumbling block which hangs in the way of the Committee on Resolutions, and remove it ourselves." Great applause followed, but a large proportion of the members seemed thrilled, and terrified by a sudden precipitation of the patent question upon them.

Infinite confusion succeeded, during which noises of all kinds were heard,—calls to order, for the regular order of business, and motions whose purport was undistinguishable in the immense volume of sound, but a vote was finally attained, and the suspension of the rules was ordered, 460 voting for and 229 against.

The States voting in the negative were Georgia, Illinois, Indiana, Iowa, Louisiana, Minnesota, Missouri, Massachusetts, Mississippi, New York, New Jersey, Pennsylvania, Ohio, South Carolina, Tennessee, Vermont and Virginia. Delaware and Rhode Island did not vote when called upon.

The vote of Delaware was cast by George Alfred Townsend, Washington correspondent of the Chicago *Tribune*. Mr. Townsend is a native of Delaware, but has not lived there since his childhood. Pennsylvania voted as a unit against the resolution, but was thought secretly to favor its adoption.

The danger of committing some fatal error seemed at this moment to be imminent, but the intelligence was conveyed to the Chair that the Committee on Platform had adopted the tariff plank.

He rose hastily and imparted the information briefly to the assembly.

"Only two votes dissenting out of the whole committee," added David A. Wells, *sotto voce.*

"Let it be read," called out an impatient delegate.

"Wait until to-morrow," exclaimed Judge Hoadley.

There were many and loud cries of "No, no; now!" during the prevalence of which J. H. Rhodes, of Cleveland, moved that the tariff resolution of the committee be referred back to them for consideration.

In response to an objection, the Chair stated that the rules had been suspended for all purposes. Mr. Rhodes moved that the resolution of Colonel Hudson be referred to the committee, with instructions to report it to the convention. There was renewed confusion, which fell into partial quiet when Cassius M. Clay appeared upon the platform.

Mr. Clay shook his gray locks, and launched boldly out upon a sea of oratory. He deprecated the debate on the tariff question, and deplored the condition of the South, "overrode" by military despotism. The latter point he thought of infinitely more importance. The former he characterized, with his usual felicity of eloquence and metaphor, as an "apple of discord."

The torrent of eloquence poured forth with such resistless energy was finally stopped by the ten minute barrier wisely erected at an early stage of the proceedings.

AN EXPLOSION.

It remained, however, for Judge Stanley Matthews to fire the train so ingeniously laid by previous speakers. He professed to deprecate the question of the tariff, sprung upon the convention while the Committee on Platforms was in session, and continued when it was fully understood that the committee had agreed upon a tariff plank with great unanimity. After these words of peace and placation, he ended his remarks in the following fiery style, his metaphors being borrowed from the slang of the lower Mississippi:

"Now, if this is to be a free fight, let us make it a fair one, and I have a counter proposition, the proposition which was used as the basis of the call for this convention, which I will read, and move as a substitute for the proposition pending before the body. It is in these words:

Resolved, That no form of taxation is just or wise which puts needless burdens upon the people. We demand a reform of the tariff, so that those duties shall be removed which, in addition to the revenue yielded to the Treasury, involve increase in the price of domestic products, and a consequent tax for the benefit of favorite interests.

[Great applause on the floor and in the galleries.]

Now, gentlemen, I will tell you one of the reasons why I entered into this movement. It was that I might assist in the work of emancipating the politics and the business of this country from the domination of rings. [Applause.] I mean political rings in Washington; I mean railroad rings, which are stealing our public lands [applause], and I mean *pig iron rings, which are robbing the people* [great applause], and which, under pretense of relieving the burdens of the people, are taking taxes off from tea and coffee in order that they may keep them up on salt and iron."

An increasing restlessness had been observed during the continuation of Judge Matthews' speech.

When he had finished the inflammatory paragraph quoted, several gentlemen into whose souls the pig iron had entered, rose to their feet with a spasmodic movement.

The points of order were innumerable. Judge Matthews attempted to hold the floor on the ground that the rules were suspended. No assistance was vouchsafed by the chairman, who fully recognized the perils of the situation. He simply said that but one rule had been suspended, which was that all resolutions should be referred without debate. Upon this the incendiary orator retired from the stand.

The next bold Roman to leap into the breach was Edward Atkinson, of Massachusetts, a courteous gentleman unused to the turmoil of active politics, and not informed with the zeal which characterizes the mere partisan. He took the stand with perceptible hesitancy, and said, speaking as a member of the committee, that the delay in the report was not caused by difference in regard to the tariff plank. Not being the chairman, he might not report the vote properly, and no copy was at hand from which he might read. The sub-committee had acted, in fine, the whole committee had acted, and the action had been nearly unanimous. Haste at a juncture like this would only hinder.

Just as Mr. Atkinson was going on to hint at what was really going on in the committee, General Cake, of Pennsylvania, rose and inquired whether it would be in order in that place for a member of the committee to report. The Chair decided Mr. Atkinson to be in order. The gentle Atkinson went on timorously and apologetically, fearing to offend, and said he was simply speaking for harmony, which certainly at that moment seemed to be a scarce article. He closed with a mixed motion to lay on the table the suspension of the rules and the pending resolution.

Various gentlemen attempted to speak, but were crushed with the statement of the Chair that the question was not debatable. Among those who struggled hardest to gain the recognition of Mr. Schurz, was Colonel McClure, of Pennsylvania, who moved to rule the question debatable. He was compelled to succumb to the rulings, although having a little spasmodic aid from Judge Hoadley.

Mr. Rhodes, of Cleveland, fearing the business would get into the committee and make trouble, moved to amend so as to lay on the table until the Committee on Platform had reported. The motion was ignored. The motion of Mr. Atkinson prevailed, amid great noise and confusion and not a little manifestation of ill temper in the Pennsylvania delegation. Colonel McClure was eager for the fray.

After voting to have a call of the States, so that each might nominate, the convention adjourned until the next morning at ten o'clock. McClure was said to have so far forgot himself in the excitement of the moment as to have said that, could he have reached Carl Schurz upon the platform, he would have put a fanciful ornament on his frontispiece.

It was further recounted that, as the satisfaction next accessible, he approached Judge Matthews, and, with a refreshing forgetfulness, asked him the leading question—"Why are you not honest?" "I am," replied Judge Matthews, neglecting to add, "but indiscreet." To which the tall Pennsylvanian responded with the assertion, "No, you are not. Your resolution was a Jesuitical cheating sham."

With such touching interchange of feeling as this between delegates, the convention ended the last session of the second day of its existence. The three sessions had been noisy without being at all enthusiastic. The spectators on the floor had applauded moderately, and the silence of the galleries had been funereal. The situation, when the delegates separated for the night, was ominous.

FACTS, RUMORS AND SPECULATIONS.

After the adjournment of the convention, rumor again became busy. Not having the concrete and tangible to deal with, recourse was had to the imagination. Before the convention met in the evening it was understood that the Committee on Platform had agreed upon the tariff plank. Therefore, surprise was common when Mr. Schurz stated that the committee were not prepared to report. It was currently reported about the city that the President was endeavoring to gain time until an answer could come to the following dispatch sent during the day:

CINCINNATI, May 2, 1872.

To Horace Greeley, Tribune Office, New, York:

We can secure the nomination of Trumbull for the first place if you will accept the second place on the ticket. Will you? Answer.

[Signed] CARL SCHURZ.

The break between Schurz and a portion of the

Missouri delegation had already occurred, the Senator not deeming Governor Brown the most eligible candidate for the Presidential office. But the Adams men had supposed Schurz to be working in their interest, and were not prepared consequently for an out and out declaration for Trumbull. The rumor of the dispatch brought Davis and Adams men here and there into council. An offer to trade from the former to the leaders of the latter elicited the reply that, if they agreed to do so, inforcement of the contract would be impossible.

The combinations most talked of were Trumbull and Greeley, and Adams and Brown. Other names were mentioned in connection, but the general indisposition of candidates to accept the second place on the ticket rendered the chances for their success hopeless. Among the possible candidates was Wm. S. Groesbeck, of Cincinnati. Mr. Groesbeck is a venerable and dignified Democrat with the instincts of a gentleman, the purse of Fortunatus, and the lingering hope of some office of importance to ennoble his declining years, and lift him into immortality. He had been too many years trimming, with a view to the disruption of existing parties, and the creation of a new one, of which he should be the stately idol. This course had continued too long, and his expectations were too well known to permit of his accepting the second place, even if he had so desired. Up to the last moment he was occasionally seen among the throng at the Burnett House, discussing the situation with interest, but still with antiquated dignity.

THE TARIFF IMBROGLIO.

The Committee on Platform were in session all day on Thursday and deep into the small hours of Thursday night. The discussions were earnest, and occasionally personal. The furniture of the parlor at the St. James, where the meetings were held, was badly abused. With much exertion John D. Defrees, delegate from the District of Columbia, secured the adoption of the following—a variation of the device submitted by Greeley, through his confidential agent, Whitelaw Reid:

A tariff being necessary to create a sufficient revenue to discharge the pecuniary obligations of the government, and its enactment and its adjustment of details being the constitutional province of the representatives of the people in Congress assembled, it should be submitted to their action unmolested by executive interference.

But, overheated with toil, and burning with thirst, he left to secure a glass of ice-water to cool his parched tongue, and the vote upon it was reconsidered.

In a sub-committee consisting of Mr. Defrees, Hon. Daniel A. Wells, and Hon. George Hoadley, the following was finally adopted after prolenged debate:

Resolved, That all taxes should be levied only for the purpose of paying the current expenses of the government, the interest on the public debt, the pensions to disabled soldiers and the widows and orphans of the late war, and a fair per cent. of annual reduction on the principal of the public debt; that none of these taxes should be levied so as to promote the interests of any particular class, or oppress the industrial pursuits of any particular section; nevertheless, assembled in this convention we declare that as the President of the United States is an executive, and not a legislative officer, the subject of taxes should be left to Congress in the belief that the President will execute the laws made by Congress."

The full committee concurred in the report of the sub-committee, and the matter was thought by most to be settled. But Colonel McClure thought differently. He swore with many oaths, and "ne'er a true one," that the tariff plank was a "wishy-washy" affair, and invoked eternal perdition if he ever accepted it. He prepared the following, which he declared he would present to the convention the following morning.

Resolved, That as the raising of a revenue for the maintenance of our national credit is a sacred obligation, imposed by the fundamental law, the levying of import duties is a duty the details of which belong to the people of the whole country through their representatives in Congress assembled, and such policy when established shall be left free from executive interference.

THE SITUATION ON THURSDAY NIGHT.

Caucusing continued until after midnight without any particular change in the situation. The Adams men were confident. The Davis men had lost hope, but still put on a bold front. The Trumbull men were disheartened by the continued aggressiveness of the Davis men, and did not hesitate to say so to their intimate friends. The friends of Greeley thought the nomination of their candidate possible; that was all. Theodore Tilton worked for him incessantly, especially among the delegates from the Southern States, with whom his sonorous periods and sophomoric eloquence had considerable weight. Whitelaw Reid had been on the ground for several days, in constant telegraphic communication with his principal. The communications were shown to a select coterie of intimates, and their contents by them from time to time disseminated. One or two were published in the papers. They generally advised the ignoring of the tariff question, or its direct reference to the people.

BLAIR AND BROWN.

Late at night it was noised about among a few that Frank Blair and Gratz Brown were in the city.

There was great surprise and not a little uneasiness. It had been authoritatively stated that Brown had too delicate a sense of honor to be at the convention, and the presence of Blair portended good to no one. What conferences the lateness of the hour permitted after the arrival of the twain, were with the Pennsylvania and New York delegates. What was really done and contemplated was known to a very limited number of persons. Outside of this circle, the life of which was supposed to be McClure, everything was strangely misconstrued. The real state of the case was not suspected. It was conjectured by most that Brown was to be put forward for the second place on the ticket either with Adams or Trumbull as principal. The influence which Pennsylvania really had in the convention, and its pivotal position, were fully determined by the events of the succeeding day. To have defended protection against the aggressive free-traders, and left the tariff question untouched in the canvas, was a great victory. Not to take the fortress which they were storming, was to the partisans of revenue reform an ignominious defeat.

Pennsylvania secured the adoption of its own platform, and put its candidates upon it. The conferences which preluded the nomination of Greeley and Brown were held with the utmost secrecy. What was agreed upon was communicated to less than a dozen miscellaneous delegates, and under a pledge of eternal silence.

The convention was called to order punctually at ten o'clock.

The Chairman sat down with disturbed looks. Colonel G. Moore, of Missouri, presented a resolution dispensing with the formal nomination of candidates. It was adopted, after some confusion.

REPORT OF THE COMMITTEE ON PLATFORM.

The Chair announced to the convention that the Committee on Platform was ready to report.

There were cries of "Good, good," and loud cheers.

Mr. Schurz further stated that he had been requested to read the resolutions on account of the vocal weakness of the Chairman of the committee, (Mr. White) and also asked to state that the concurrence of the committee in the report was *almost* unanimous.

The President read the report as follows:

The administration now in power has rendered itself guilty of wanton disregard of the laws of the land in the exercise of powers not granted by the Constitution. It has acted as if the laws had binding force only for those who are governed, and not for those who govern. It has thus struck a blow at the fundamental principle of constitutional government and the liberties of the citizen.

The President of the United States has openly used the powers and opportunities of his high office for the promotion of personal ends. He has kept notoriously corrupt and unworthy men in places of power and responsibility, to the detriment of the public interest.

He has used the public service of the government as a machinery of partisan and personal influence, and interfered, with tyrannical arrogance, in the political affairs of States and municipalities.

He has rewarded, with influential and lucrative offices, men who had acquired his favor by valuable presents, thus stimulating the demoralization of our political life by his conspicuous example.

He has shown himself deplorably unequal to the tasks imposed upon him by the necessities of the country, and culpably careless of the responsibilities of his high office.

The partisans of the administration, assuming to be the Republican party and controlling its organization, have attempted to justify such wrongs and palliate such abuses, to the end of maintaining partisan ascendency.

They have stood in the way of necessary investigations and indispensable reforms, pretending that no serious fault could be found with the present administration of public affairs, thus seeking to blind the eyes of the people.

They have kept alive the passions and resentments of the late civil war, to use them for their own advantage. They have resorted to arbitrary measures in direct conflict with the organic law, instead of appealing to the better instincts and latent patriotism of the Southern people by restoring to them those rights, the enjoyment of which is indispensable for a successful administration of their local affairs, and would tend to restore a patriotic national feeling. They have degraded themselves and the name of their party, once justly entitled to the confidence of the nation, by a base sycophancy to the dispenser of executive power and patronage unworthy of Republican freemen. They have sought to silence the voice of just criticism, to stifle the moral sense of the people, and to subjugate public opinion by tyrannical party discipline ; they are striving to maintain themselves in authority for selfish ends by an unscrupulous use of the power which rightfully belongs to the people, and should be employed only in the service of the country.

Believing that no organization thus led and controlled can longer be of service to the best interests of the Republic, we have resolved to make an independent appeal to the sober judgment, conscience, and patriotism of the American people.

We, the Liberal Republicans of the United States, in national convention assembled at Cincinnati, proclaim the following principles as essential to just government :

1. We recognize the equality of all before the law, and hold that it is the duty of government in its dealings with the people to mete out equal and exact justice to all of whatever nativity, race, color, or persuasion, religious or political.

2. We pledge ourselves to maintain the Union of the States, emancipation

and enfranchisement, and oppose any re-opening of the questions settled by the Thirteenth, Fourteenth, and Fifteenth amendments of the Constitution.

3. We demand immediate and absolute removal of all disabilities imposed on account of the rebellion, which was finally subdued seven years ago, believing that universal amnesty will result in complete pacification in all sections of the country.

4. Local self-government, with impartial suffrage, will guard the rights of all citizens more securely than any centralized power. The public welfare requires the supremacy of the civil over the military authority, and the freedom of person under the protection of the *habeas corpus*. We demand for the individual the largest liberty consistent with the public order, for the State self-government, and for the nation return to the methods of peace and the constitutional limitation of power.

5. The civil service of the government has become a mere instrument of partisan tyranny and personal ambition, and an object of selfish greed. It is a scandal and reproach upon free institutions, and breeds a demoralization dangerous to the prosperity of republican government.

6. We therefore regard a thorough reform of the civil service as one of the most pressing necessities of the hour; that honesty, capacity and fidelity constitute the only valid claims to public employment; that the offices of the government cease to be a matter of arbitrary favoritism and patronage, and that public stations become again a post of honor. To this end it is imperatively required that no President shall be a candidate for re-election.

7. We demand a system of Federal taxation which shall not necessarily interfere with the industry of the people, and shall provide sufficient means to pay the expenses of the government, economically administered, pensions, and the interest on the public debt, and a moderate annual reduction of the principal thereof; but, recognizing the existence in our midst of honest, but irreconcilable, differences of opinion upon the merits of the respective systems of protection and free trade, we remit the discussion of the subject to the people in their congressional districts and to the decision of Congress thereon, wholly free from executive interference or dictation.

8. The public credit must be sacredly maintained, and we denounce repudiation in every form and guise.

9. A speedy return to specie payment is demanded alike by the highest considerations of commercial morality and honest government.

10. We remember with gratitude the heroism aud sacrifices of the soldiers and sailors of the republic, and no act of ours shall ever detract from their justly earned fame or the full rewards of their patriotism.

11. We are opposed to all further grants of land to railroads or other corporations. The public domain should be held sacred to actual settlers.

12. We hold that it is the duty of the government, in its intercourse with foreign nations, to cultivate the friendship of peace by treating with all on fair and equal terms, regarding it alike dishonorable either to demand what is not right, or to submit to what is wrong.

13. For the promotion and success of these vital principles, and the support of the candidate nominated by this cenvention, we invite, and cordially welcome, the co-operation of all patriotic citizens, without regard to previous political affiliations.

General Burnett, of Cincinnati, moved the adoption of the "second Declaration of Independence" by acclamation. The motion prevailed amid riotous enthusiasm caused rather by the consciousness of really having a platform safe and sound after much tribulation, than by the nature of the principles presented.

After the turmoil partially subsided, the President said, "The Chair announces, with gratification and pride, that the resolutions are adopted by a unanimous vote." The gratification of the vast assembly at having at last touched bottom again welled to the surface in fainter efforts at applause.

The Chair stated that the question recurred on the nomination of candidates.

A spasmodic effort was made to secure formal nominations. The Chair directed the roll-call to proceed.

FIRST BALLOT.

The first ballot resulted as follows.

STATES.	ADAMS.	TRUMBULL.	DAVIS.	GREELEY.	BROWN.	CURTIN.
Alabama	--	3	2	7	--	--
Arkansas	1	1	--	--	10	--
California	--	--	6	--	6	--
Connecticut	12	--	--	--	--	--
Delaware	6	--	--	--	--	--
Florida	6	--	--	--	--	--
Georgia	2	2	2	4	12	--
Illinois	--	21	21	--	--	--
Indiana	8	14	6	--	--	--

States.	Adams.	Trumbull.	Davis.	Greeley.	Brown.	Curtin.
Iowa	--	9	2	7	4	--
Kansas	--	10	--	--	--	--
Kentucky	16	--	--	2	6	--
Louisiana	4	8	--	2	--	--
Maine	14	--	--	--	--	--
Maryland	2	1	13	--	--	--
Massachusetts	22	4	--	--	--	--
Michigan	18	--	--	--	--	--
Minnesota	--	9	1	--	--	--
Mississippi	4	4	2	6	--	--
Missouri	--	--	--	--	30	--
Nebraska	--	3	--	2	1	--
Nevada	--	--	--	--	6	--
New Hampshire	--	--	--	8	--	--
New Jersey	5	--	--	5	7	--
New York	2	--	--	66	--	--
North Carolina	--	--	12½	5	--	--
Ohio	44	--	--	--	--	--
Oregon	--	--	--	--	6	--
Pennsylvania	--	--	--	--	--	56
Rhode Island	8	--	--	--	--	--
South Carolina	--	2	12	--	--	--
Tennessee	11	6	1	--	4	--
Texas	2	--	--	14	--	--
Vermont	1	--	--	7	--	--
Virginia	--	6	5	5	--	6
West Virginia	5	--	3	2	--	--
Wisconsin	10	5	4	1	--	--
Total	203	108	92½	129	92	62
Chase, 2½.						

When Judge Casey, of the District of Columbia, offered the vote of his delegation, the chairman expressed the opinion that as the present was a liberal convention, and all national conventions had admitted the territories to vote, they should be so allowed on this occasion.

Objections were made, and the territories were excluded from the ballot.

ENTER GRATZ BROWN.

At this point occurred the most remarkable episode of the convention. Gratz Brown, of Missouri, had been for some time sitting with the Missouri delegation, whose place was a few seats from the platform, and to the left of the chairman. He was now observed to have risen, and to be endeavoring to gain the eye of that official. The chair seemed disinclined to recognize the governor of Missouri. After having once or twice enunciated the formula, "Mr. President," Mr. Brown slowly skirted the reporters' platform, picking his way with difficulty through the narrow lane, closely hemmed in by excited people, and making his way with difficulty toward the steps of the platform. The chair seemed startled and uncertain how to act. When the intruder was nearing the steps, and recognition could be no longer postponed, Mr. Schurz said: "A gentleman, who is recognized by the chair as not a member of this convention, desires to make a personal explanation to the convention, and being a gentleman who had been voted for by a large number of delegates as a candidate for President of the United States, the chair submits to the convention whether or not leave should be granted him by unanimous consent. That gentleman is Governor Gratz Brown, of Missouri."

As this was delivered, there was an appealing wave of the hand, and a glance of the eye, that swept the house to the farthest seat. No whisper of objection was wafted to the anxious ear of the speaker. Had there been a breath of remonstrance, the speech of Mr. Brown would never have been made. But the only sounds heard were, "leave, leave!" and applause. The voice of dissent was delicately silent. The majority were too much astonished to take action, not having even the faintest idea of what was to occur.

BROWN'S SPEECH.

As Brown ascended the steps to the platform, the sunlight, finding entrance through some opening in the lofty roof, struck fully upon his red hair, giving it an intenser fiery tinge, and making his head seem not as if encircled by a golden aureole, but as though it were really the flaming torch of discord. Having attained his position, and turned his haggard face toward the audience, he said:

"MR. PRESIDENT AND GENTLEMEN OF THE CONVENTION: Although a delegate to this convention, it has not been possible for me to meet with you until to-day, as I have been detained at home by official business. And now when I come in for the first time, I find myself in an embarrassing position. Some of my friends from my own State, and many from other States, have done me the honor to cast their votes for me for the highest office in the gift of the nation. [Applause.] Now, I do not disguise it from myself that this is a prize worthy of the ambition of any man on the broad face of this globe. [Applause.] I also recognize the fact that it requires ability, culture, experience, age, and many qualities which my modesty forbids me to believe, and which my judgment convinces me, I do not possess. [Cheers.]

I therefore, after tendering to you, gentlemen, my thanks for the compliment which you have given me, desire to say in brief that I came to this convention with no personal ends to accomplish; that I am animated sincerely and solely by a desire of victory in this contest. [Applause.] We want a man nominated who will carry the largest Republican vote in this nation in defiance of the regular Grant organization [applause], and that man, in my judgment, is Hon. Horace Greeley, of New York. [Applause and hisses.]"

The voice of the orator was shaky. It would be impossible to describe the immediate effect of his speech upon the majority of the convention. There was a sudden pause, a momentary paralysis, a temporary deprivation of speech. The whole corrupt bargain of the previous night—the meaning of the Brown and Blair irruption, was apparent. There was a spasm of intense indignation. Had the delegates been less dignified, had they been men on a level with the ordinary workingmen in culture, they would have risen in the might of their wrath and cast Gratz Brown beyond the threshold of the hall. That was, without exaggeration, the feeling of the moment. The Missouri delegation shared in the momentary revulsion of feeling, and glared at their late leader in astonishment. It was only the Pennsylvania and New York delegations that looked upon the scene unmoved, and with a show of approbation. Friends of Greeley outside of these States would have been glad to see the success of their candidate, but they hoped for less questionable means.

Several gentlemen endeavored to get the floor in order, it was supposed, to change their votes, but were not successful.

The vote was announced as follows: Adams, 293; Davis, 92½: Brown, 95; Chase, 2½; Trumbull, 110; Greeley, 147; Curtin, 62.

A Kentucky delegate attempted to add fuel to the excitement by insinuating that Cassius M. Clay, chairman of the delegation, had not correctly stated the vote.

Mr. Clay said he had been too long in public life to reply to the imputation upon his honor. He had stated the vote as he understood it.

SCHURZ'S SPEECH IN THE MISSOURI DELEGATION.

The delegation from Missouri asked leave to retire for consultation. Mr. Schurz relinquished the chair to Mr. Julian, and followed into the north wing of the Industrial building.

The Missouri delegation were gathered loosely about one of the long tables. On one side of it stood Schurz, speaking in an animated manner. His face was flushed, and his appearance nervous and agitated. Gratz Brown was stalking about on the edge of the crowd, his dejected looks bent on the ground, and his cloak hanging carelessly from one shoulder. After a few preliminary remarks Mr. Schurz said:

> "I think the convention would make a fatal error in nominating Greeley for the presidency. Instead of being the strongest candidate that can be put forward, I regard him as the weakest. It is not possible for him to win the German vote. He has been a life-long temperance man, and his name has been associated with the most ultra and unreasonable acts of which they have been guilty. He is therefore most objectionable. The Liberal ticket cannot be elected without Ohio and Illinois. Neither of these States can be carried by Mr. Greeley. I have known Mr. Greeley for fifteen years, and our relations during that time have been of the most friendly character. But he is not by nature or by education suited to fill the presidential office. His lack of dignity, his idiosyncracies, his many crotchets, eminently unfit him for appropriately occupying so high and honorable a position."

Mr. Schurz returned to the Adams chair, looking depressed and several years older than when he left it.

Several unavailing efforts were made to have the territories recognized in the balloting, but they were disposed of by cries of "ballot, ballot!" "no, no, that wont do," "put them out," and such elegant invocations to the orators, as "spit it out again."

The name of Andrew G. Curtin was withdrawn after the first ballot.

THE SECOND BALLOT.

The call of states for the second ballot was at length commenced by the clerk, Mr. McClane. It proceeded to the noisy accompaniment of rebel yells and discordant shouts in all keys.

California cast her vote thus: "Six votes for honest David Davis."

A voice sneeringly called out "*Honest* David Davis—Oh, yes!" at which there was general laughter.

New Jersey cast her thirteen votes for the "friend of humanity." A parenthetic voice, desiring to know who the universal friend might be, was answered, "Horace Greeley." The remainder of the votes of New Jersey were cast for another candidate.

With great effort the chairman brought sufficient order out of the chaos to permit the result of the second ballot to be heard. It stood:

STATES.	Adams.	Trumbull.	Davis.	Greeley.
Alabama	--	--	--	18
Arkansas	2	--	--	10
California	--	--	6	6

STATES.	ADAMS.	TRUMBULL.	DAVIS.	GREELEY.
Connecticut	12	--	--	--
Delaware	--	6	--	--
Florida	--	--	6	--
Georgia	2	--	--	18
Illinois	--	21	21	--
Indiana	9	16	2	1
Iowa	10	5	1	6
Kansas	--	10	--	--
Kentucky	19	--	--	5
Louisiana	4	8	--	2
Maine	14	--	--	--
Maryland	2	3	10	1
Massachusetts	22	4	--	--
Michigan	22	--	--	--
Minnesota	--	9	4	--
Mississippi	--	8	--	8
Missouri	4	16	--	10
Nebraska	--	5	--	1
Nevada	--	--	--	6
New Hampshire	--	--	--	8
New Jersey	5	--	--	13
New York	2	1	--	65
North Carolina	--	9	3	8
Ohio	42	--	--	2
Oregon	--	--	--	6
Pennsylvania	26	--	11	18
Rhode Island	8	--	--	--
South Carolina	--	2	12	--
Tennessee	11	9	1	1
Texas	3	--	--	13
Vermont	1	--	--	7
Virginia	2	14	2	4
West Virginia	6	--	3	1
Wisconsin	15	2	2	1
Total	243	148	75	245

Brown, 2; Chase, 1.

Whole number of votes cast, 714; necessary to a choice, 355.

Before the vote was announced, California changed six votes from Davis to Greeley.

On the third ballot the totals were but little changed, standing: Adams, 246; Trumbull, 146; Greeley, 258; Davis, 44. On the fourth they stood: Adams, 279; Trumbull, 141; Greeley, 251; Davis, 41.

FIFTH BALLOT.

States.	ADAMS.	TRUMBULL.	DAVIS.	GREELEY.
Alabama	--	--	--	18
Arkansas	2	--	--	10
California	--	--	--	12
Connecticut	12	--	--	--
Delaware	6	--	--	--
Florida	6	--	--	--
Georgia	2	--	--	18
Illinois	--	21	21	--
Indiana	11	7	--	10
Iowa	16	--	--	6
Kansas	10	--	--	--
Kentucky	19	--		5
Louisiana	5	3	--	6
Maine	14	--	--	--
Maryland	[illegible]	1	--	--
Massachusetts	22	4	--	--
Michigan	22	--	--	--
Minnesota	--	9	1	--
Mississippi	5	3	--	8
Missouri	4	8	--	18
Nebraska	--	6	--	--
Nevada	--	--	--	6
New Hampshire	--	--	--	8
New Jersey	5	--	--	13
New York	5	1	--	62
North Carolina	5	7	3	5
Ohio	42	--	--	2
Oregon	--	--	--	6
Pennsylvania	32	1	4	18
Rhode Island	8	--	--	--
South Carolina	--	--	--	--
Tennessee	12	9	--	1
Texas	3	--	--	13
Vermont	4	--	--	4
Virginia	1	8	--	4
West Virginia	6	--	1	3
Wisconsin	18	--	--	2
Total	309	91	30	258

Brown—Georgia, 2.

Chase—Pennsylvania, 1; South Carolina, 14; Virginia, 9. Total, 24.

SIXTH BALLOT AND NOMINATION.

States.	Adams.	Trumbull.	Davis.	Greeley
Alabama	--	--	--	18
Arkansas	2	--	--	10
California	--	--	--	12
Connecticut	12	--	--	--
Delaware	6	--	--	--
Florida	--	--	--	--
Georgia	--	--	--	22
Illinois	27	1	--	14
Indiana	8	--	--	19
Iowa	17	--	--	5
Kansas	5	2	--	3
Kentucky	5	--	--	19
Louisiana	7	--	--	7
Maine	14	--	--	--
Maryland	11	2	--	3
Massachusetts	22	--	--	--
Michigan	20	--	--	2
Minnesota	--	9	1	--
Mississippi	8	--	--	8
Missouri	10	2	--	18
Nebraska	--	--	--	6
Nevada	--	--	--	6
New Hampshire	--	--	--	8
New Jersey	5	--	--	13
New York	5	1	--	62
North Carolina	3	--	--	17
Ohio	42	--	--	2
Oregon	--	--	--	6
Pennsylvania	32	1	4	17
Rhode Island	8	--	--	--
South Carolina	--	--	--	2
Tennessee	9	3	--	10
Texas	3	--	--	13
Vermont	1	--	--	7
Virginia	8	--	--	7
West Virginia	1	--	1	7
Wisconsin	18	--	--	2
Total	309	21	6	346

Brown—Pennsylvania, 1.

Chase—Florida, 6; Massachusetts, 4; Pennsylvania, 1; South Carolina, 12; Virginia, 7.

Palmer—Indiana, 1.

The influence of Schurz upon the Missouri delegation was shown by its vote in the second ballot,—sixteen for Trumbull, ten for Greeley. The vote for Greeley gradually increased until in the last two ballots it reached 18; the remainder casting their votes persistently for Adams. During one of the most exciting scenes of the balloting, a Missouri delegate uttered the pithy sentence already become historical,—" Sold, but not delivered." When the state vote was made up on the occasion of each ballot, it was always with bickering and bitterness apparent to the entire convention.

The second and third ballots were completed without the occurrence of anything notable. There were occasional spasms of excitement, which yielded to comparative order.

The fourth ballot showed a small gain for Adams, and a diminution in the votes for Greeley. The friends of Adams were jubilant. Davis's vote steadily diminished from the first ballot.

WHAT MIGHT HAVE BEEN.

At the end of the fifth ballot, Illinois might have nominated Adams by changing her vote to him unanimously. Her own vote alone would have accomplished the result, but the moral effect of the transfer would have been further accessions of strength. The friends of Davis changed to Greeley in the successive ballotings, or scattered on impossible candidates. Trumbull's strength diminished to ninety-one on the fifth ballot. At this time the end was apparent.

The states were called on the sixth ballot, amid unprecedented confusion. The chair tried to preserve the semblance of order with a useless expenditure of strength on the gavel. A motion to take a recess of twenty minutes was badly defeated. The aisles were full of excited delegates and others. Men were everywhere talking excitedly, mounted upon benches, and standing on chairs. Speeches were being made in all parts of the hall at the same moment. Illinois retired for consultation, and returned with the vote divided between Adams and Greeley; Trumbull having a solitary retainer. The announcement was received with derisive laughter.

New Jersey, rich in benevolent nomenclature, cast her vote on the last ballot for "the Philosopher, Horace Greeley."

The sixth ballot, as tabulated above, shows the result before the final change that nominated Greeley. Pennsylvania was the first to change when the crisis arrived, going solidly for the high tariff reformer. The announcement of this change, by Col. McClure, was received with extraordinary enthusiasm. Kentucky changed next, then Minnesota, Kansas, Mississippi, South Carolina, and other states. The exact result will probably never be known, but the majority was overwhelming for Horace Greeley.

When it became apparent to the convention that Greeley would be the nominee, there was great enthusiasm in certain quarters, and an extraordin-

ary lack of it in others. The local sympathy was with Adams, therefore the gallery was ominously silent.

When the nomination was announced from the chair, not a handkerchief was lifted, and not a cheer heard from the balcony. The cheering on the floor was principally confined to Pennsylvania, and the Southern "delegations;" Ohio, and the extreme Eastern members not participating. After a brief interval for thought, consciousness of what they had done seemed to fill the convention with amazement. The friends of Adams and Trumbull were the most aggrieved. They seemed stunned and blinded by their sudden downfall. Some of them were so staggered that they were obliged to seek the nearest means of physical support. Like the lady collegian, in the "Princess," they "stared with great eyes, and laughed with alien lips."

FOR VICE PRESIDENT.

The balloting for Vice President was tame after this scene of excitement. The names of Trumbull, Cox, Cassius M. Clay, and Palmer were successively withdrawn. It is possible that Trumbull might have won the second place on the ticket had he desired it. Hon. John Hickman, of Pennsylvania, moved the nomination of Gratz Brown by acclamation, both before and after the first ballot.

The following is the result of the first ballot: Whole number of votes cast, 702; necessary to a choice, 352; B. Gratz Brown received, 237; Lyman

Trumbull received 156; George W. Julian received 134½; Cassius M. Clay, 44.

The Chair announced the second ballot in the following terms: Whole number of votes, 647; necessary to a choice, 349; Brown received 435; Walker, 75; Palmer, 8; Julian, 75; Tipton, 3.

A motion to make the nomination unanimous was greeted with a storm of indignant "noes."

Brown was called upon for a speech, but was found to have left the hall.

The National Executive Committee of the new party was formally appointed. The following are the names of its members:

South Carolina, S. A. Pierce; Texas, E. M. Pease; West Virginia, Hon. M. C. Church; District of Columbia, C. M. Alexander; Maine, J. L. Leford; Nevada, George C. Lyon; Ohio, J. T. Brooks; North Carolina, L. R. Goodloe; Montana, J. C. Everts; Pennsylvania, Hon. Wm. H. Raddiman; Louisiana, H. C. Warmoth; Minnesota, Thomas Wilson; Arkansas, John Kirkwood; New Hampshire, Henry O. Kent; Iowa, James D. Campbell; Florida, J. C. Drew; New Jersey, James M. Scovill; Colorado, S. C. Brown; New York, Ethan Allen; California, Frank M. Pixley; Maryland, Samuel M. Gouverneur; Connecticut, David Clark; Indiana, Isaac T. Gray; Tennessee, J. S. Fowler; Nebraska, T. W. Tipton; Kansas, S. A. Biggs; Illinois, L. Swett; Kentucky, L. N. Dembitz; Wisconsin, A. Scott Sloan; Vermont, John P. Ladd; Massachusetts, Charles G. Davis; Oregon, Jasper W. Johnson; Alabama, W. T. Hatchett; Mississippi, E. Jeffords; Delaware, George Alfred Townsend; Missouri, Geo. W. Anderson; Michigan, George L. R. McWhorter; Rhode Island, E. Corbett.

During the final proceedings the spectators had been leaving, and few even of the delegates were in their places.

Mr. Schurz, being repeatedly called upon for a final speech, said with evident unwillingness, and with obvious hesitation of manner:

"This convention has overwhelmed me with kindness, and I have especially to thank them for the indulgence with which they have borne with me while I was endeavoring, to the best of my ability, to conduct, with fairness and impartiality, the deliberations of this large and—let us confess it—sometimes a little unruly body. [Applause and laughter.]

"We have now completed our work. It will now be our duty to proclaim to all the land the principles we have embodied in our platform, and to go forward and solicit, with all the entreaties which our minds and hearts are capable of making, the support of the people of the United States for the candidates we have nominated.

"I have already done so much speaking in this convention, and may be I shall still have to do so much during the impending campaign, that you will certainly bear with me if I close my last speech in the same manner in which I closed my first, when seconding a motion to adjourn, and now declare the Liberal Republican Convention adjourned *sine die.*"

Mr. Julian was called upon to speak, but declined on the ground of ill health. Theodore Tilton and Cassius M. Clay were also called for, but did not respond, and the remains of the immense crowd dispersed.

The executive committee met in the evening, and elected as permanent officers Ethan Allen, of New York, (no relation of the Revolutionary hero) Chairman, and Daniel R. Goodloe, of North Carolina, Secretary.

The aspect of Cincinnati was almost funereal after the convention. Everything was gloom and uncertainty. Few were hopeful enough to think that the Liberal party could elect the ticket nominated, and all were disgusted at the shameful trickery by which the result had been reached. Judges Stallo, Matthews and Hoadley, the two Brinkerhoffs, and others, were understood to have left the convention before adjournment, utterly repudiating its acts and filled with mortification.

Some of the Indiana delegates were said to have left when Brown made his speech of bargain and sale. All the local talk upon the streets was bitter and acrimonious. Everywhere the greatest contempt was felt for the nominees, and the deepest anger mingled with sorrow at the action of the convention. For several hours it seemed as if the ticket would find no supporters of influence in the West.

THE GERMANS.

The Germans were most of all vexed and turbulent. They declared that they would not support Greeley under any circumstances. The local German papers were unanimous in their opposition. Carl Daenzler, editor of the *Anzeiger des Westen*, published at St. Louis, telegraphed to his editor in charge the following:

"The corruptionists, under the lead of Blair and Brown, have carried the day. It was a regular bargain and sale, in which Missouri spoil hunters and adventurers from other States, self-styled delegates, have played a prominent part. The liberal German element is unanimously opposed to the nominations; and the *Anzeiger* will fight them to the bitter end. Bolt the nominations at once, and as energetically as you can, and publish this over my own signature."

It was thought on the night succeeding the nomination that not a single German newspaper throughout the length and breadth of the land could be induced to support Greeley, for reasons well expressed in Carl Schurz's speech to the Missouri delegation; and the surmise has been almost verified.

The Reunion and Reform convention, which

had been sitting simultaneously to the main convention, and as an auxiliary of that body, broke up, demoralized and disgusted, and nothing has since been heard of Judge Stallo and its other influential members, mostly Germans, except in denunciation of the results of the convention. The speeches with which the nominations were immediately received by the Reunited Reformers were very violent.

SECESSION OF THE OHIO DELEGATION.

The Liberal Convention had proved to the Ohio delegation a dead sea apple,—dust and ashes to the core. While the balloting was progressing, and when Greeley's chances looked exceedingly favorable, a meeting was appointed, to occur soon after the convention completed its labors. The delegation assembled at College Hall, at four o'clock, with a tolerable full attendance. Very bitter speeches were made by Judge Spaulding, Gen. Burnett, Judge Brinkerhoff, Judge Hoadley and others. The last named gentleman said he was authorized to speak for Judge Matthews, John W. Sohn, and the United German delegation. His language was, in part, as follows:

"I have heretofore expressed the opinion that we have to-day seen the candidates of an organized fraud put on a platform which we believe to be an honest and fair one. The administration of Greeley and Brown would be the most corrupt with which this country was ever afflicted. It would be carried on by a new Tammany Ring. We may not succeed in defeating their nominations, but we are after them, and if they get elected we will at least help to knife them in the midst of their villanies. They are a pair of scoundrels—of infernal scoundrels. I am after them now, and intend to be after them till next November, and I shall vote and work for Grant to help defeat these thieves. Others who have been called away to their homes in the country think and speak just as I do. We need take no formal action here. The reporters are present, and the doings of this meeting will go out to the world. I am glad of it. The more public it is made the better. We must, however, keep up an organization and be ready for future action. We have many good men on our rolls, and we will yet make our power felt. We were only a little too late or we should have had no John Sherman to misrepresent us in the United States Senate. We will accomplish good results in this State, and shall eventually triumph in the Nation."

The meeting adjourned without stated action.

THE NEWSPAPER SYNDICATE.

The action of the principal newspaper men present at the convention has been given considerable prominence since the convention. This has not been without reason. But for their opposition to the administration of Grant, the convention would never have been. The Cincinnati *Commercial* had been pronounced for Adams, and worked up the feeling day after day with skill and energy. To the last moment Mr. Halstead was confident of success. His most active co-worker in the Adams cause was Samuel Bowles, of the Springfield *Republican*. Bowles was to be seen at the *Commercial* office at all hours of the day and night. Godkin, of the *Nation*, was in favor of Adams, and from the first intolerant of any other candidate. Horace White preferred Trumbull, in whose interest he was all the while quietly laboring, but would have accepted any available candidate. Henry Watterson, of the Louisville *Courier-Journal*, had from the first advocated the claims of Adams, although without acrimony.

All of these gentlemen were intensely mortified

at the result. For some hours after the nomination of Greeley was precipitated, these men were in doubt whether they would or would not bolt the nominations. As night drew on, there were in some of them faint signs of adhesion. The name of Horace White was appended to the platform. He was, therefore, bound to the cause with hooks of steel. He seemed in honor compelled to adhere to its decision. His journalistic confreres were not so inextricably bound in the tangled mesh of Liberalism.

In the evening, there was a supper of delicate edibles, at the Saint Nicholas, about which the five gentlemen named gathered for the discussion of results, and the formation of plans. The topics were as distasteful as the supper was savory. Whitelaw Reid, first lieutenant of Greeley's paper, is said to have been an invited guest. Over the viands the disappointments, the hopes, the fears, the anticipations of each were expressed with freedom. The result was that all but Godkin and Halstead promised to support the ticket cordially, but to censure the manner in which the nominations were brought about. How they did so will be inferred from following extracts of their utterances:

Bowles told in the Springfield *Republican* of Saturday what had happened on Friday, as follows:

"Frank Blair became alarmed at the growing prospect of Adams' nomination, in which he and his family naturally had no sympathy, and brought over Gratz Brown from St. Louis last night, to undertake its defeat. How they did it the record shows. Brown withdrew in favor of Greeley; and though at first the move seemed likely to prove a failure, the slowness of the friends of Trumbull to appreciate the danger and act aggressively against it, allowed it to aggregate strength, arouse the friendly heart of the convention for Greeley, and give him a brilliant victory. The logic and the judgment of the convention were for Adams—not its enthusiasm. * * * *

Mr. Greeley's wisest freinds then tried to change the plan of the architects of this result or giving the Vice-Presidency to Gratz Brown. They saw how much this would look like a bargain, and they greatly felt the personal objection to Mr. Brown. But in the *demoralized and flabby state of feeling in the convention*, it was impossible to concentrate the votes of his opponents on any one acceptable. Mr. Julian would have been especially agreeable to Mr. Greeley; but the convention was impatient and hungry; many didn't care what happened; Mr. Trumbull's and Mr. Cox's friends refused to allow those gentlemen to be pressed for the second place; Brown had many earnest personal friends at work for him; the thoughtless among Mr. Greeley's friends were grateful to him; and so the little sinful game of Frank Blair was played out successfully to the end.

"The blow falls very heavily upon the free traders of the West. They were the originators of this reform movement; to them it meant, almost first of all, tariff reform, and they struggled long and earnestly to put their ideas on this aubject in the front. But partly by the betrayal of a portion of their Missouri associates; partly by their own over-persistence in the verbal struggle for the platform on the question, *they have lost everything*. The tariff resolution is practically, and almost in words, Greeley's compromise, and the candidate is the one man in all the country who believes most sincerely in protection, and fights its battle most ably."

Horace White, of the Chicago *Tribune*, the chief of these free traders, expressed his grief in the following terms:

"The Gratz Brown performance has given the whole affair the appearance of a put-up job, but it was merely a lucky guess. The Blairs and Browns do not like Schurz. To defeat a candidate who was likely to be on confidential terms with Schurz, as either Adams or Trumbull would have been, was the thing nearest to their hearts, and for this purpose Brown made his appearance here. His speech in the convention fell like dishwater on the whole assemblage.

* * * * * * * * *

"Then gush and hurrah swept everything down, and almost before the vote of Illinois had been recorded by the Secretary, the dispatches came rushing to the telegraph instruments that Greeley was nominated. For a moment the wiser heads in the convention were stunned, though everybody tried to look perfectly contented. Of all the things that could possibly happen, this was the one thing which everybody supposed could not happen. Not even the Greeley men themselves thought it could happen. The only able politician who seemed to be really for Greeley, was Waldo Hutchins, of New York, and even his sincerity was questioned by Greeley's back-bone friends as long as the Davis movement was regarded as still alive."

"The politicians, for the most part, either left the convention, to bathe their heads, or sat still, as idle and indifferent spectators. It was freely charged and believed that the nomination of Greeley was a put-up job of Brown's, and so delighted were the innocents at the success of the supposed scheme, that they hastened to ratify it.

After the convention adjourned, the streets were filled with a Babel of the most sorely puzzled individuals that the world has ever seen."

From the morning on which this dispatch was published the *Tribune* never mentioned the name of Gratz Brown editorially, except in a manner merely incidental. The Cincinnati *Volksblatt*, the ablest of the German papers which had inclined to Liberalism, received the result with ineffable disgust. It said, on the following morning:

"The Liberal Convention has thrown away the opportunity it had. We regret this, not merely on account of the forfeited success, but on account of the bungled management of the movement. In a contest for correct principles, and conducted by a rcal representative of the same, we could, if need be, have even submitted to a defeat. It is nothing new to us to struggle with minorities. The old Freesoil, afterwards Republican, party, was originally a minority party. But it was a minority party which had to become a majority party, because it had Truth and Justice on its side. We cannot say the same thing of a Greeley party."

How the Reformers were put to ignominous route on their main issue—the Tariff—is thus told by Mr. Bowles, a member of the syndicate and the best possible authority on this subject:

" But here we must consider how these people threw away their first and great opportunity. So soon as the delegates began to assemble on Saturday, the agitation of the tariff question commenced. Through Monday, Tuesday and Wednesday, there was, as it were, a protracted meeting for discussion and consultation upon this subject. It threatened at one time to disrupt the convention. But it soon grew obvious that the great majority of the revenue reformers themselves were indisposed to insist upon a radical declaration for free trade. It was clearly felt that the reform movement had passed beyond this special question, had reached to new elements of power, who held antagonistic views as to the tariff, and that the question of general reform, of a higher tone in the administration, of a more generous policy toward the South, of a burial of past issues, and the revolution and reconstruction of parties, were the more pressing and absorbing points of the movement. But a few of the revenue tariff doctrinaires—such men as Mr. Atkinson, of Boston, and Judge Hoadley and Stanley Matthews, of Cincinnati—would not yield their faith to these considerations. This was the corner-stone of their politics; it had grown in their minds to the first place in all reform; they felt that it would be disgrace and treason to yield it up, and they insisted upon it beyond the patience almost of their associates—certainly beyond the patience of the great body of the convention. Had they seen what such men as Horace White and David A. Wells saw, what independent outsiders saw and warned them of, and had they come frankly forward on Tuesday or Wednesday, or even on Thursday morning, and said to Mr. Greeley's friends and the Pennsylvania delegates—"We will yield this difference, we will accept the relegation of this disputed question to the congressional elections, and agree with you to its decision by congressional votes; but in view of the history of this movement, and in return for this concession, you must take a candidate from among our representative men—you must take Mr. Adams, or Mr. Trumbull, or Mr. Cox, or Mr. Brown"—doubtless the offer would have been accepted, and platform and candidate would have grown out of an honorable compromise. But they fought the platform against fate. They urged, first, positive declarations for free trade or revenue reform; next, they sought to juggle the question with fine words; and they only yielded the only honorable compromise, when they had lost the good-will of the convention, and lost the opportunity to make terms on the ticket."

SCHURZ SOOTHES HIS SORROW WITH A SYMPHONY.

We make room for one other extract from Mr. Bowles's letter, narrating how the man of the best ability, clearest view and most sincere purpose among them, vented his disgust after the crash and chaos came:

"The conduct of Governor Brown and its resultant nomination of Mr. Greeley were indeed a sad surprise and serious blow to Carl Schurz. Pledging in faltering voice his support of the nomination to the convention, he left it, weary with labor and sad in spirit, for the house of his friend, Judge Stallo. Entering there a circle of equally disappointed friends, he said: 'I am overwhelmed and discouraged.' There were no words of consolation or cheer to offer him, and a sad silence reigned for a few moments. Then he turned to the piano, and with his master hand poured out his feeling through one of Auber's most touching compositions. It seemed as if the composer's thought had never been so fitly rendered before, and tears filled the eyes of the whole company. But in a more noble way than he was wounded will the country revenge Carl Schurz. His high and generous course at this convention and his noble address to it won him the added respect of both friend and foe. Never did he stand so high in the estimation of the American people as at this moment, and he well deserves the compliment which Charles Francis Adams paid to him more than a year ago, in saying, 'that the one man who seemed to understand our institutions, their spirit, their history, their dangers and their possibilities, better than any other citizen, was of foreign birth, and his name, CARL SCHURZ.'"

CHAPTER XXI.

HORACE GREELEY.

Birth of the Hero—His Youthful Experiences—A Statesman in Leading Strings—Almost Drowned—The Mystery of Ox-yoking too Great for Him—Apprenticed to a Printer—Migrates to New York—Makes an Impression upon a Boss Printer—Begins to Develop his Eccentricities—His Grahamite Experience—An Eating Exploit not Down in Graham's Bill of Fare—Divers Instructive Anecdotes—Rise of the "Tribune"—Greeley's Characteristics as a Journalist—What Horace White Said of Him—Greeley Travels—His Imprisonment at Paris—His Terrible Ride to Placerville.

It seems almost foolhardy to commence at this stage of our book the biography of a man of such multiplex characteristics, and of such a public record as belong to Horace Greeley—the man whose name is better celebrated than that of perhaps any other American; the man who has been most intimately concerned in nearly half a century of New York and national politics; who has written a dozen ponderous volumes and uncollected matter enough to fill ten times as many; who has been on both extremes of nearly every important public question, and received alternately the encomiums and the curses of every free-speaking American citizen; who may truthfully be said to have brought on the late civil war, insisted upon conducting it both politically and militarily, nearly brought it to

HORACE GREELEY.

a disgraceful close more than once during its progress, and finally officiated as its most popular historian. It is plain that to crowd the events and the lessons of such an active and instructive life into the space now at command will be great violence to the subject—yet it has to be done; and any who may be disposed to grieve over the brevity of Mr. Greeley's "life," as herein contained, must console himself with reflecting that Greeley's friend, Mr. Parton—most charming of biographic whitewashers—has furnished to the world a history of this famous man's life, only less fascinating than the same biographer's panegyric of Aaron Burr, or of Benj. F. Butler—a history, too, which the present writer has perused too well to contentedly forego a frequent reference to its pages in the preparation of this sketch.

BORN.

Horace Greeley, sometimes called the *Tribune* Philosopher, sometimes the Sage of Chappaqua, sometimes the Peacemaker of Niagara, was born on the 3d of February, 1811, and was therefore, at the time of his nomination for President, somewhat over sixty-one years old. Seven cities would doubtless have contended for the honor of his birth-place, had not the town of Amherst, N. H., shown such incontestible proofs of title to that honor as to squelch utterly all rivals. It is noteworthy that the nascent statesman began, even before he ever breathed, that policy of puzzling uncertainity which has characterized him since looming upon the public view. Up to the time when he was fifteen minutes old, Horace had by no means made up his mind whether to accept this world as a fitting tenement for his occupancy, or to "spit upon it" (figuratively, his salivary apparatus being not then well developed) as he has since done for the platforms of his party, and thus leave it to wag on as best it might without him.

To be more explicit, it is related by his faithful biographer that Horace, when first ushered into,—well, the reader knows what is meant, without repeating the trite phrase,—was found to be a dark problem indeed; presenting a skin of cimmerian blackness and a body as lifeless as that of the Democratic party before it was galvanized at Cincinnati. "But the little discolored stranger had articles to write," observes Parton, most happily, "and was not permitted to escape his destiny." Through the efforts of an experienced aunt, whose name richly deserves handing down to fame, the incipient (and we might almost add, inchoate) philosopher and Presidential candidate soon began to breathe and to undergo that change of color from red to black experienced by a lobster in boiling.

BECOMES A PRODIGY.

Being named Horace, in remembrance of a relative "on his father's side," the infantile statesman soon took upon himself the proper abbreviation, "Hod," and bore it triumphantly until manhood arrived. "Hod" soon became the intellectual prodigy of the community in which he lived. It is related that he could read any ordinary book when four years of age, and he was certainly the champion speller of a large area of New Hampshire territory. At six he had already resolved to become a printer; and at fifteen he was allowed by his father to put this resolution into practice. The conversion of the elder Greeley to this plan of disposing of his ambitious boy may have been facilitated by the fact that, although "Hod" was an intellectual prodigy, and could hold any man in town a tearing discussion on political economy, he would not learn which was the "off" ox and which was the "near" one, and therefore was wont to waste a great deal of valuable time, both of himself and the oxen, in a useless endeavor to persuade "Buck" to come under the yoke in the place where "Bright" ought to be.*

ADVERSITY.

Horace's mother was a woman of many excellences, and contributed much, by her training, to bring the boy rapidly forward. Of his father, Zaccheus, we do not hear very much, except that he was a good-natured, improvident man, who kept his help (and himself, too, for that matter) too well supplied with New England's favorite beverage, rum. As a consequence, he was sold out by the sheriff, and fled with his family to Westhaven, Rut-

* Parton's Panegyric, page 67.

land county, Vermont, where he took a farm of a nabob of those parts, and operated it on shares.

A POSSIBLE (BUT NOT PROBABLE) EPISODE.

It must have been while on the Amherst farm that Horace took those first lessons in agriculture to which he alludes in "What I Know about Farming." He there tells how he commenced his career as an agriculturist by riding the old mare to furrow between his father's corn, when he was only five years old. Already his genius for acquiring knowledge had shown itself in his exploits with the reading book, and the neighbors had already marked him as the boy who was one day to be President (one of the million American youths who have been thus marked, though we have had only eighteen Presidents.) If marvels such as we read about in ancient Roman history had not gone out of fashion long ago, we might have looked in that memorable cornfield for a repetition of the omen experienced by the Tarquinian Lucius, whose cap, the veracious fable tells us, was removed by an eagle, and then, after that fowl had cut a pigeon-wing in the air, was gracefully replaced. We might imagine the juvenile Horace—Hod, for short—thus visited; but if so, the bird should have been the pelican—type of the Southern Confederacy, to which Horace will be indebted for the supreme place in the nation's councils, if he ever obtains it.

Zaccheus Greeley's exodus took place in 1821, when Horace was ten years old. He continued to help about the farm—to

"Mow and hoe and hold the plow,
And long for one-and-twenty,"

and to absorb the contents of all the books and newspapers which came within seven miles of him (we follow the figures of his Boswell in this narrative) until he had got well into his sixteenth year. The experiences of the farm were only varied by the exploits of the spelling school, the lyceum, and the village tavern, where "Hod" was often trotted out by admiring old codgers who there sat in perpetual congress, and whose earnest applause, while developing in the boy a streak of vanity which has never left him, doubtless did him much good, by also developing in him the quality of self-reliance, and encouraging him on a path which boys usually find thorny, rough and unattractive.

A NARROW ESCAPE.

To these incidents were added few out of which the biographer can construct a thrilling episode—absolutely none, in fact, except one, wherein, it appears, the young philosopher's thread of life came near being nipped prematurely. When he was thirteen years old occurred an adventure which Parton designates as "Horace's first experience at log-rolling." (Cincinnati may be termed his last, thus far.) Himself and his younger brother were floating across a mill-pond upon saw-logs, which appears to have been the regular means of making the transit. The younger one suddenly found himself plumped into the pond, in water far beyond his depth. Horace sailed to his relief upon his own log, but was soon floundering in the water with his brother. Neither could swim; but the younger one had the sagacity to escape to a more tenable mooring by clambering over Horace, who still struggled with the treacherous log, yelling lustily for help. This came at last, and the editor of the *Tribune* was rescued from what had threatened to be his watery grave.

ANOTHER.

It would appear that the young philosopher did not, even through this thrilling experience, master the science of riding saw-logs successfully; for since his nomination at Cincinnati, a correspondent of the Warren (Pa.) *Mail* has contributed to history the following similar incident, with which he endeavors to point a moral:

"In 1841 the correspondent was working at a saw-mill in Wrightsville. Greeley being in that section on a visit to his father's family, came along canvassing for his paper. He started to cross the pond on loose logs. 'Now,' says the correspondent, 'such logs never will keep still. They bolt, and the bolting philosopher soon found himself on two logs and two legs spreading wider and wider apart the longer he tried to stand still! The writer called to him to go ahead, but he didn't; he only went in up to his neck, and that's all he knows about riding a saw-log. Now if he can't ride two saw-logs in one direction, how can he ride two horses running in different directions, without going under? That's the question.'"

At fourteen, the precocious youth had already become a profound politician, and could put to rout almost any of the Democratic politicians of those parts. He had also become a confirmed Universalist in religion; nor has his Whiggism nor his Universalism ever wavered a hair-breadth since that day, though other isms by the dozen have risen and subsided in his fermenting brain.

HE GOES TO BE A PRINTER.

At fifteen,* Horace was bound as an apprentice to the publisher of the *Northern Spectator*, a weekly paper published at East Poultney, Vermont, having walked from Westhaven, all by himself, to secure a situation advertised in that paper—the stereotyped "Boy Wanted," so familiar at the head of the editorial columns of many country weeklies. Horace seems to have had the faculty of impressing himself upon everybody whom he met for the first time as an unmitigated idiot. He so impressed the editor of the *Northern Spectator*, who nevertheless consented to take him, and was soon proud of the budding faculties of his apprentice.

MUSTERED OUT.

Here Horace worked over four years, having been released from the conditions of his apprenticeship about a year before its expiration, by the failure of the newspaper and of the firm which conducted it. This occurred in spite of the fact that Horace had contributed many paragraphs to its columns during the last year or two of his service. The dissolution of this concern mustered Horace Greeley out of service at East Poultney, with twenty dollars in cash, a wardrobe which he

* Viz., in the spring of 1826.

might have stuffed in his pocket, and a fair knowledge of the typographic art. Released from his apprenticeship and "out of a sit," as the printers term it, he set out for a visit to his parents, who had then removed "away out West," into the wilds of Pennsylvania.* He did not leave the scenes of his struggles with the art of Guttemberg and of his many debating-school triumphs, without receiving a testimonial from admiring friends.

The landlord of the tavern in which Horace had boarded, seeing the young man about to set out on his journey, scantily clad and with a sore leg (which the curious reader will find duly depicted on the 16th page of Mr. Parton's book) felt so moved in his heart toward the youthful pilgrim that he urged one of his other boarders, then sitting by, to give Horace an old overcoat which he (the boarder) then had on; and so contagious did this generous emotion of the landlord prove that the garment was immediately stripped off and conferred upon Horace, who, being much smaller than his benefactor, walked away quite overwhelmed with (and in) his newly acquired possession.

IN NEW YORK.

This ends the boyhood history of Horace Greeley. He next appears as a young man in his twenty-first year, applying for work at the case in New York. It is safe to say that young Greeley was not at this time so lacking in confidence as

* Where his father died, aged 80 and upwards, about 1870.

many young men who make their way to the city in pursuit of work. He had acquired some of the habits of journeymen printers—among them, card playing and a fluency in swearing and obscenity which have since, as exhibited in and about the *Tribune* office, been the admiration of outsiders and the terror of employees. He had but recently beaten Joe Wilson, of Cattaraugus county, at a game of chequers, and——well, it could no longer be disguised from a young man of Horace's keen perception, that he was "no slouch" of a fellow, take him for all in all. But this impression was not readily shared by casual observers; and hence, when Horace appeared to take a "sit" in the office of a Mr. West, at No. 85 Chatham street, he was the subject of no little cacchination on the part of the printers there employed, and of the following remark from the proprietor to the foreman:

"What! did you hire that —— fool?*

PARTNER IN A JOB OFFICE.

"That —— fool" proved, however, to be one of the best printers in the shop, and came forward rapidly in his trade. At the beginning of 1833 we find him forming a partnership with a Mr. Story, in the proprietorship of a job printing establishment on a small scale. The firm of Greeley & Story was originated by the latter named partner, for the purpose of publishing a two-penny morning paper for one Dr. Sheppard, and doing such other

*Parton, page 124.

job work as could be obtained. The paper, called the *Morning Post*, was the first one of its price ever conceived in this country or elsewhere; indeed, it was never born as a penny paper, the printers having persuaded the Doctor to place his price at two cents for a time. The enterprise failed in its third week, but the firm of Greeley & Story went on swimmingly until dissolved by the death of Story, in the middle of the first year. The chief revenue of the concern was derived from lottery printing, which the firm made a specialty. It seems that, though Greeley had imbibed a great many isms—among them Washingtonianism, anti-Masonism (on which he is very much set to this day), Grahamism, Communism, etc., he had not acquired any such antipathy to the lottery business—then infesting the lower *strata* of society with particular virulence—as to prevent his soliciting business auxiliary to this species of gambling. The death of Story did not break up the business, as the lottery printing had already begun to be quite remunerative. Greeley took in two more partners, named Jonas Winchester and E. Sibbett, and the firm name became Greeley & Co. He subsequently alludes to these men, in a letter which he printed in the *Tribune*, as "bad partners"—not a chivalrous phrase, in view of the facts.

HIS AFFECTATIONS.

It was about this time (1833–4) that Greeley began to develop some of the personal eccentricities which form so large an element of his notoriety. For instance, he was very slovenly about his dress, and it is recorded by his faithful Boswell that the ladies of Mr. Winchester's household had great difficulty "in inducing him to keep his shirt buttoned over his white bosom." It is also related by the same chronicler that he was in the habit of forgetting whether he had been to dinner, and that he would often be sent off after superfluous meals, or fooled into fasting altogether by the practical jokers of the office. This indication of genius was not lost upon his admiring friends, who swore by him as an oracle, whereas some of his old New England neighbors would probably have been more than ever disposed to brand as a (blank) fool, a grown man who "didn't know enough to go to dinner."

A GRAHAMITE.

If, however, Horace did not know enough to go to dinner, he knew a thing or two about what should be eaten on arriving there. In 1834 he embraced the doctrines of Dr. Graham concerning food, and, as was his wont with regard to other theories which struck him favorably, he became completely possessed by them for a time, carrying them to their farthest extreme. He became a vegetarian of the strictest sect, and reveled in bran-meal mush and apples, to the exclusion of everything succulent and savory, especially meat. To carry this doctrine into practical effect, and also to place himself conspicuously before the world as one who had renounced the lascivious pleasures of the chop and steak, Greeley went to the Graham Hotel to board.

CUPID SMITES.

It was here that he first encountered the lady who soon afterward became his wife—Miss Mary Y. Cheney, of North Carolina, a young woman of the strong intellectual type, and a school teacher, who also doted upon Graham breads, and who had come even further than her lover to carry out her theories of living. Their marriage occurred on the 5th of July, 1836, and has never been dissolved, though there have always been rumors that it did not prove entirely a happy one. These rumors have probably been exaggerated. At all events, the fruits of the marriage have been five children, of whom only one—a daughter, Ida, now twenty odd years old—survives. In view of the possibility of Mr. Greeley's being chosen President, there may be some curiosity about the future lady of the White House. This will undoubtedly be Miss Ida, as society has not known her mother at all, notwithstanding Mr. Greeley's prominence, his idiosyncracies and his genial sociality have made him a favorite in many parlors, and especially at public banquets.

THOSE SILK STOCKINGS.

While on the subject of Mr. Greeley's personal eccentricities, particularly of dress, we must not forget the story of his wedding stockings. Horace had imbibed from some source—probably from some of the books which he had read in Vermont—an idea that the only correct costume for a gentleman to be married in, should include a pair of silk stockings. He accordingly ordered a gorgeous pair along with the wedding suit. Arraying himself in the outfit, in rehearsal for the event, he was disgusted to the point of profanity to find that the pantaloons came down so well upon the foot as to bury the silk stockings in total eclipse. His radically philosophical mind immediately preceived that there was no use in sporting silk stockings for nobody to look at—to "blush unseen" beneath the shadow of black doeskin. And here the inventive genius of our philosopher came into play. While a common mind, or one tied down, like that of General Grant, for instance, to the conventionalities of society, would have gone to the wedding, and few of the spectators been aware whether their bridegroom's hose were of silk or cotton, Greeley severed the Gordian knot of the situation, and won an easy triumph. He ordered the tailor to cut a sort of half moon into the bottom of the pantaloons, large enough to exhibit the gorgeousness of the stockings so plainly that the wayfaring man, though a fool, need not err therein. The silken hose appeared in all their glory, and the trowsers were, to say the least, of a cut which no man had ever worn before, so that the device may be pronounced a complete success. "The way to resume specie payment is *to resume*," says our philosopher. "The way for everybody to be happy and wealthy is *to associate*"; and the way to exhibit your stockings to advantage is explained in the foregoing lines.

THE WHITE COAT.

It was also during or about this eventful period of Greeley's life that the famous white coat first made its appearance. The young adventurer had not failed to perceive that his awkwardness of appearance had, on the whole, worked rather in his favor than against him, since they had enhanced his individuality, and made him a "marked man," as the saying is. He evidently resolved to cultivate this feature of his personality, and cast about him for some sort of garment which would serve the purpose better than any other. He found it upon a newly arrived immigrant—a long grey coat of wool, which, not being made under the protecting wing of Henry Clay tariffs, was well made, and lasted an astonishingly long time. When it was gone, another was found, and thus Greeley was distinguished until his metamorphosis occurred, on the occasion of his visiting Europe in 1851. Then he plunged to the opposite extreme, but soon lapsed back into a slip-shod, though not absolutely eccentric style of costume.

A MEAL FOR A GRAHAMITE.

Having wandered away from our chronological bearings, we may as well relate (still on the authority of Greeley's own biographer) an anecdote which his friends tell in illustration of the eccentricities above referred to. It was during the famous campaign of 1840. Let us have the story in the charming language of Mr. Parton, who vouches for it as literally true:

"Time,—Sunday evening. Scene,—the parlor of a friend's house. Company,—numerous and political, except the ladies, who are gracious and hospitable. Mr. Greeley is expected to tea, but does not come, and the meal is transacted without him. Tea over, he arrives, and plunges headlong into a conversation on the currency. The lady of the house thinks he 'had better take some tea,' but cannot get a hearing on the subject; is distressed, puts the question at length, and has her invitation hurriedly declined; brushed aside, in fact, with a wave of the hand.

" 'Take a cruller, any way,' said she, handing him a cake basket containing a dozen or so of those unspeakable, Dutch indigestibles.

"The expounder of the currency, dimly conscious that a large object was approaching him, puts forth his hands, still vehemently talking, and takes, not a cruller, but the cake-basket, and deposits it in his lap. The company are inwardly convulsed, and some of the weaker members retire to the adjoining apartment, the expounder continuing his harangue, unconscious of their emotions or it cause. Minutes elapse. His hands, in their wandering through the air, come in contact with the topmost cake, which they take and break. He begins to eat; and eats and talks, talks and eats, till he has finished a cruller. Then he feels for another, and eats that, and goes on, slowly consuming the contents of the basket till the last crumb is gone. The company look on amazed, and the kind lady of the house fears for the consequences. She had heard that cheese is an antidote to indigestion. Taking the empty cake-basket from his lap, she silently puts a plate of cheese in its place, hoping that instinct will guide his hand aright. The experiment succeeds. Gradually the blocks of white new cheese disappear. She removes the plate. No ill consequences follow. Those who saw this sight are fixed in the belief that Mr. Greeley was not then, nor has since become, aware that on that evening he partook of sustenance."

THE "NEW YORKER."

Meantime, Greeley has made his debut and his first success as an editor. On the 22d of March, 1834, appeared the first number of the *New York-*

er, of which the firm of Greeley & Co., above described, were the proprietors and Greeley himself chief editor. The joint capital of the firm was then about $3,000. The paper which they proposed to print was a political, (but not partisan) literary and family weekly, of a class much higher than any then published in this country; and few will deny that they carried out their idea with great zeal and fair ability. The *New Yorker* was a model of typhographical neatness; its selected matter was choice, its compilations of news uncommonly full and accurate for the time, and its editorials pointed, energetic and original. Its first endeavor to be impartial in politics did not succeed very well. Still, its Whiggism was much more moderate than that of Mr. Greeley's subsequent ventures in the journalistic line. One of the features of the *New Yorker* was the publication of a piece of music each week. The first number contained "Meet me by moonlight alone;" the next, "Still so gently o'er me;" and the next two were devoted to Rossini's "All by the shady greenwood tree;" and in view of the narrow space at the disposal of the editor, it is evident that the musical feature of the *New Yorker* was intended to be an important one. The plan underwent some change as time wore on; but through all the circulation increased, until it reached at one time 9,000. Yet, through the failure of any of its proprietors to grasp the practical and financial situation, the enterprise never *paid*, and the publishers buried in it, during the seven years of its existence, all the money they could make out of their job office, and all they had accumulated at the beginning.

During the campaign of 1840, Greeley published and edited the *Log Cabin*, a Whig campaign paper, in addition to the *New Yorker*, then still in existence. In the autumn of the following year they were both merged in the *Weekly Tribune*.

STARTS THE "TRIBUNE."

It was on the morning of the 10th of April, 1841, that the first number of the *Tribune* was issued, as a cheap Whig daily, with a purpose to be more decent as well as more enterprising than the *Sun* and *Herald*—then the leading penny papers in New York. The *Tribune* was sold at one cent a copy, or $4 a year. Its capital was $1,000, borrowed by Greeley of James Coggeshall; the talent of himself and Henry J. Raymond, then new to New York daily journalism; and the real need, which then existed, of such a paper. The *Tribune* began with 600 subscribers, and printed an edition of 5,000 the first day, only a portion of which were sold. The circulation of the *Tribune* increased apace, and well it might; for besides being the cheapest of all respectable papers in the city, it was as newsy, spicy and able as the best of the ten-dollar journals. Both Greeley and Raymond performed prodigies of work, the former usually writing about three columns per day of editorial matter. Nevertheless the paper did not attain financial success during the first few months, for a reason which is obvious. It lacked a good business head. This it fortunately found in Thomas McElrath, who took an interest in the concern and assumed the business management on July 31, following the foundation of the *Tribune.* Raymond should have been made a partner also; but he was kept on a salary of $8 per week, and was, after a year or two, allowed to leave the paper. The course of Greeley toward both Raymond and McElrath has been criticised; but upon what data we shall not undertake here to say. The best authority upon this subject is Maverick's Life of Raymond, which, however, has a slight bias of personal favoritism for the lamented subject of the biography.

Mr. Greeley embraced Fourierism as early as 1839; but it did not crop out in the *Tribune* until near the end of the first year of that paper's existence. The most important facts of Mr. Greeley's career in behalf of Communism are reserved for a separate chapter in this history. The fact of such a connection is mentioned here as an episode of the *Tribune's* history—and a very important episode it was, since it had much to do with the suddenly gained notoriety of that paper.

GREELEY AS AN EDITOR.

Mr. Parton, in expressing his regrets that Greeley allowed Raymond to leave him, remarks, "Horace Greeley is not a born journalist. He is too much in earnest to be a perfect editor. He has too many opinions and preferences. He is a born Legislator, a Deviser of Remedies, a Suggester of Expedients, a Framer of Measures." But Parton is manifestly wrong in ruling Greeley out of the sphere of journalism upon these qualities and characteristics. It is obvious from this schedule of his biographer, as well as from his life generally, that Mr. Greeley is a theorist, rather than a practical man; an observer who takes a birds-eye view of humanity, rather than one who comes amongst it and learns the character and qualities of each specimen; and a ready and fertile inventor of things practicable and impracticable, rather than an organizer and handy operator of affairs. The qualities which he has are needed in the journalist; of those needed by the Legislator he has but few, as he proved when in Congress; and of those needed by the Executive he has next to none. Tact he has not; but genius in a certain direction, viz., of accumulating facts, constructing theories, and communicating ideas, he certainly has. In this direction runs the path of the journalist; and although Mr. Greeley is deficient in the judicial faculty, which every journalist should have, yet it cannot be denied that he is, or rather was, until the Presidential mania seized him, the most brilliantly successful, and, on the whole, the chief of all journalists in America.

HIS INTEMPERANCE OF LANGUAGE.

Mr. Greeley's career, as editor of the *Tribune*,

cannot here be traced in detail. Only such points as illustrate his individual peculiarities will be alluded to. One of these peculiarities is his intemperate use of invective, showing his lack of practical charity, and his uncontrollable tendency to become flagrantly belligerent upon any case submitted for his consideration. His penchant for vituperative language toward his opponents developed itself early in the history of the *Tribune*, and continued up to the latest recorded utterance. It is as natural for him to call names in his newspaper as it is for a Billingsgate fishwoman at her stand; and the only excuse to be offered for such violation of dignity and decency is the same in each ease, viz., that no fights ever come of it, as would happed if another had used the epithet. Scarcely a day passes during a compaign season, when Mr. Greeley is habitually engaged at writing editorials for the *Tribune*, that he does not brand some statement as "a lie." Somewhat less frequently he dubs some person "a villain," etc. He used to pursue Major Noah. of a rival paper, with especial vindictiveness. In one paragraph referring to him he would commence with, "We ought not to notice this old villain again." In another, he would refer to him as a "superannuated renegade from all parties." a "worn-out tool," etc. Here are other delicate morsels of *Tribune* repartee:

"The villain who makes this charge against me well knows its falsehood."

"We defy the Father of lies himself to crowd more stupendous falsehoods into a paragraph than this contains."

"Mr. Benton! Each of the above observations is a deliberate falsehood, and you are an unqualified villain!"

GREELEY AND WHITE EXCHANGE COMPLIMENTS.

And it was only last summer that Mr. Greeley dubbed the editor of the Chicago *Tribune*—now perforce his principal advocate in the West—as "a sublime liar;" but the editor referred to had got ahead of Greeley in this respect by saying of him some months before:

"For twenty-five years he has been a marplot in council; an unreliable commander in action; a misanthrope in victory, and a riotous disorganizer in defeat. He has always been fanatical in his demands for the extremest measures, and when the party has reached the eve of triumph, invariably thrusts himself forward as a negotiator of terms of surrender to the enemy. His course during the war was but a repetition of his course in politics. In 1861 he was an open defender of secession; he changed to a vigorous champion of the war, and thereafter was forever recklessly making proposals for peace and as recklessly withdrawing them—making war in spite of Mars, and negotiating in spite of Minerva.

"For twenty years he has been an uncompromising advocate for a square fight with the pro-slavery party, and when that kind of a fight was forced upon the Republicans in 1860, he was here in Chicago, voting not for Lincoln, nor for Chase, but for old Edward Bates, of Missouri, one of the fossils of the slave party. He was then the associate and co-laborer of that other impracticable and unreliable squad, the Blair family. The country at this time wants no inspired Harlequins in the national councils. Still less does it want men with statesmanship so microscopic that they can see nothing in public business but the mileage and *per diem* of their fellow members. If Mr. Greeley is not satisfied with his position as a journalist—a position which ought to be equal, in point of influence, power, and dignity, to that of six average Senators—and if the Republicans of New York want to do something for him, let them make him State Prison Inspector, or even Governor, anything that will not make the people outside of the State responsible for his follies."

Mr. Greeley continued his connection with the *Tribune* up to the 15th of May, 1872, when, following the advice of friends proffered in view of his recent nomination for President, he published in that paper the following card:

" The *Tribune* has ceased to be a party organ, but the unexpected nomination of its editor at Cincinnati, seems to involve it in a new embarrassment All must be aware that the position of a journalist who is at the same time a candidate, is at best irksome and difficult ; that he is fettered in action and restrained in criticism by the knowledge that whatever he may say or do is closely scanned by thousands, eager to find in it what may be so interpreted as to annoy or perplex those who are supporting him as a candidate, and to whom his shackled condition will not permit him to be serviceable. The undersigned, therefore, withdraws absolutely from the conduct of the *Tribune*, and will henceforth, until further notice, exercise no control or supervision over its columns.

"(Signed,) HORACE GREELEY.

"May 15, 1873."

GREELEY'S WORKS.

During his service on the *Tribune* and *New Yorker* he fonnd time to enage in lecturing and other enterprises, out of which he earned several fortunes, though he has never amassed great wealth, owing partly to improvidence, and partly to his promiscuous generosity with money.* In 1838-9,

*Some idea of the looseness of Mr. Greeley's habits in the management of money affairs may be formed from an incident which Mr. Parton relates as characteristic: " If a boy stole his letters from the Post-office, he would admonish him and let him go, or try him again. On one occasion, he went to the Post-office himself, and, receiving a large number of letters, put them, it is said, into the pockets of his overcoat. On reaching the office, he hung the overcoat on its accustomed peg, and was soon lost in the composition of an article. It was one of the last chilly days in spring, and he thought no more either of the overcoat or its pockets till autumn. Letters kept coming in complaining for the non-receipt of papers which had been ordered and paid for ; and the office was sorely perplexed. On the first cool day in October, when the editor was shaking the summer's dirt from his coat, the missing letters were found, and the mystery was explained."

Under the same head the Chicago *Times* tells the story, which is doubtless authentic in substance:

" It has long been notorious that whenever any unprincipled adventurer, confidence man, or dead beat desired to 'make a raise,' he could readily devise the way to bamboozle H. G. into indorsing his note or lending him the required note. When one of the proprietors of the auxiliary Grant organ of

he edited the *Jeffersonian*, a Whig campaign organ, designed for New York State circulation; he also wrote leading articles for the *Daily Whig*, another campaign organ. He has published numerous books, mostly reprinted from the *Tribune* and other papers. Principal among these are his "Hints Toward Reform" (1850), "Glances at Europe" (1853), "History of the Struggle for Slavery Extension or Restriction in the United States, from 1718 to 1856, (1856). "Recollections of a Busy Life" (1866), "The Great American Conflict," a history of the War of Rebellion, in 2 volumes, (1865), a book in Advocacy of Protection, published in 1868, and "What I Know of Farming," (1870). "Hints Toward Reform" was his maiden book. It contains more condities of manner than the others, and is at the same time more exempt from some of the peculiar faults of Mr. Greeley's methods of treat-

this city met the philosopher in New York some months ago, he took the liberty of an old acquaintanceship to ask him how much he was worth. 'Well,' said the philosopher, 'I don't know. I've got ten shares in the *Tribune;* I've got a farm up here in the country, and I've got some other things, but I don't know what they're worth. 'What does your *Tribune* stock pay you?' 'I think about $10,000 a year.' 'How much does it cost you to live?' 'About $5,000 a year.' 'Well, what becomes of the other $5,000?' 'I pay my debts with it.' 'What revenue does your farm yield?' 'From what I know about farming, I should say not much. I contrive to get a part of my living from it.' 'Which leaves something over five thousand with which you pay your debts?' 'Well, I think likely.' 'How much did you make out of your book?' 'I should say about a $100,000.' 'What became of that?' 'Oh, I paid my debts with it. 'Of course you draw a salary from the *Tribune?*' 'Oh, yes; I use that to pay my debts. You see, Joe, the fact is, some of these fellows who get me to indorse for them, turn out to be liars, villains, and scoundrels!' The *Times* ventures the observation that it is not economy in money matters, any more than it is political economy, which H. G. represents."

ment. There is perceptible throughout this series of essays a free gush of sentiment, or of sentimentality, and the writer often indulges in a flight of fancy which would probably have astonished him at a later period of his development. "Hints Toward Reform" is "affectionately" inscribed, with many typographical flourishes, "To the Generous, the Hopeful, the Loving who, firmly and joyfully Believing in the Impartial and Boundless Goodness of our Father, Trust that the Errors, the Crimes and the Miseries which have long rendered Earth a Hell, shall yet be Swallowed Up and Forgotten in a Far Exceeding and Unmeasured Reign of Truth, Purity and Bliss."

In one of the essays of this volume—that on "Human Life"—he pictures the scene which should present itself "to the piercing gaze of an unfettered spirit, unmindful of space, who should scan this fair globe from the central orb of our system," with such detail as to make a sort of geographical epic of the whole. From the "tiger-haunted jungles of India" and the "swarming vales of China and Japan," he marches on, past the "scorched and glowing deserts of Africa, shining in silvery worthlessness and desolation," to this country, with the "prairie openings in its center, which nature, or rather, the red man's annual conflagration, has sufficed to hollow out by imperceptible gradations," and the great lakes, of which he says the "last is surpassing in profundity and beauty;" and thence to the "broad placid surface of the unvexed Pacific, sprinkled with isles of deepest emerald, where flowers perennial bloom."

GREELEY AS A POET.

It should be known, also, that Mr. Greeley has often "dropped into poetry," and that nearly forty published poems, the product of his muse, are now extant in print. They are less meritorious than his prose, but that is not saying that they are bad verses; for Horace Greeley is certainly one of the most vigorous and felicitous prose writers in America. Of these poems, the most interesting and carefully constructed (and, as it happens, the only love poem in the lot) is called "Fantasies," and bears date May 31, 1834. Therein, after stating that,

> "They deem me cold, that through the years departed,
> I ne'er have bowed me to some form divine,"

he goes on to explain:

> "No! in my soul there glows but one bright vision,
> And o'er my heart there rules but one fond spell,
> Brightening my hours of sleep with dreams Elysian
> Of one unseen, yet loved, aye, cherished well.
> Unseen? Ah! no: her presence round me lingers,
> Chasing each wayward thought that tempts to rove,
> Weaving affection's web with fairy fingers,
> And waking thoughts of purity and love."

At the time of composing this, Horace was boarding at the Graham House; and it is more than likely that he never had but one "bright vision" to haunt him in the manner described, and she the veritable one for whom the silk stockings were donned two years afterwards.

Some facts of Mr. Greeley's connection with American politics will be touched upon in the next chapter; and as his life has been one prolonged political campaign, there are but few incidents or episodes which we need stop to relate here. One of these was the *Tribune* editor's voyage to Europe in 1851, where he served as a juror at the World's Fair in London, and attracted considerable attention as a prominent American politician and agitator—a class which always obtains demonstrative recognition in England. In 1859, Mr. Greeley made the journey overland to California, lecturing and delivering addresses at almost every considerable town. These are the principal travels of our hero, and the principal episodes of his life, outside of politics.

CAPTURED BY THE FRENCH.

An incident of Greeley's European tour has recently been related by Don Piatt (a personal friend and supporter), and is amusing enough to warrant its transcription here:

One sunny summer's afternoon, nearly twenty years since, in beautiful Paris, we were dressing for a dinner party. We had progressed liesurely so far as the immaculate linen, the buff-colored pantaloons with the broad gold braid running the length of each leg, and the patent leather boots, when further adornment was arrested by a row upon the pavement in front of the Legation. Looking through the window we saw our valued friend, Horace Greeley, struggling in the hands of six ruffians, while a gathering crowd looked on with the quiet indifference so peculiar to the French.

It was not wise to rush into that conflict without our diplomatic coat. Could we have added the cocked hat, with national tail feathers of the American rooster, it would have been well. The French mind respects the diplomatic position, being a civilized, a polite nation, and find in the

JANUS GREELEY.

Within the past thirty-nine months the Republican Party, under President GRANT

clothes thereunto belonging conclusive evidence of mysterious powers. Now our diplomacy did not get beyond the legs. From the feet to the waist we were in the eyes of Paris a diplomatic power. From the waist up we were only a private citizen. We might have kicked a French official, but he in return, while respecting our diplomatic legs, could have punched our unofficial head.

We have never ceased to regret this false move on our part. Oh! if we had only put on that coat, what different results would now go to make up the Recollections of a Busy Life and the history of the world. As it was, our arrival upon the scene did not have the effect it ought to have had. The French myrmidons did not fall back in respectful awe before us. Not much. They only went on more vigorously with their infamous work. This consisted in an attempt to get Mr. Greeley into a very common and disreputable *voiture*. Two stout Frenchmen were swung each to the great journalist's arms, and he held back in the most bashful and diffident manner. The six Parisians were all talking at once in the purest French. Mr. Greeley was responding in the purest English—that is, interspersed with some profane language, of which he was, and is, a consummate master. We recollect he called these officious officials "damned hogs," showing at the moment his agricultural turn. We did not suggest at the time that he had better translate that into "*maudit cochon*," and so touch the souls of the *miserables*, as the hour for discussion had passed, and that of action arrived. We shook off one of the assailants, and interposed our diplomatic person between our journalistic friend and his other enemy, and while doing so we cried:

"Run into the bureau, Mr. Greeley—run!"

We knew that if he once took sanctuary in that way, he would stand as it were upon the sacred soil of free America, and could bid the minions of an effete despotism defiance. But he would not, this infatuated quill driver, take the hint.

"What must I run for?" he demanded in his querulous, shrill voice. "I have done nothing to run from; only ask these damned scoundrels what they want."

We did not believe our guileless friend; we must say that we did not put a particle of confidence in his assertions of innocence. We believed he had committed murder. From reading Mr. Greeley's editorials we had been impressed with the belief that he was capable of great violence. We thought then that he had got into controversy with some poor Frenchman on the tariff, and had assassinated him because of the difficulty of making himself understood. Mr. Greeley is troubled with this, and gets very violent when the fit is on him.

We continued our friendly efforts in his behalf. Not wishing to accompany our dear friend to prison when we were expected to a charming dinner, we did not murder the six assailants; we did not even knock them down, but we did make it very lively for them, and gave Mr. Greeley several excellent chances escape. He declined accepting them, and knowing that we would be too late for dinner, we desisted at last, and through our tears saw the old white hat and venerable coat chucked by the ruffians into that vulgar *vioture*, where two sat by him and one on him. The dirty vehicle was driven away with such violence that the horse actually took fright and for the first time in the history of Paris a horse of this sort ran away. It was not much of a run, but so amazed the driver that he lost his head and let the crazy animal collide with one of the trees in the camps Elysees. when the *Tribune* and the officers were all spilled out.

The police of Paris are world-famous for their efficiency, and on this occasion they arrested the *voiture* and driver and marched them off, leaving the officers and prisoner to find another vehicle to carry them to the debtors' prison, known as Clichy.

This all occurred on Saturday afternoon, and I learned that night the meaning of it. It seemed that the World's Exposition, held in New York a few years before this event, the directors, wishing to encourage the concern, pledged themselves to not only return safely the articles not sold, but pay for transportation of the same. This encouraged a French artist to send a life-sized statue of Venus de Medicis, and whether in marble or plaster we fail to remember. All French artists indulge in Venuses, and this one came to grief. The Exposition proved a failure, the transportation was not paid, and, worse yet, the Venus de Medicis had her nose knocked. Now the Venus in Paris with a damaged nose is common, but not attractive, and the indignant artist wanted pay for the same. He did not get pay to any great extent, and learning that Mr. Greeley, one of the directors, was in Paris, the artistic stone-cutter had him arrested late on Saturday afternoon, so as to incarcerate him in prison until Monday at least, believing that the free-born American would pay the amount rather than submit to the outrage. He mistook his man.

We left that little dinner party at an early hour. We saw Judge Mason and secured his efforts in behalf of the imprisoned journalist. We had an interview with the Minister of Foreign affairs, and I must say for my chief, that he stated the case with much earnest force, so much indeed, that Mr. Greeley's release was promptly ordered, and on Monday, the able journalist came out a free man.

CHAPTER XXII.

GREELEY AS A FOURIERITE.

The Sage of Lackawaxen—He Espouses the Philosophy of Fourier—What That Means—Socialism in America—Greeley as its Great Apostle—His First Bull Run—"On to Lackawaxen"—His Colony Fails Miserably and he Calls the Members hard Names—Greeley's Utterances in Favor of Communism—His Discussion with Raymond.

By no means the least interesting part of Horace Greeley's life is his experience as a prominent advocate of Fourierism, and a zealous laborer in the work of planting these unfortunate colonies, or "phalanxes," which began to dot the country about thirty years ago, and the wrecks of which are still to be seen in almost every State. The story of these enterprises would be comical if it were not so sad a record of credulous, crack-brained mortals, duped by designing knaves or (more frequently) misled by others more brilliant, and also more crack-brained than themselves.

GREELEY THE FOUNDER OF FOURIERISM IN AMERICA.

Early in his journalistic career, Mr. Greeley espoused the cause of the Socialists—they who sought to reorganize society on a far better plan than that which the Creator ordained; to abolish, in great measure, the sacred ties of family, and to substitute the Community in its place; to repeal the natural laws which guarantee personal independence in the enterprise of accumulating wealth and spending it, and to substitute therefor a principle which Mr. Greeley calls *interdependence.*

John Humphrey Noyes, the leading apostle of the Oneida Community, a strictly free-love association which grew out of these earlier attempts at Communism, says in his "History of American Socialisms" [page 14]:

"Fourierism was introduced into this country by Albert Brisbane and Horace Greeley in 1842, and then commenced another great national movement similar to that of Owenism, [a previously exploded *ism*] but far more universal and enthusiastic. Many of them never undertook to carry into practice Fourier's theories in full; but they all originated in a common excitement, and that excitement took its rise from the publications of Brisbane and Greeley."

WHAT FOURIERISM MEANS.

Before narrating (chiefly from facts obtained in Noyes's book and from a carefully prepared account by A. J. MacDonald, embodied therein) the career of Mr. Greeley as a Fourierite and Communist, we will quote from Henry J. Raymond—a man noted, in his day, for fairness to his opponents—a statement of the vital tenets of the American Socialists. It is taken from the concluding article of a notable discussion which took place in 1846–7 between Raymond and Greeley, and which was printed in the New York *Times* and *Tribune*, commencing Nov. 20, 1846. Mr. Raymond says:

"We have proved, in preceding articles of this discussion, that the whole system of association is founded upon, and grows out of, the fundamental principle known as the law of passional attraction. The arguments by which this position is established remains untouched; and we shall not therefore repeat it. In our last article we proved that in this system the law of man's nature is made the supreme rule of his conduct and character; that it recognizes no higher law than that of inclination, no authority above that of passion; and of course no essential distinction between right and wrong—no standard of duty except that of impulse. Of course the idea of human responsibility is utterly destroyed; and all the sanctions of moral and religious truth, as derived from the Word of God, are abrogated and cast aside. These deductions flow inevitably from the law of passional attraction."

The inevitable particular tendencies of the socialistic theory advocated by Mr. Greeley, not only as elaborated by Fourier and others, but as following logically upon the main principles avowed by Greeley, are further pointed out by Mr. Raymond in his concluding article. He shows how in attempting to reform labor, by breaking down what he calls the monopoly of land, Mr. Greeley would virtually throw all the land into the hands of a few capitalists, and make those less thrifty by nature their dependent tenants and serfs. He shows how, in abolishing the isolated households which characterize the natural condition of civilized society, and throwing everybody into droves, Mr. Greeley would deprive men and women of that desire for a comfortable separate home, which constitutes the main spur to industry and good habits. He shows how, in the communistic plan of taking children from the care of their parents and nurses, and entrusting the community with their education from the first, a deadly blow is struck at the parental relation as ordained in the Word of God. He shows how, in the abolition of the marriage relation, and leaving women free from either marital obligation or responsibility for the care of their offspring, Mr. Greeley, or those who defend this communistic theory, introduce into society a worse form of polygamy, or of that and polyandry combined, than has ever been attempted in any nation or any age of the world.

Such is a clear, cool, logical statement of the doctrines of an order of which Albert Brisbane said: "Greeley has created the cause in this country."

THE TRIBUNE THE ORGAN OF FOURIERISM.

How did he do this? Let us follow events in their chronological order.

In 1842, when Brisbane and Greeley introduced Fourierism into America, the New York *Tribune* was in its infancy. It was, as Mr. Greeley is accustomed to call the Pennsylvania iron mills, and the New England woollen and cotton factories, a "struggling" institution. A portion of its space was then surrendered to the Communists, who occupied it daily with good effect—that is, good from their point of view. To be sure, there was an editorial explanation on the first day of the *Tribune's* service in this cause, to the effect that the proprietors of the paper were not to be held responsible for what they printed in these columns. But this was evidently on account of Mr. Greeley's partner, Mr. McElrath, as "it was known," says Noyes, "that Greeley was much in sympathy with Fourierism, so that Brisbane had the help of his popularity" with the laborers, whose organ the *Tribune* also was). And the historian adds: "Whether the *Tribune* lifted Fourierism or Fourierism lifted the *Tribune*, may be a matter of doubt;" but he inclines to the latter opinion.

ON TO LACKAWAXEN !

In May, 1843, we hear of Mr. Greeley as Treasurer of the Sylvania Phalanx, a Fourierite community, which ran a brief and by no means brilliant career at Lackawaxen, Pike county, Pennsylvania, and of which Thomas Whitley was President. An address issued in the form of a pamphlet, and signed by Horace Greeley, amongst others, contained the following announcement:

"This association was formed early in 1843 by a few citizens of New York, mainly mechanics, who, deeply impressed with the present defective, vice-engendering and ruinous system of society, with the wasteful complication of its isolated households, its destructive competition and anarchy in industry, its constraint of millions to idleness and consequent dependence or famine for want of employment, and its failure to secure education and development to the children growing up all around and amoug us in ignorance and vice, were impelled to immediate, energetic action in resistance to these manifold and mighty evils. Having earnestly studied the system of industtial organization and *social reform propounded by Charles Fourier, and been led to recognize in it a beneficent, expansive and practical plan* for the melioration of the condition of man and his moral and intellectual elevation, *they most heartily adopted that system as the basis and guide of their operations.*"

"Vice-engendering" is a good phrase, especially when, as a remedy for the vice-engendering system, Mr. Greeley proposed to substitute a plan of social organization which abolishes the *home*, and throws the human beings upon whom he experiments into a promiscuous boarding-house in which each works for his keeping merely; and in which the only moral law recognized is "passional equilibrium"!

Into this scheme about 150 persons were decoyed by the Greeley prospectus and by the glowing description of the "domain," published in the *Phalanx*, organ of the association, which last represented the said domain as being handily accessible, and having for soil "a deep loam, well calculated for tillage and grazing." How the poor Lackawaxenites fared, and what were the practical workings of Mr. Greeley's "beneficent, expansive" system, is best told in a dialogue reported by Mr. MacDonald, as having been held between C., an inquirer after wisdom, and A., a member of the Phalanx.

HOW THE "EXPANSIVE SYSTEM" WORKED.

C.—What were the qualifications of the men who were appointed to select the location? I think this very important.

A.—One was a landscape painter, another an industrious cooper, and the third was a homœpathic doctor!

C.—And not a farmer among them! Well, this must have been a great mistake. At what season did they go to examine the country?

A.—I think it was in March; I am sure it was before the snow was off the ground.

C.—How unhappy are the working classes in having so little patience. Everything they attempt seems to fail because they will not wait the right time. Had you any capitalists among you?

A.—No; they were principally working people, brought up to a city life.

C.—But you encouraged capitalists to join your society?

A.—Our constitution provided for them as well as laborers. We wished to combine capital and labor, according to the theory laid down by Charles Fourier.

* * * * * * * * * * * *

C.—But about the committee which you say consisted of an artist, mechanic and a doctor; what report did they make concerning the land?

A.—They reported favorably of a section of land in Pike County, Pa., consisting of about 2,394 acres, partly wooded with yellow pine and small oak trees, with a soil of yellow loam without lime. It was well watered, had an undulating surface, and was said to be elevated fifteen hundred feet above the Hudson river. To reach it from New York and Albany, we had to take our things first to Rondout, on the Hudson, and thence by canal to Lackawanna; then five miles up hill on a bad stony road. [In the prospectus the canal is said to be "*directly across from* the domain."] There was plenty of stone for building purposes lying all over the land. The soil being covered with snow, the committee did not see it, but from the small size of the trees, they probably judged it would be easily cleared, which would be a great advantage to city-choppers. Nine thousand dollars was the price demanded for this place, and the society concluded to take it.

C.—What improvements were upon it, and what were the conditions of sale?

A.—There were about thirty acres planted with rye, which grain, I understood, had been successively planted upon it for six years without any manure. This was taken as a proof of the strength of the soil; but when we reaped, we were compelled to rake for ten yards on each side of the spot where we intended to make the bundle, before we had sufficient to tie together. There were three old houses on the place; a good barn and cow-shed; a grist-mill without machinery, with a good stream for water-power; an old saw-mill, with a very indifferent water-wheel. These, together with several skeletons of what had once been horses, constituted the stock and improvements. We were to pay $1,000 down in cash; the owner was to put in $1,000 as stock, and the balance was to be paid by annual instalments.

C.—How much stock did the members take?

A.—To state the exact amount would be somewhat difficult; for some who subscribed liberally at first, withdrew their subscriptions while others increased them. On examining my papers, I reckon that in Albany there were about $4,500 subscribed in money and useful articles for mechanical and other purposes. In New York I should estimate that about $6,000 were subcribed in like proportions.

C.—When did the members proceed to the domain, and how did they progress there?

A.—They left New York and Albany for the domain about the beginning of May; and I find from a table I kept of the number of persons, with their ages, sex and occupations, that in the following August there were on the place twenty-eight married men, twenty-seven married women, twenty-four single young men, six single young women, and fifty-one children; making a total of one hundred and thirty-six individuals. These had to be closely packed in three very indifferent two-story frame houses. The upper story of the grist-mill was devoted to as many as could sleep there. These arrangements very soon brought trouble. Children with every variety of temper and habits, were brought in close contact, without any previous training to prepare them for it. Parents, each with his or her peculiar character and mode of educating children, long used to very different accommodations, were brought here and literally compelled to live like a herd of animals. Some thought their children would be taken and cared for by the society, as its own family; while others claimed and practiced the right to procure for their children all the little indulgences they had been used to. Thus jealousies and ill-feelings were created, and in place of that self-sacrifice and zealous support of the constitution and officers, to which they were all pledged (I have no doubt by some in ignorance), there was a total disregard of all discipline, and a determination in each to have the biggest share of all things going, except hard labor, which was very unpopular with a certain class. Aside from the above, had we been carefully selected from families in each city, and had we been found capable of giving up our individual preferences to accomplish the glorious object we had in view, what had we to experiment upon? In my opinion, a barren wilderness; not giving the slightest prospect that it would ever generously yield a return for the great sacrifices we were making upon it. The land was cold and sterile, apparently incapable of supporting the stunted pines which looked like a vast collection of barbers' poles upon its surface. I will give you one or two illustrations of the quality of the soil: We cut and cleared four and a half acres of what we thought might be productive soil; and after having plowed and cross-plowed it, we sowed it with buckwheat. When the crop was drawn into the barn and threshed, it yielded eleven and a-half bushels. Again, we toiled hard, clearing the brush and picking up the stones from seventeen acres of new land: we plowed it three different ways, and then sowed and harrowed it with great care. When the product was reaped and threshed, it did not yield more than the quantity of seed planted. Such experiences as these made me look upon the whole operation as a suicidal affair, blasting forever the hopes and aspirations of the few noble spirits who tried so hard to establish in practice, the vision they had seen for years.

C.—How long did the Association remain on the place?

A.—About a year and a half, and then it wás abandoned as rapidly as it was settled.

C.—They made improvements while there. What were they, and who got them when the society left?

A.—We cleared over one hnndred acres and fenced it in; built a large frame-house forty feet by forty, three stories high; also a two-story carpenter's-shop, and a new wagon-house. We repaired the dam and saw-mill, and made other improvements which I cannot now particularize. These improvements went to the original owner, who had already received two thousand dollars on the purchase; and (as he expressed it) he generously agreed to take the land back, with the improvements, and release the trustees from all further obligations!

And MacDonald adds to this narration, as the fruit of his observations and reflections upon the subject, the following remarks:

"There were too many children on the place, their number being fifty-one to eighty-five adults. Some persons went there very poor, in fact, without anything, and came away in a better condition; while others took all they could with them, and came back poor. Young men, it is stated, wasted the good things at the commencement of the experiment; and besides victuals, dry-goods supplied by the Association were unequally obtained. Idle and greedy people find their way into such attempts, and soon show forth their character by burdening others with too much labor, and, in times of scarcity, supplying themselves with more than their allowance, of various aritcles, instead of taking less.

"Where such a failure as this occurs, many persons are apt to throw the blame upon particular individuals as well as on the principles; but in this case, I believe, nearly all connected with it agree that the inferior land and location was the fundamental cause of ill success.

"It was a loss to nearly all engaged in it. Those who subscribed and did not go, lost their shares; and those subscribed and did go, lost their valuable time as well as their shares. The sufferers were in error, and were led into the experiment by others, who were likewise in error. Working men left their situations, some good and some bad, and, in their enthusiasm, expected not only to improve their own condition, but the condition of mankind.

They fought the fight, and were defeated, Some were so badly wounded that it took them many years to recover; while others, more fortunate, speedily regained their former positions, and now thrive well in the world again. The capital expended on this experiment was estimated at $14,000."

This funeral sermon is corroborated in its substantial statements by the *Phalanx*, (the same paper which had published the rose-colored description of the Sylvania " domain " a year before,) which in announcing the failure and utter confusion of the enterprise, treated it as due to "the fact that the domain is located in a thinly inhabited region, cut off almost entirely from a market for its surplus productions," and that the association had "become satisfied of its inability to contend successfully against an ungrateful soil and ungenial climate, which unfortunately characterize the domain on which it settled." The notice is exceedingly laconic for the Communists, who had developed a great fertility of words; no "ungrateful soil" or "ungenial climate" were their fermenting brains. So laconic indeed was the obituary of the Lackawaxen Phalanx that there appears to have been no room in it for an invitation for the ruined Communists to "apply to the Treasurer, Horace Greeley, Esq., for the return of the $14,000 cash sunk in the enterprise"! And yet such a transaction as this, whatever we may say of the "passional equilibrium," was absolutely necessary to the financial equilibrium of the Phalanx.

WHO WAS RESPONSIBLE?

We cannot forbear making one more quotation

relative to the history of this cruel experiment. It is a reflection indulged in by one who feels kindly toward Socialism, but who does not approve of such a reckless rushing into experiments, with illy digested plans, or such an unscrupulous confidence game as that practiced by the agents of this Lackawaxen enterprise:

"What, then, shall we say of the rank and file that formed themselves into phalanxes and marched into the wilderness to the music of Fourierism? Multitudes of them, like the poor Sylvanians, lost their all in the battle. To them it was no mere matter of theory or of pleasant propagandism, but a miserable 'Bull Run.' And surely there was a great mistake somewhere. Who was responsible for the enormous miscalculation of times and forces, and capabilities of human nature, that is manifest in the universal disaster of the experiments? Shall we clear the generals, [Greeley, Whitley, *et al.*,] and leave the poor soldiers to be called volunteer fools, without even the comfort of being in good company?"

And yet this is precisely what Greeley called his colonists in his *Tribune* not long after the retreat from Lackawaxen. He referred to himself, Whitley, and other "generals," as "noble, lofty souls," and to their unhappy dupes as "the conceited, the crotchety, the selfish, the headstrong, the unappreciative, the played out, the idle, and the good-for-nothing generally," upon whom the blame of the failure rested! Here is true charity for you! Here is an illustration of the practical philanthropy of some who set themselves up as philanthropists on a grand scale!

GREELEY CONTINUES TO RECONSTRUCT MANKIND.

But this disastrous and humiliating experience did not quench the fire of philanthropy which burned in the breast of the sage of Lackawaxen.

Greeley was still recognized by the Socialists as a strong tower of their system; and at the National Convention of Associationists, held at New York, April 4th, 1844, he was one of the Vice-Presidents, and was re-elected one of the editors of the *Phalanx* newspaper, (the *Harbinger*, to which Greeley also contributed, having been founded later.) This convention was very much of a love-feast and jubilee, the order being at the time in the heyday of its financial prosperity. Among the members were Brisbane and Greeley, the twin leaders of the movement; George Ripley, one of Greeley's editorial writers at the present time; Charles A. Dana, who has since developed into the champion blackguard of America, but who was then a very devout and self-abnegating representative of the Brook Farm Phalanx; and Parke Godwin, who furnished a remarkably pious and ingenious address, attempting to trace to the Bible the principles of the order.

A FAMOUS BANQUET.

On the evening of the 6th, the Convention had a banquet at the Apollo Saloon. Mr. Greeley was toasted by Brisbane in a fervent speech, in which the toaster said: "He [Greeley] has done for us what we never could have done. He has created the cause on this continent. He has done the work of a century." This extravagant eulogium Mr. Greeley accepted with a smile, and launched out in a speech wherein he said:

"When I took up this cause, I knew that I went in the teeth of many of my patrons, in the teeth of the prejudices of the great mass, in the teeth of religious prejudices; for I confess I had a great many more clergymen on *my* list [no credit for poor McElrath] before than I have now, as I am sorry to say; for had they kept on, I think I could have done them a little good. [Laughter.] But in the face of all this I have gone on, pursuing a manly, and at the same time a circumspect course, treading wantonly on no man's prejudice; telling, on the contrary, universal man, I will defer to your prejudices as far as I can consistently with my duty; but when duty leads me you must excuse my stepping on your corn if it be in the way." [Cheers.]

This speech is printed in the official report given by the *Phalanx* at the time, and bears internal evidence of having been written out by Mr. Greeley for this purpose. It will be seen that the philosopher and presidential candidate avows very emphatically his purpose to fly in the teeth of the prejudices of the great masses whenever he sees fit. Of course, he at once dubs as "prejudice" all opposition to his views, and proceeds to "fly in the teeth" of the people, "tread on their corns," etc., as he pleases. This is not the kind of man whom the people want for President, especially since their experience of Andrew Johnson.

The day on which this banquet was held was the anniversary of Fourier's birth-day. The regular toasts were all to the memory of this theorist, and to the twelve several passions, which, according to Fourier, constitute the active forces of human nature. The brethren became so wrought up with some of these passions that after one of the toasts, Mr. MacDaniel proposed that the thing be repeated with clasped hands. "This proposition," says the *Phalanx*, "was instantly accepted, and, with a burst of enthusiasm, every man rose, and locking hands all round the table, the toast was repeated by the whole company, *producing an electric thrill of emotion through every nerve.*" This phenomenon is strictly according to Fourier, who has much to say about the passional effect of Touch. It is doubtless a recollection of this thrilling moment which impels Mr. Chas. A. Dana, after years devoted to writing down Mr. Greeley, to turn about and give him a solemn support (if Dana's advocacy can be called a support) in his candidacy for President.

Of course, after such a season of mutual admiration and "electric thrill" as this, the faithful band returned to their task of propagandism with redoubled zeal. Dana returned to "menial and repulsive work" at Brook Farm, and Greeley straightway indulged in another Phalanx, and another prospectus. This was the North American Phalanx which had its location at Monmouth, N. J., about forty miles from New York city. Greeley was Vice President and a large stockholder. Special efforts were made to fill up the ranks of this phalanx with true and trusty soldiers, and to weed out with scrupulous care all "the selfish, the conceited, the played-out," etc., whom their leader at Lackawaxen had so severely execrated. But human nature proved too much for the "beneficient and expansive" system of Association, and after eleven years of trial, during which the financial prosperity of the Communists had not been bad, the members suddenly discovered, with one consent, that they would prefer to return to the "vice-engendering systems" of civilized society, and the "wasteful complications of its isolated households."

Mr. Greeley's demeanor toward these enterprises was characterized by the same reckless generosity with money which has been observed in his private life. The Philosopher has ever been ready to lend a man five dollars, even though he had but four to lend him. It is imputed to him that, in contributing material aid to the struggling associations, he was far more forward than his fellow laborer, Brisbane. In his address to the fraternity, published in the *Harbinger* of Oct. 25, 1845, he wrote:

"Fellow Associationists! I shall do whatever I can for the promotion of our common cause. To it whatever I have or may hereafter acquire, of pecuniary ability is devoted; may I not hope for a like devotion from you?"

The response does not seem to have been very encouraging; for the system, already dead at the core and fast going to decay, continued to droop in all its branches.

THE DISCUSSION WITH RAYMOND.

This did not, however, deter Greeley from taking up the cudgels in behalf of Socialism whenever opportunity offered. In 1846 and '47 occurred the famous discussion with Henry J. Raymond, already quoted from.

In the first of his twelve articles of this series, Mr. Greeley contended that the landless have an inherent right to their "due share" of land, and the right of constant employment; and that these rights cannot be guaranteed without a radical change in our social economy. In the second he outlined the system of co-operation by phalanxes. In the third he unfolded the same fully, and enunciated substantially the theory of Fourier; *i. e.*, common property, etc. And so on, to the end of the last chapter, wherein he yearned for "the association of two or three hundred families, after the similitude of a bank or a whale-ship (!) inhabiting a common edifice." He "saw in the benevolent movements of the present time the portents of a good time coming. In this faith," he declared, "I labor and live; share it or scout it, as you will. Adieu." And here he appended those awe-inspiring initials, "H. G." with which the public has become so familiar.

It was generally pronounced that Raymond had the better of his antagonist in this discussion; but in estimating the intellectual merits of the performance, it must be borne in mind that Raymond had the sympathy of the entire public, to begin with.

However well he may have argued, he did not convince "H. G."—that is certain; for ten years later we find that staunch disputant still "flying in the teeth of prejudice," and incontinently tendering a loan of $12,000 to the North American Phalanx—an offer which does more credit to his heart than to his head, since the Phalanx was then in the throes of dissolution, and was soon sold out at sixty cents on the dollar.

REPUBLICAN PARTY

CHAPTER XXIII.

GREELEY AS A POLITICIAN.

His Political Life Characterized—Greeley's First Experience at "Relegating"—The Tippecanoe Campaign—The Clay Fiasco—"Isms" of the Philosopher—In Congress—His Career as a Legislator—The Partnership with Seward and Weed—Greeley Indignantly Withdraws—Cause of his Wrath—The Famous Seward Letter—Greeley Favors Secession—Defeats Seward at Chicago—The War Comes On—"Forward to Richmond!"—Thorning Lincoln—The Cleveland Convention—"Anybody to Beat Lincoln"—Greeley Winks at the Movement—The Niagara Falls Affair—Greeley Hobnobs with Bogus Rebel Commissioners—Blames Lincoln and Misrepresents Him—Noble Letter of the Martyr President—The War Ended—Greeley Does go On to Richmond—What he Does There—Indignation of the Public—Greeley's Opinion of Himself and Other Presidency-Hunters—Greeley and Tammany.

Horace Greeley's public career as a politician—all the while as an influential writer and the most of the time as an inside manager of politics—already stretches over a period of about thirty-eight years, commencing with the founding of the *New Yorker* in 1834. It did not, however, put on that very actice phase which has for the most part, characterized it, until the Presidential campaign of 1840, when Harrison and Tyler were running, on the Whig ticket, against Van Buren and Johnson.

The campaign was an unprecedently active one, being known as the Hard Cider and Log Cabin Campaign. The canvass commenced as early as the December preceding the election—nearly eleven months being thus allowed for "working up" the candidates.

THE RELEGATING BUSINESS.

The convention which nominated Harrison took place at Harrisburg, and it, like the campaign, was long and bitter. At this convention recurred Mr. Greeley's first experience at "relegating" troublesome questions to the several localities—something which may have struck our younger politicians as a new trick in politics, when introduced by Greeley as a stepping-stone to the candidacy at Cincinnati. We read in one of the earliest issues of the *Tribune* an explanation of this matter, in response to a question which had been raised as to whether the Whig party then had any platform. It seems that the Convention broke up and went home without adopting any platform at all; the *Tribune* explaining that on the last day of the session, "every thought was turned to the healing of disappointments and the solution of a Vice President" [and the one that they elected proved soon that they had better turned more careful thoughts in that direction]; and that "each delegation should," on returning home, "communicate to their constituents the nomination and the reasons for sustaining it in such manner as they should think proper." It was generally understood, however, that Mr. Greeley and his fellow-zealots of the Whig faith were fighting mainly for a high protective tariff, a consolidated national bank in the hands of a corporate monopoly, and under the "protection" of the government, and a profuse expenditure of national funds for building local improvements, such as wharves, railroads, etc. Of the doctrine we have nothing to say at present; but we call attention to the *school* of politics in which the present Democratic candidate received his first lessons.

GREELEY ON D. S. DICKINSON.

During the early history of the *Tribune*, Greeley was at Albany a good deal, and sent thence copious "editorial correspondence" to his paper. In one of these letters we read his opinion of Daniel S. Dickinson—a man of much nobler aims and purer ideas of public management than himself. Putting on a sweet smartness of style, with a little smattering of French which he had picked up somewhere and seemed anxious to air, our young editor wrote:

"I hear that my very sensitive friend, Daniel S. Dickinson, of Broome (familiarly, Scripture Dick), is a candidate for Secretary of State, Attorney General, or almost anything that is comfortable. I hardly credit it. Mr. Dickinson's talents are rather of a forensic than executive order. He ought to go to Congress manifestly; his peculiar style of oratory would create more amusement than a puppet show, and his words would suffice at any time to still the fiercest words of disorder,—the angriest burst of passion, at the first sound of his voice would subside in a horse laugh. There was a rare low comedian (the French would say *farceur*) spoiled when he became a statesman. He must not come here, therefore, but go to Congress."

The description certainly did not fit Mr. Dickinson. Would it not fit Mr. Greeley better?

GOES TO CONGRESS.

In the fall of 1848, Mr. Greeley was elected to Congress on the same ticket with James Brooks, of the *Express*—Mr. Greeley to serve out the remainder of a deceased member's term, which expired on the 4th of March following, and Mr. Brooks to fill the whole term succeeding that. This arrangement does not seem to have satisfied Mr. Greeley's idea of what was due him from the party, or rather the party managers, for in the famous letter to Governor Seward, in 1854, he uses this language: "I was once sent to Congress for ninety days, merely to enable Jim Brooks to secure a seat therein for four years. * * * James White (you hardly know how good and true a man he is) started my name for Congress, and Brooks's packed delegation thought I could help him through, so I was put on behind him."

Greeley's career in Congress does not appear to have been very successful. He proposed measures enough, and was especially active in behalf of his hobby of then—abolition of mileage—but never got any proposition before the House in a way or at a time to receive consideration. At the same time, he was constantly berating his fellow members through his correspondence for the *Tribune*—a course which could not be expected to conciliate them toward him, or any of his favorite measures. One of his epistolary attacks, of which a member named Rust, of Arkansas, was the object, brought that gentleman down upon Mr. Greeley with a cane, in a very dastardly attack—the only one, we believe, which the philosopher has ever received, notwithstanding he has applied "fighting" epithets to a majority of his fellow citizens, either individually or by class.

WISHES TO BE GOVERNOR.

In 1854 Greeley experienced one of the severest disappointments of his life. He then desired intensely the nomination of the Whigs for Governor of New York, and his failure to get that nomination may be said to have embittered his political life and changed the whole future course of the *Tribune*. His paper had, up to this time, been a truthful party organ, working implicitly for the nominations of the Whig party; but from this time it became a habitual bolter of nominations and a spitter upon platforms. The *animus* of its subsequent course is easily learned from the letter which Mr. Greeley addressed to Mr. Seward, on the 11th of November, immediately following the election which assured Seward's return to the Senate.

Greeley had, as already mentioned, desired the nomination of the Whigs for Governor. His almost Herculean efforts in behalf of Whig principles had, as he urges in the letter referred to, deserved some such recognition as this from the party. But there were considerations which prevented his nomination—chief of which was the almost absolute certainty of his being defeated, and with him Governor Seward for the Senate, if he should run. For ten years his paper had been the "organ," not merely of the Whig party, but of all the *isms* which had found lodgment in the big scraggy brain of its editor. And whatever Greeley had advocated, he had advocated in the most belligerent and extreme fashion, giving no quarter to his opponents, nor charity to their motives or opinions. These ten years had been probably the most prolific period of the *Tribune's* history in the development of *isms*—the crop including Fourierism, Grahamism, Maine-law-ism, Spiritualism, Woman's Rights-ism, (which Greeley was then, but not now, disposed to favor) and an infinite number of minor crotchets in which the philosopher indulged, perhaps no more than a journalist and reformer of society ought (several of them he did not fully adopt—only favoring them enough to enable his opponents in the press to stigmatize him with them), but still much more than is advisable in a candidate for the chief magistracy of a State in which political parties are balanced as evenly as the most delicately poised scale. On this account, Mr. Thurlow Weed, the most adroit and influential of Mr. Seward's friends, waited upon Mr. Greeley and urged him to abandon the idea of running for Governor. He was successful in this, but Greeley added, "Suppose you try my name for Lieutenant Governor, and see whether I am so odious."

When the convention assembled at Albany, it was found advisable to give the second place upon the Gubernatorial ticket to some gentleman whose action, in an emergency, could be depended upon more implicitly than that of Greeley could be. For instance, Greeley had given notice, in the *Tribune*, that he should support "Maine Law" candidates for the legislature, no matter what their political principles or their general character. This course might easily throw the majority of one branch of the legislature into the hands of the Democrats, (or "Locos," as Greeley then called them) and defeat Seward, the tower of strength of the Liberal Whigs and (as all old citizens remember) the champion of the anti-slavery element of politics. The result was that Myron H. Clark, a poor stick, but a man who happened to be in favor with all wings of the party, was nominated for Governor, and Henry J. Raymond, a journalistic rival of Greeley, was put in nomination for Lieutenant Governor.

The ticket won; but the manner of making it up had proved the last feather that broke the back of Greeley's patience, long groaning, it seems, under real or fancied wrongs. These wrongs consisted in the neglect of Seward to provide Greeley with a fat office at several opportunities which had occurred. These opportunities Greeley mentioned in his letter, referred often to his "extreme poverty," rebuked Seward with having been hard upon him in a judicial decision upon a libel case (!) and announced "the dissolution of the political firm of Seward, Weed and Greeley, by the withdrawal of the junior partner." Here is one paragraph out of his letter:

"Now (1841) came the great scramble of the swell mob of coon minstrels and cider-suckers at Washington—I not being counted in. Several regiments of them went on from this city; but no one of the whole crowd, though I say it who should not, had done so much toward General Harrison's nomination and election as *yours respectfully*. I asked nothing—expected nothing; but you, Governor Seward, ought to have asked that I be postmaster of New York. Your asking would have been in vain; but it would have been an act of grace neither wasted nor undeserved."

The reader should peruse this extract once more, or, indeed, read here the whole letter, which is found to be a complaint, not because Seward did not testify his gratitude to Greeley for what few personal favors he had received from him (this he admits the Governor did do, in many professional favors and other "acts of kindness"); but the complaint is that Seward *did not give him office.* Seward, a man of good breeding and of conscientious devotion to the people's interest, sought to reward Greeley for his labors by favors which came from his own pocket or his own labor—which really testified by their cost to the bestower, his good will toward the recipient. Greeley, on the contrary, wanted Seward to reward him in the people's coin—to bestow on him an office which cost the giver nothing, but which would make the receiver a pensioner on the public. Seward judged Greeley, as many verdant people have since judged him, by his protestations in the *Tribune*, and thought he was above any susceptibility to the allurements of a fat office. He mistook his man, and incurred the vindictive opposition of one who was able, six years after, to retaliate at Chicago for his imaginary grievances.

GREELEY AT CHICAGO.

Greeley went to the Chicago convention of 1860 with the grand purpose of defeating Seward, then by far the most prominent candidate of the Republicans for Presidential nominee. The South had already threatened secession in the event of the nation's refusal to extend slavery *ad infinitum*, and the issue had to be met boldly. To meet it thus, Seward was the man upon whom the Republicans of every section felt they could best depend. But Greeley, having obtained a seat as a delegate from Oregon (though he was far more influential in the lobbies as a delegate from the *Tribune*, and a supposed friend of Seward, since his letter of 1854 had not then been published, and he was continually asseverating to those whom he buttonholed his personal devotion to Seward,) went to work vigorously for Edward Bates, of Missouri—a man whom Greeley's present Chicago organ calls "one of the fossils of the slave party," a labor in which he was associated, as he now is, with those Machiavillis of politics, the Blair family. The result was the defeat of Seward, and the gratification of a grudge which the "magnanimous," universal-amnesty-ranting philosopher had cherished within his bosom for six long years. He could forgive in a day the traitors who had struck at the heart of the nation, and who, thanks to on-to-Richmond and other like efforts of his own, had brought woe into a million loyal households; but he could not in a life-time forgive a man who had failed to name him as Postmaster of New York! Behold, young man, ambitious to win a name as a patriotic statesman, how fine a thing it is to be magnanimous on paper, in withholding the justice which belongs to a higher authority, and at the same time wreak all your own private revenges in the stolen name of that same authority!

HE FAVORS SECESSION.

In securing by such means the nomination of Lincoln, Mr. Greeley builded better than he knew. It is one of those cases in which the Lord hath made the wrath of man to praise him. The Southern States seceded, encouraged thereto, as their statesmen claim, by the utterances of Greeley's *Tribune*, and their belief, founded thereon, that there was a large party of political free-thinkers at the North who sympathized with Greeley in the views expressed in the following extracts:

[From the New York Tribune, of November 9, 1859.]

"If the cotton States shall become satisfied that they can do better out of the Union than in it, we insist in letting them go in peace. The right to secede may be a revolutionary one, but it exists nevertheless. * * * We must ever resist the right of any State to remain in the Union and nulify and defy the laws thereof.

"To withdraw from the Union is quite another matter; and whenever a considerable section of our Union shall deliberately resolve to go out, we shall resist all coercive measures to keep them in it. We hope never to live in a Republic where one section is pinned to another by bayonets."

[From the New York Tribune, of November 26, 1859.]

"If the cotton States unitedly and earnestly wish to withdraw peacefully from the Union, we think they should be allowed to do so. Any attempt to compel them by force to remain would be contrary to the principles enunciated in the immortal Declaration of Independence—contrary to the fundamental ideas on which human liberty is based."

GREELEY AS A MILITARY COMMANDER.

Next in chronological order, of Mr. Greeley's disastrous attempts to run the United States government, was his "On-to-Richmond" fiasco of July, 1861. The circumstances of that heart-sickening affair are too well known to the public to need repitition here. He had been thorning the Government for weeks to order an advance upon the Rebel capital. Of course he knew nothing about the military situation or about military maxims or military possibilities; but he had a crotchet in his head, he had the ear of the public, and he could not refrain from acting upon his impulse to dictate upon all questions which engaged his interest. Accordingly, he kept urging, in labored editorials, a speedy advance upon Richmond, before the Union army had been drilled or fairly organized. In addition to these leaders, he kept up the following cry from day to day—the paragraph being reiterated, word for word, in successive issues of the *Tribune*, set in italics and capitals:

"THE NATION'S WAR CRY.

"*Forward to Richmond! Forward to Richmond! The Rebel Congress must not be allowed to meet there on the 20th July!* BY THAT DATE THE PLACE MUST BE HELD BY THE NATIONAL ARMY!"

On the 16th of July, mainly in obedience to this

clamor, the Union army was set in motion. The terribly disastrous result is well known. How many thousand lives, how many millions of treasure it cost us, no one can tell; but all admit that the war was greatly prolonged and made greatly more burdensome by the disastrous defeat of Bull Run. Most military men are of opinion that if a battle could have been won in Virginia that fall, instead of the utter rout which did occur, the war would have been closed without calling out one-quarter of the troops that were used, and with one-tenth of the loss of life that did occur.

On the morning of the 17th of July, 1861, the *Tribune*, elated with the idea that *its* military policy had been enforced upon the Government, assured the country that victory was certain, and the Confederacy about to gasp its last. "This day," it said, "is to have important results. * * * Where the victory will rest, there can be no doubt." In a few days more the editor of the *Tribune*, cringing under the public indignation which his "Forward to Richmond" cry and its lamentable result had worked, was seeking, in a personal card, to fasten the blame upon his subordinates. "Still," he said, "I wish to be distinctly understood as not seeking to be released from any responsibility for urging the advance of the Union army into Virginia." And the public, after hearing his defence, with its whining plaint that if some one must die to appease the popular rage, it might as well be himself as anybody, concluded not to release him. They have, perhaps with too impetuous justice, held him responsible for that disaster to this day; and their natural arrangement, when it comes to voting upon Mr. Greeley's application for the Presidency, will be this: those who rejoiced at the result of Bull Run will vote for Greeley; those who lamented that result will vote against him.

Views like those cited from the *Tribune* on page 468 were reiterated by Greeley at intervals during the war, and served, like his efforts in behalf of a dishonorable peace, to stimulate in the breasts of the Rebels, a belief that the Northerners were weakening in their determination to enforce the Union. "The pro-slavery Democrats we have on our side anyway," they argued with themselves; "if we have also the Radical abolitionists represented by the *Tribune*, we can certainly hold out and whip them yet." And so more blood, more blood, more blood was poured out.

DICTATING TO LINCOLN.

In the summer of 1862, Greeley led in a grand attack upon Lincoln, because he had not yet got ready to launch his policy of Emancipation.* He was more anxious than they to destroy slavery; but he knew when the military situation would enable him to enforce such a policy—they didn't. In

* A correspondence which took place between Lincoln and Greeley concerning the emancipation of the negroes may be found in Raymond's Life and Letters of Abraham Lincoln, and in McPherson's History of the Rebellion; but Greeley in his American Conflict, and in his (Parton's) biography, garbles his own letter fearfully, since certain passages of it read badly in the light of subsequent events.

good time the proclamation came. Then Greeley refrained from his turbulent criticism for awhile, especially as 1863 was a year of overwhelming Republican victories, showing that the people held the Administration in high esteem.

The spring and summer of 1864 appear to have been a very uncomfortable period in Mr. Greeley's political career. A Presidential campaign was coming on; Greeley was, as usual, fretting and fuming for a change; and at the same time the people were so determined to fight it out under the leader whom they then had, that they would tolerate scarcely a word in opposition to "Old Abe." Nevertheless, Mr. Greeley found courage to slip into the *Tribune* sly inuendos against the administration of Lincoln, and to cherish tenderly the movement for an independent nominiation at Cleveland. He secretly favored that operation of his present partner, Gratz Brown, his fellow Communist Cluseret and other hot-heads and sore-heads of the period, and when the Convention came off he published their bombastic Address in large type in the *Tribune*, with some kind words in its behalf. A meeting was held at Cooper Institute, New York, on the 13th of May, against Greeley's solemn advice, and addressed by Governor Oglesby and Hon. I. N. Arnold, of Illinois, Senator Doolittle and others, whose speeches favored the nomination of Lincoln. Its proceedings were totally ignored—the *Tribune*, notwithstanding that journal had room on the same day for an elaborate report of a "dress reform" convention, on the morning when it should have reported this meeting.

ANYBODY TO BEAT LINCOLN.

After it was found that the Cleveland convention was a flat failure, the anti-Lincoln factionists, looking to Greeley as their most valued sympathizer, cast about for a candidate more available than Fremont, and fixed upon Grant, then in the Wilderness, as their man. (" The man on horseback" was not so objectionable an idea to Greeley then as it seems to be now.) They appointed a meeting, to be held in New York a few days before the Republican convention was to be held at Baltimore, and intended to develop such a feeling of enthusiasm for Grant as could be used upon the national assembly of Republicans—Greeley had not then invented his great device of calling them " Renominationists" to force the nomination of Grant, instead of Lincoln. This meeting was held, and its callers had the temerity to invite Lincoln himself to attend. That noble statesman wrote a generous letter closing in a manner, which shows that he apprehended the object of the meeting. It was to this effect: " I trust that your meeting will be a success in developing an expression of the gratitude which is due so brave and skillful a commander; and that you will so shape your good words that they will turn to men and guns marching to his (Grant's) aid in the field."

The result of the meeting was not satisfactory to

the malcontents. A great many speeches eulogistic of Grant were made, but they were equally strong in behalf of sustaining the existing policy of the national government that they could not be used at Baltimore, especially as Grant himself had caused it to be understood that he would, on no account, be used for any such purpose as the engineers of this meeting contemplated.

The "Renominationists" met at Baltimore and endorsed Lincoln, in effect, unanimously. The people proved to be Renominationists too, and Lincoln was chosen by the largest popular and electoral majorities ever recorded. But Greeley did not allow this glorious result to be brought about without resorting to every device in his power to prevent it. On the morning after the nominations had been announced, Greeley had remarked in his paper:

"We cannot but feel that it would have been wiser and safer to spike the most serviceable guns of our adversaries by nominating another for President and thus dispelling all motives save that of naked disloyalty, for further warfare upon this Administration. We believe the Rebellion would have lost something of the cohesion and venom from the hour in which it was known that a new President would surely be inaugurated on the 4th of March next, etc."

He continued to intrigue against the Republican nominations during the summer. First, it was proposed, with infinite braggadocia, to have both Lincoln and Fremont withdrawn (and Fremont, glad to get out of the scrape with any show of grace, soon did so); then, on the 2d of September, finding Lincoln still in the field, in spite of the probs of the *Tribune* quill and the disgraceful and damaging operations at Niagara Falls (to be mentioned below), Greeley addressed the following letter to the Governors of the loyal States (a call for 500,000 troops being then but partially answered):

NEW YORK, Sept. 2, 1864.

Hon. ——:

YOUR EXCELLENCY: The undersigned have been requested by a body of influential Unionists to communicate with the loyal Governors for the purpose of eliciting replies to the following queries:

1. In your judgment, is the re-election of Mr. Lincoln a probability?

2. In your judgment, can your own State be carried for Mr. Lincoln?

3. In your judgment, do the interests of the Union party, and so of the country, require the substitution of another candidate in place of Mr. Lincoln?

In these queries, we give no opinion of our own, and request yours only for the most private and confidential use.

Yours truly,

HORACE GREELEY,

Editor of the *Tribune*, (and two others.)

This device failed entirely, except as it may have served to retard the recruiting of troops in some of the States. If the answers to this letter had afforded any encouragement to their purpose, there is no telling what new *coup d' etat* this "influential body of Unionists" might have sprung upon the country.

GREELEY'S NIAGARA FALLS EXPLOIT.

It was during the summer of 1864, about a month after Lincoln had been renominated, that Greeley—pretending to be friendly to the President—attempted to draw him into a proposition to the Rebel Government for peace. We will give the history of this operation of Greeley's in the language of another, who has epitomized it in a manner suitable to our purpose:

So late as the 23d day of February, 1864, he reiterated in the New York *Tribune*, in this language, his views concerning the right of the South to secede:

"We have repeatedly said, and we once more insist, that the great principle embodied by Jefferson in the Declaration of Independence, that governments derive their just powers from the consent of the governed, is sound and just, and that if the slave States, the cotton States, or the Gulf States only, choose to form an independent nation, they have a clear, moral right to do so. * * * Whenever it shall be clear that the great body of the Southern people have become conclusively alienated from the Union, and anxious to escape from it, we will do our best to forward their views."

Recognized by the South as a leading Republican, it is not strange that Mr. Greeley should be regarded by them as the most fitting person to whom to address peace propositions. His views differed in no essential particular from theirs. Every failure of the Union armies was continually magnified by him. His views of the situation were most gloomy and despondent, and he took good care that through the columns of his paper they should be widely circulated. Early in July, 1864, correspondence was opened with Mr. Greeley by an irresponsible and half crazy adventurer known as "Colorado Jewett." On the 5th of July, Jewett writes Greeley, in reply to a note previously received from him, in which he says: "I am authorized to state to you, for our use only, not the public, that two embassadors of Davis & Co. are now in Canada, with full and complete powers for a peace, and Mr. Sanders requests that you come on immediately to me at Cataract House, to have a private interview, or if you will send the President's protection for him and two friends they will come on and meet you."

On the next day Jewett telegraphed Greeley as follows:

"Will you come here? Parties have full power."

On the 7th of July Greeley inclosed Jewett's letter and telegram to the President, accompanied by a letter of his own, in which occurs this remarkable passage:

"*And, therefore, I venture to remind you that our bleeding, bankrupt, almost dying country, also longs for peace, shudders at the prospect of fresh conscription, of further wholesale devastation, and of new river of human blood; and a widespread conviction that the government and its prominent supporters are not anxious for peace, and do not improve proffered opportunities to achieve it, is doing great harm now, and is morally certain, unless removed, to do far greater in the approaching elections.*"

[In this letter were also embodied the terms on which Greeley proposed to effect a peace. Among these conditions were the payment of $400,000,000 to the Slave States, rebel and loyal alike, for the

TRIBUNE
What I say is true
What others say is
A LIE
"whoever say's you ain't honest
is a liar & a slanderer"
REPUBLIC
1000 MILES TO WASH

value of slaves emancipated, and the concession to them of the right to be represented in Congress according to their "total, instead of their federal population." The bonds for the $400,000,000 were to be paid over to each State " upon the ratification by *its* legislature of this adjustment!"]

"To this letter Mr. Lincoln at once, on the 9th of July, replied, saying to Greeley: " If you can find any person, anywhere, professing to have any proposition of Jefferson Davis, in writing, for peace, embracing the restoration of the Union and abandonment of slavery, whatever else it embraces, say to him he may come to me with you, and that if he really brings such proposition, he shall at the least have safe conduct with the paper (and without publicity if he chooses) to the point where you shall have met him. The same if there be two or more persons."

"On the 10th of July, Greeley wrote the President suggesting that the rebel envoys would decline to exhibit their credentials to him, and on the 13th advised the President that he then had information on which he could rely, that Clay and Thompson were then in Canada, *duly commissioned and empowered to negotiate for peace.*

"Hearing nothing further from Greeley, Mr. Lincoln, on the 15th, wrote him that he had sent Mr. Hay, his private Secretary, to him, and said to him: 'I am disappointed that you have not already reached here with those commissioners. If they would consent to come on being shown my letter to you of the 19th inst., show that and this to them, and if they will come on the terms stated in the former, bring them. I not only intend a sincere effort for peace, but I intend that you shall be a personal witness that it is made.'

"Mr. Hay reached New York on the morning of the 16th, met Greeley, who promised to start on his mission immediately if he could have an absolute safe conduct for four persons to be named by him, whereupon, under the direction of the President, Hay wrote for the safe conduct, and Greeley started for Niagara Falls. Arriving there on the 17th, he addressed a note to the supposed rebel commissioners, in which he stated that he had been informed that they are duly accredited from Richmond as the bearers of propositions looking to the establishment of peace, and that they desired to visit Washington in fulfillment. He then adds: 'If my information be thus far substantially correct, I am authorized by the President of the United States to tender you his safe conduct on the journey proposed, and to accompany you at the earliest time that will be agreeable to you.'

"THE NEGOTIATIONS FAIL.

"And here occurred the first hitch in these extraordinary negotiations.

The only assurance that Greeley ever had that these gentlemen were duly accredited from Richmond, or possessed any authority whatever to negotiate for peace, he derived through Colorado Jewett. In answer to this letter these rebel gentlemen informed Mr. Greeley that they had not been accredited from Richmond, but they thought that they might be. The substance of this letter Greeley telegraphed to the President, who sent by the hand of Major Hay this celebrated paper:

"To whom it may concern:—Any proposition which embraces the restoration of peace, the integrity of the whole Union and the abandoment of slavery, and which comes by and with an authority that can control the armies now at war against the United States, will be received and considered by the executive government of the United States, and will be met by liberal terms on substantial and collateral points, and the bearer or bearers thereof shall have safe conduct both ways."

On the 20th of July, accompanied by Greeley, Maj. Hay delivered this document to Prof. Holcombe, one of the supposed rebel commissioners. No reply was vouchsafed to Mr. Hay; Greeley at once returned to New York, and a most elaborate reply was sent to him through the irrepressible Jewett.

In this reply, with great force of statement, the President was charged with a sudden and entire change of views; the rebel envoys insisted that having been assured at the outset that the safe conduct for which they applied would be granted without conditions, very properly complained that the paper handed them was a clear violation of any such assurance, and adjured their Southern brethren to fight to the death, rather than submit to such insults.

AND GREELEY PREVARICATES.

The paper addressed "To whom it may concern," and the reply to it were at once published, together with the statement that Greeley "regrets the sad termination of the initiatory steps taken for peace in consequence of the change made by the President in his instructions to convey commissioners to Washington for negotiations unconditionally." The administration was thus placed clearly in the wrong, and incalculable mischief was worked both North and South.

The other portions of the correspondence which I have read to you were not then published, and the country knew nothing of its existence. The attitude in which Mr. Lincoln was thus placed was that of an Executive in the interests of peace, offering unconditionally safe conduct to the rebel commissioners, and then suddenly withdrawing his officer and substituting unheard of and unanticipated conditions. This impression was false—utterly and altogether false. Horace Greeley knew that it was false. He knew that the prevalence of any such false impression must result in serious injury to the Union cause. He knew that the terms proposed by Mr. Lincoln were those which he had himself proposed at the very outset of the correspondence. He knew that the first letter addressed to him by the President, placed any peace negotiations upon the basis of restoration of the Union and the abandonment of slavery. He knew that the President had requested him to exhibit that letter to any one holding the position of Confederate commissioner, and that any negotiations were based upon the readiness of the rebels to treat on those terms. He knew that a word from him would relieve the President of the serious charges made against him, would strengthen his administration and the Union cause, and, yet he failed to speak that word. Nay, more. He not only suppressed the truth, but he stated in the interests of self-constituted rebel negotiators, and against the Union, an unequivocal falsehood, wilfully, wickedly and deliberately.

He stated that the negotiations had terminated in consequence of the change made by the President in his instructions, when he knew that there had been no change whatever, and that those negotiations had disgracefully failed merely because he had failed to communicate to his rebel friends precisely what the President desired at the outset they should know, to wit, the terms upon which propositions for peace would be considered. He misrepresented the facts to the President when he assured him that he had reliable information that the rebel commissioners were duly authorized to treat for peace. He had no such information, and such was not the fact. He deceived and misled his rebel friends when he told them that he was authorized by the President to tender them safe conduct to Washington to negotiate for peace. He had no such authority, except that they were willing to negotiate on the basis of a restored Union and the abolition of slavery. Thus he deceived and misled both sides, and to cap the climax refused to permit Mr. Lincoln to place himself right before the country. The President requested that the whole correspondence be published, except those portions of Mr. Greeley's letter where he spoke of our bleeding, bankrupt and almost dying country, the publication of which, at that time, Mr. Lincoln urged would do injury to the cause, and was not necessary to understand the correspondence, but this concession Horace Greeley obstinately refused to make. Abraham Lincoln, rather than add one particle to the burdens which were then weighing down the public heart, preferred to suffer himself—preferred that the country should misjudge him, and the correspondence was not published until after the close of the war, when Horace Greeley's white-livered complaints could work no harm.

The passages which Mr. Lincoln wished expunged from the correspondence on publishing it were, the ones quoted above (in italics) from Greeley's letter of July 7th; another in the same letter, saying, "it may save us from a Northern insurrection;" and one or two others, wherein a coming election in

North Carolina is hinted at as the objective point of the negotiations. It will be perceived that there was nothing in Lincoln's requirements which was really prejudicial to Greeley, and the only conclusion is that the latter stood out for unworthy reasons, making the really patriotic conditions imposed by Lincoln merely a pretext for not consenting to the publication. No patriot can read without emotion the *fac simile* autograph copy of the private letter which Lincoln wrote to his friend, Henry J. Raymond, at this time, and which is published in the "Life of Lincoln" by that gentleman already referred to. It is as follows:

EXECUTIVE MANSION, WASHINGTON, Aug. 15, 1869.

HON. HENRY J. RAYMOND:

My Dear Sir:—I have proposed to Mr. Greeley that the Niagara correspondence be published, suppressing only the parts of his letters over which the red pencil is drawn in the copy which I herewith send. He declines giving his consent to the publication of his letters unless these parts be published with the rest. I have concluded that it is better for *me* to submit for the time to the consequences of the false position in which he has placed me, than to subject the *country* to the consequences of publishing these discouraging and injurious parts. I send you this, and the accompanying copy, not for publication, but merely to explain to you, and that you may preserve them until their proper time shall come.

Yours truly, A. LINCOLN.

A HOME THRUST FROM GRANT.

So much for the disgraceful peace negotiations. We will only add, as supplementary to this statement and to that of Greeley's letter to the loyal Governors, a dispatch from Grant, of nearly even date with the latter document:

CITY POINT, September 13, 1864,
10:30, A. M.

Hon. Edwin M. Stanton, Secretary of War:

We ought to have the whole number of men called for by the President in the shortest possible time. Prompt action in filling our armies will have more effect upon the enemy than a victory over them. They profess to believe, and make their men believe, there is such a party North in favor of recognizing Southern independence, that the draft cannot be enforced. [The *Tribune's* homily of February 23d, 1864, and other similar utterances from the same source, had been extensively republished in the South.—E. C.] Let them be undeceived. Deserters come into our lines daily, who tell us that the men are nearly universally tired of the war, and that desertions would be much more frequent, but that they believe peace will be negotiated after the fall election.

The enforcement of the draft and prompt filling up of our armies will save the shedding of blood to an immense degree.

U. S. GRANT, Lieutenant-General.

THE BAILING OF JEFF. DAVIS.

The next spring peace was obtained, thanks to Grant, not Greeley, *without buying it.* Then Jeff. Davis was captured, and, his trial being delayed, Greeley rushed down to Richmond to sign the bail bond which exempted Davis from any further punishment for the greatest of possible crimes. This was not even necessary to save Davis from suffering, as there were many Southern gentlemen of means anxious to go upon the bond. It was merely a little piece of sensational sentimentality, which gratified Greeley; which might have done some good if the signer's record had been more unequivocally loyal during the war; and which certainly did no harm except to the feelings of a great proportion of the loyal people of the North, especially the soldiers, and those whose sensibilities, lacerated by the loss of dear relatives, had not yet been soothed and deadened by time. Greeley was greatly feted by the "chivalay" of Richmond, and made them a gushing speech twelve yards long; but he came back North to find most of the loyal press of the country denouncing in unmeasured terms his impetuous course. It was this general denunciation which drew from Greeley that phrase characterizing the editors of the country as "the little creatures whom God, for some inscrutable purpose, permits to edit a majority of our minor journals"—a phrase which we quote from a letter addressed by Greeley to the Union League Club of New York, and published in the *Tribune* about May 25th, 1867.

During the campaign of 1868, the *Tribune* favored Grant, and the many eloquent words which it then uttered in praise of the honored soldier are now doubly true, while the equally many which it then recorded against the Democratic party are at least equally true.

GREELEY ON GREELEY.

In the fall of 1868, Mr. Greeley attended a banquet at Montreal. There he made a speech, of which the following is an extract, concerning the baneful effects upon public men of that political disease called Presidency-mania—an ailment to which he has himself finally succumbed:

"Mr. Webster was not only a gentleman, but he had the elements of moral greatness; and he had faults as well. He failed only in one respect, and in this respect I differ from him; he wanted to be President, and I don't [But you did.] But for that one misfortune he would have been the greatest man America ever produced. We have seen our greatest man, Mr. Chase, making the same blunder. I have seen men who had the disease early and died of it at a very old age. Gen. Lewis Cass died at about 82, and up to the day of his death he wanted to be President. *No one ever escapes who once catches the disease;* he lives and dies in the delusion. Being a reader and an observer at an early age, I saw how it *poisoned and paralyzed the very best of our public men*, and I have carefully avoided it. It is easy then to speak for truth and justice, when they need an advocate, when those who threatened could execute no vengeance that you dreaded. So, then, I think you are happy in that respect, if no other, for none of you in Canada expect to become sovereign of your country. That enables you to have a purer press and more fearless public men than perhaps you would otherwise have. We at least, in our day, *have a President elect who did not try to be President. He was elected mainly on that account.* Let a public man honestly go forward, saying what he believes to be just, doing what he thinks is right, and, though he may not probably be President, he can enjoy a very large measure of freedom of opinion, as well as freedom of action, though freedom of opinion is the very last thing that a free people is disposed to concede to its public men."

So poor Mr. Greeley thought, doubtless, at Cincinnati, where he sold or "relegated" his whole birthright for a mess of Democratic pottage.

GREELEY AND "BAYONET LEGISLATION."

The Cincinnati platform condemns in the severest language (and Mr. Greeley endorses it in his letter of acceptance) the so-called Ku-Klux legislation of Congress. But on the 21st of April, 1871, the *Tribune*, in publishing the Ku-Klux bill then just passed, said editorially:

"It is a great point gained that there has been legislation of any character upon this question. The lawlessness at the South has been greatly fostered by the heretofore seeming indifference of Congress and the North to the outrages committed upon loyal citizens. Legislation, however imperfect, was calculated to restore the confidence of the friends of the Union and to warn its enemies. The bill, now become a law, should be enforced with such power and firmness as to intimidate those who seek to regain political power by outrage and crime, and to protect fully all friends of order and peace, irrespectively of party or of political considerations. The Democrats in

Congress have fought the Ku-Klux bill as party measure directed against their adherents in the South. The Republican administration will enforce it as a measure of peace to the country and security to all its citizens."

The only objection that Mr. Greeley even intimated at the time consists in the fact that the law, in his view, was not sufficiently stringent. He would have had a still stronger law. He found no fault with the section which authorizes the President to suspend the privilege of the writ of *habeas corpus*, when the necessity existed therefor. Previously to the enactment of the law he had filled the columnes of the *Tribune* from day to day with the evidences of outrages and murders committed by the Ku-Klux Klans, showing the extent of these nefarious organizations, and proving the absolute necessity of interference by the General Government for their suppression.

To show that the language of the *Tribune*, cited above, embodied Mr. Greeley's own sentiments, we quote from his speech before the Lincoln club on the 12th of June, 1871:

"But I have been asked, 'Are there any Ku-Klux down South?' 'Yes, gentlemen, there are. They didn't come up to me, and tell me they were Ku-Klux very often. * * * I hold it to be the duty of the Government of the Union to oppose, with all its power and all its force, every such execrable proceeding as this. Do you tell me that those men are liable to the State laws for the assaults and batteries which they have committed. I don't doubt it; but I say they are also in substance and purpose traitors to the government, *rebels against its authority*, and the most cowardly, skulking rebels ever known to this or any other country. I hold our government bound by its duty of protecting our citizens in their fundamental rights, to pass and enforce laws for the extirpation of the execrable Ku-Klux conspiracy; and if it has not power to do it, I say our government is no government, but a sham. I therefore, on every proper occasion, advocated and justified the Ku-Klux act. I hold it especially desirable for the South; and if it does not prove strong enough to effect its purpose, *I hope it will be made stronger*."

And he showed how his present Southern friends had carried Louisiana in 1868 for Seymour, notwithstanding there was 30,000 Republican majority in the State, adding, "You know perfectly well that this result was secured only by terrorism and violence."

GREELEY AND TAMMANY.

In following Mr. Greeley through some of his wanderings after strange gods, and his dangerous lapses from the excellent rules and principles with which he commenced political life, we have only space left to point to his flirtations with Tammany, the most desperate of political prostitutes. The record of the *Tribune* on this subject is unquestionably bad. On many occasions of local elections it has been found veering about in strange ways, like a compass needle in the vicinity of a hidden lodestone. It would favor all manner of queer coalitions with the Democracy, and the nominees thus united upon would be found, when installed in office, to be suspiciously lenient toward the practices of Tammany. It would be continually embroiled with the management of the Republican party in its own State, and would rarely have any serious quarrel with the monster of corruption that was eating up the store of New York city tax-payers. Pretending to be a tribune of the people, an independent and fearless journal, ready to lash evil-doers wherever it found them, and to carry out the high-sounding precept of its editor to young Americans—"Be no man's man but Truth's and your country's"—(borrowed from Shakspeare's Wolsey, but still none the less a fine precept,) it sat in its easy chair, never budging, except to thwack the Custom House officials once a day pretty regularly—sat until the rascals in Tammany

Hall and the City Hall had *stolen* $60,000,000 out of the treasury of the city and county of New York—stolen dollars where a cent was wasted at the Custom House.

When, finally, the other New York journals, led by the *Times*, commenced the scathing exposition and denunciation of the Tammany frauds, which led to the expulsion of Tweed and his ring from the offices which they had abused, and which, besides causing many of them to disgorge their spoils, came near landing them in the penitentiary, the *Tribune* was all the while pulling back and exclaiming, "Let us be calm; let us not make any assertions until we can have incontestible proofs," etc. When the *Times* came out with transcripts from the Comptroller's books, which showed a fearful record of wholesale thieving, with *data* to indicate just where the money went, who audited the bills, and what the pretext was, Mr. Greeley still cried, "Hold!" "These accounts are surreptitiously obtained," said he; and he published Oakey Hall's quibbling answers, and treated the complaint as nothing more than a newspaper sensation. It was not until forced into it by the denunciations and threats of its patrons that the *Tribune* rallied and made a show of helping to expose Tammany. Meantime how more than cat-like was it in its vigilance toward the Custom House authorities! How quick to pounce upon the merest mouse that was suspected of gnawing at the revenues of Uncle Sam!

THE WHEREFORE.

Why this discrimination in favor of the greatest, most barefaced robbery ever perpetrated under political protection, and against an administration (meaning that of the New York custom house) more efficient than any of its predecessors had been? It is not enough to argue that the $50,000 a year which (according to the New York *Times*) the *Tribune* derived from Tammany printing jobs served to control its course in this manner. Those who know Mr. Greeley know he cannot be bought with money. They also know that he *can* be wheedled into almost any project by a due application of flattery, protestation and cajolery, and that he is especially susceptible to the blandishments of those who promise him high office.

Greeley saw the debt of New York city increased, in the face of enormous taxes, $66,500,000 in thirty-one months, and never so much as growled. He saw the debt of the United States diminished by $242,128,401 in twenty-nine contemporaneous months, and yet rent the air with his vociferous complaints.

This achievement was the work of General Grant's administration, and Greeley "knew a man" whom he preferred to see in Grant's place. *That* achievement was the work of Tammany's administration, and Greeley knew a man who would soon need Tammany's votes. *Verbum sat.*

CHAPTER XXIV.

GREELEY AS A BOOK FARMER.

A Chapter Consisting of what Mr. Greeley Knows About Farming, and which, therefore, has Nothing In It.

We had intended to go somewhat into detail in describing Mr. Greeley's method of farming and enunciating his peculiar theories concerning agriculture—all this mainly as a curiosity, and as an illustration of how easy it is for a born philosopher to construct half a dozen theories without possessing one fact; but our space is too far overrun for this, and the chapter will therefore have to be very brief.

Mr. Greeley has a farm at Chappaqua station, town of Newcastle, Westchester county, New York, some 35 miles from the city. This farm, mostly marsh and unpromising upland, cost him $140 an acre; and he has been at work on it twenty years trying to make a model farm of it. Its total area, as increased by late purchases, is seventy acres; and of this, fifty acres is a hill-top. He visits it every Saturday, and gives the man who carries it on for him a good top-dressing of profanity and a rich mulching of theory; and the man has, by diligently avoiding the latter and benignantly forgiving the former, been able to keep himself and wife alive on the product of the seventy acres.

As everybody knows, Greeley has been a very voluminous writer upon agriculture. His book, called "What I Know About Farming," has obtained a large circulation by being given away as a premium for subscribers, when the portrait of the Sage of Lackawaxen himself had no further charm for rural readers. It is beyond cavil, one of the most entertaining books in the language It fills a place in American literature somewhat akin to that occupied in English by a'Beckett's "Comic History of England." In it the reader is afforded the luxury of seeing a great mind turn itself inside out, and evolve things from the focal point of what it does not contain. It is a complete refutation of the ancient maxim, *ex nihilo, nihil fit.* This may have been true in ancient Roman times, but no man who sees Horace Greeley evolve a bookful of agricultural aphorisms out of his own internal consciousness, will longer believe that "out of nothing, nothing can be made." This circumstance affords further evidence of Greeley's leading principle that the world is all awry, and has got to be reconstructed altogether, from keel to topmast.

Horace tells us that during the fifteen years of apprenticeship which he served on his father's farm, he "learned no more about farming than a plow-horse ought to know"; but he thinks if he could have had such a book as "What I Know About Farming," to read, he would have become so fascinated with his calling that he would have continued a good agriculturist to this day; and he closes his book, at the 52nd chapter, "with the joyful hope that its perusal will inspire in the mind of the young agriculturist a desire for something better"—a hope that is doubtless realized. At least the *old* farmers, who are not to be caught with book chaff, have usually signified, after reading Horace's essays, that they "desire something better," or nothing at all.

Mr. Greeley's great hobby as an agriculturist, is *deep plowing*. He will not stop a barley-corn short of thirty inches; and the brindle steers that perish in the attempt to haul subsoil plows through the stony hard-pan at this depth are of no more account to him than the thousand soidiers who got their death at Bull Run. He has also strong ideas upon the subject of irrigation, and actually delivered a lecture in the Wabash Valley of Indiana—a district almost constantly flooded from the river, and malarious from alluvial deposits, recommending elaborate apparatus for this purpose!

Being compelled to summarize Mr. Greeley's agricultural platform very briefly, we will adopt his own style of re-laying the planks of the Cincinnati platform, and throw it into a letter to the illustrious author—thus:

ANYWHERE, July 4, 1872.

HON. HORACE GREELEY:

Sir:—I have received your work entitled "What I know of Farming," which contains your gospel of agriculture. Being a young farmer without experience—one of those young men whom you have so impetuously advised to "take $250 and go West"—your book will, I anticipate, prove of inestimable value to me in supplying those precepts of which a lamentable defect in my early training places me so greatly in need. Your precepts aforesaid, as I understand them from a careful reading, may be fairly epitomized as follows:

CONCERNING PLOWING.—That thirty inches is the requisit depth, no matter whether we are raising strawberries or oaks. That the man who plows shallower than this is an idiot or a knave, and that State's prison is too good for him. That we really can't have any successful farming until somebody invents a steam plowman who whistles as he goes, and pulverizes crosswise and otherwise, ten to twenty acres per day. I am reserving all my plowing till that happy day.

CONCERNING WHERE TO FARM.—That if I "cannot coax it (my farm) to grow decent crops of anything," I must "run away from it or work out by the day" for my "more fortunate neighbor," and that you and I are in favor of "a law compelling him" (the more fortunate neighbor) to employ me whenever I demand employment. That I must n't go West with a family on my hands, nor must I buy a farm on credit; but that I must take $2,000 and buy up somebody's improvements and farm it in peace and comfort. (By the way, Mr. Greeley, must n't we have a law compelling somebody to give me that $2,000? Some "more fortunate neighbor," for instance?)

CONCERNING TREES.—That "for every tree cut down, two should be planted." This rule is invariable. That you are in favor of chestnut, walnut, hickory, white oak, locust and white pine as the proper trees to be planted; that you don't know whether they will grow or not, but that they ought to, and should be compelled to do their duty. (*What I Know, etc.*, page 54.)

CONCERNING DRAINING.—That water will not, as you formerly supposed, run on level ground. (*Ibid p.* 65). That the way to make a good drain is to find out how you made yours at Chappaqua, and then proceed as unlike you as possible, (*Ibid p.* 66); and that to get a drain well laid, I should go to "Messrs. Chickering & Gall," New York, (*Ibid p.* 67); and that it wont pay to wall in a brook as you did, at the expense of $3,000, when the spring floods carry the walls away every year.

CONCERNING IRRIGATION.—That, next to deep plowing, this is the first law of nature; that *irrigating dams* like yours, which cost $90—"twice what it ought to have been,"—and which don't work then, are productive of *irritating damns*, even in Philosophers.

CONCERNING GUANO.—That it is a very reprehensible beverage for the soil to make use of—in fact, as you felicitously style it, "the brandy of vegetation;" and that being, moreover, the product of the pauper labor of pigeons in savage islands, it should not be allowed to come in competition with protected American gypsum.

CONCERNING APPLE TREES.—That no limb should extend more than eight feet from the trunk; that "for shedding wind barren trees are best;"

that caterpillars are incongenial to apples, and that "no man who harbors caterpillars has any moral right to apples." That apples are often lost through the too early blossoming of the trees, and the subsequent appearance of Jack Frost, and that the placing of ice under the roots of the trees will obviate this evil. (*Ibid p.* 141.)

CONCERNING POTATOES.—That the aspiration of the age is toward a Perfect Potato; and that "he who originates a really valuable new Potato deserves a recompense for his industry"—perhaps to have your next book dedicated to him, as the present is "to the future inventor of the steam plow," whereby "Not Less than Ten Acres per Day shall be Pulverized to a Depth of Two Feet, at a Cost of not more than Two Dollars per Acre." I find, also, to quote your valuable Work, that potatoes cannot be honestly raised without treating them to Swamp Muck.

CONCERNING BEETS AND CARROTS.—That these are proper vegetables, which deserve encouragement; that you yourself have never succeeded with Beets (no political insinuation) but that you "confidently expect to be able soon to raise 1,000 bushels of Carrots, and 1,500 bushels of Beets per acre." I will defer my experiments with those roots until you tell me how you did this.

CONCERNING ANIMALS.—That you have understood sheep to be valuable animals to the farmer; but that you know nothing about Animals, of your own positive knowledge, and therefore relegate that subject to the several Congressional districts; but that concerning Dogs, you have no hesitation in counting them as disreputable, and recommend strychnine for the whole species.

CONCERNING PASTURING.—That it is "a process I (you) detest;" that it is a radical, incurable vice, "(*Ibid p.* 19, 20,) etc.; and that a prohibitory law, making pasturing a penal offence, and authorizing the seizure and destruction of all pastures, would therefore, according to the Greeley philosophy, be a good thing. This is a subject which I feel should not be "relegated."

CONCERNING GRAIN RAISING.—That the prettiest way to raise Wheat is to take $72,000 and buy 400 acres of desert in New Jersey, put on $24,000 worth of Marl, $20,000 worth of Swamp Muck, $5,000 worth of Oyster Shell Lime, and $5,000 worth of Bone Flour, and sow Wheat upon the compost thus formed, (*Ibid p.* 767.) I am now looking for a man to loan me $72,000 on security of the probable crop. Several have refused. Will you please brand them in the *Tribane* as liars, cut-throats and villains?

Yours admiringly,

JONAS PEAPOD.

GREELEY'S BATTLE OF DORKING.

The vagaries of Mr. Greeley on the subject of

agriculture have been made the subject of many broad burlesques (which the foregoing, made up largely of actual extracts from Mr. Greeley's book, is by no means intended to be). They have also given rise to several clever hits in a more delicately satirical way, one of which, a parody on the English sketch, "Battle of Dorking," also hits off some of Mr. Greeley's other weaknesses and eccentricities. The story (which we reproduce below) is supposed to be told, fifty years hence by a father to his inquiring child:

THE FALL OF AMERICA.

You ask me to tell you, my children, of the events which immediately preceeded the destruction of the once great American Union and the capture of the country by its present European rulers, and to say something, also, of the cause which led to these deplorable results. I undertake the task with a heavy heart, for when I revert to that terrible time I cannot help contrasting our proud condition up to that fatal year with the humiliating position occupied now by the American people. The story is a short one. In the fall of 1872 Horace Greeley, the editor of a newspaper in New York, was elected President of the United States, The people voted for him because they thought he was an honest man. And so he was. But he was also vain and weak, and he entertained certain fanatical and preposterous notions—about agricultural matters, for instance—which he was determined to force upon the people at all hazards and despite all opposition. He believed, among other things, that every man ought to go west to earn his bread, and long before he was chosen President he used to advise everybody to move to that region, as a cure for all the disasters that could befall the human family.

As soon as he reached the executive mansion, which we used to call the White House, President Greeley organized an army of two hundred thousand men, and proceeded to force the entire population of the seaboard States westward at the point of the bayonet. The utmost violence was used. Those who resisted were shot down, and their dead bodies were carried off to a national factory which the President had established for making some kind of fantastical fertilizer. All the large cities of the East were depopulated, and the towns were entirely empty. The army swept before it millions of men, women and children, until the vast plains west of Kansas were reached, when the pursuit ceased and the army was drawn up in a continuous line, with orders to shoot any person who attempted to visit the East.

Of course hundreds of thousands of these poor creatures perished from starvation. This seemed to frighten President Greeley, and he sent a message to Congress recommending that seven hundred thousand volumes of a book of his entitled "What I Know about Farming," should be devoted for the relief of the starving sufferers. This was done, and farming implements and seeds were supplied ; and then the millions of wretched outcasts made an effort to till the ground. Of the result of this I will speak further on.

In the meantime the President was doing infinite harm to the country in another way. His handwriting was so fearfully and wonderfully bad that no living man could read it. And so when he sent his first annual message to Congress—the document was devoted wholly to the tariff and agriculture—a sentence appeared which subsequently was ascertained to be, "Large cultivation of rutabagas and beans is the only hope of the American nation, I am sure." The printers, not being able to interpret this, put it in the following form, in which it went to the world: "The Czar of Russsia could'nt keep clean if he washed himself with the whole Atlantic ocean once a day!" This perversion of the message was immediately telegraphed to Russia by the Russian Minister, and the Czar was so indignant that he immediately declared war.

"Just at this time President Greeley undertook to write some letters to Prince Bismark upon the subject of potato rot, and, after giving his singular views at great length, he concluded with the statement that if the Emperor William said that subsoil plowing was not good in light soil, or that guano was better than bone-dust, he was 'a liar, a villain and a slave!' Of course the Emperor immediately declared war, and became an ally of Russia and England, against which latter country Mr. Greeley had actually begun hostilities already, because the Queen, in her speech from the throne, had declared the *Tribune's* advocacy of a tariff on pig iron incendiary, and calculated to disturb the peace of nations.

"Unhappily, this was not the full measure of our disasters. The President had sent to the Emperor of Austria a copy of his book, 'What I Know," etc., with his autograph upon a fly-leaf. The Emperor mistook the signature for a carricature of the Austrian eagle, and he readily joined in a war against the United States ; while France was provoked to the same act by the fact that when the French minister came to call on Mr. Greeley, to present his credentials, the President, who was writing an editorial at the time, not comprehending the French language, mistook the Ambassador for a beggar, and without looking up handed him a quarter and an order for a clean shirt, and said to him, 'Go West, young man—go West.'

"So all these nations joined in making war upon the United States. They swooped down upon our coasts and landed without opposition, for those exposed portions of our unhappy country were absolutely deserted. The President was afraid to call away the army from Kansas at first, for fear the outraged people upon the plains would come East in spite of him. But at last he did summon the army to his aid, and it moved to meet the enemy. It was too late. Before the troops reached Cincinnati the foreigners had seized Washington and all the country east of the Ohio, and had hung the President, the Cabinet, and every member of Congress. The army disbanded in alarm, and the invaders removed to the far West, where they found the population dying of starvation because they had followed the advice of Greeley's book, to 'Try, for your first crop, to raise limes; and don't plant more than a bushel of quicklime in a hill?' Of course, these wretched people were at the mercy of the enemy, who—to his credit be it said—treated them kindly, fed them, and brought them back to their old homes.

"You know what followed—how Prince Frederick William of Prussia ascended the American throne, and the other humiliations that ensued. It was a fearful blow to Republicanism—a blow from which it will never recover. It made us, who were freemen, a nation of slaves. It was all the result of our blind confidence in a misguided old man, who thought himself a philosopher, but who was actually a fool. May heaven preserve you, my children, from the remorse I feel when I remember that I voted for that bucolic old editor."

CHAPTER XXV.

IS HE FIT?

Traits of Horace Greeley's Character—For what his Genius Fits him—For what it Does Not—How an Honest Man Can Do Dishonest Acts—Some Faults and How they Might be Cured—Can the Country Afford it?—How his One-Term Theory Kills His Own Chances—H. G., his Plea at the Jubilee—H. G. as an Administrator—Eleven Specific Points—Wm. C. Bryant's Portraiture of Greeley.

It is to be hoped that no reader has received an impression from the preceding chapters, or from any other source, that Horace Greeley is a man destitute of admirable personal qualities. He certainly has several such. In the first place, he is a man of genius—genius in a certain direction, to which his success as an agitator and reformer, and as a writer for the patriotic American public, bears sufficient testimony. His best trait—indeed the best trait which any man, public or private, can have, is honesty: or rather, we must say in this particular case, the intention to be honest; and this intention is always executed except where it is overborne by his strong and impetuous prejudices, or by his inordinate personal vanity, or by some other motive, in itself not dishonorable, but which warps the man's conscience, unconsciously to himself.

This paradox often occurs in men of irregular

education, of uncontrolled impulse, and of a predisposition to theorizing and to making all events and actions square themselves by their theories. we have already seen this illustrated in the case of Charles Sumner, asserting what was not true with regard to Stanton, and denying what was true with regard to himself. It rarely appears in Mr. Greeley's history, except in connection with public affairs—as in the case of the Niagara peace negotiations, wherein he not only misrepresented Lincoln, and caused him to be misrepresented still more widely by the *quasi* Rebel commissioners, but misrepresented his own status to the public through the *Tribune*. On the morning of the 22d of July, 1864, five days after his fiasco at the Clifton House, he said, at the head of his editorial columns:

"Of course all reports that the writer has been engaged in proposing, or receiving or discussing hypothetical terms or basis of peace, whether with accredited agents of the Richmond authorities *or others*, are utterly mistaken,"

On the same day he published those portions of the correspondence which accuse Lincoln of prevaricating.

Having in youth few really vicious impulses, and none, perhaps, which manifested themselves to his parents, Mr. Greeley never felt obliged to put forth effort to control his impulses; hence it is, doubtless, that we find him yielding so readily to them throughout his career.

There is no doubt that a term of public service in an office of dignity and responsibility, would be beneficial to him—would make him less flighty, less fidgety, less ready to go into a passion and speak hard words, less ready to yield to the importunities of friends without reference to the character of those friends, less ready to adopt every new vagary which presents itself to him of a summer morning in a plausible aspect. In short, his constitutional radicalism might be toned down into a partial conservatism by a term of office as chief magistrate of the nation. But can the nation afford to take him as a leader, just for the training it would give him, when it has others already trained? And especially when there is great risk that the qualities which now unfit the man for the place might, by the force of circumstances extremely liable to occur, be exaggerated, rather than cured by the process? Even if it were not for this risk, a very strong argument against trying Greeley in the Presidency would be furnished by his own rule of One Term, which would muster him out of service before he had become well fitted for his duties.

Mr. Greeley himself argues* that, since he has been a good journalist, he may be reasonably expected to make a good President; but this is a most palpable *non sequitur*. In the first place, he is not a good journalist†—he is simply an able writer and speaker, a bold innovator and a doughty disputant upon mooted points of politics, who can command the ear of the public, and whose style is peculiarly adapted to the needs of the newspaper "leader" or

*Speech at the Boston Jubilee, July 3, 1872.

†Mr. Parton concurs in this view. See Biography, p. 205.

editorial paragraph. Whenever he has had the absolute management of the *Tribune*, its list and its profits have fallen off. One year since the beginning of the war, under such conditions, the net receipts of the paper were reduced to less than $12,000, whereas they should have been upwards of $200,000.

But supposing Mr. Greeley were a good journalist, the fact would not argue that he would make a good President any more than that he would be a skillful watchmaker. Some of the qualities which militate seriously against Mr. Greeley's fitness for the Presidential office are these:

1. He is inconstant of purpose. Evinced in his vacillating course on many questions of social economy in the period previous to 1860, and his hot-and-cold blowing during the war—favoring one day the right of the South to secede, counseling amnesty, peace-on-any-terms, etc., and on the next day shouting "On to Richmond!" "The Rebels have been too leniently treated!" "They must, on returning, find their homes desolate, their wives and children starving," etc.

2. He is intolerant, rabidly intolerant, of the opinion of others, even in non-essentials. He himself tells us* how he was at serious variance with Margaret Fuller, during months of her stay in his household, because she chose to drink tea and coffee. Of his intolerance in more serious matters, numerous instances have been given in these pages.

* Parton, page 257.

3. He tends to violent theories and *isms* as a duck tends toward the water. Instance his sudden embracement of Communism (which he has not yet really abandoned), his ultra views concerning sumptuary legislation, his dalliance with Rebels during the War, his "affinity" for Margaret Fuller, Theodore Tilton, and such extremists, for Weston, the pedestrian, "Lord Gordon Gordon," and such humbugs, and his general eagerness to revolutionize society.

4. He is rude to boorishness in manners, a fact springing not less from his lack of breeding than from his inordinate self-conceit and affectation of individuality. Instance his habitual profanity, his appearance upon the street in rags and filth,* his commencing a reply to the *Evening Post* in 1849, with these words:

"*You lie, villian! willfully, wickedly, basely lie!*" and other like illustrations cited in chapter twenty of this book.

5. He is the worst judge of men. Instance his choice of political associates at home, and his almost daily experience in being duped by designing fellows, recommending rascals for office, etc.

6. He is ignorant of the qualities and capacities of human nature. Instance his "worse than crimes"—his blunders—in the Lackawaxen expedition and other Fourierite experiences.

7. He does not know the American people, nor respect their opinions. Instance his wayward

* Parton, pp. 574 and 576.

course in the war, and his declaration at the Fourier banquet of his purpose to "fly in the teeth" of public opinion whenever he chose.

8. He lacks the organizing and administrative faculty. See *Tribune* experiences as above, failure in all newspaper ventures before he picked up McElrath, failure of his farming, frittering away of his million of personal revenues, failure of his political schemes, etc.

9. He is a Radical by temperament, which a President should never be, though may entertain progressive views.

10. He cherishes personal revenges and is constantly in half a dozen quarrels, and Charles Sumner's Eleventh Commandment (which Greeley is circulating by the hundred thousand) says, "A President should never quarrel." (See Seward letter, Lincoln episodes, *Tribune* of almost any date relative to Senator Conkling, etc.)

11. And worst—he has a morbid laxity of conduct toward evil-doers—not because he is prone to evil himself, nor solely because of his sentimental notions about universal amnesty, but because the public condemns robbery and corruption, and Greeley's habitual belligerency toward public opinion places him instinctively on the opposite side from the general public. Instance his course toward Tammany from a remote date, toward the Southern Rebels, and toward many isolated and individual malefactors.

Of these eleven articles of impeachment none

would perhaps serve to oust Greeley *after* should be placed in the Presidential chair; there is therefore all the more need of the public considering them well, *before* elevating him to such a responsible place. If any two or three of them are true, they should disqualify him for the popular suffrages. Which *one* of them is not?

We will close this chapter with two quotations from high authority in reinforcement of our characterization of Mr. Greeley. First, from Mr. George William Curtis, most candid and generous of New York journalists, and editor of *Harper's Weekly*. He says:

"Mr. Greeley undoubtedly has elements of strength, but he is not a strong candidate. His name does not suggest to the country either of the two great executive qualities—discretion and decision. Bred in the school of Henry Clay, whose memory he piously reveres, he is naturally timid and a compromiser. He has the credulity which belongs to a certain simplicity of nature, and which destroys all sound judgment of person. His sympathies are limited; his prejudices deep and strong. He has been always a politician, and of an unsuspected personal honesty. Yet he is not free from suspicion of personal grievance, for he undoubtedly considered himself betrayed by the action of the New York Republican Convention in 1870; and it is plain that he has felt the want of what is called influence with the administration."

And next, from that Nestor of the press, Mr. William C. Bryant, who writes in his *Evening Post* (a paper which had been in sympathy with the Cincinnati movement up to the time of its wreck upon the old rock of political trickery):

"We shall, therefore, put together a few reasons that occur to us why the nomination of Mr. Greeley is unworthy of support.

"He lacks the courage, the firmness, and the consistency which are required in a chief magistrate of the nation. He showed this in a remarkable manner when, at the outbreak of the civil war, he desired to let the South have its way and dissolve the Union of the States. He was frightened, and feared to face the consequences of rejecting the demands of the Southern politicians. The war, however, went on, and soon, though claiming to be a Unionist, he became frightened again. He wanted to make terms with the rebel government at Richmond; he wanted to negotiate with George Saunders and other agents of the rebel government who had sought refuge in Canada. He was for stopping the war and letting the South depart with the chance of preserving slavery. His whole career during the war was irresolute and cowardly, and his counsels impolitic and unwise to the last degree.

"Mr. Greeley's political associations and intimacies are so bad that we can expect nothing from him, in case, to his own misfortune and ours, he should be elected, but a corrupt administration of affairs. Everybody is aware of his close intimacy with Mr. Fenton, of the Senate. If there is a corrupt and dishonest politician in the land, there is no man who has a better claim to be so considered than Reuben E. Fenton. His character is well known to Mr. Greeley; yet is he Mr. Greeley's bosom friend and counsellor in politics. Without a single idea of what public virtue or principle means, he is a most shrewd and skillful political manager. It was probably through his intrigues more than through any other influence that Mr. Greeley succeeded in obtaining his nomination. The same facility for entering into close association with dishonest men has marked the whole of Mr. Greeley's career. He began his political life as a disciple of Thurlow Weed, and only rebelled against his master when he found that he was not to have any of the offices for which political parties were quarreling. In a letter, which found its way to print, he expressly declined to hunt any longer in company with that virtuous individual, Weed, because there was no proper division of the game. He now hunts in company with Fenton, who is more generous. If he should be elected, it is very likely that Fenton would be the principal member of his Cabinet, and that the other heads of departments would be little better. As for the subordinate offices, they would probably be filled by the men whom he makes his companions, such as John Gridley, Waldo Hutchins, Benjamin Wood, John Morrissey and Hank Smith, the lesser lights of Mr. Greeley's social firmament.

"Mr. Greeley has no settled political principles, with one exception. It is a serious objection to any candidate for an office of high political trust that he has no well defined standard of right in his own mind by which to try any measure or any course of proceeding that may be proposed. This is one of Mr. Greeley's great deficiencies. Any aspect of a public measure which looks plausible satisfies him, and drifts backward and forward upon the shifting currents of expediency. It has been said of him as a politician, and we believe with some truth, that he has been on every side of every public question that has come up save one, and that brings us to another objection to him as a candidate.

"He is a thoroughgoing bigoted protectionist, a champion of one of the most arbitrary and grinding systems of monopoly ever known in any country. Mr. Greeley is nothing if not a protectionist.

"The last objection to Mr. Greeley which we shall here mention is the grossness of his manners. General Grant is sometimes complained of as not filling the executive chair with the decorum and dignity which properly belong to the place; but his deficiency in this respect is the deficiency of one not accustomed to polished society, giving little heed to certain conventionalities which really become the high sphere he moves in, as Mr. Greeley so often is.

"These are some of the objections which will occur to thoughtful men when they hear of Mr. Greeley's nomination; and allowing these the weight which they fully deserve, we must advise our readers to refuse the nomination their support. With such a head as is on his shoulders the affairs of the nation could not, under his direction, be wisely administered; with such manners as his, they could not be administered with common decorum; with such associates as he has taken to his bosom, they could not be administered with common integrity."

CHAPTER XXVI.

THE DEMOCRATIC PARTY.

Its Record During and Since the War—Some Nice Tidbits from the History of Greeley's Present Allies—The Essence of their Poliey Then the Same as Now—A Democratic Club of 500,000—Greeley's New York Associates —Who and What They Are—Greeley the Ring Candidate—That Good, Honest Soul—What he has Promised to Do for Them—Frank Blair as Painted by H. G.—The Southern Aristocrats, Ditto—Some of Greeley's Western Friends—Democratic Record on Financial Questions—On Congressional Abuses—The Original Nominator of H. G.—He Favors Repudiation of the Yankee War Debt and a Return of Negroes to Slavery—A Question by H. G. in 1864—Will he Answer it in 1872?

The action of the Democratic party at Baltimore, in nominating Horace Greeley as its candidate upon his secession record and his amnesty principles, has two effects. It completely stultifies the course of those "Liberal Republicans" who claim to be still Republicans, and who arrogate to themselves much virtue for *breaking up* the Democratic party; and it also makes Greeley distinctively the *Democratic* candidate for the Presidency, just as Judge Chase would have been in 1868, if he had secured the nomination which he then so ardently coveted. Greeley is the candidate of the regular Democratic organization. Democratic discipline will be brought to bear to whip voters into his ranks, and Democratic money, doled out by Augustus Schell and Cyrus H. McCormick, will be used to buy such as will yield to no other incentive. The friends of the Democratic party, therefore, are Greeley's friends, and the friends of Greeley are its friends.

RECORD OF THE DEMOCRACY.

The record of the Democratic party prior to the Administration of James Buchanan, is not of much account in this connection, since all national issues assumed a new phase with the dawn of secession and civil strife. It will be recollected, however, that the Democratic party (so called because it was not democratic but oligarchic) was the party of Slavery before the war, and that ever since the firing upon Sumpter, it has been the opponent of all measures for putting down the Slaveholders' Rebellion, and for realizing the results of the defeat of that rebellion. Its *personnel.* is practically the same now as then; and its perpetuation of itself at Baltimore—its refusal to adopt the "possum" policy signifies nothing less than the determination to keep alive the aspirations and purposes of 1861–63–64–66, and those years; a determination which is doubtless reinforced by confidence in Greeley's devotion as a neophyte to their cause, and especially by his promise in a recent letter to a Hartford gentleman, to deal out the loaves and fishes of office to copperhead Democrats in proportion to the number of votes which they cast for him.

We will refresh the recollection of the reader with a few facts in the record of the Democracy—and but a few, since they are all so notorious and so uniformly unpatriotic as to be an uninviting theme for the chronicler.

BUCHANAN AND HIS CABINET.

In the winter of 1860–1, when the rebellion broke out, the Democratic party was in power, as it now seeks to be. It had in the Presidential chair an old fussy man, such as it now seeks to put in, who held, as Greeley holds, that the national government had no right to coerce a State into loyalty. That fussy old man, James Buchanan, had very much such a pro-Southern cabinet as Greeley may be expected to appoint if he succeeds in being elected next November. In this cabinet the Secretary of War was J. B. Floyd—the same who afterwards ran away from Grant at Fort Donelson. Among the exploits of Floyd, in behalf of the Southern Confederacy and the Democratic party, just before the storm broke, was to transfer from Northern to Southern arsenals 105,000 stand of muskets and 10,000 rifles. At the same time forty columbiads and four 32-pounders were moved from Pittsburgh to Ship Island, La., and seventy columbiads and seven 32-pounders from the same foundries to Galveston, although the fortifications at Galveston, on which the guns were to be used, were not to be done in five years. At the same time, also, the navy of the United States was by the the Secretary of that Department scattered and the vessels assigned either to Southern ports, where they could be captured by the Rebels, or to remote stations, whence they could not be recalled in months.

Buchanan's other cabinet officers also rallied in support of the rebellion. Jeremiah S. Black—one of Greeley's supporters—then Attorney General, decided solemnly that the President had no power to call out the militia; though a committee of Congress appointed that winter said "Yes, the power is distinctly conferred by the statute of February 28, 1795."

President Buchanan informed the country, in his last message, Dec. 4, 1860, that "the Constitution did not delegate to Congress or to any other department of the Federal Government, the power to coerce a State into submission which is attempting to withdraw, or has actually withdrawn from the Union."

THE DEMOCRATS IN CONGRESS.

It will be recollected that the members of the House of Representatives which was chosen in 1860, did not take their seats until after the session of March 4th of the following year, and that the members from the seceding states maintained their seats for a time, thus leaving the Democrats a large vote in each house until near the close of the 37th Congress. The propositions made in Congress during that eventful winter, with a view of settling with the South by compromise, were many of them disgraceful to American patriotism. Among others, John A. McClernand, now Greeley's chief stump orator for Illinois, and who came near being President of his Baltimore Convention, introduced a resolution in favor of a bill indemnifying, at the expense of the government, the owners of all slaves who had escaped from freedom, and providing for a special police, paid by the general government—Massachusetts contributing to the fund alike with South Carolina—for the prevention of any further escapes.

Noell, of Missouri, introduced a resolution proposing to abolish the office of President of the United States and establish instead a triumvirate, to be chosen from three sections—the East, West and South (this with a view to keeping New England under), and also to restore to the South her former prestige in the Senate by subdividing the Southern states.

On the 27th of February, 1861, every Democrat in the House voted for a constitutional amendment which should say that "No amendment shall be made to the Constitution which shall authorize or give to Congress the power to abolish or interfere with slavery."

John Cochrane is a specimen of the "Liberal Republicans" who have joined the Democratic ranks because the Republican party could not in decency recognize their impertinent claims for preferment. He was only an interloper in the Republican camp at best. In December, 1860, being then a Democratic Member of Congress, he defended Buchanan's cowardly message, and introduced a joint resolution "fully concurring with the President, that no department of the Federal Government has the right to wage war against a seceding State," and declaring that "a just conception of the Constitutional authority of Congress combines with other and more commanding motives [meaning love for slavery and slaveholders] to prescribe other means than aggressive and coercive warfare to remedy the *inconveniences* of such secession."

This unvarying policy of favoring the South and truckling to the worst demands of the fire-eaters, continued to characterize the party, even after active hostilities were in progress. On the 5th of December, 1862, S. S. Cox, also one of Mr. Greeley's supporters, and one of his intimates, introduced an amendment to another member's resolution, which amendment defined as "assassins" "all men, whether of the North or South, who have been instrumental in producing the present war, and especially those, in or out of Congress, who have been guilty of flagrant breaches of the Constitution, and who are not in favor of establishing the Union as it was and the Constitution as it is;" and all the Democrats, except two, voted for this amendment!

INSULT TO INJURY!

Buchanan, in his last message to Congress, proposed the enactment of "an explanatory Constitutional amendment, containing, 1. An express recognition of the right of property in slaves where it now exists, *or may hereafter exist;* 2. The duty of protecting this right in all our territories; and 3. "A like recognition of the right of the master to his slave," and a forcing of the Fugitive Slave Law upon all the States, as a part of their State codes. Here is Democratic State Rights for you in all its original purity!

Propositions like this came in by the dozen during the first few months of the Rebellion. Fortunately, the very impetuosity of the Southern traitors defeated their cause, by preventing the enactment of any of these suicidal propositions. It did not, however, prevent the Democrats in Congress and elsewhere from evincing, on all convenient occasions their sympathy with the South. The Democratic Members of Congress voted solid, or nearly so, against a committee to inquire into the alleged abuse of the executive power as to the South; against a resolution censuring the Secretary of the Navy for sending off men-of-war, so that they could not be used to put down the rebellion; against the construction of seven steam war vessels; against a resolution approving the course of Major Anderson in defending Fort Sumpter; and, in general, against every measure proposed during the prevalence of the Rebellion, for putting down that Rebellion or strengthening the Government.

OUTSIDE OF CONGRESS.

Outside of Congress the Democrats were equally

active. Mr. Greeley's friend and advocate, Fernando Wood, then mayor of New York, sent a special message to the Common Council of that city, proposing to *secede from the Union and join the Confederacy*—the latter clause of the proposition being implied. In 1863 the New York *News* (Ben. Wood's paper) and the Brooklyn *Eagle*—both of them among the earliest and most earnest advocates of Greeley for the Presidency, were presented by the grand jury of their respective counties for trial for disloyalty.

In the year last mentioned, the Democrats were better organized than they have been of late. It appears from testimony taken by a Commission over which Judge Advocate General Holt presided, that there were in the Northwestern States 500,000 staunch Democrats compacted into organizations known variously as the Order of American Knights, Sons of Liberty, Knights of the Golden Circle, etc., two-thirds of whom were furnished with arms,* and all of them banded together by stringent oaths and working under elaborate forms, like the White Brotherhood, or Ku-Klux Klan, of later days in the South. The number above given is the estimate of C. L. Vallandigham, who was himself a high officer of the order. The object of this fine Democratic organization, as elicited from the testimony of numerous witnesses and summarized by Mr. Holt, were as follows:

1. To aid soldiers of the Union army to desert and to harbor and protect deserters.

* See testimony of witness Clayton and others in Mr. Holt's report.

2. To discourage enlistments and to help resist drafts.
3. To circulate disloyal and treasonable publications.
4. To furnish intelligence of Union movements to the enemy.
5. To aid the enemy by recruiting for them within our lines.
6. To furnish the Rebels with arms, etc.
7. To co-operate with raids and invasions from the South.
8. The destruction of government property.
9. The destruction of private property.
10. Assassination and murder
11. The establishment of a Northwestern Confederacy.

There have been studious efforts made since the war to cry down the facts about these organizations and represent them as mere myths. They were undoubted realities. The draft riots of Wisconsin and New York city, the Camp Douglas plot in Chicago, and other like demonstrations, were specimens of their handiwork. The members of the O. A. K., the K. G. C., etc., are still at large* and at work for Greeley.

IN CONGRESS SINCE THE WAR.

The Thirteenth Constitutional Amendment, abolishing slavery, was adopted by the U. S. Senate on February 10, 1864, *every Democratic member voting against it except two, and those are now shelved by their party.* In the House, 65 Democrats voted against it, and only 3 in its favor. Among the noes were Brooks, Cox, Wood, Randall, Eldridge and others, now at work for Greeley.

In 1868 the Democrats, though still maintaining their reactionary policy on Southern questions, abandoned their time-honored position on the tariff, and declared for incidental protection.

*See Chicago *Tribune* of December 4, 1871, for murders committed by the Indiana Ku-Klux, now important allies of the newspaper named.

In January, 1870, the entire Democratic vote of the House of Representatives in Congress was cast in favor of a resolution requiring the payment of the Five-twenty bonds in greenbacks (then at about 25 per cent. discount) and declaring that the Government "squanders millions" by paying par upon these bonds. On the 16th of May, 1870, a resolution declaring the 14th and 15th amendments to the Constitution valid and obligatory upon all the departments of the Government, received the votes of only *four* Democrats in the House, while *thirty-two* voted against it.

Indeed, the uniform record of the party upon the questions thus far referred to and as illustrated by the examples cited, is well recollected by all who have followed the political history of our country during the past twelve years. With regard to those public vices which it has been their custom (and it is now) to charge upon the Republican party, such as legislative jobbery, the abuse of the franking and other Congressional privileges, the Democrats have been much more reckless and unscrupulous than the Republicans, and it is to *their* practices that a large measure of the odium is due.

WHO ARE GREELEY'S FRIENDS?

The record of some of these has been already celebrated in the foregoing paragraphs. Before ever Greeley sold himself out to the Democracy, and while making his loudest plaints as the most virtuous and an unproperly suppressed member of the Republican organization, his affiliations were of the most scandalous sort. When he tried to split up the Republican party in New York in 1871, and descended upon the Syracuse Convention with the purpose of capturing that organization, and with it some spoils for the Fenton crowd, he was backed by a bogus Central Committee, recently organized under his lead, and which contained *forty-one* pensioners of Boss Tweed and his Tammany Ring. Among the most conspicuous of Greeley's adherents at that time were Benj. F. Manniere, "Hank" Smith, Fire Commissioner Galway, D. D. Conover, Rufus F. Andrews, Tom. E. Stewart, Waldo Hutchins and John Cochrane, all beneficiaries of Tammany. These were his associates and the men in whose behalf he labored when claiming to represent the double-refined purity of Republicanism; what can be expected now that he has fallen absolutely into the arms of Democracy?

Among the first reinforcements to join his standard after the Cincinnati affair were the members of the Brooklyn Ring—a more compact organization of robbers than Tammany, and equally successful. The head of this is Wm. C. Kingsley, owner of the Brooklyn *Eagle*, and "King of the Ring." His paper favored Greeley (why?) even before the Cincinnati convention.

To the Tammany and Brooklyn rings, add, as specimens of Greeley's supporters in his own state, such men as Orange S. Winans, the renegade Republican legislator who sold out his party for $5,000 at Albany, in the spring of 1871; John Morrissey, the professional gambler, who has always clung to Greeley as a political affinity, and who, like most professional gamblers, "knows his man"; Jo. Howard, forger of proclamations, who was sent to Fort Lafayette for one of his acts of wanton disloyalty; and ——. But the list defiles our pages.

Geo. N. Saunders, the notorious rebel agent, who was connected with a plot to burn Northern cities and rob Northern banks as a Confederate war measure, has lately returned from Europe to make the canvass for his friend Greeley, He flew at once to Chappaqua on arriving on these shores, and has since been an intimate associate of the great Reform canoidate, both in private and public.

Among the most active participants in the Cincinnati convention was Alexander Long, expelled from Congress for disloyalty in 1863.

On the National Executive Committee which is to direct the campaign (and placed there because he is expected to contribute $100,000 to make votes with) is Cyrus H. McCormick, of Chicago, who attempted to found a political theological seminary at Chicago, and did contribute $25,000 toward General Lee's military school at Lexington, Virginia, for the education of soldiers for the next Confederate army.

A man without whom Greeley could not have been nominated at Cincinnati, is Henry C. Warmoth, the most corrupt of the Southern carpet-bag governors, and the head of the most absolute local monarchy ever known in the United States—the man who engages in public brawls, and who says of his constituency that "they are all demoralized; that they are either —— knaves or —— fools, and that he, by —— knows how to handle them" (!) Warmoth is the Louisiana member of the "Liberal" Executive Committee, and will have any place that he wants under Greeley *when* the latter is elected.

In Missouri, Mr. Greeley's most active supporter is the Lexington *Caucasian*—a paper which, indeed, claims the merit of having been the only one to propose beforehand the precise ticket which was nominated at Cincinnati. This paper keeps standing at the head of its editorial columns, displayed in very bold letters, the following stuff:

STATE SOVEREIGNTY!!

WHITE SUPREMACY!

—AND—

REPUDIATION!!

THIS IS LIBERTY!!

OUR MOTTO:

NEVER DESPAIR OF THE REPUBLIC!

OUR PLATFORM:

THE CONSTITUTION OF 1860, AND THE RIGHTS OF THE STATES!

OUR DOCTRINES:

THIS IS A WHITE MAN'S GOVERNMENT, MADE BY WHITE MEN FOR WHITE MEN, AND THEIR POSTERITY FOR EVER!

DOWN WITH THE FIFTEENTH BEDAMNEDMENT!!

Total Repudiation of the Monstrous Yankee War Debt!—That Accursed, Unconstitutional Burden, accumulated by an Unconstitutional Mob styling itself a Congress, in the prosecution of an Unconstitutional Crusade, for the Accomplishment of an Unconstitutional and Horrid Purpose!

DOWN WITH BOND-HOLDERS AND TAXATION!

Subordination of the Military to the Civil Authorities!

DOWN WITH THE SATRAPS!

EQUAL TAXATION AND THE RIGHTFUL REPRESENTATION OF ALL THE STATES, OR

ANOTHER REBELLION!!

Revolution must be met by Counter Revolution!—Force by Force! Violence by Violence!—And Usurpation should be overthrown, if need be, by the Bayonet!

Down with Test Oaths and Registrations!

And Horace Greeley is the man through whom it proposes to carry out this extraordinary programme!

There are some men to be counted in the Greeley party (at least were, early in the campaign) who have respectable, or semi-respectable, records in politics. They are, however, chiefly of the class called soreheads—disappointed Federal office seekers, or men shelved by their local party associates.

The most valued of Greeley's allies, perhaps, are the Blair family, of whom the Washington correspondent of the Boston *Globe* (an independent sheet) writes:

"It is curious to notice how the Blair family come in as marplots and Catalines. It was the presence of Montgomery Blair in Mr. Lincoln's Cabinet that brought about the revolt of Wade aud Winter Davis, as well as the Cleveland Convention with the Fremont nomination. The removal of that Blair was the price paid by Mr. Lincoln for the withdrawal of General Fremont as a Presidential candidate. It was the Blairs who played Mephistopheles to Andrew Johnson. After his drunken fiasco on inauguration day, he retired to Silver Springs, and there passed entirely under the Blair influence. Montgomery was his chief kitchen cabinet adviser; the effect of such advice has since become history. Now they appear again; this time to break up the party both Montgomery and Frank P. helped to make and mold, and which they have ever since been seeking to betray."

GREELEY ON THE MAN WHO NOMINATED HIM.

It has already been shown that Frank Blair was the principal intriguer along with Gratz Brown, to log-roll Greeley's nomination through the Convention, along with Brown's. Here is what Greeley said of Blair in the *Tribune* of May 7, 1864:

"An outright secessionist is wickeder and more dangerous than Frank Blair; but his position seems to us meaner and more glaringly inconsistent than that of Jeff. Davis. He would first use the blacks to subjugate the traitors, and then combine with the traitors to trample on and deny all political rights to the blacks."

When Greeley says of Blair that "his position is meaner and more glaring that that of Jeff. Davis," he justifies the inference that he Greeley would not go so far to bail Blair as he did to bail Jeff. Davis; and yet, after all this denunciation of the blatant Missourian, and a thousand times as much more, which he heaped upon him after his famous Brodhead letter, and during the campaign of 1868, Mr. Greeley does not hesitate to accept, chiefly from these same traitors, a nomination which he owes mainly to the good offices of this same "mean," disreputable and "glaringly inconsistent" Blair!

BLAIR TO BRODHEAD.

The "Brodhead letter" referred to—written a few days before Blair's nomination by the Democrats at New York for Vice-President, contained this passage, which was not qualified or toned down in the least by the context, nor afterwards explained by Blair:

"The reconstruction policy of the Radicals will be complete before the next election; the States so long excluded will have been admitted, negro suffrage established and the carpet-baggers installed in their seats in both houses of Congress. There is no possibility of changing the political character of the Senate, even if the Democrats should elect their President and a majority of the popular branch of Congress. We cannot therefore undo the Radical plan of reconstruction by Congressional action; the Senate will continue a bar to its repeal; must we submit to it? How can it be overthrown? *It can only be overthrown by the authority of the Executive*, who is sworn to maintain the Constitution, and who will fail of his duty if he allows the Constitution to perish under a series of Congressional enactments which are in palpable violation of its fundamental principles.

"If the President elected by the Democracy enforces, or permits others to enforce, these reconstruction acts, the Radicals, by the accession of twenty spurious Senators and fifty Representatives, will control both branches of Congress, and his Administration will be as powerless as the present one of Mr. Johnson.

"There is but one way to restore the Government and the Constitution, *and that is for the President* (Greeley?) *to declare these acts null and void*, compel the army to undo its usurpation at the South, disperse the carpet-bag State Governments, allow the white people to reorganize their own governments and elect Senators and Representatives."

A PERTINENT QUESTION.

In the *Tribune* of May 4, 1864, on one of the days when Mr. Greeley felt more like helping the Republican party than he did like beating Lincoln, he wrote these words, which especially the last clause, with names in brackets, altered a trifle, is well suited to the present time:

"Some of us think Slavery might and should have been crowded to the wall much faster and more sternly than it has been," [the trouble with "some of us" this year, however, is of an opposite sort, viz.: That Slavery, in the form of terrorism, has been pushed too hard]; "Supposing," continues Mr. Greeley, "supposing this true; should we make anything by substituting for our present Administration one whereof [Frank Blair, Beauregard, Warmoth, Letcher of Virginia, Sat. Clark, Boss Tweed, the Brooklyn Ring, *et id omne genus*] are the chief spokesmen and champions?"

GREELEY ON HIS SOUTHERN SUPPORTERS.

One great end of Greeley's candidacy, as claimed

by his advocates, is to "break the sway of the carpet-baggers" at the South, and to set up the "respectable element" of the Southern population in their place. From this respectable element they expect such support as will enable them to carry most of the Southern States. Here is Greeley's opinion of this "respectable element," after he had been among them in 1871—only a year ago. We extract it from an "H. G." letter in the *Tribune*, published about the time that Greeley returned from his trip through the South.

"The ancient aristocracy of the South remind me of the Federal Squirearchy of our country after Jefferson's election as President. Instead of studying the new situation and seeking to master it, they content themselves with endless and fruitless complainings. They lament the sway of the "carpet-baggers" over their late slaves, but take no effective measures to counteract it. Rogues as some of the "carpet-baggers" are, they are all zealous for the education of the Blacks, while the submerged aristocracy grudge every penny assessed on them for building school-houses and paying teachers as though it were thrown into the sea. The noblest, purest, most intelligent women of New England, who have come down here to teach Black children, are shunned and banned by the aristocracy, as though they were camp followers of Sherman's army, and being thus doomed to associate only with Blacks, and live with them, are actually charged with this as a betrayal of low tastes when it is a dictate of stern necessity."

And more to the same effect.

CHAPTER XXVII.

THE BALTIMORE CONVENTION.

Its Composition—A Cut and Dried Affair—To Nominate or to Endorse:—That is the Question—Organization—"Dixie" for Music—Greeley Swallowed—Likewise the Cincinnati Platform—Delaware, Pennsylvania, Georgia, Remonstrate in Vain—A Sudden Adjournment.

The Baltimore Convention is a short horse, soon curried. The delegates had, nearly all, been instructed to vote for Greeley and Brown, and there was nothing left for them to do but to meet and go through with the form. The only question was what that form should be—whether to nominate formally or to simply endorse the Cincinnati nominations and platform, appoint an auxiliary committee, and adjourn. The latter policy was urged with great earnestness by the "Liberal" leaders present, but the Democrats proper would not listen to it for a moment. The "endorsing" policy obtained no show at all in the Convention, and the four-year-long efforts of Horace White and others to persuade the Democracy to go out of business were thus brought to naught. The Democrats reasoned that Greeley was a good enough Democrat for them—that recent converts usually proved more zealous in enforcing the party creed than older members; and that the Democracy, whose platform now was *anything to beat Grant*, and reverse his policy—a platform to which Greeley heartily subscribed, could afford to hold up its head as high as ever.

THE LIBERAL PLAN SCORNED.

This course prevailed. The convention met at twelve o'clock on the 9th of June, in Ford's Opera House. It was called to order by August Belmont, Chairman of the National Executive Committee, who had been the chief manipulator of the party in Seymour and Blair days—in McClellan and Pendleton days, and so on back. The leaders generally were equally veterans in the service; though some effort had apparently been made to leave out from the published proceedings the names to which odious records are attached.

THE OLD, OLD STORY.

Mr. Belmont, in his opening speech, of course made pathetic allusions to the "Cæsarism and centralization," which, he said, "are undermining the very foundations of our federal system, and are sweeping away the constitutional bulwarks erected by the wisdom of the fathers of the republic. These abuses," said Belmont, "have become so glaring that the wisest and best men of the Republican party have severed themselves from the Radical wing, which is trying to fasten upon the country another four years' reign of corruption, usurpation and despotism, and whatever individual opinion we may entertain as to the choice of the candidates," we must, etc., etc.

ORGANIZATION.

Mr. Belmont nominated a Mr. Randolph, of Virginia, said to be a grandson of Jefferson, as temporary Chairman. Afterwards the convention was permanently organized by the election of Hon. James R. Doolittle, of Wisconsin—the right hand man of Andrew Johnson during the administration of that worthy, as permanent Chairman, with E. O. Perrin, of New York, A. T. Whittlesey, of Indiana, Thos. H. Moore, of Maryland, and Jno. C. Barr, of Pennsylvania, for Secretaries. The Vice-Presidents were as follows:

Alabama, Wm. M. Bird; Arkansas, D. W. Carroll; California, Hon. Eugene Casserly; Connecticut, D. A. Daniels; Delaware, J. H. Payne; Florida, Thos. Rundell; Georgia, H. L. Benning; Illinois, Wm. M. Gonard; Indiana, Bayless W. Hanna; Iowa, Jno. H. Peters; Kansas, Isaac Sharp; Kentucky, G. H. Dore; Louisiana, B. F. Taylor; Maine, Wm. H. McCrelles; Maryland, R. T. Banks; Massachusetts, D. D. Brodhead; Michigan, E. H. Lathrop; Minnesota, Wm. Lee; Mississippi, J. W. D. Watson; Missouri, Silas Woodson; Nebraska. Jno. Black; Nevada, N. B. Weyman; New Hampshire, G. M. W. Pitman; New Jersey, Albert H. S. Lape; New York, Thomas Kinsella; North Carolina, R. T. Armfield; Ohio, Alfred Gaither; Oregon, E. F. Colby; Pennsylvania, Wm. McMullen; Rhode Island, Lyman Pierce; South Carolina, Wm. Aiken; Tennessee, Neils Brown; Texas, J. W. Henderson; Vermont, W. T. Horiben; Virginia, Robt. Ould; West Virginia, Allen T. Caperton; Wisconsin, H. H. Gray; Dakota, Bartlett Thripp; District of Columbia, Richard T. Merrick; Idaho, B. F. Patterson; New Mexico, Chas. P. Chaveo.

After a half hour speech from the Chairman, a Committee on Resolutions was constituted, a great flood of independent resolutions presented, and the National Executive Committee appointed, after which an adjournment was had.

THE COMMITTEE.

The members of the National Committee are as follows:

Alabama, Thos. A. Walker, Jacksonville; Arkansas, S. R. Cockrell, Pine Bluffs; California, F. McCoppin, San Francisco; Connecticut, Wm. H. Barnum, Lime Rock; Delaware, Chas. Beasten, Odessa; Florida, Chas. E. Dyke, Talahessee; Georgia, A. R. Wright, Augusta; Illinois, Cyrus H. McCormick, Chicago; Indiana, Thos. Dowling, Terre Haute; Iowa, M. M. Hall, Dubuque; Kansas, Isaac Eaton, Leavenworth; Kentucky, H. D. McHenry, Hartford; Louisiana, H. D. Ogden, New Orleans; Maine, D. T. M. Sweet, Portland; Maryland, A. Leo Knott, Baltimore; Massachusetts, F. O. Priner, Boston; Michigan, Wm. A. Moore, Detroit; Minnesota, Wm. Lochren, Minneapolis; Mississippi, J. H. Sharp, Columbus; Missouri, John G. Priest, St. Louis; Nebraska, G. L. Miller, Omaha; Nevada, Thos. H. Williams, Virginia City; New Hampshire, M. V. B. Edgerly. Manchester; New Jersey, T. F. Randolph, Morristown; New York, A. Schell, New York; North Carolina, M. W. Ransom, Weldon; Ohio, J. G. Johnson, Columbus; Oregon, R. J. Ladd, Portland; Pennsylvania, Jas. D. Barr, Pittsburgh; Rhode Island, Gideon Bradford, Providence; South Carolina, Thos. G. Simmons, Charleston; Tennessee, Wm. R. Bales, Nashville; Texas. F. S. Stockdale, Indianola; Vermont, H. B. Smith, Milton; Virginia, Jno. Goode, Norfolk; West Virginia, J. B. Hoge, Martinsburg; Wisconsin, Geo. H. Paul, Milwaukee.

The displacement of Mr. Belmont from the committee and the substitution of Mr. Schell created some hard feelings among the New York delegation, but was smilingly acquiesced in by Mr. Belmont, who is doubtless glad to be relieved from the large pecuniary obligations which have hitherto rested upon him as chairman and moneyed man of the committee, and also from the odium which so prominent an advocacy of Greeley would bring him in financial circles. Mr. Schell is a very wealthy man, having made millions of dollars in a government contract, under Andrew Johnson. Mr. Storey, of the Chicago *Times*, a former valuable member of the committee, had chosen to forego that honor henceforth, rather than support the nomination of Greeley. The members of this committee, so far as known to the writer, are of Copperhead antecedents.

THE PLATFORM—AND TROUBLE.

In the evening the Committee on Resolutions met and voted to adopt the Cincinnati philippic as a platform. Only three States—Delaware, Mississippi and Georgia—voted against this. The programme thus agreed upon was ratified by the Convention on the following day; but not until Senator Bayard, of Delaware, a member of the Platform Committee, and speaking for the Delaware delegation, had made a very earnest speech against "the adoption of the language of a platform made by other men not of the same political faith with the convention." Other members rose to remonstrate in the same manner, but a call for the previous question had been made and carried; which shut off debate, and carried the second-hand platform through under the gag law. The vote by which the previous question was seconded was 573 to 159; and the platform was adopted by 662 to 70. The scene, pending the discussion and voting, was one of great turbulence.

A NOMINATION—AND CLAP-TRAP.

After the platform was swallowed, the next thing in order was to swallow the candidate which had been prepared for the patient; and an Illinois gentleman named Snowhook, who had been bobbing up at frequent intervals and nominating Horace Greeley off-hand, was now allowed to do so *pro forma*, and the convention proceeded to swallow its leek, "in token of revenge." The vote resulted as follows:

Horace Greeley	686
Jeremiah S. Black	21
James A. Bayard	16
W. S. Groesbeck	2
Blank	7
Total	732

Upon the announcement of this result an attempt was made to imitate the thrilling dramatic features which accompanied the renomination of General Grant at Philadelphia. A motion was made, by a heart-sick Pennsylvanian (who afterwards swore point blank that he would not vote for Greeley) to make the nomination unanimous; but this was negatived by the staunch Delawareans and by many Southern delegates. Then a canvass was lowered away from the flies of the theater stage, on which was a vision of the White House; and the band struck up "The Battle Cry of Freedom." A newspaper correspondent, writing from the scene immediately afterwards, said of the musical feature of the Convention and the result upon that body's enthusiasm:

"A significant feature in the convention to-day was the manner in which the popular airs were received. Previous to opening the convention this morning the band played "Yankee Doodle," "Red, White and Blue," "Marching Through Georgia," etc., but they received no notice. Finally, however, when "Dixie" and "The Bonnie Blue Flag," were performed, the audience broke out in a most violent manner, and cheered the airs to the echo. In fine, the convention did not display enough enthusiasm over anything of a national character to charge a bottle of pop. But all allusions to the south and southern soldiers were loudly applauded, showing clearly enough the composition and spirit of the convention."

With a few further formalities, the convention adjourned *sine die*, after a painfully short and embarrassed session.

This convention also had its side-show—an assembly of Irreconcilables who met in a neighboring hall, under the presidency of another Bayard—Hon. Samuel J., of New Jersey. They adopted an address and voted to call a national convention to be held at Louisville on the 3d of September to take advantage of any new phase which the situation might assume at or before that time. There were many members of the regular convention in sympathy with this movement, but the number who actually participated was not great.

HENRY WILSON.

BAKER-CO. CHI.

CHAPTER XXVIII.

HENRY WILSON.

His Humble Birth—Apprenticed to a Farmer—Learns the Shoemaker's Trade After Becoming Twenty-one—Pursues an Academical Course After That—Becomes a Stump Orator—Great success—Enters Public Life—In the Legislature—An Ardent Free Soiler—An Editor for Two Years—Chosen United States Senator in 1850—His Career in the Senate—Challenged by Bully Brooks—Service on the Military Committee—Joins the Army—His Labors for the Colored Race—Why he Would Not Join the Working-men's Party—An Answer Worth Reading—A Busy Career.

Our sketch of Henry Wilson, Republican candidate for Vice-President, is mainly a hasty compilation from recent newspaper sketches, of which the New York *Times* and the Philadelphia *Telegraph* have published the best which have come to hand. The origin of Wilson, like that of Lincoln, Grant, Johnson and others whom the whole nation has seen fit to elevate to the highest places within its gift, was extremely humble; more so, indeed, than any of the others. His manner of struggling upward against adversity was very like that of Horace Greeley; but as the temperaments and minds of the two men are essentially different, the parallel does not extend to their respective careers after attaining manhood.

Henry Wilson was born at Farmington, N. H.,

February 16th, 1812, and is now, therefore, in his sixty-first year. On account of the extreme poverty of his parents, he was at ten years of age apprenticed to a farmer in the vicinity for eleven years. His master was a kind and generous man, who sent the young hard-working boy to school in the intervals of agricultural labor, and here he soon developed a great taste for reading. He hungered after knowledge, and his evident desire to learn induced a lawyer of Farmington to offer him the free use of his library, which was fortunately a very extensive one. Here the statesman in embryo reveled, and, in after life he has declared to friends that he believes he read during those eleven years a hundred volumes a year. When he became twenty-one he had exhausted the library. We continue the narrative in the words of another:

LEARNS A TRADE.

"His indentures were now completed, and if he had chosen to become a farmer, opportunities of advancement were not wanting, for everybody liked the shy awkward youth, with his broad, high forehead, his honest eyes and his immense but somewhat desultory stores of information. But he had resolved upon quitting Farmington and seeing the world. Putting his few clothes and his books, his only treasures, into a bundle, he slung it across his shoulder and walked gayly off to Natick, in Massachusetts, where he hired himself to a shoe-maker, with the resolution of working at this trade until he had accumulated a fund sufficient to maintain him in some good academy. It took three years to do this, when he returned to New Hampshire and studied for a time in the academies at Stafford, Wolfsborough and Concord. Most unfortunately, the man to whom he had confided his little heap of savings became insolvent, so Henry Wilson was obliged to return to the shoemaker's bench at Natick.

"Mr. Wilson himself gives, in one of his speeches, the following account of his rugged experience as a boy and young man:

"'I left my home at ten years of age and served an apprenticeship of eleven years, receiving a month's schooling each year, and at the end of eleven years of hard work, a yoke of oxen and six sheep, which brought me eighty-four dollars. Eighty-four dollars for eleven years of hard toil! I never spent the amonnt of one dollar in money, counting every penny, from the time I was born until I was twenty-one years of age. I know what it is to travel weary miles and ask my fellow-men to give me leave to toil. I remember that, in October, 1833, I walked into your village from my native town, went through your mills, seeking employment. If anybody had offered me nine dollars a month, I should have accepted it gladly. I went to Salmon Falls, I went to Dover, I went to New Market, and tried to get work, without success, and I returned home footsore and weary, but not discouraged. I put my pack on my back and walked to where I now live, in Massachusetts, and learned a mechanic's trade.'

BECOMES A STUMP ORATOR.

"He was now twenty-six, and noted everywhere in the neighborhood as a modest, well-educated young man, with a great turn for debating. He delighted in discussion, and was so redoubtable an opponent that no one in the academies or among his comrades at Natick cared to enter into an argument with one who was so logical, so keenly alive to the weak points of others, and who had, moreover, so powerful a flow of language. Everybody predicted that at the next election the people would hear of Henry Wilson. They did. In 1840 General Harrison was the Whig candidate, and young Wilson's feelings were warmly enlisted on his side. He spoke with great effect at Natick in his favor, and afterward in other towns of Massachusetts and New Hampshire. He was at once recognized as a genuine orator, and his services were engaged by the Whig party, for whom he delivered no less than sixty speeches during that campaign.

AND AN EDITOR.

In the next five years he was himself elected three times a member of the Legislature of Massachusetts, and was twice State Senator. Here he quickly distinguished himself as a bitter hater of slavery, and, when a State Senator from Middlesex county, was selected to carry the great protest of Massachusetts against the evils of slavery and against the annexation of Texas to Washington. The poet Whittier was connected with him in this characteristic embassy. He was a delegate to the Whig National Convention of 1848, being now thirty-six, and he took the opportunity of proposing and presenting to the Convention a series of anti-slavery resolutions which were declared by many authorities to be the most comprehensive and the most unsparing that the brain of man could devise. The Convention, however, was too timid to accept them, and Henry Wilson, on their rejection, at once withdrew and devoted himself to assisting in the formation of the Free Soil Party. Believing that the public mind wanted educating on the subject, he purchased the Boston *Republican* and for two years agitated the question without fear or flinching.

In 1849 he was chosen Chairman of the Free Soil State Committee of Massachusetts, which post he held for four years. In 1850 he was sent to the State Senate, and unanimously elected President. Two years afterward he was elected by acclamation President of the great Free Soil Convention, which was held in Pittsburg, Penn., when he electrified the members by the most wonderful displays of eloquence. The Free-soilers put him up as candidate for Representative in Congress, and though defeated, he ran ahead of his ticket by thousands of votes. Next year the same party put him up for Governor, but he was again defeated, though still running largely ahead of his ticket. Two years afterward, 1855, things changed, and the Free-soilers being in the ascendant, Henry Wilson was elected United States Senator in the place of Edward Everett.

IN THE UNITED STATES SENATE.

No sooner had he taken his seat than he made the Senate Chamber ring with the most eloquent denunciations of slavery. He made a great speech advocating the repeal of the Fugitive Slave law, and for the abolition of slavery in the District of Columbia. He next took an active part in organizing the Republican Party on the basis of equal and exact justice to all. In May, 1856, Mr. Sumner, his colleague, was assailed in the most dastardly manner by Preston Brooks, of South Carolina. He rose to his feet and denounced the assault as " brutal, murderous and cowardly." The South Carolina fire-eater sent him a challenge, which he disregarded, on the ground that dueling was a remnant of barbarism, branded by the law, and that it ill became law-makers to violate law so grossly. At the same time he intimated that should any one assault him as his colleague had been assaulted, it would be seen that he believed most fully in the right of self-defense.

AT THE HEAD OF THE MILITARY COMMITTEE.

" In March, 1861, Mr. Wilson was assigned to the chairmanship of the Committee on Military Affairs. For four years previous he had been a member of that committee, when Jefferson Davis was its chairman, and, though a in minority, had profited by his position in becoming thoroughly familiar with all the details of the condition of the arms and defenses of the country, and the state of the army and its officers. To it he now brought his indomitable energy and tireless industry. Its duties were multiplied a hundred fold in the four years that followed.

"The important legislation for raising, organizing and governing the armies originated in that committee, or was passed upon by it, and eleven thousand nominations, from the second lieutenant to the lieutenant-general, were referred to it. The labors of Mr. Wilson as chairman of the committee were immense.

" Being in Washington when Fort Sumter fell, he was one among the few who advised that the call should be for three hundred thousand instead of seventy-five thousand men. On the day that call was made, he induced the

Secretary of War to double the number of regiments apportioned to Massachusetts.

"On the second day of the extra session of Congress, July 4, 1861, Mr. Wilson introduced five bills and a joint resolution. The first bill was a measure authorizing the employment of five hundred thousand volunteers for three years, to aid in enforcing the laws; the second was a measure increasing the regular army by the addition of twenty-five thousand men; the third was a measure providing for the "better organization of the military establishment," in twenty-five sections embracing very important provisions. These three measures were referred to the Military Committee, promptly reported back by Mr. Wilson, slightly amended, and enacted into laws. The joint resolution to ratify and confirm certain acts of the President for the suppression of insurrection and rebellion was reported, debated at great length, but failed to pass, though its most important provisions were, on his motion incorporated with another measure.

"Mr. Wilson, at the called session, introduced a bill in addition to the "Act to authorize the employment of volunteers," which authorized the President to accept five hundred thousand more volunteers, and to appoint for the command of volunteer forces, such number of major and brigadier-generals as in his judgment might be required; and this measure was passed.

"He introduced bills "to authorize the President to appoint additional aids-de-camp," containing a provision abolishing flogging in the army; "to make appropriations;" "to provide for the purchase of arms, ordnance and ordnance stores;" and "to increase the corps of engineers;" all of which were enacted. He introduced also a bill, which was passed, "to increase the pay of privates," which raised the pay of the soldiers from eleven to thirteen dollars per month, and provided that all the acts of the President respecting the army and navy should be approved, legalized and made valid.

"At the close of the session General Scott emphatically declared that Senator Wilson had done more work in that short session than all the chairmen of the military committees had done in the last twenty years.

"After a brief period of actual military service (having raised a brigade of troops in Massachusetts in 1861, and afterwards served on General McClellan's staff as a volunteer aid-de-camp) pressing duties in Congress forced him to tender his resignation, and he returned to his legislative duties.

ORIGINATES ARMY LEGISLATION.

"During the second session of the Thirty-seventh Congress, Mr. Wilson originated, introduced and carried through, several measures of vital importance to the army and the interests of the country. Among these measures, were the bills 'relating to courts-martial;' 'to provide for allotment certificates;' 'for the better organization of the signal department of the army;' 'for the appointment of sutlers in the volunteer service, and defining their duties;' 'authorizing the President to assign the command of troops in the same field or department, to officers of the same grade, without regard to seniority;' 'to increase the efficiency of the medical department of the army;' 'to facilitate the discharge of enlisted men for physical disability;' 'to provide additional medical officers of the volunteer service;' 'to encourage enlistments in the regular army, and to volunteer forces;' 'for the presentation of medals of honor to enlisted men of the army and volunteer forces, who have distinguished, or who may distinguish themselves in battle during the present rebellion;' 'to define the pay and emoluments of certain officers of the army, and for other purposes,'—a bill of twenty-two sections of important provisions; and 'to amend the act calling forth the militia to execute the laws, suppress insurrection and repel invasion.' This last bill authorized for the first time the enrolment in the militia, and the drafting of negroes, and empowered the President to accept, organize, and arm colored men for military purposes. During the session, Mr. Cameron, the Secretary of War, resigned, and, on leaving the department, he said, in a letter to Senator Wilson:

"No man, in my opinion, in the whole country, has done more to aid the War Department in preparing the mighty army now under arms, than yourself; and, before leaving this city, I think it my duty to offer to you my sincere thanks, as its late head. As chairman of the Military Committee of the Senate, your services were invaluable."

"In the last session of the Thirty-seventh and the whole of the Thirty-eighth Congress, Mr. Wilson labored with the same vigor and persistency to organize and develop the military resources of the nation, to do justice to the officers and to care for the soldiers. Aside from the numerous bills which, though originating with him, were offered by others, and the amendments which he suggested to bills originating with other Senators, or with the House of Representatives, the following important measures were introduced and advocated by him, and passed through his efforts: 'An act to faciiitate the discharge of disabled soldiers, and the inspection of convalescent camps and hospitals;' 'to improve the organization of the cavalry forces;' 'to authorize an increase in the number of major and brigadier-generals;' 'for enrolling and calling out the national forces, and for other purposes' (this act contained thirty-eight sections, and was one of the most important passed during the session); 'to amend an act entitled 'An act for enrolling and calling out the national forces' (this bill contained the provision that 'colored persons should, on being mustered into the service, become free'); 'an act to establish a uniform system of ambulances in the armies;' 'to increase the pay of soldiers in the United States army, and for other purposes' (this increased the pay of a private soldier to sixteen dollars a month;) 'to provide for the examination of certain officers of the army;' 'to provide for the better organization of the Quartermaster's Department;' 'an act in addition to the several acts for enrolling and calling out the national forces;' 'to incorporate a national military and naval asylum for the relief of totally disabled men of the volunteer forces;' 'to incorporate the National Freedmen's Saving Bank;' 'to incorporate the National Academy of Sciences;' 'to encourage enlistments, and promote the efficiency of the military and naval forces, to making free the wives and children of colored soldiers;' and a joint resolution 'to encourage the employment of disabled and discharged soldiers.' The important legislation securing to colored soldiers equality of pay from the 1st of January, 1864, and to officers in the field an increase in the commutation price of the ration, and three months' extra pay to those who should continue in service to the close of the war, was moved by Mr. Wilson upon Appropriation bills.

HIS LABORS FOR THE NEGRO.

"But while laboring, with ever-watchful care, for the interests of the army and the support of the government in its gigantic efforts to suppress the Rebellion, Mr. Wilson did not lose sight, for a moment, of slavery, to the ultimate extinction of which he had consecrated his life more than a quarter of a century before slavery revolted against the authority of the nation. In that remarkable series of anti-slavery measures which culminated in the anti-slavery amendment of the Constitution, he bore no undistinguished part. He introduced the bill abolishing slavery in the District of Columbia, which became a law on the 16th of April, 1862, and by which more than three thousand slaves were forever made free, and slavery became forever impossible in the nation's capital. He introduced a provision, which became a law on the 21st of May, 1862, providing that persons of color in the District of Columbia should be subject to the same laws to which white persons were subject; that they should be tried for offenses against the laws in the same manner as white persons are tried, and if convicted, be liable to the same penalty, and no other, as would be inflicted upon white persons for the same crime. On the 12th of July, 1862, he introduced from the Military Committee the bill, which became a law on the 17th, to amend the act of 1795, calling for the militia to execute the laws. This bill made negroes a part of the militia, authorized the President to receive, into the military or naval service, persons of African descent, and made free such persons, their mothers, wives, and children, if they owed service to any persons who gave aid to the rebellion. On the 24th of February, 1864, he caused the enrollment act to be so amended as to make colored men, whether free or slave, part of the national forces; and the masters of slaves were to receive the bounty when they should free their drafted slaves. On the committee of conference, Mr. Wilson moved that the slaves should be made free, not by the act of their masters, but by the authority of the government, the moment they entered the service of the United States, and this motion prevailing, the act passed in that form. General Palmer reported that in Kentucky alone more than twenty thousand slaves were made free by it. He subsequently introduced, and in the face of the most persistent opposition, carried through, a joint resolution making the wives and children of all colored soldiers forever free.

Six months after the passage of this bill, Major-General Palmer reported that in Kentucky alone, nearly seventy-five thousand women and children had received their freedom through it.

"Senator Wilson also moved and carried an amendment to the Army Appropriation bill of June 15, 1864, providing that all persons of color who had been or who might be mustered into the military service should receive the same uniform, clothing, arms, equipments, camp equipage, rations, medical attendance and pay, as other soldiers, from the 1st day of January, 1864.

"His efforts in behalf of the Massachusetts colored regiments are well known, and it was due to his persistency, that they received a part of what was their just due. The Freedmen's Bureau bill was originally reported by him, and in all the subsequent legislation on that subject, he was active and decided in favor of its organization and maintenance. He defended with great ability and secured the adoption of negro suffrage as a part of the Congressional plan of reconstruction, and in both the thirty-ninth and fortieth Congresses, he has maintained fully his old reputation as the champion of the oppressed and downtrodden.

"Mr. Wilson was a prominent candidate for the Vice Presidency in the political campaign of 1868, and though, eventually, Mr. Colfax received the nomination, the vote for Mr. Wilson was 61 on the fifth ballot, on which Mr. Colfax was nominated.

A THIRD TIME ELECTED SENATOR.

"In 1871 Mr. Wilson was again re-elected to the Senate, without any organized opposition, for the full term of six years ending March 4, 1877, and was again placed at the head of the Committee on Military Affairs, a position which he still retains. Although his colleague in the Senate, Mr. Sumner, joined in the crusade against the administration of President Grant, he held fast to the party and its regular organization, and, in a letter addressed, in November, 1871, to the Committee on the Organization of the Labor Reform movement, in Washington, announced his continued adherence to the party in the following words:—

"I cannot, with my 'views of propriety, join in this movement.' I am a Republican by conviction as well as by association. Born in extreme poverty, bound as an apprentice at an early age, I learned by bitter trials and hardships the poor are doomed to suffer from boyhood. Every pulsation of my heart has been in sympathy with the sons and daughters of toil of all races. My early experiences made me abhor wrong and oppression, so I early became any enemy of slavery and of the rule of the slave-masters. I saw and felt the degrading influences of a system that held working-men in enforced toil, that allowed capital to own labor. For more than twenty years I strove to make a political power to emancipate the slave and end the iron rule of the master.

"The Republican party came into being to break the power of the owners of labor and to deliver the laborer, to lift from the brows of workingmen the dishonor of enforced toil, and to make our country a glorious land where labor can look up and be proud amidst its toil. I did what I could to bring it as a party into being. It has done grand work for the country and for the toiling men of the country, and of the world, too. History records no nobler achievements. Its work is not yet secure, nor is it completed. I can do nothing to endanger that work ; nor can I do anything to arrest the completion of the work imposed upon the Republican party by the needs of the country and the logic of its own principles, that require it to be as true to the interests of white workingmen as it has been to the interests of black workingmen. I am constrained by an imperitive sense of duty to stand by the Republican party till its great work is secured and finished. But whatever I can do shall ever be done to aid in improving, elevating and rewarding labor."

Mr. Wilson is now writing, and has published one volume of an elaborate "History of the Slave Power in America," which promises to be a monumental work on the subject.

CHAPTER XXIX.

BENJAMIN GRATZ BROWN.

Of Aristocratic Family—Graduates at Yale—Studies Law—Moves to St. Louis—Cultivates the Germans—Goes to the Legislature—Starts the "Democrat"—Elected to the United States Senate—Governor of Missouri—His Characteristic Traits—A Habitual Bolter and Extremist—How he Doubled on his Track as to Amnesty—Brown and the Schoolma'ams—Some of his Flights Accounted for.

The Democratic candidate for Vice-President is Benjamin Gratz Brown, of Missouri. Mr. Brown is not, as Greeley called him, not long since, "a third-rate lawyer." He is a man of ability, and his career has been a brilliant one,—erratic, perhaps, but still brilliant. Some points of it follow.

Unlike the three other gentlemen whose names appear upon the national ticket of 1872 as candidates for the Presidency or Vice-Presidency, Mr. Brown is of what we may call aristocratic birth; and this fact in Kentucky was unquestionably of great service to him. His father was the late Judge Mason Brown, of Frankfort, a lawyer and jurist of note, and the son of John Brown, the first person ever chosen Senator from Kentucky. He is a kinsman of the Prestons, Breckenridges, Blairs. McDowels, Bentons and other well-known families, whose members have been prominent in national

B. GRATZ BROWN.

and State affairs since the formation of the Government.

EARLY HISTORY.

Gratz was born on the 28th of May, 1826, at Lexington; graduated at the Transylvania "University," and at Yale College, taking his bachelor's degree at the latter institution when he was only twenty-one years of age. He next studied law at Louisville, whence he moved to St. Louis in 1850 and commenced the practice of this profession. At law he was successful, but preferred politics. He was chosen to the State Legislature in 1852, and served there for several terms. In St. Louis were many Germans, and Brown was sagacious enough to see in them an element of power for any politician who could obtain recognition as their representative. They were mostly radical—so was he. They were for the abolition of slavery—so he became, although he had been brought up by slave nurses. He has the distinction of making the first speech for emancipation in the Legislature of a slave State, and of founding the first anti-slavery journal in a slave State. Thus we have three editors in the Presidential field—Greeley, Wilson, Brown.

BECOMES A SENATOR.

The journal referred to was the *Missouri Democrat*, which Brownestablished at St. Louis, in 1854, in conjunction with Frank Blair and others, Brown being the chief editorial writer. His articles were fiery and powerful, and he not only succeeded in advancing the cause of the Benton democracy, but in establishing his journal on a firm, broad basis. In 1862, Mr. Brown was elected to the United States Senate for the incomplete term extending from 1863 to 1867. (He was afterwards instrumental in elevating Carl Schurz and Frank Blair to seats in the same body.) Retiring from public office at the expiration of this term, he remained in comparative seclusion until 1870, when he appeared before the State Republican Convention of Missouri as a candidate for the gubernatorial nomination. His pet issue then was complete amnesty to Rebel citizens of the State, who were disfranchised by the then existing State constitution—an instrument which, as will afterwards appear, Brown had helped to get adopted. Failing to secure the nomination, he, with Schurz and others, organized a bolt and a coalition with the Democracy. This proved immensely successful, and Brown became Governor,—an office which he still holds.

CHARACTERISTIC TRAITS.

By temperament and talent, Brown is a sensationalist. Upon whatever course he may resolve, he goes at once to the extreme of it, that he may thereby startle the community and attract its notice. He is not so much a pioneer of the army of progress, keeping in front a clearing away the obstacles, as he is a volunteer aid-de-camp or a privileged straggler, galloping about, finding conspicuous and commanding heights, ascending them and shouting to the marching masses, "See here! Here I am—Brown! You daren't come up here, boys!" Brown is a fire-eater, and the direction of his extremism depends upon that of the current of thought upon the community upon which he proposes to operate. He is now, and has been since the agitation in Missouri, in 1870, fierce for complete amnesty. It would hardly be thought by Brown's present partisans, except by those who know the ultraism of the man's character, that he would have uttered such words as these in a public speech:

"It is not within the thought of this nation and this people that they who have engaged in this resistance and rebellion, whether openly in arms or stealthily by device and falsehood shall EVER in the future have the means of controlling our institutions or shaping our policies. FRANCHISE IS NOT FOR SUCH—CANNOT BE FOR SUCH—WILL NOT BE FOR SUCH. Power and position belong of right to the loyal, for self-preservation knows no higher law. In the revolted states this is peculiarly the case—but the limit will not be territorial; it will go wherever rebellion has gone or shall go, *or shall enkindle a kindred sympathy to manifest itself.* The valor of the nation has gone forth to peril life—all of life—to carry forward that progress which promises a nationalty of freedom to our union; and think ye that it is within the endurances of human nature that they who remain at home to thwart such high purposes will be permitted to repose on beds of peace and fructify in the abuse of power and influence? God's providence has not so ordered it heretofore in this world, and there is no reason to believe otherwise than that, as it has been in other annals and like progressions from the people, so will it be in ours *to the fullest measure of* RETALIATION. Escape will be the exception, visitation the rule, for the evidences of treason, rebellion, sympathy, are too plain to escape detection."

ETERNAL PROSCRIPTION STILL HIS POLICY IN 1865.

And yet he said precisely this—and his whole speech on the subject was of the same purport—at St. Louis on the 27th of August, 1863. But this, it may be said, was during the prevalence of the war, and under the stimulus of Mr. Brown's loyal feeling, and peace would bring a revulsion of his sentiments. But let those who think thus read also Brown's letter to J. R. Winchell, Esq., of Hannibal, written in 1865, *after the close of the war*, and republished in Mr. Winchell's paper, the Hannibal *Courier* of May 8, 1872. The following is an extract. He is arguing with his correspondent in favor of the new Constitution, and adduces as its first point the precise provision which was so odious to him a little while after—at least by opposing which he then got into office. He says:

"Upon reading it, however, I find two provisions that go very far to redeem it, and that certainly make it preferable to the old. First, the provision authorizing the Legislature to amend, by a majority vote, approved by the people. Second, the registration of voters, and the disfranchisement of Rebels, on proofs submitted to the registers. My remark about eternizing our hostilities was an epitome of the idea that oaths had failed to exclude Rebels, and only keep alive their identity and irritation in our midst, and if the Constitution intend hereafter to rely on oaths alone, it would be a failure. *I need scarcely say that I am one of those who have from the beginning believed that the loyal and the disloyal can NEVER live in Missouri together, and the latter must be FORCED to depart, and I believe that registration is the only mode that will accomplish it.* * * * Will you be kind enough to return or destroy my note to you some days since, as it may fall into the hands of those who would not know the qualifications that attend it, and might use it dangerously."

And but for Mr. Brown's care to cover his tracks by having the earlier letter destroyed, it is quite likely that we might find something therein still more highly flavored with the doctrine of *eternal hate* which he was then inculcating. There is no law against a man's changing his opinions; but the rule of common sense dictates, where a man's opinion undergoes such frequent and such violent changes as those of Governor Brown, noted in this case, the value of those opinions decrease with each change.

BROWN ON EDUCATION.

We have said that Brown is a sensationalist. This quality of his mind was illustrated in the summer of 1871 by a remarkable address which he made before the National Convention of School-Teachers, which met at St. Louis. Wishing to advocate to them a greater proportion of moral culture in their courses of instruction, he overshot his mark entirely, and gave them a discourse which must have been revolting to the sentiments of his hearers, denouncing the whole system of American education, and declaring that the public schools of the country were the firebrands of society, and much more conducive to immorality than absolute ignorance; his theory being that education makes a youth ambitious—and that ambition makes him unprincipled! He seemed to forget that children have any other means of moral instruction except the public school, and slashed away, thick and heavy, in behalf of some sort of a moral-precept machine whereby the evils of which he complained might be remedied, and the teachers whom he addressed deprived of their poisonous fangs. This speech was applauded by the Chicago *Tribune*.

WHY SOME THINGS ARE THUS.

It is generally understood among those familiar

with the habits of Governor Brown, that the extraordinary theories and sentiments which he is apt to advance in public ways are not so much the result of the consumption of midnight oil, as of some other liquid, more volatile in its properties. St. Louis is a convivial city, and politics, as run by Brown, is a demoralizing business to the habits of its votaries. The result upon a man of sanguine temperament can be easily imagined. Some of Mr. Brown's most brilliant and startling oratory has been delivered on banquet occasions, at an hour when reporting is impracticable, hence they have been lost to the world. It is related that Frank Blair, whose habits are also convivial, and who is not himself noted for his continence of language, has been seen to pluck the Governor by the coat, in the midst of the latter's most extravagant flights of oratory, when the table was in a roar, and exclaim spiritedly, "Good, Governor! Good, by ———! Go ahead, Governor! make a —— —— fool of yourself. That will read well in the morning. (Hic) hurrah!"

It must in candor be admitted by Governor Brown's enemies that he reforms his habits frequently, and is every few months as rabid a teetotaler and Maine law man as he was the opposite a month before, and it is more than likely that, at least until the present campaign is over, he will be as good a temperance man as his companion upon the Democratic ticket.

In person, Governor Brown is of the medium

hight, very slender of figure and immediately noticeable for his wealth of red hair and beard. The color is very pronounced, and hence our engraving, in plain black and white, cannot adequately portray his most distinguishing feature. In short, he is, like his companion upon the Democratic ticket, exactly the man whom an observer would not select for a place requiring, as the Presidency or the Vice Presidency does, a large degree of dignity, reserved force, calmness of manner, consistency of purpose and equability of temper. None of these can justly be attributed to B. Gratż Brown.

APPENDIX.

DOCUMENTS, STATISTICS, CAMPAIGN NOTES.

Greeley's Letter of Acceptance—Henry Wilson's Ditto—Scraps From Greeley's Paper—A Secessionist through 1860, '61, '62—Converted to Republicanism—Eulogizes Grant's Administration Repeatedly—What the Tribune Said for Grant in 1870 and 1871—Sumner's Falsehood Concerning Stanton Exposed—"Bayonet Legislation"—Of What it Consists—The New Tax Law—Burdens Lifted from the People—Interesting National Debt Statement—Election Statistics—National and State Governments—Presidential Tickets in the Field—Expose of Greeley's Intriguing for the Democratic Nomination in 1871.

HORACE GREELEY'S LETTER OF ACCEPTANCE:

New York, May 20, 1872.

Gentlemen: I have chosen not to acknowledge your letter of the 3d inst. until I could learn how the work of your Convention was received in all parts of our great country, and judge whether that work was approved and ratified by the mass of our fellow citizens. Their response has from day to day reached me through telegrams, letters, and the comments of journalists independent of official patronage and indifferent to the smiles or frowns of power. The number and character of these unconstrained, unpurchased, unsolicited utterances satisfy me that the movement which found expression at Cincinnati has received the stamp of public approval, and been hailed by a majority of our countrymen as the harbinger of a better day for the Republic.

I do not misinterpret this approval as especially complimentary to myself, nor even to the chivalrous and justly esteemed gentleman with whose name I thank your Convention for associating mine. I receive and welcome it as a spontaneous and deserved tribute to that admirable Platform of principles, wherein your Convention so tersely, so lucidly, so forcibly, set forth the convictions which impelled and the purposes which guided its course—a Platform which, casting behind it the wreck and rubbish of worn-out contentions and by-gone feuds, embodies in fit and few words the needs and aspirations of To-Day. Though thousands stand ready to condemn your every act, hardly a syllable of criticism or cavil has been aimed at your Platform, of which the substance may be fairly epitomized as follows:

1. All the political rights and franchises which have been acquired through our late bloody convulsion must and shall be guaranteed, maintained, enjoyed, respected, evermore.

2. All the political rights and franchises which have been lost through that convulsion should and must be promptly restored and re-established, so that there shall be henceforth no proscribed class and no disfranchised caste within the limits of our Union, whose long estranged people shall re-unite and fraternize upon the broad basis of Universal Amnesty with Impatial Suffrage.

3. That, subject to our solemn constitutional obligation to maintain the equal rights of all citizens, our policy should aim at local self-government, and not at centralization; that the civil authority should be supreme over the military; that the writ of *habeas corpus* should be jealously upheld as the safeguard of personal freedom; that the individual citizen should enjoy the largest liberty consistent with public order; and that there shall be no Federal subversion of the internal polity of the several States and municipalities, but that each shall be left free to enforce the rights and promote the well-being of its inhabitants by such means as the judgment of its own people shall prescribe.

4. There shall be a real and not merely a simulated reform in the Civil Service of the Republic; to which end it is indispensable that the chief dispenser of its vast official patronage shall be shielded from the main temptation to use his power selfishly, by a rule inexorably forbidding and precluding his re-election.

5. That the raising of Revenue, whether by Tariff or otherwise, shall be recognized and treated as the People's immediate business, to be shaped and directed by them through their Representatives in Congress, whose action thereon the President must neither over-

rule by his veto, attempt to dictate, nor presume to punish, by bestowing office only on those who agree with him or withdrawing it from those who do not.

6. That the Public Lands must be sacredly reserved for occupation and acquisition by cultivators, and not recklessly squandered on the projectors of Railroads for which our people have no present need, and the premature construction of which is annually plunging us into deeper and deeper abysses of foreign indebtedness.

7. That the achievement of these grand purposes of universal beneficence is expected and sought at the hands of all who approve them, irrespective of past affiliations.

8. That the public faith must at all hazards be maintained, and the National credit preserved.

9. That the patriotic devotedness and inestimable services of our fellow-citizens who, as soldiers or sailors, upheld the flag and maintained the unity of the Republic shall ever be gratefully remembered and honorably requited.

These propositions, so ably and forcibly presented in the Platform of your Convention, have already fixed the attention and commanded the assent of a large majority of our countryman, who joyfully adopt them, as I do, as the basis of a true, beneficient National Reconstruction—of a New Departure from jealousies, strifes, and hates, which have no longer adequate motive or even plausible pretext, into an atmosphere of Peace, Fraternity, and Mutual Good Will. In vain do the drill-sergeants of decaying organizations flourish menacingly their truncheons and angrily insist that the files shall be closed and straightened; in vain do the whippers-in of parties once vital because rooted in the vital needs of the hour protest against straying and bolting, denounce men nowise their inferiors as traitors and renegades, and threaten them with infamy and ruin. I am confident that the American People have already made your cause their own, fully resolved that their brave hearts and strong arms shall bear it on to triumph. In this faith, and with the distinct understanding that, if elected, I shall be the President not of a party, but of the whole People, I accept your nomination, in the confident trust that the masses of our countrymen, North and South, are eager to clasp hands across the bloody chasm which has too long divided them, forgetting that they have been enemies in the joyful consciousness that they are and must henceforth remain brethren

Yours, gratefully,
HORACE GREELEY.

To Hon. Carl Schurz, President; Hon. George W. Julian, Vice-President; and Messrs. William E. McLean, John G. Davidson, J. H. Rhodes, Secretaries of the National Convention of the Liberal Republicans of the United States.

HENRY WILSON'S LETTER OF ACCEPTANCE.

WASHINGTON, June 14, 1872.

Hon. Thomas Settle and others, President and Vice-President National Republican Convention, held at Philadelphia:

GENTLEMEN: Your note of the 10th inst., conveying to me the action of the Convention in placing my name in nomination for the office of Vice-President, is before me. I need not give you assurance of my grateful appreciation of the high honor conferred upon me by this action of the fifth National Convention of the Republican party. Sixteen years ago, in the same city, was held the first meeting of men who, amid the darkness and doubts of that hour of slaveholding ascendancy and aggression, had assembled in National Convention to confer with each other on the exigencies to which that fearful domination had brought their country. After a full conference, the highest point of resolve they could reach, the most they dared to recommend, was an avowed purpose to prohibit the existence of slavery in the Territories.

Last week the same party met, by its representatives from thirty-seven States and ten Territories, at the same great centre of wealth, intelligence, and power, to review the past, take note of the present, and indicate its line of action for the future. As typical facts and headlands of the nation's recent history, there sat on its platform, taking a prominent and honorable part in its proceedings, admitted on terms of perfect equality to the leading hotels of the city, not only the colored representatives of the race which were ten years before in abject slavery, but one of the oldest and most prominent of the once despised Abolitionists, to whom was accorded, as to no other, the warmest demonstrations of popular regard and esteem, an ovation, not to him alone, but the cause he had so ably, and for so many years represented, and to men and women living and dead, who had toiled through long years of obloquy and self sacrifice for the glorious fruition of that hour. It hardly needed the brilliant summary of its platform to set forth its illustrious achievements. The very presence of those men was alone significant of the victories already achieved, the progress already made, and the great distance which the nation had traveled between the years of 1856 and 1872.

But grand as has been its record, the Republican party rests not on its past alone. It looks to the future, and grapples with its problems of duty and danger. It professes, as objects of its immediate accomplishment, complete liberty and equality for all; the enforcement of the present amendments to the national constitution; reform in the civil service; the national domain to be set apart for homes to the people; the adjustment of duties on imports so as to secure remunerative wages to labor; extention of bounties to all soldiers and sailors who in the line of duty became disabled; continued and careful encouragement and protection of voluntary immigration and guarding with zealous care the rights of all adopted citizens; abolition of the franking privilege, and speedy reduction of the rates of postage; reduction of the national debt and rates of interest and resumption of specie payment; encouragement of American commerce and of ship-building; suppression of violence and protection of the ballot-box. It also placed on record the opinions and purposes of the party in favor of amnesty, against all forms of repudiation, and indorsed the humane and peaceful policy of the administration in regard to the Indians.

But while clearly defining and distinctly announcing the policy of the Republican party on these questions of practical legislation and administration, the Convention did not ignore the great social problems which are pressing their claims for solution, and which demand the most careful study and wise consideration.

Foremost stands the labor question.

Concerning the relations of capital and labor, the Republican party accepts the duty of so shaping legislation as to secure full protection and the amplest field for capital and for labor, the creation of capital, the largest opportunities and just share of the mutual profits of these two great servants of civilization.

To woman, too, and her new demands, it extends the hand of grateful recognition, and proffers its most respectful inquiry. It recognizes her noble devotion to the country and freedom; welcomes her admission to wider fields of usefulness, and commends her demands for additional rights to the calm and careful consideration of the nation.

To guard well what has already has been secured, to work out faithfully and wisely what is now in hand, and to consider the questions which are looming up to view but a little way before us, the Republican party is to-day what it was in the gloomy days of slavery, rebellion, and reconstruction—a national necessity. It appeals, therefore, for support to the patriotic and liberty-loving; to the just and humane; to all who would dignify labor; to all who would educate, elevate, and lighten the burdens of the sons and daughters of toil. With its great record, the work still to be done, and under the great soldier whose historic renown, and whose successful administration for the last three years begot such popular confidence, the Republican party may confidently, in the language of the Convention you represent "start on a new march to victory."

Having accepted, thirty-six years ago, the distinguishing doctrines of the Republican party of to-day; having during years of that period, for their advancement, subordinated all other issues, acting in and cooperating with political organizations with whose leading doctrines I sometimes had neither sympathy nor belief; having labored incessantly for many years to found and build up the Republican party, and having during its existence taken an humble part in its grand work, I gratefully accept the nomination thus tendered, and shall endeavor, if it shall be ratified by the people, faithfully to perform the duties it imposes.

Respectfully yours,
HENRY WILSON.

GREELEY FOR SECESSION.

THE "TRIBUNE" DEFENDS THE RIGHT TO SECEDE.

[From the N. Y. Tribune, November 9. 1860.]

And now, if the cotton States consider the value of the Union debatable, we maintain their perfect right to discuss it. Nay, we hold with Jefferson to the inalienable right of communities to alter or abolish forms of government that have become oppressive or injurious; and, if the cotton States shall decide that they can do better outside of the Union than in it, we insist in letting them go in peace. The right to secede may be a revolutionary one, but it exists, nevertheless; and we do not see how one party can have a right to do what another party has a right to prevent. We must ever resist the asserted right of any State to remain in the Union, and nullify or defy the laws thereof; to withdraw from the Union is quite another matter. And, whenever a considerable section of our Union shall deliberately resolve to go out, we shall resist all coercive measures designed to keep it in. We hope never to live in a republic whereof one section is pinned to the residue by bayonets.

AS MUCH RIGHT AS THE COLONISTS HAD TO REVOLT IN 1776.

[From the N. Y. Tribune, Dec. 13, 1860].

We have repeatedly asked those who dissent from our view of this matter to tell us frankly whether they do or do not assent to Mr. Jefferson's statement in the Declaration of Independence, that Governments "derive their just powers from the consent of the governed; and that whenever any form of government becomes destructive of those ends, it is the right of the people to alter or abolish it, and to institute a new Government," &c., &c. We do heartily accept this doctrine, believing it intrinsically sound beneficent, and one that, universally accepted, is calculated to prevent the shedding of seas of human blood. And if it justified the secession from the British Empire of three millions of colonists in 1776, we do not see why it would not justify the secession of five millions of Southrons from the Federal Uuion in 1861. If we are mistaken on this point, why does not some one attempt to show wherein and why? For our own part, while we deny the right of slaveholders to hold slaves against the will of the latter, we cannot see how twenty millions of people can rightfully hold ten, or even five, in a detested union with them, by military force.

Of course, we understand that the principle of Jefferson, like any other broad generalization, may be pushed to extreme and baleful consequences. We can see why Governor's Island should not be at liberty to secede from the State and nation and allow herself to be covered with French and British batteries commanding and threatening our city. There is hardly a great principle which may not be thus "run into the ground." But if seven or eight contiguous States shall present themselves authentically at Washington, saying, "We hate the federal Union; we have withdrawn from it; we give you the choice between acquiescing in our secession and arranging amicably all incidently questions on the one hand, and attempting to subdue us on the other"—we could not stand up for coercion, for subjugation, for we do not think it would be just. We hold the right of self-government sacred, even when invoked in behalf of those who deny it to others. So much for the question of principle.

Now as to the matter of policy:

South Carolina will certainly secede. Several other cotton States will probably follow her example. The border States are evidently reluctant to do likewise. South Carolina has grossly insulted them by her dictatorial, reckless course. What she expects and desires is a clash of arms with the Federal government, which will at once commend her to the sympathy and co-operation of every slave State, and to the sympathy, at least, of the pro-slavery minority in the free States. It is not difficult to see that this would speedily work a political revolution, which would restore to slavery all, and more than all, it has lost by the canvass of 1860.

We fear that Southern madness may precipitate a bloody collision that all must deplore. But if ever "seven or eight States" send agents to Washington to say, "We want to go out of the Union," we shall feel constrained by our devotion to human liberty to say, Let them go! And we do not see how we could take the other side without coming in direct conflict with those rights of man which we hold paramount to all political arrangements, however convenient and advantageous.

NO RIGHT TO COERCE THE SOUTHERN STATES.

[From the N. Y. Tribune, Dec. 24, 1860.]

Most certainly we believe that governments are made for peoples, not peoples for governments—that the latter "derive their just power from the consent of the governed," and whenever a portion of this Union, large enough to form an independent, self-subsisting nation, shall see fit to say, authentically, to the residue, "We want to get away from you," we shall say—and we trust self-respect, if not regrad for the principle of self-government, will constrain the residue of the American people to say—"Go?" We never yet had so poor an opinion of ourselves or our neighbors as to wish to hold others in a hated connection with us. But the dissolution of a government cannot be effected in the time required for knocking down a house of cards. Let the cotton States, or any six or more States, say, unequivocally, "We want to get out of the Union," and propose to effect their end peaceably and inoffensively, and we will do our best to help them out—not that we want them to go, but that we loathe the idea of compelling them to stay. All we ask is that they exercise a reasonable patience, so as to give time for affecting their end without bloodshed. They must know, as well as we do, that no President can recognize a mere State ordinance of secession, nor neglect to enforce the laws of the United States throughout their whole geographical extent. It takes two to make a bargain, whether of admission or secession; but with reasonable forbearance all may be brought about.

THE MORAL RIGHT OF SECESSION.

[From the N. Y. Tribune of 23d of February, 1861, Five days After the "Inauguration" of Jeff. Davis].

We have repeatedly said, and we once more insist, that the great principle embodied by Jefferson in the Declaration of American Independence, that Governments derive their just powers from the consent of the governed, is sound and just; and that if the slave States, the cotton States, or the Gulf States only choose to form an independent nation, they have a clear moral right to do so. We have said, and still maintain, that provided the cotton States have fully and definitively made up their minds to go by themselves, there is no need of fighting about it; for they have only to exercise reasonable patience and they will be let off in peace and good will. Whenever it shall be clear that the great body of the Southern people have become conclusively alienated from the Union, and anxious to escape from it, we will do our best to forward their views.

MR. GREELEY IN 1862.

[In a letter to H. McChesney, of Troy, N. Y., dated September 23, 1862, and published in the New York Tribune of the 26th of the same month, Horace Greeley, speaking of the right of secession, thus declared himself:]

"But I still insist that, if it had been proved that the people of the slave States—or even of the cotton States alone—had really desired to dissolve the Union, and had peacefully, deliberately and authoritatively expressed that wish, we should have assented to it. At all events, *I* should."

Adult readers will rememper that when the secession fever broke out in the South, the Hon Alexander H. Stephens opposed the vile heresy, and delivered one of the ablest speeches of his life in the Georgia Convention in opposition. It may not be known to them that the only answer ever made to that eloquent appeal to remain in the Union and support the government was the reading to the Convention by Robert Toombs of an editorial written by Horace Greeley, from the New York *Tribune*, wherein the right of the South to secede was conceded and placed on the same high plane of conduct with that of our revolutionary fathers when they seceded from Creat Britain.

GREELEY EULOGIZES GRANT'S ADMINISTRATION.

[From the N. Y. Tribune, March 4, 1870.]

The quotations of gold, which have been steadily and rapidly going down during the past fortnight, fell yesterday till the premium reached the vicinity of 113, fluctuating the greater part of the day a few fractions above that point, but at one time striking a fraction below it. The quotations of government bonds indicated, during the day, that they were on the verge of par in gold, most of the varieties being worth but little less than gold, while one variety was at a gold premium over its face value.

That the day of which we are able to chronicle these highly favored financial facts was also the day that marks the termination of the first year of President Grant's administration of public affairs, is a circumstance which the country will not lose sight of, and which the friends of the President will witness with unfeigned joy.

No one who has observed the fluctuations will believe that there is any more likelihood of gold returning to 130 than there is of its returning to 200. It has not gone down through speculative combinations, but through the operations of general causes that are not within the control of the Gold Room.

The things, however, for which the administration deserves the highest credit in connection with the improvement in our financial condition, are such as relate to the carrying out of Grant's policy of honesty and retrenchment. When, by his election, the country and the world received assurances that the financial honor of the government would be maintained; when the policy of repudiation was spurned by the people, and Congress gave its pledge to support the public credit by paying the principal and interest on the debt in gold—the first great steps towards financial redemption were taken. When Grant announced his brief and simple policy for remedying the confusion of our financial state; when he began carrying out practically the programme he had announced, it was evident that we were about to take a long stride toward the settlement of our troubles. But a year's experience of this policy had gone far beyond public expectation. To say that the debt had been decreased during the year of his administration $100,000,000 is but to represent a small part of what has actually been achieved. To say that during the first half of the current year the revennes were increased by more faithful collection, at the rate of $30,000,000 a year over the previous year, does not indicate the actual result gained for the public treasury. To say that the expenses of the government have been vastly reduced, and that the interest has been decreased by the diminution of the debt is only to give a hint of the retrenchment that has been carried out. But these things have told with immense effect upon our financial condition, and it is to the admirable policy and action of the administration that we owe the improvement which is now going on to its consummation.

A Democratic paper recently took the trouble to attempt to show that neither Grant nor his policy deserved any credit for the brightening financial outlook. But Grant and his policy deserve the very highest credit. Suppose his policy had been of a different kind from what it has been. Suppose he had collected the revenue in the reckless manner of which we had so much previous experience. Suppose the debt had been increased as it was in the latter part of Johnson's administration—suppose the wasteful expenditures of Johnson's time had been continued—suppose we were experimenting with greenback theory and the repudiation fraud—does anybody suppose that our bonds would now be at or near par, or that gold would be quoted at the present price, or that our credit would stand where it does abroad? To ask the question is to answer it, and to show the absurdity of the reasoning of the Democratic organ.

It is not by the display of any immense genius, or of any gigantic or mysterious "plan" that these great results have been wrought. It is by the carrying out of a few simple principles, the principles of *honesty* and *economy*, which President Grant announced one year ago. There can be no more beneficent natural genius than is found in the power to perceive and enforce those principles. And having aided in the election of Grant, it gives us pride and joy to be able, at the close of the first year of his administration, to point the country to the results that have already been achieved—to speak of the growth of the national welfare, as shown in the financial improvement no less than in the consummation of the peaceful policy of reconstruction.

MEANING OF A DEMOCRATIC VICTORY.

[From the N. Y. Tribune, February, 1871.]

We like Gen. Grant; but we care more for Republican ascendancy than for any man's personal fortunes. It is in our view of great importance that the opposition shall be kept out of power, whilst it is of comparatively small moment that A or B should tenant the White House. For a Democratic national triumph means a restoration to power of those who deserted their seats in Congress and their places under the last Democratic President to plunge the country into the Red Sea of Secession and Rebellion. Though you paint an inch thick, to this complexion you must come at last. The brain, the heart, the soul, of the present Democratic party is the rebel element at the South with its Northern allies and sympathizers. It is rebel to the core to-day, hardly able to reconcile the defeats of Lee, Johnson, Bragg, Hood and Price, and the consequent downfall of its faith in Divine Providence. It would hail the election of a Democratic President in 1872, as a virtual reversal of the Appomatox surrender. It would come into power with the hate, the chagrin, the wrath, the mortification, of ten bitter years, to impel and guide its steps. It would devote itself to taking off or reducing tax after tax until the Treasury was deprived of the means of paying interest on the national debt, and would hail the tidings of national bankruptcy with unalloyed gladness and unconcealed exultation. Whatever chastisement may be deserved by our national sins, we must hope that this disgrace and humiliation will be spared us.

GRANT'S GENIUS.

A DEMOCRATIC TRIBUTE —— "SOLID WORK"— NOT MERE SHOW.

[From the N. Y. World, April 11, 1865.]

Gen. Grant's history should teach us to discriminate better than we Americans are apt to do between glitter and *solid work*. Our proneness to run after demagogues and spouters may find a wholesome corrective in the study of such a character as his. The qualities by which great things are accomplished are here seen to have no necessary connection with showy and superficial accomplishments. When the mass of men look upon such a character they may learn a truer respect for themselves and each other; they are taught by it that *high qualities and great abilities* are consistent with the simplicity of taste, contempt for parade, and plainness of manners with which direct and earnest men have a strong natural sympathy. Ulysses Grant the tanner, Ulysses Grant the unsuccessful applicant for the post of City Surveyor of St. Louis, Ulysses Grant, the driver into that city of his two-horse team with a load of wood to sell, had within him *every manly quality* which will cause the name of Lieutenant General Grant to live forever in history. His career is a lesson in practical democracy; it is a quiet satire on the dandyism, the puppyism and the shallow affectation of our fashionable exquisites as well as upon the swagger of our plausible, glib-tongued demagogues. Not by any means that great qualities are inconsistent with cultivated manners and a fluent elocution; but that such superficial accomplishments are no measure of worth or ability.

THE GREATEST OF ALL COMMANDERS.

General Grant's last brilliant campaign sets the final seal upon his reputation. It stamps him as the superior of his able antagonist as well as of all the commanders that have served with or under him in the great campaigns of the last year.

* * * * * * * * * * * *

Grant stands *pre-eminent among all the Generals* who have served in this war in the completeness of his final results. He has owed nothing to accident; and, both in the West and the East, he has accomplished the most arduous things that were to be done. Gen. Grant has exhibited the utmost strength of will of which the *highest type of manhood* is capable. The defenses of Vicksburg and the defenses of Richmond were both deemed impregnable, and were defended with a proportionable confidence and obstinacy; but they both yielded, at last, to Grant's matchless persistence and unequalled strategy. And, in both cases, he not only took the long-contested positions, but compelled the surrender of the whole force defending them. Nothing could be more clean and complete, even in imagination, than Gen. Grant's masterly execution. He did not merely, in each case, acquire a position which was the key of a wide theatre of operations; he did not merely beat or disable the opposing force; he left no fragment of it in existence except as prisoners of war subject to his disposal.

HIS "SURENESS OF JUDGMENT."

If anybody is so obtuse or so wrong-headed as to see nothing great in Gen. Grant beyond his marvelous tenacity of will, let that doubter explain, if he can, how has it happened that, since Grant rose to high command, this quality has always been exerted in conspicuous energy precisely at the point on which everything in his whole sphere of operations hinged. There has been no display of great qualities on small occasions; no expenditure of herculean effort to accomplish objects not of the first magnitude. It is only a very *clear-sighted and a very comprehensive mind* that could always thus have laid the whole emphasis of an indomitable soul so precisely on the emphatic place. How, if he be not a General of the first order of intellect, as well as the most heroic determination, does it happen that in assigning great and brilliant parts to his subordinate commanders, he has never, when the results of his strategy were fully unfolded, appeared in the picture except as the central figure? However it may seem during the progress of one of his great combined campaigns, it always turns out at last, when it reaches that completeness and finish in which he contrives to have his campaigns end, that we see him standing in the foreground, and that the grouping is always such that the glory of the other generals, instead of eclipsing his own, gives it additional luster?

It is this sureness of judgment which sees precisely what are the objects that justify the utmost stretch of persistence; it is this ability to take in the whole field of view in just perspective and due subordination of parts, that is the mark of a superior mind. Gen. Grant has taken out of the hands of critics the question whether it belongs to him. He has won his greatest triumph over the most skillful and accomplished general on the other side; over a general who foiled him long enough to prove his great mastery of the art of war; and the completeness of whose defeat is a testimony to Grant's genius such as a victory over any other general of the Confederacy, or even an earlier victory over Lee himself could not have given. Apply to Gen. Grant what test you will; measure him by the magnitude of the obstacles he has surmounted, by the value of the positions he has gained, by the fame of the antagonist over whom he has triumphed, by the achievements of his most illustrious co-workers, by the sureness with which he directs his indomitable energy to the vital point which is the key of a vast field of operations, or by that supreme test of consummate ability, the absolute completeness of his results, and he vindicates his claim to stand next after Napoleon and Wellington, among the great soldiers of this country, if not on a level with the latter.

SUMNER'S FALSEHOOD CONCERNING STANTON.

[From Sumner's speech in U. S. Senate, May 31. 1872.]

"Something also must be attributed to individual character; and here I express no opinion of my own; I shall allow another to speak in solemn words echoed from the tomb.

"My last visit [to Stanton] was marked by a communication never to be forgotten. As I entered his bedroom, where I found him reclining on a sofa, propped by pillows, he reached out his hand, already clamy cold, and in reply to my inquiry, 'How are you?' answered, 'Waiting for my furlough.' Then at once with singular solemnity he said, 'I have something to say to you.' When I was seated he proceeded without one word of introduction: 'I know General Grant better than any other person in the country can know him. It was my duty to study him, and I did so night and day, when I saw him and when I did not see him, and now I tell you what I know, he cannot govern this country.' I observed, 'What you say is very broad.' It is as true as it is broad,' he replied promptly. I added' 'You are tardy: you tell this late; why did you not say it before his nomination?' He answered that he was not consulted about the nomination, and had no opportunity of expressing his opinion upon it, besides being much occupied at the time by his duties as Secretary of War and his contest with the President. I followed by saying, 'But you took part in the presidential election, and made a succession of speeches for him in Ohio and Pennsylvania.' 'I spoke,' said he, 'but I never introduced the name of General Grant. I spoke for the Republican party and the Republican cause.' This was the last time I saw Mr Stanton. A few days later I followed him to the grave where he now rests."

[Extract from Stanton's Speech at Steubenville, O., Sept. 25, 1868.]

"Grant stands this day before us the foremost military commander in the world, with peace for his watchword. [Applause.] Why should he not be elected? What reason has any lover of his country for not voting for him? By his side stands Schuyler Colfax, who, by his own energy, good character and industry, advanced from the printing office to the Speaker's chair, and for three successive terms has filled that high office with honor and distinction. Honest and upright men have been nominated for your representatives in Congress, pledged to stand by Grant and the country. Why, then, again I ask, should he and they not receive your support? The history of Grant is known to you and the whole world. Educated at West Point, he served with distinction through the Mexican war, and when it was ended, unwilling to be a drone, resigned his commission, and engaged in the pursuits of civil life. Leaving his peaceful pursuits at the commencement of the rebelllon, he joined the army, and soon advanced to the rank of major general commanding an army. After varied and important services, he moved upon the enemy's works at Donelson, and compelled their commander, Buckner, to surrender with 18,000 prisoners of war. Soon after he grappled with Beauregard, on the field of Shiloh, and drove him and his routed army from the field. Resolved to open the navigation of the Mississippi river, he ran its batteries, fought and defeated Gen. Johnson, chased the rebel general Pemberton into Vicksburg, and forced him to surrender with 30,000 prisoners of war. [Applause.] Advanced to the command of all the armies of the West, he fought and defeated Bragg at Chattanooga, shattered his army and delivered that vast territory from the hands of the rebels. Advanced still higher, as Lieutenant-General he changed his headquarters to the Potomac. Forty days' marching and fighting through the Wilderness drove Lee and his army into Richmond. Compelled to evacuate that city, Lee was chased to Appomattox Court-House, and forced to surrender himself and his arms and men as prisoners of war, which practically brought the war to an end. [Applause.] And now I ask, what reason has any man to vote against Gen. Grant? *His capacity and integrity for civil administration were equally manifest in the vast territories in which he operated.*"

[Mr. Stanton continued in the some strain some minutes further, and in other speeches during the campaign—particularly one at Philadelphia, enforced upon his hearers the merits of Gen. Grant as a patriot, a general and a wise administrator. Senator Carpenter in his speech in the Senate, June 3d, 1872, thus further exposes the falsehood of Sumner's statement: "I know," he says, (and Mr. Carpenter was an intimate associate of Stanton's in those days,) "that in the serious illness which terminated so disastrously, he frequently had occasion to refer to the course of the Administration, to matters that were pending in Congress, and I do know, and I can testify, and I hold it to be my solemn duty to testify, that in all those interviews, from first to last, from the time I first made his accquaintance down to the hour of his death, I never heard him say of General Grant anything that was not of the kindest nature and of the highest praise * * * *

But the quotations I have made are sufficient to show either that Mr. Stanton on his death-bed uttered a falsehood to the Senator from Massachusetts, a falsehood which he must have known to be susceptible of easy contradiction by reference to the reports of his speeches during that campaign, or that the Senator from Massachusetts deliberately falsified Mr. Stanton; and I am content that the American people shall judge between them."]

BAYONET LEGISLATION.

OF WHAT IT CONSISTS.

[From the Utica (N. Y.) Herald.]

Some of the pretexts which are given for opposition to the national administration and the Republican party, come with a particularly ill grace from those who make them. Conspicuously, the charge of centralization of power, of "bayonet-legislation," illustrates the weakness of those who have taken active part in all the acts for establishing order at the South, and who now denounce those measures in the height of their success. The great steps toward "centralization," if any have been taken, are the amendments to the National Constitution, perfecting emancipation, conferring civil rights, maintaining the National credit, and assuring a free ballot. Is it against these that assault is now to be directed? If this is the offense of the Republican party, let a proclimation be issued, and let the verdict of the country be pronounced. For in those amendments are written the victories of the war. Beginning there, a cry against centralization is intelligible. The persons who deny the validity of these new guaranteees of freedom, which, for the first time, under our Republican system complete and symmetrical, submit for adjudication a question which the American people will not be slow to decide.

Out of these amendments have sprung two, and only two, laws of especial importance. A constitution will not inforce itself. Statutes must apply their principles, and assign the duties of Courts. So far as criticism is directed against the administration, it runs against laws enacted, and no pretense is put forward that the President has exceed by an iota his legal authority. The two laws to which partisans now take exception are the enforcement act and the Ku-Klux act. Neither of these involves a claim for federal sovreignty so broad and sweeping as is embodied in the internal revenue law. That puts the strong hand on the citizen and his property, and enters his home and extorts the inmost secrets of his life. The Republican party makes haste to mitigate and remove that necessity of the war, with little help from Democrats or their new allies. Of that inqusitorial and arbitary exercise of national power, our enemies say little, for the speedy removal of it is one of the greatest triumphs of the present administrations and of the Republican party in Congress.

Upon two laws, then, the indictment must proceed, if at all. The enforcement act was passed, May 31, 1870, and its purpose and character are designated by its title: "To enforce the right of citizens of the United States to vote in the several States of the Union who have hitherto been denied that right on account of race, color or previous condition of servitude." The law naturally and wisely limited and defined the methods by which the rights of our new citizens should be secured, and one of its leading features is the placing in the courts of powers which might have been confided to the exeeutive. Eor example, the officers designated to watch and verify registry and elections, are appointed by the courts. Observe the time and circumstances which called for this law. The validity of the amendments was denied by a great party and by many States. They must be enforced. The mode was not left to the choice of the President. It was carefully defined by written statute, and so far as could be, the duty was imposed on the courts. Even Senator Trumbull supported the bill on its passage. His intense dread of "bayonet legislation" took no alarm at its provisions. Clearly the "Liberals" do not base their charges against the Republican party upon the enforcement act of 1870.

In 1871 the Democratic minority of a committee of the Senate of the United States, speaking of North Carolinia, said: "All the disorders which exist in that State, were created by the unjustifiable and unconstitutional legislation of Congress, in regard to its government." So Democratic Senators admitted that disorders existed, and they were political in character. What was true of North Carolina, was true in a worse degree of other States. Murder, mutilation, and outrages were perpetrated on unnoffensive citizens only because they were Republicans. An investigation committee was appointed; the KuKlux law was passed; and to many States, almost wholly, and to all in good part, quiet and order have been restored. This has been done by due process of law, except that an executive proclamation of warning was issued in two cases. This law after full discussion, was passed. The *Tribune* earnestly demanded it. Among others Senators Fenton, Schurz, Trumbull, Tipton, who are now "Liberal" apostles, and denounce bitterly "bayonet legislation," claimed to be good Republicans after its passage. Clearly their antagonism is not to the Ku Klux act of 1871, which has achieved such benificent results.

Nor is such criticism based on the reconstruction laws, by which the several States were restored to loyalty and representation; for these men participated in their passage. Moreover, those acts have accomplished their purpose, and passed into history. As things of the past, they cannot divide parties in the present action.

What, then, is the "bayonet legislation," which alarms the timid nerves of persons, who, failing to control patronage, seek pretext for opposition to the Republican party? The issue has been created during the past session of Congress. The moderation of the Republican party could not be more strongly expressed than in the fact, that the only provision of law, even in pretext, repressive, passed at the recent session, authorizes witnesses of the election of representatives and presidential electors. In some southern States intimidation and violation, at elections, are alleged, Difficulty has existed to obtain testimony, and threats and danger are assigned as the reason. Here is an evil which might bring into dispute a presidential election or the political complexion of Congress. The remedy proposed is not "bayonets," is not the interference of the President. It is simply that the United States courts, when requested, shall designate two witnesses, one from each party, to observe the proceedings at elections so that in contested cases, sure evidence can be obtained. Should they be driven away, violence will be apparent. Their presence will go far to guarantee regular balloting and honest returns. Is there a reasonable citizen, who says that the eye of the Republic shall not be over the elections in which its very existence is involved? Could there be a less objectionable method to guard against alleged intimidation and violence? Yet absolutely this is the whole sum of legislation, repressive, centralizing, despotic, which Congress, at its recent session, placed on the statute books. The pretext of "bayonet legislation" advanced for opposition to the Republican party, has less basis than the mists of the morning.

THE AMENDED TAX LAW.

THE PRINCIPAL CHANGES IN THE TARIFF.

The new tariff bill, recently passed by Congress, contains forty-seven sections. Most of the changes prescribed will take effect on the first day of August next.

The following are some of the new duties provided in the first section of the bill, with a comparative statement of the duties in the present law:

	Tariff of 1870.		Tariff of 1872.
Bituminous coal, ton	$1 25		$ 75
Slack coal or culne, per ct	25	bush.	40
Salt. in bulk, per 100 lbs	18		8
Salt in sacks, barrels, &c., per 100 lbs	24		12
Oatmeal, per cent	10	per lb.	½
Potatoes	25	bush.	15
Bend, or belting leather, per cent	35		15
Calfskins, tanned or dressed, per cent	30		25
Upper leather and dressed skins, N. O. P., per cent	25		20
Morocco skins tanned, but unfinished, per cent	--		10
Chicory, ground or unground, per lb	4a5		1
Timber, hewn or sawed, per cent	20		--
Timber used in buildiug wharfs, per cent	20		--
On garden seeds and other seeds for agricultural purposes, not otherwise provided for, per cent	30		20
Ginger, ground, per lb	5		3
Ginger, preserved or pickled and essence, per cent	50		35
Chocolate, per lb	7		5
Cocoa, prepared or manufactured	[illegible]		2

The second section of the new bill contains the ten per cent reductions on many of the articles in the present tariff. The principal articles affected by this section are: All manufactures of cotton; all wools, hair of the alpaca goat and other animals, and all their manufactures; all iron and steel, and on all manufactures of iron and steel, excepting cotton machinery; all metals not herein otherwise provided for, and on all manufactures of metals of which either of them is the component part of chief value, excepting percussion caps, watches, jewelry and other articles of ornament; all paper and manufactures of paper, except unsized printing paper; all manufactures of India rubber, gutta percha or straw, and on oilcloths, glass and glassware, and on unwrought pipe clay, fine clay and fuller's earth; all leather, and all manufactures of skins, bone, ivory, horn and leather, except gloves and mittens, and on liquorice paste and on liquorice juice. Most of these duties apply only where the articles named are the component part of the chief value in the manufactures.

The fourth section specifies many changes in the rate of duty on certain articles, chiefly used in manufacturing and on what the tariff is slightly reduced.

The fifth section contains the free list, which is enlarged by the addition of many articles, although most of them are unimportant to the general reader.

The sixth section provides that for two years after the passage of the act, machinery and apparatus designed for steam towage on canals, and not now manufactured in the United States, may be imported by any State or by any person duly authorized by the Legislature of any State, free of duty, subject to such regulations as may be prescribed by the Secretary of the Treasury.

The seventh section establishes the standard of vinegar to be that strength which requires thirty-five grains of bicarbonate of potash to neutralize one ounce troy of vinegar.

Sections 9, 10 and 11 provide for drawbacks in favor of materials used in American manufactures, such as firearms, scales, shovels, axes, harness and agricultural machines, generally; nearly all the articles used in ship building, when the ships are to be used in the foreign trade; and salt used in curing fish.

REDUCTION OF EXCISE TAXES.

Section 12 increases the tax on distilled spirits from 50 to 70 cents. This section amends the system of collecting the tax, and is very long. It also provides that all wines, liquors or compounds, known or denominated as wine, and on all liquors not made from grapes, currants, rhubarb or berries grown in the United States, paying a tax of ten cents per bottle or package containing not more than one pint, or of twentv cents per bottle or package, containing more than one pint and not more than one quart, and at the same rate for any larger quantity of such merchandize, however the same may be put up, or whatever may be the package, to be paid by stamps.

Sections 13 to 39 contain voluminous directions to brewers and distillers for the conduct of their business.

Section 31 establishes a uniform tax of twenty cents on tobacco; and the next three sections provide numerous amendments regulating the collection of taxes and penalties.

Section 35 repeals the tax on coal gas.

Section 36 provides that on and after the first day of October, 1872, all the taxes imposed by stamps under and by virtue of schedule B of scetion 170 of the said act, approved June 20, 1864, and the several acts amendatory thereof, be and the same are hereby repealed, excepting only the tax of two cents on bank checks, drafts or orders; provided that where any mortgage has been executed and recorded, or may be executed and recorded before the first day of October, Anno Domini, 1872, to secure the payment of bonds or obligations that may be made and issued from time to time, and such mortgage not being stamped, all such bonds or obligations so made and issued on or after the said first day of October, Anno Domini 1872, shall not be subject to any stamp duty, but only such of their bonds or obligations as may have been made and issued before the day last aforesaid.

The remainder of the bill is occupied with details amending the time of paying bank taxes, extending the benefits of ths charitable exemptions, abolishing and regulating informers' moieties, remitting the shipbuilders' taxes, reducing and consolidating the revenue districts, and providing means for recovering delinquent taxes.

STAMPS ABOLISHED.

The following stamps are abolished by the new tax law, after first October next.

Contracts for insuranee against accidental injuries.

Affidavits.

All *agreements or contracts*, or renewals of the same.

Appraisements, of value or damage, or for any other purpose.

Assignments of a lease, mortgage, policy of insurance, or anything else.

Bills of Exchange, foreign, inland, letters of credit, or anything of that kind now taxed by stamps.

Bills of lading and receipts, in the United States or for anywhere else.

Bills of Sale, of any kind.

Bills of Indemnification, of any kind.

Bond Administrator or guardian, or anything that has the name of bond in it, and now taxed by stamp.

Broker's notes.

Certificates of Measurement of anything.

Certificates of stock, profit, damage, deposit or any other kind of certificate now taxed by stamp.

Charter, or its renewal, or a *charter-party* of any kind.

Conveyance, any part of the work of conveying.

Endorsement of any negotiable or not negotiable instrument.

Entry, for consumption, warehousing or withdrawal.

Gauger's returns.

Insurance policies, contracts, tickets, renewals, &c., (life, marine, inland and fire).

Lease. All through the lease list is abolished.

Legal documents. Writ or other process, confession of jugdment, cognovit, appeals, warrants, &c., letters of administration, testamentary, &c.

Manifests at Custom House, or anywhere else, or for any purpose.
Mortgage of any kind.
Pawners' checks.
Probate of will of any kind.
Protest of any kind.
Receipt. Now generally exempt, and if included in present law in any case, will be hereafter exempt.
Trust deed.
Warrant of attorney.
Passage ticket to any place in the world.
Power of attorney for any purpose.
Promissory note for anything.
Quit claim deed.
Sheriff's return.
Warehouse receipt.
Weigher's return of any character.

THE NATIONAL DEBT.

OFFICIAL STATEMENT OF ITS REDUCTION UNDER GRANT'S ADMINISTRATION.

	Debt of the U. S. less cash in the Treasury	Dec. of debt during the preceding month.	Total Dec. from March 1, 1869, to date.	Decrease in annual interest charge
1869.				
March 1	$2,525,463,260 01	....	....	....
April 1	2,525,196,461 74	$266,798 27	....	$74,694 00
May 1	2,518,797,391 09	6,399,070 65	$6,665,868 92	115,521 00
June 1	2,505,412,613 12	13,384,777 97	20,050,646 89	304,467 00
July 1	2,489,002,480 58	16,410,132 54	36,460,779 43	667,467 00
August 1	2,481,566,736 29	7,435,744 29	43,896,523 72	1,786,725 00
September 1	2,475,962,501 50	5,604,234 79	49,500,758 51	2,387,325 00
October 1	2,468,495,072 11	7,467,429 39	56,968,187 90	3,354,345 00
November 1	2,461,131,189 36	7,363,882 75	64,332,070 65	4,050,705 00
December 1	2,453,559,735 23	7,571,454 13	71,903,524 78	4,822,041 00
1870.				
January 1	2,448,746,955 31	4,812,781 92	76,716,306 70	5,651,475 00
February 1	2,444,813,290 92	3,933,664 39	80,649,971 09	6,119,571 00
March 1	2,438,328,477 17	6,484,811 75	87,134,782 84	6,301,707 00
April 1	2,432,562,127 74	5 766,349 43	92,901,132 27	6,601,350 00
May 1	2,420,864,334 35	11,697,793 39	104,598,925 66	6,908,436 00
June 1	2,406,562,371 78	14,301,962 57	118,900,888 23	7,268,397 00
July 1	2,386,358,599 74	20,203,772 04	139,104,660 27	7,747,797 00
August 1	2,369,324,476 00	17,034,123 74	156,138,784 01	8,133,954 00
September 1	2,355,921,110 41	13,403,325 59	169,542,109 60	8,614,470 00
October 1	2,346,923,652 28	9,007,498 13	178,549,607 73	9.162,270 00
November 1	2,341,784,355 55	5,129,296 73	183,678,904 46	9,768,311 04
December 1	2,334,308,494 65	7,475,860 90	191.154,765 36	10,155,576 96
1871.				
January 1	2,332,067,793 75	2.240,700 90	193,395,466 26	10,661,026 44
February 1	2,328,026,807 00	4,040,986 75	197,436,453 01	11,064,916 44
March 1	2,320,708,846 92	7,317,960 08	204,754,413 09	11,537,461 08
April 1	2,309,697,596 27	11,011,250 65	215,765,663 74	12,062,997 96
May 1	2,303,573,543 14	6,124,053 13	221,889,716 87	12,870,039 96
June 1	2,299,134,184 81	4,439,358 33	226,329,075 20	13,489,202 04
July 1	2,292,030,834 90	7,103,349 91	233,432,425 11	14,440,219 56
August 1	2,283,328,857 98	8,701,976 92	242,134,402 03	14,761,404 00
September 1	2,274,122,560 38	9,206,297 60	251,340,699 63	14.950.164 48
October 1	2,260,663,939 87	13,458,620 51	264,799,320 14	15,413,528 04
November 1	2,251,713,448 03	8,950,491 84	273,749,811 98	16,368,108 96
December 1	2,248,251,367 85	3,462,080 18	277,211,892 16	16,741,436 04
1872.				
January 1	2,243,838,411 14	4,412,956 71	281,624,848 87	17,165,927 52
February 1	2,238,204,949 50	5,633,461 64	287,258,310 51	17,568,834 48
March 1	2,225,813,497 98	12,391,451 52	299,649,762 03	18,203,915 04
April 1	2,210,331,529 34	15,481,968 64	315,131,730 67	20,484,552 00
May 1	2,197,743,440 72	12,588,088 62	327,719,819 29	21,472,089 00
June 1	2,193,517,378 94	4,226,061 78	331,945,881 07	22,002,519 00

Total Decrease, 9 months, ending Dec. 1, 1869.................$ 71,903,524 78
Total Decrease, 12 months, ending Dec. 1, 1870................ 119,251,240 58
Total Decrease, 12 months, ending Dec. 1, 1871................ 86,057,126 80
Total Decrease, 6 months, ending June 1, 1872................ 52,733,988 91

Total Decrease, 39 months of Grant's Administration..........$331,945,881 07

The foregoing is a correct statement of the Public Debt, as appears from the books and Treasurer's returns in the Department at the close of business, May 31, 1872.

GEORGE S. BOUTWELL,
Secretary of the Treasury.

ELECTION STATISTICS.

ELECTORAL VOTE OF 1872.

The additions authorized by the new apportionment bill passed by Congress will make the House of Representatives consist of 292 members. Adding the Senators from the thirty-seven States, there will be an electaral college of 366 members, appointed as follows:

State	Votes	State	Votes
Alabama	10	Missouri	15
Arkansas	6	Nebraska	3
California	6	Nevada	3
Connecticut	6	New Hampshire	5
Delaware	3	New Jersey	9
Florida	4	New York	35
Georgia	11	North Carolina	10
Illinois	21	Ohio	22
Indiana	15	Oregon	3
Iowa	11	Pennsylvania	29
Kansas	5	Rhode Island	4
Kentucky	12	South Carolina	7
Lousiana	8	Tennessee	12
Maine	7	Texas	8
Maryland	8	Vermont	5
Massachusetts	13	Virginia	11
Michigan	11	West Virginia	5
Minnesota	5	Wisconsin	10
Mississippi	8		
Total			366

HOW IT STOOD IN 1868.

The electoral vote of 1868 was divided as follows:

FOR GRANT.

State	Votes	State	Votes
Alabama	8	Missouri	11
Arkansas	5	Nebraska	3
California	5	Nevada	3
Connecticut	6	New Hampshire	5
Florida	3	North Carolina	9
Illinois	16	Ohio	21
Indiana	15	Pennsylvania	26
Iowa	8	Rhode Island	4
Kansas	3	South Carolina	6
Maine	7	Tennessee	10
Massachusetts	12	Vermont	5
Michigan	8	West Virginia	5
Minnesota	4	Wisconsin	8
Total			214.

FOR SEYMOUR.

State	Votes	State	Votes
Delaware	3	Maryland	7
Georgia	9	New Jersey	7
Kentucky	11	New York	33
Lousiana	7	Oregon	3
Total			80

The three States of Mississippi, Virginia, and Texas were not in a condition to vote. The popular vote amounted that year to about 5,700,000, out of which the Republicans had a majority of 300,000.

POPULAR VOTE IN 1868 AND 1870.

The following table shows the majorities in each State for the respective candidates for President in 1868, also in the gubernatorial or other State election nearest to November, 1871. It should be borne in mind that the full vote is never got out except in Presidential years, and that Republican majorities always make a poor showing on the off years:

States.	Rep. maj. 1868.	Dem. maj. 1868.	Rep. maj. 1870.	Dem. maj. 1870.
Alabama	4,280	------	------	------
Arkansas	3,074	------	------	------
Caifornia	514	------	5,474	------
Connecticut	3,054	------	------	------
Delaware	------	3,357	103	------
Florida	------	------	------	------
Georgia	------	45,688	------	------

States.	Rep. maj. 1868.	Dem. maj. 1868.	Rep. maj. 1870.	Dem. maj. 1870.
Illinois	51,150	------	22,589	------
Indiana	9,572	------	------	------
Iowa	46,359	------	41,254	------
Kansas	17,030	------	------	------
Kentucky	------	64,301	------	37,153
Louisiana	46,962	------	------	------
Maine	28,030	------	10,631	------
Maryland	------	31,918	------	15,135
Massachusetts	77,069	------	13,465*	------
Michigan	31,481	------	------	------
Minnesota	15,470	------	14,984	------
Mississippi	------	------	24,049	------
Missouri	25,883	------	------	------
Nebraska	4,290	------	4,408¶	------
Nevada	1,262	------	------	1,053
New Hampshire	6,967	------	------	510†
New Jersey	------	2,880	------	5,979
New York	------	10,000	18,907	------
North Carolina	12,136	------	------	9,345
Ohio	41,428	------	20,168	------
Oregon	------	164	------	------
Pennsylvania	28,898	------	14,575	------
Rhode Island	6,445	------	3,471	------
South Carolina	17,064	------	------	------
Tennessee	30,446	------	------	24,279
Texas	------	------	------	------
Vermont	32,122	------	------	------
Virginia	------	------	------	------
West Virginia	8,719	------	------	2,150
Wisconsin	25,447	------	9,329	------

* Six candidates in the field.
† Plurality. Result reversed in April, 1872.
¶ Congressional Election of 1870.

THE NEGRO VOTE.

The number of electors, white and black, in the eight Southern States wherein the colored population is chiefly gathered, is as follows:

States.	*Whites.*	*Colored.*	*Per Ct. Col.*
Virginia	712,089	512,841	41.86
North Carolina	678,470	391,650	36.5
South Carolina	284 667	415,814	58.8
Georgia	638,926	545,142	48.
Florida	96,057	91,689	48.8
Alabama	521,384	475,510	47.6
Mississippi	382,896	444,201	53.6
Lousiana	362,065	364,210	50.1
Total	3,681,554	3,241,057	46.9

OTHER NATIONALITIES.

The German vote is estimated in four States as follows: Pennsylvania, 32,029; Ohio, 36,578; Indiana, 15,611; Illinois, 40,750; total, 124,968. The heaviest Irish vote is in Pennsylvania, 140,625; New York, 88,134; Illinois, 20,027; and New Jersey, 14,164.

STATE GOVERNMENTS, ELECTIONS, &c.

STATES. (37)	Population. 1870.	CAPITALS.	GOVERNORS.	Term Expires.	Legislatnres Meet.	State Elections.
Alabama	996,992	Montgomery	*Robert B. Lindsay*	Nov. 1872	3 M. Nov.	Tu. aft. 1 M. Nov.
Arkansas	484,471	Little Rock	O. A. Hadley, *ex-officio*	Jan. 1873	1 M. Jan.	1 Monday, Nov.
California	560,247	Sacramento	Newton Booth	Dec. 1875	*1 M. Dec.	1 Wed. Sept.
Connecticut	537,454	Hartf'rd & N. Hav'n	Marshall Jewell	May, 1872	1 W. May.	1 Monday, April.
Delaware	125,015	Dover	*James Ponder*	Jan. 1875	*1 Tu. Jan.	1 Tu. Aug.
Florida	187,748	Tallahassee	Harrison Reed	Jan. 1873	T. a 1 M. Jan.	Tu. aft. 1 M. Nov.
Georgia	1,184,109	Atlanta	*James Milton Smith*	Jan. 1873	*1 W. Jan.	Tu, aft. 1 M. Nov.
Illinois	2,539,891	Springfield	John W. Palmer	Jan. 1873	*1 M. Jan.	Tu. aft. 1 M. Nov.
Indiana	1,680,637	Indianapolis	Conrad Baker	Jan. 1873	*1 W. Jan.	2 Tuesday, Oct.
Iowa	1,191,792	Des Moines	Cyrus C. Carpenter	Jan. 1874	*2 M. Jan.	2 Tuesday, Oct.
Kansas	364,399	Topeka	James M. Harvey	Jan. 1873	2 Tu. Jan.	Tu. aft. 1 M. Nov.
Kentucky	1,321,011	Frankfort	*P. H. Lesley*	Sept. 1874	*1 M. Dec.	1 Monday, Aug.
Louisiana	726,915	New Orleans	Henry C. Warmoth	Jan. 1873	1 M. Jan.	1 Monday, Nov.
Maine	626,915	Augusta	Sidney Perham	Jan. 1873	1 W. Jan.	2 Monday, Sept.
Maryland	780,894	Annapolis	*Wm. Pinkney Whyte*	Jan. 1876	*1 W. Jan.	Tu. aft. 1 M. Nov.
Massachusetts	1,457,351	Boston	Wm. B. Washburn	Jan. 1873	1 W. Jan.	Tu. aft. 1 M. Nov.
Michigan	1,184,059	Lansing	Henry P. Baldwin	Jan. 1873	*1 W. Jan.	Tu. aft. 1 M. Nov.
Minnesota	439,706	St. Paul	Horace Austin	Jan. 1874	T. a 1 M. Jan.	Tu. aft. 1 M. Nov.
Mississippi	827,922	Jackson	Ridgley C. Powers, *ex.offi'o*	Jan. 1874	T. a 1 M. Jan.	Tu. aft. 1 M. Nov.
Missouri	1,721,295	Jefferson City	B. Gratz Brown, Ind.	Jan. 1873	*Last M. Dec.	Tu. aft. 1 M. Nov.
Nebraska	122,993	Lincoln	Wm. H. James, *ex-officio*	Jan. 1873	*Th. a1M. Ja.	2 Tuesday, Oct.
Nevada	42,491	Carson City	*L. R. Bradley*	Jan. 1874	*1 M. Jan.	Tu. aft. 1 M. Nov.
N. Hampshire	318,300	Concord	E. A. Straw	June 1873	1 M. June.	2 Tuesday, March.
New Jersey	906,096	Trenton	*Joel Parker*	Jan. 1875	2 Tu. Jan.	Tu. aft. 1 M. Nov.
New York	4,382,758	Albany	*John T. Hoffman*	Jan. 1873	1 Tu. Jan.	Tu. aft. 1 M. Nov.
N. Carolina	1,071,361	Raleigh	T. R. Caldwell, *ex-officio*	Jan. 1873	1 Th. Nov.	1 Thursday, Aug.
Ohio	2,665,260	Columbus	Edward F. Noyes	Jan. 1874	*1 M. Jan.	2 Tuesday, Oct.
Oregon	90,923	Salem	*L. F. Grover*	Sept. 1874	2 M. Sept.	1 Monday, June.
Pennsylvania	3,521,791	Harrisburg	John W. Geary	Jan. 1873	1 Tu. Jan.	2 Tuesday, Oct.
Rhode Island	217,353	Newport & Provid.	Seth Padelford	May, 1873	May & Jan.	1 Wed. April.
S. Carolina	705,606	Columbia	Robert K. Scott	Jan. 1873	3 W. Oct.	4 Monday, Nov.
Tennessee	1,258,520	Nashville	*John C. Brown*	Oct. 1874	*1 M. Oct.	1 Monday, Aug.
Texas	818,579	Austin	Edmund J. Davis	Nov. 1873		
Vermont	330,051	Montpelier	John W. Stewart	Oct. 1872	*2 Th. Oct.	1 Tuesday, Sept.
Virginia	1,225,163	Richmond	*Gilbert C. Walker*	Jan. 1874	1 M. Dec.	Tu. aft. 1 M. Nov.
West Virginia	442,014	Charleston	*John J. Jacob*	Mar. 1874	2 Tu. Jan.	4 Thursday, Oct.
Wisconsin	1,054,670	Madison	Cadwallader C. Washburn	Jan. 1874	1 W. Jan.	Tu. aft. 1 M. Nov.
Total	38,113,253		Democrats in *Italic*.		* Biennial Sessions and Elections.	

Territories.	Capitals.	Governors.
Alaska	Sitka	
Arizona	Tucson	A. P. K. Safford.
Colorado	Denver	Edward M. McCook.
Dakota	Yancton	J. A. Burbank.
Idaho	Boise	Thomas. W. Bennett.
Indian	Tahlequah	Cyrus Harris.
Montana	Virginia City	Benjamin F. Potts.
New Mexico	Santa Fe	Marsh Giddings.
Utah	Salt Lake City	George L. Woods.
Washington	Olympia	Edward S. Salomon.
Wyoming	Cheyenne	James A. Campbell.
District of Columbia	Washington	Henry D. Cooke.

UNITED STATES GOVERNMENT.

Ulysses S. Grant, of Illinois, *President*	Salary $25,000
Schuyler Colfax, Indiana, *Vice-President*	" 8,000
Hamilton Fish, of New York, *Secretary of State*	Salary $3,000
George S. Boutwell, of Massachusetts, *Secretary of the Treasury*	" 8,000
William W. Belknap, of Iowa, *Secretary of War*	" 8,000
George M. Robeson, of New Jersey, *Secretary of the Navy*	" 8,000
Columbus Delano, of Ohio, *Secretary of the Interior*	" 8,000
George H. Williams, of Oregon, *Attorney-General*	" 8,000
John A. J. Creswell, of Maryland, *Postmaster-General*	" 8,000

SUPREME COURT OF THE UNITED STATES.

Salmon P. Chase, of Ohio, *Chief Justice* ---- Salary $8,500

Samuel Nelson, of N. Y., *Associate Justice.*	David Davis, of Illinois, *Associate Justice.*
Nathan Clifford, of Maine, " "	Stephen J. Field, of Cal. " "
Noah H. Swayne, of Ohio, " "	William M. Strong, of Pa. " "
Samuel F. Miller, of Iowa, " "	Joseph P. Bradley, of N. J., " "

Salary of Associate Justices, $8,000. Court meets first Monday in December, at Washington.

MINISTERS TO FOREIGN COUNTRIES.

Country.	*Capital*	*Ministers.*	*Salary.*	*Appointed.*
Austria	Vienna	John Jay, N. Y.	$12,000	1868
Brazil	Rio Janerio	James R. Partridge, Md.	12,000	1871
Chili	Santiago	Joseph P. Root, Kansas	10,000	1869
China	Pekin	Frederick F. Low, Cal.	12,000	1860
France	Paris	Elihu B. Washburne, Ill.	17,500	1869
Great Britain	London	Robert C. Schenck, Ohio	17,500	1870
Italy	Florence	George P. Marsh, Vt.	12,000	1861
Mexico	Mexico	Thomas H. Nelson, Ind.	12,000	1869
Peru	Lima		10,000	1871
Germany	Berlin	George Bancroft, Mass.	17,500	1867
Russia	St. Petersburg	Andrew G. Curtin, Penn.	12,000	1869
Spain	Madrid	Daniel E. Sickles, N. Y.	12,000	1869
Argentine Republic	Buenos Ayres		7,500	1869
Belgium	Brussels	J. R. Jones, Ill.	7,500	1869
Bolivia	Cochabamba	Leopold Markbreit, Ohio	7,500	1869
Costa Rica	San Jose	Jacob B. Blair, W. Va.	7,500	1868
Denmark	Copenhagen	M. J. Cramer, Ky.	7,500	1870
Ecuador	Quito	E. Rumsey Wing, Ky.	7,500	1870
Guatemala	Guatemala	S. A. Hudson, Iowa	7,500	1869
Hawaiian Islands	Honolulu	Henry A. Pierce, Mass.	7,500	1869
Honduras	Comayagua	Henry Baxter, Mich.	7,500	1869
Japan	Yedo	C. E. Delong, Oregon	12,000	1869
Netherlands	Hague	Chas. T. Gorham, Mich.	7,500	1870
Nicaragua	Nicaragua	Charles N. Riotte, Texas	7,500	1869
Paraguay	Asuncion	See Uruguay	7,500	
Portugal	Lisbon	Chas. H. Lewis, Va.	7,500	1870
San Salvador	San Salvador	Thomas Biddle, Penn.	7,500	1869
Sweden and Norway	Stockholm	C. C. Andrews, Mass.	7,500	1869
Switzerland	Berne	Horace Rublee, Wis.	7,500	1869
Turkey	Constantinople	George H. Boker, Penn.	7,500	1870
Uruguay and Paraguay	Montevideo	John L. Stephens, Me.	11,250	1871
U. S. of Colombia	Bogota	S. A. Hurlburt, Ill.	7,500	1869
Venezuela	Caracas	William A. Pile, Mo.	7,500	1869
Hayti	Port-au-Prince	E. D. Basset, Pa.	7,500	1869
Liberia	Monrovia	J. Milton Turner	4,000	1871

DEPARTMENT AND BUREAU OFFICERS.

Assistant Secretary of State	Charles Hale.
Second Assistant "	William Hunter.
Assistant Secretary of the Treasury	William A. Richardson.
" " " "	John F. Hartly.
First Comptroller	Robert W. Taylor.
Second "	J. M. Brodhead.
Commissioner of Customs	W. T. Haines.
Register of the Treasury	John Allison.
First Auditor	David W. Mahon.
Second "	Ezra B. French.
Third "	Allen Rutherford.

Fourth Auditor	Stephen J. W. Tabor.
Fifth "	J. H. Ela.
Sixth "	J. J. Martin.
Treasurer of the United States,	Francis E. Spinner.
Comptroller of the Currency,	H. R. Hulbird.
Commissioner of Internal Revenue,	J. W. Douglass.
General of the Army,	W. T. Sherman.
Adjutant General,	E. D. Townsend.
Inspector General,	Col. Randolph B. Marcy.
Quartermaster General,	Montgomery O. Meigs.
Commissioner General,	Amos B. Eaton.
Surgeon General,	Joseph K. Barnes.
Judge Advocate General,	Joseph Holt.
Assistant Secretary of the Interior,	Benjamin R. Cowen.
Commissioner of the Land Office,	Willis Drummond.
Commisssioner of Pensions,	J. H. Baker.
" Patents,	M. D. Leggett.
" Indian Affairs,	Francis A. Walker.
" Education,	John Eaton, jr.
First Assistant Postmaster Genl.,	Jas. W. Marshall.
Second " " "	John L. Routeral.
Third " " "	W. H. H. Terrell.
Assistant Attorney General,	Clement H. Hill.
Commissioner of Agriculture,	Frederick Watts.
" Public Buildings	O. E. Babcock.
Chief Justice U. S. Gourt of Claims	Charles D. Drake.

SENATORS TO BE REPLACED.

The terms of Spencer of Alabama, Rice of Arkansas, Cole of California, Ferry of Connecticut, Osborn of Florida, Hill of Georgia, Trumbull of Illinois, Morton of Indiana, Harlan of Iowa, Pomeroy of Kansas, Davis of Kentucky, Kellogg of Louisiana, Vickers of Maryland, Blair of Missouri, Nye of Nevada, Patterson of New Hampshire, Conkling of New York, Pool of North Carolina, Sherman of Ohio, Corbett of Oregon, Cameron of Pennsylvania, Sawyer of South Carolina. Morrill of Vermont, and Howe of Wisconsin, all expire on the 4th of March, 1872. All of these are yet to be chosen except John Sherman of Ohio, who has been already re-elected. The United States Senate now stands; Democrats 17; Republicans 57. Of the retiring members, 21 are Republican, and three are Democrats.

PRESIDENTIAL TICKETS.

The following is a full list of the various tickets placed in nomination, or likely to be, up to the time of putting this book to press:

	For President.	*For Vice President.*
1. Republican,	Ulysses S. Grant	Henry Wilson
2. Democratic and Bolters,	Horace Greeley	B. Gratz Brown
3. Labor Reform,	David Davis	Joel Parker
4. Temperance,	James Black	James Russell
5. Revenue Reform,	Wm. S. Groesbeck	Fred Law Olmsted
6. Anti Masonic,	Chas. Francis Adams	J. L. Barlow*
7. Free Love,	Victoria Woodhull	Frederic Douglass

Of these the third and fifth are aleady out of the field, while the seventh is not of any moment—the candidate for Vice President, very justly deeming the gathering which nominated him, too trivial an affair even to bestow a letter of declination upon. The convention of Labor Reformers was held at Columbus,O., on the 22nd of February. It was thought at first that this nomination by the ostensible representatives of the Labor interest, could be brought to bear on the Cincinnati Convention, or on the Democratic party; and Judge Davis, on being notified of his nomination, hit upon the happy expedient of replying laconically to the committee, "The office of President is one which should be neither sought nor declined by an American citizen," and there letting the matter rest. After it bceame evident that the nominations at Columbus would not be endorsed by any body representing a more numerous constituency, both the candidates formally withdrew. (It should be mentioned that the Workingmen's Union of New York, representing a larger actual constituency than the Cincinnati gathering, nominated Grant and Wilson about a fortnight before the assembling of the Philadelphia Convention.)

*Vice Chas. H. Howard, declined. Mr. Adams (said to be a Royal Arch Mason,) has paid no attention to this nomination.

SUMNER REBUKED BY A FELLOW-ABOLITIONIST.

William Lloyd Garrison, the noted anti-slavery pioneer, has sent the following letter to Senator Sumner:

ROXBURY, June 1, 1872.

DEAR MR. SUMNER—I owe it to you to say, with all the frankness which a sincere friendship justifies, that I have carefully read your speech in sharp arraignment of the President, and my conviction is that it is ill judged, ill-timed and so extravagant in its charges and bitter in its personalities as to neutralize whatever of just criticism can be found in it. It will assuredly serve the purposes of the worst foes the cause of impartial freedom has most to fear, very many of them now rallying under the deceptive banner of "Liberal Republicanism," but the loyal, liberty-upholding party with which you have hitherto been proud to be identified will peruse it with deep regret, if not with unfeigned astonishment. Certainly you do not represent Massachusetts in this sweeping impeachment. Her Republican people are almost a unit for the re-election of the man whom you attempt to stain with crime and cover with infamy.

You cannot separate General Grant from the party which put him in the Presidential chair, and which means to keep him in it, if possible, another term, being satisfied as to his ability, integrity and patriotism; and therefore in stigmatizing him as a venal self-seeker and an unscrupulous usurper you virtually pronounce it to be equally corrupt and untrustworthy. This you have a right to do on your own responsibility if you must, but in so doing you will find yourself for the first time in marked opposition to the sentiment of Massachusetts, as its Senator in Congress, and surrounded by allies who have been heretofore your deadliest enemies. Occupying, as I do, an outside position, I write this under no party bias, and only because I feel constrained in this manner to free my mind as a proof of my friendship. Receive it in the spirit which has dictated it.

Faithfully and regretfully yours,
WILLIAM LLOYD GARRISON.

GREELEY'S INTRIGUES WITH THE DEMOCRACY.

The Cincinnati Nomination the Result of a Plot to which Greeley and Horatio Seymour were Parties, Extending Back Nearly a Year.

The following are the essential facts of an intrigue whereof Horace Greeley, Horatio Seymour, Waldo Hutchins and Lewis Carmichael were the principal agents, and which resulted in a bargain between Greeley and the Democratic party of New York, for mutual support in the present campaign. The particulars, as related by Carmichael to the editor of the Binghampton *Republican*, are certified to by many persons of unquestioned veracity and by the affidavits of two such, which are appended hereto.

CARMICHAEL'S STATEMENT.

Lewis Carmichael is a farmer, probably between 50 and 55 years of age, who owns and resides upon a tract of 240 acres of improved land, two miles west of the village of Unadilla, in Otsego county. For over twenty years he has enjoyed the reputation of being a politician of influence and sagacity, and was consulted in times of important political movements by Dickinson and other eminent men.

Carmichael wrote to Mr. Greeley, last September, giving him his view about the then coming presidential campaign, and inviting Greeley to become a candidate. Carmichael's letter was addressed inside to "Hon. Horace Greeley, the next President of the United States." Carmichael told Mr. Greeley that the time had come to "raft over," and he thought the Democratic leaders would drop old issues and support him.

Mr. Greeley answered this letter in a short time. He expressed [then or afterward—the writer is not certain as to time here] his willingness to become a candidate, but was fearful that the Democratic leaders would not support him. A letter from him invited Carmichael to an interview with him.

Carmichael said he went down to New York soon after receiving that letter, and had a long talk with Greeley in the *Tribune* office. Greeley told Carmichael that Horatio Seymour was a standing candidate with the Democratic party, and that Mr. Seymour would not step aside for him. Carmichael answered that he could not tell about that, as Governor Seymour had not been asked, and had not said what he would do. Carmichael then offered to undertake to secure Seymour's consent and co-operation to the movement, and Mr. Greeley agreed to be a candidate provided he succeeded with Mr. Seymour and other prominent Democrats.

Within a short time after the interview with Greeley, Carmichael saw Governor Seymour. He was not inclined to receive the proposition with much favor. Carmichael gave him his views, and left him to think the matter over. At that time Seymour thought that perhaps Hutchins could be agreed upon as a candidate.

It was not long before Carmichael saw Seymour again, by appointment, and he said he had made up his mind that Carmichael was right, and that the Democrats could support Greeley; or if a portion of the Republican party preferred making a change in the administration, the Democrats should not take advantage of the movement.

Carmichael informed Mr. Greeley, as soon as convenient, of his success with Governor Seymour; and went about the State, immediately, to consult the Democratic leaders. The proposition met with very strong opposition, but the fact that it was about the only thing they could do, convinced the party leaders that they had better do it. If they should elect a prominent man from their ranks he would have political associations, and friends that he could not help serving, and they could not get such an administration as they could by taking up a man with no former political associations he would be under obligations to recognize. The leaders of both parties are corrupt. Such Democratic leaders as Belmont, Marble and others, have been making money and political capital out of our following, and the party has continually lost. Three millions of Democratic votes had become useless for want of proper management of them, and we thought it was time to turn the tables and compel the leaders to follow for a while.

In 1860 we might have elected Houston, if we had nominated him, over Lincoln, because Houston claimed that the territories were the common property of all the States, and the Democrats all over the United States could have united on that principle. In 1864 we could have elected Reverdy Johnson over Lincoln. And in 1868 we could have elected Chase over Grant. We had fooled away so many opportunities that we concluded it was best to drop some of the old, unpopular doctrines this fall and come out in shape to succeed.

Carmichael refused to show any letters, alleging that he had already shown letters to the editor of this paper. He said he did not understand Mr. Greeley as desiring there should be secrecy about the movement. [Precisely how he desired to be understood here, is uncertain.] The first plan, Carmichael said, was to call a convention in Otsego county to nominate Mr. Greeley, and start the campaign in that manner.

Last April Mr. Greeley, true to his usual vacillating habit, wrote to Carmichael saying that he believed the Democrats preferred a candidate from their own ranks, and would not unite in his support; therefore he desired to be withdrawn from the canvass. But Carmichael prevailed upon him to stick to it until they knew what the Democratic leaders would do. It was not best to back down before they had time to work the thing up.

AFFIDAVIT OF C. S. CARPENTER.

[Of Mr. Carpenter, who makes the following affidavit, the Binghampton *Republican* says "he is a young man of unusual ability, and probity; was reared in Unadilla; is respected by all who know him; and he is widely known. As the editor of the Oneonta *Herald*, one of the best and most trustworthy weekly journals of the State, he is highly esteemed. With his own readers, no certification could be stronger than his owu word."]

ONEONTA, July 17, 1872.

C. S. Carpenter, being duly sworn, deposes and says that he is a resident of Oneonta, Otsego county, in the Sate of New York, and that he is well acquainted with Lewis Carmichael, of Unadilla, in said county. That Carmichael has for many years been a Democrat, interested in county, State and national conventions, which he frequently attended; and that he has for about a year past been engaged in seeking a Democratic candidate for the presidency. That Carmichael was last fall in correspondence with Horace Greelev and Horatio Seymour, on the question of making new issues; one of which was the payment of pensions to disabled rebel soldiers, as well as to Union soldiers; and that deponent saw letters from said Greeley and from Seymour, on that question. That one of Greeley's letters, which deponent recognized by what he knows of Greeley's handwriting, and by the *Tribune* heading (this letter being an answer to a letter of Carmichael, asking his views on the Confederate pension question), expressed the *views of Mr. Greeley as favorable to the passage of a law providing that the general government pay pensions to Southern disabled soldiers;* although he (Greeley) doubted whether Congress would pass such a bill. That deponent read the letter carefully, and this was its true expression and meaning; and it was freely discussed between Carmichael and deponent. That this letter was, according to deponent's best recollection, dated in August or early in September, 1871. Deponent saw a letter from Horatio Seymour on the same subject, at about the same time. Mr. Seymour expressed himself in opposition to making the pension an issue then.

That deponent also saw another letter of Horace Greeley, addressed to Carmichael, in which Greeley *invited Carmichael to call on him in New York*, to talk over political issues that had been broached between them; and a separate part of that letter, which deponent did not have opportunity of reading carefully, expressed, as deponent casually noticed, and was distinctly informed by Carmichael, *the possibility that Greeley would accept the nomination for president*, if the nomination were tendered to him in 1872. That Carmichael was absent from Otsego shortly afterward, and received from Greeley, as Carmichael distinctly and emphatically stated to him, *Mr. Greeley's positive consent to be the Democratic candidate* for president in 1872, if the nomination were given to him. The date of this letter was in October, 1871.

That Carmichael endeavored to induce deponent to consent to advocate paying pensions to Southern soldiers, as a measure of conciliation between North and South, and to support Mr. Greeley for the presidency.

That it was fully understood between deponent and Carmichael that Greeley was to be pressed for Democratic nomination. That deponent regarded Carmichael as a candid man who treated these subjects with the utmost seriousness; and that deponent is fully convinced that this correspondence and interviews, and their meaning and results, were described by him honestly and faithfully.

C. S. CARPENTER.

Sworn before me this 17th day of July, 1872.
E. M. CARVER, Notary Public.

Dr. Ireland, who makes the other affidavit, is a citizen of high character; enjoys the esteem of everybody; and by the clearness and very essential importance of his affidavit, contributes much to the completeness of the case. He, with Mr. Carpenter, was averse to personal prominence in the matter; but a sense of duty admitted of no other course than that they have pursued.

AFFIDAVIT OF DR. IRELAND.

Louis E. Ireland, of Unadilla, Otsego county, New York, being sworn, says that Lewis Carmichael, also of Unadilla, whom he has known for six years, has frequently been in deponent's office in Unadilla, and has shown deponent letters from Horace Greeley, of New York, five or six in number; and one letter of Horatio Seymour; that deponent did not readily read Greeley's letters, except the heading and signature—Carmichael's being addressed as "Friend Carmichael" in one or more of them—which letters deponent held in his hand. Their contents related to matters understood between Carmichael and Greeley, some of the letters passing on as though connected with previous business; and one of the letters *invited Carmichael to go to Cincinnati*. These letters were shown to deponent in the last of March or first of April, 1872. Carmichael then said to deponent that *Greeley would be nominated at Cincinnati*, and *the Democrats would adopt him*; that the only point there was, *that Greeley should get the Cincinnati nomination*. Deponent perused Horatio Seymour's letter, which he read easily, and recognized the handwriting, according to his previous knowledge of it, as Seymour's. The subjects of that letter were as follows: It mentioned an *interview of Carmichael and Seymour*, and an *interview of Carmichael and Greeley*; saying he (Seymour) *was more favorably impressed* with the turn of matters, with which he seemed satisfied; mentioned the tariff question, and said the best way was *to leave the issue a vague one, as Carmichael had proposed*, so as to unite persons of different views *in the coalition movement*; suggested that if Greeley favored this, it would *smooth the way to the end*. Deponent's strong impression is that Greeley's candidacy was mentioned; but of that he does not say positively. The time when this letter was read by deponent was about the last of March or first of April, 1872.

The subject had previously been brought to deponent's attention by Carmichael; but when the letters were shown, particularly Greeley's letters, deponent thought the matter too absurd to notice; but after the Cincinnati nomination he understood their importance, and endeavored to procure copies. He would have exposed the matter, except that he had hopes of procuriug the letters or copies of them.

Deponent was informed in December, 1871, from the statement of Carmichael, that Greeley had promised Carmichael the tone of the *Tribune* would be changed about the first of the year 1872; and the deponent, on noticing, saw the change—which statement of Carmichael deponent can prove on competent testimony of a public officer.

Deponent further remembers that in one of Greeley's letters, Chase was mentioned as now feeble and broken down.

Deponent makes this statement on his honor as a citizen, and because he believes the facts he has mentioned should be exposed.

L. E. IRELAND.

Sworn to and subscribed before me, this 17th day of July, 1872.
FREDERICK A. SANDS,
Notary Public of Otsego county, N. Y.

THE TWO CHARGES AGAINST PRESIDENT GRANT.

[From Senator Conkling's Speech at New York, July 23, 1872.]

GIFT TAKING.

But let us go back a moment to Grant before he seriously thought of being President and when he was only the idol of the nation. Returning from the field covered with glory, but poor in money, the affluent, whose fortunes he had saved, met him with munificent offerings. In this they followed the customs of ancient and modern times. The austere republics of antiquity enriched and ennobled their heroes returning from victory. England, with an unwritten constitution and an omnipotent Parliament, which a lawyer once said "could do anything but to make a man a woman," has enriched her Generals both by acts of Parliament and by voluntary subscriptions. In the United States the constitution does not permit Congress to act in such matters. Here they rest wholly in the voluntary action of individuals, and that public presentations to heroes involved turpitude in givers or recipients has been first found out by the spurious reformers and libellers now clamoring for notice. Wellington received from his government and his neighbors more than three million dollars. British citizens of Calcutta made him presents, the officers of the army gave him $10,000, the House of Commons voted him $1,000,000, and a mansion and estate were purchased for him by subscription, at a cost of $1,300,000. Besides this he was three times ennobled, twice by England and once by Spain. Oliver Cromwell, for deeds done in civil war, received $32,500 a year in gifts. Marlborough was given a stately palace and a splendid fortune. Nelson and his family were ennobled and received $70,000. Jewels and money were given to Fairfax for services in civil war. The generals and admirals of England and France have generally been recipients of great pecuniary benefits. In England and elsewhere the custom of presents to public men has gone beyond the army and the navy. Richard Cobden, a civilian, in token of political service only, was given by subscription $350,000. John Bright has just received costly gifts. America, younger and poorer, with few wars to breed heroes, has been less lavish than older nations; but Americans have not been stingy. General McClellan, perhaps, begins the list of largely rewarded generals. His active service ended before the war was over, and his democratic admirers, prior to nominating him for the Presidency, presented him a costly house and a large purse, amounting in all to $100,000. To Sherman, Sheridan, Farragut and Grant large sums were given. To Stanton's family and to Rawlins' were given more than a hundred thousand each. Were these things dishonorable? Was it wrong for General Grant to accept such gifts? The charge is an insult to the nation who witnessed and applauded the proceeding; it is an imputation upon those who gave, as much as upon him who received. It can not have been dishonorable or improper for him to accept a gift without being dishonorable and improper to offer it. How must the cant and snivel we hear seem to the people of Germany just now. Bismarck, though Chancellor and Prime Minister, has just received as a gift, in token of his services in the recent war, a magnificent landed estate, worth more than was given to all our generals; and Bismarck in like token, has been made a Prince. General Von Moltke, for his services in the German-Franco war, has been given $300,000; and Germany has set apart from the French indemnity fund $4.000,000 to be distributed in gifts to her heroes. Do you believe any German, or any man with a German heart in his bosom, will ever be mean enough to throw these gifts in the face of those who earned and accepted them? If there is a man mean enough to do it he will be safer in the Greeley menagerie than he would be in any hiding place in Germany. Yet gift-taking, forsooth, is paraded by political Pharisees. One thing is noticeable:—The men who screech about gift-taking are those who never gave a cent, and who were never openly offered a cent—certainly not for any honorable service rendered to their country. The charge that Grant accepted any gift after he became President, or after he was nominated, is wholly false. He has accepted nothing of value since his first nomination—not even a carriage and horses—although Lincoln, and Buchanan, and Pierce, and Taylor, and other Presidents, did accept carriages and horses after their election.

NEPOTISM.

Let me go on with the charges against the President. Few of them figure more largely than appointing relatives to office. Mr. Sumner has staggered the nation by the weight of the dictionaries, encyclopædias and other big books which he has dumped upon us, to show what "nepotism" is. He finds it charged that Popes had children, and called them nephews, and lavished upon them the moneys of the Church; and he thinks that where a public office is to be filled and a good man is appointed at the same pay any other man would receive, a case has occurred like that of the Popes, provided the man who makes the appointment and the man who gets it are related to each other. This, if not a useful, is a wonderful discovery.

From the morning of time common sense has distinguished between creating a useless and lucrative sinecure and bestowing it on a relative, and selecting a relative to do a service required to be done. When Hannibal and Frederick the Great and Napoleon and Emperor William put a brother or a son at the head of an army, with rank and titles, or even placed him on a throne, the world never thought it was like a sinecure for a Papal nephew. On the contrary, in public and private business, nothing has seemed more natural than for those entrusted with affairs to employ and associate with themselves persons in whom they most confided, whether relatives or not. In all such cases, if the person be fit, little harm can be done; but if he is unfit, a great wrong is done, whether he be a relative or not. If the appointment of relatives be a crime, a great many men, including the busiest and most blatant "liberals," must be great criminals. Andrew Johnson, his Cabinet and chief officers must have been huge offenders, for reasons which no one thought of at the time though every one knew of them. President Johnson's son was his chief Private Secretary. Governor Seward's son was Assistant Secretary of State. Edwin M. Stanton's son was a clerk in the War Department. Giddeon Welles' son was Chief Clerk of the Navy Department; and when Giddeon Welles employed a relative at a great remuneration to buy ships the scandal was not that he paid just sums to a relative, but that he paid such sums at all. Reverdy Johnson, Minister to England, made his son Assistant Secretary of Legation. John A. Dix, Minister to France, did the same thing with his son. All this was under Andrew Johnson, but when a drag net of criticism and impeachment was cast over him these things were not caught up.

"LIBERAL" RELATIVES.

The rueful "reformers" themselves will not bear examination on this point. Mr.

Schurz pressed his brother-in-law upon the President, and obtained for him a lucrative office, and when Mr. Trumbull caused his removal upon statements impeaching his fitness Mr. Schurz raged against the President for removing his brother-in-law. Mr. Trumbull seems to have procured appointments for his brother-in-law, his sons and his nephews, and he broke, it is said, with the President because he refused to appoint Mr. Trumbull's son to an office. That shrill and frisky "reformer," Mr. Tipton, although not colossal himself, would need a hay scales to be weighed along with all his relatives he has helped to get office. Three brothers-in-law, a nephew and a son in office, with other things for other relatives, did not satisfy his "liberal" inclinations, but he vigorously plied the President and the Secretary of State to give a valuable consulship to another son, and after they declined he frequently avowed—once pipingly to the President himself—that the refusal was the cause of his opposition. Mr. Fenton saw no objection to giving to his adopted son his influence for an office, nor to obtaining it from Tammany Hall, and keeping it through all the exposures of Tweed and the rest, although no service was attached to it equivatent to the pay. Mr. Sumner, with a brother-in-law in office under Andrew Johnson, was inflamed by his removal, and did not hesitate to make known his displeasure. Even Mr. Greeley did not scruple to countenance his brother-in-law in obtaining the most lucrative collectorship of internal revenue in the United States. Nor has he hesitated to urge appointments, clearly unfit, on the ground of the intimate terms between himself and those he urged.

[Mr. Conkling then goes on to cite cases of nepotism on the part of Democratic office-holders—among them that of Governor Hoffman, who, when Mayor of New York, caused the appointment of his father-in-law, Starkweather, to a place which yielded him $561,-000 in four years.]

But if General Grant has done wrong, the crime of others cannot help him. Let us look into his case. You might suppose from the noise, that he had used a relative as a peg for every hole in the country, and that he had put round pegs in square holes, and square pegs in round holes, everywhere. It has been said that he has appointed 50 relatives, 40 relatives, 30 relatives, and Mr. Sumner estimates 13 relatives, to office. None of these statements are true. Since President Grant came in, but nine persons in all, connected in the remotest degree with him or with his wife, have held political office under the United States.

I have a list of them, and do not speak without information. Nine is the total number in political office. This does not include a son of the President, sent as a pupil to West Point, long before his father became President; nor does it include his brother-in-law, Dent, who has long held a commission in the army by the same tenure under which Sherman and Sheridan, and every other officer of the army holds his place, and which the President has no more power to give or take away than the man in the moon.

Of the nine relatives or connections in office, two were appointed by Andrew Johnson, viz.: The President's father, postmaster at Covington, Ky., and his brother-in-law, the Rev. Mr. Cramer, Consul to Leipsic. Mr. Cramer was transferrred from Leipsic to Denmark by President Grant, on the recommendation of Bishop Simpson, Bishop Jaynes, and many other well known persons, friends of Mr. Cramer. Being the brother-in-law of the President, he, of course became a mark for "liberal" abuse, and was charged with drinking beer, and being refused the membership of a social club.

But now comes the Cincinnati Methodist Conference, about as respectable a body as has met in Cincinnati lately, and certifies after full investigation, the utter falsity of the charges. Their report is fortified by letters from Copenhagen, and by statements of the official journal and other newspapers there, indignantly repelling the aspersions cast at Mr. Cramer, and pronouncing him a blameless officer and man.

Deducting Jesse R. Grant and M. J. Cramer, appointed by Johnson, seven instances of relatives appointed to political affice remain, and of these but two were in truth and in fact abpointed by the President as I will show you.

Orlando H. Ross, a cousin of the President, holds a clerkship, under the third Auditor of the Treasury. He was a soldier in the war, and Gen. Logan, as he stated in Senate, procured his appointment at the Treasury Department without the knowledge of the President who. in fact, never heard of it until he read it in a newspaper. This leaves six, and of these four hold local offices, viz.: George W. Dent, Appraiser at San Francisco; James F. Casey, collector at New Orleans; one a brother and the other a brother-in-law of Mrs. Grant; Peter Casey, Postmaster at Vicksburg, Miss., a brother of a brother-in-law of Mrs. Grant; and George B. Johnson, Assessor of the third District of Ohio, who married a third cousin of the President. These men hold local offices, and were selected and put forward, as has been universal in both political parties for 50 years, by the local Representatives.

When the member of Congress from a District certifies the character of an applicant for a post-office or any other office local in his district, and recommends his selection, the practice of the Government has always been to rely and act upon such representations, holding the member of Congress responsible to the Government and to his constituents, if he obtains unfit appointments.

It was in this way that the four persons just named were selected, the President having no part in the matter, if he believed the applicant fit and worthy, except to consult the wishes of the people made known through their representatives, or else to overrule their wishes, upon the grouud that it might be better for himself not to run the risk of having the matter some time or other flung in his face.

Two appointments remain, and upon these the President did undoubtedly exercise his own choice and his own judgment.

The first is Alexander Sharp, a connection of Mrs. Grant, who was appointed Marshal of the District of Columbia. This officer is virtually a member of the President's household—he receives company with the family, introduces visitors, and generally helps along. For these reasons some relative or friend of the President's family has always been found for this position.

The remaining relative is Silas Hudson, Minister to Guatemala. He is cousin to the President. Iowa, the Siate in which he lives, had the mission to Guatemala before President Grant came in; Fitz Henry Warren held it; and on his retirement Iowa claimed it still, and presented Mr. Hudson, who is desciibed as an able and accomplished man. The President might have refused to appoint him, without giving just offence to the Republicans of Iowa, because he might have taken a man from some other State, but he did appoint him, and thus he furnished the needy "Liberals" with one awful example.

GREELEY INELIGIBLE.

Mr. Greeley is assailed on all sides, but the latest bit of gossip is furnished by a dispatch published in the Boston *Traveler* to the effect that "one of the reasons for which Carl Schurz is silent on the Greeley question is supposed to be the belief on his part that the Axeman of Chappaqua is ineligible to office, because in all the amnesty bills passed by Congress for the removal of political disabilities, the name of Horace Greeley does not appear. His voluntary advice and encouragement which he gave to the seceding States, now counts against him, for as matters stand no person can hold any office whatsoever, who can not make oath that he has never given any aid or countenance, counsel or encouragement to parties engaged in avowed hostilities against the government of the United States, and that he has never yet aided or voluntarily supported any pretended government, authority, power or constitution within the United States, hostile or inimical thereto. It is well known that Horace Greeley can not, without perjury, subscribe to such an oath, and his ineligibility to the presidential office is therefore an established fact."

A DARKEY'S VIEW OF THE SITUATION.

A correspondent of the Cincinnati *Commercial*, a Greeley organ, traveling in Kentucky, interviewed his barber on the political situation, with the following result:

Barber. What is the name of your paper?

Correspondent. *The Commercial.*

B. Oh, yes; I've seen that. It's a Grant paper, ain't it?

C. No, it's a Greeley paper.

B. Oh, I thought it was Republican.

C. So it is.

B. What? Republican and for Greeley?

C. Certainly.

B. It supported Seymour, didn't it?

C. Not at all.

B. That sounds curious to me. How could a paper be against Seymour and for Greeley?

C. Because Seymour was a Democrat.

B. Well, so is Greeley.

C. You are much mistaken; Greeley is a Republican.

B. (*Looking amazed*, and opening his eyes as big as shaving mugs:) I don't understand it; I can't see how a Republican can be running on a Democratic ticket.. There is something loose somewhere.

C. He is not running on a Demoeratic ticket.

B. Then the Democrats are mightily fooled, for they think he is.

C. No, indeed, they don't.

B. But they are all going for him about here. Just look how it is; every Republican is for Grant, and every Democrat for Greeley. It looks to me like he is running the same way Seymour did. The people are divided, just like they were then, only in place of Seymour, Greeley has come out. I don't know anything about the platform, as they call it; I look at the thing just as it is before the people.

THE END.

www.ingramcontent.com/pod-product-compliance
Lightning Source LLC
LaVergne TN
LVHW021233110826
845150LV00002B/324

* 9 7 8 1 4 2 5 5 6 2 2 4 3 *